D0583926

THEORIZING COMMUNICATION

THEORIZING COMMUNICATION,

A History

Dan Schiller

New York
Oxford University Press
1996

Oxford University Press

Oxford   New York
Athens   Auckland   Bangkok   Bogotá   Bombay
Buenos Aires   Calcutta   Cape Town   Dar es Salaam
Delhi   Florence   Hong Kong   Istanbul   Karachi
Kuala Lumpur   Madras   Madrid   Melbourne
Mexico City   Nairobi   Paris   Singapore
Taipei   Tokyo   Toronto

and associated companies in
Berlin   Ibadan

Copyright © 1996 by Dan Schiller

Published by Oxford University Press, Inc.,
198 Madison Avenue, New York, New York 10016

Oxford is a registered trademark of Oxford University Press

Library of Congress Cataloging-in-Publication Data
Schiller, Dan, 1951–
Theorizing communication : a history / Dan Schiller.
p.   cm.   Includes bibliographical references and index.
ISBN 0–19–510199–5
1. Communication—Philosophy—History.   I. Title.
P90.S348   1996   302.2'01—dc20   95-42072

1 3 5 7 9 8 6 4 2

Printed in the United States of America
on acid-free paper

To Marcus and Vinny, who hold the roads open

[M]en fight and lose the battle, and the thing that they fought for comes about in spite of their defeat, and when it comes turns out not to be what they meant, and other men have to fight for what they meant under another name. . . .

William Morris, *A Dream of John Ball*

Preface

Today the sweep and import of communication have become virtually uncontained. To study communication, it is now widely evident, is not only to be concerned with the contributions of a restricted set of media, either to the socialization of children and youth or to buying and voting decisions. Nor is it only to engage with the ideological legitimations of the modern state. It is, rather, to make arguments about the forms and determinants of sociocultural development as such. The potential of communication study, in short, has converged directly and at many points with analysis and critique of existing society across its span.

This book is a sustained effort to trace this extraordinary transit of ideas. Useful historical exegeses of thinking about communication, of course, already exist—one thinks first of Hanno Hardt's *Critical Communication Studies* and of Dan Czitrom's chapters in *Media and the American Mind*. I have taken it upon myself to add to this body of work principally for two reasons. First, the specialized literature, with its often unprecedented quality of scholarship, is quickly altering our received sense of the past; indeed, the issues are open at such a number of points that it becomes necessary to think afresh about the overall historical record. Second, I believe that such an extended historical map of our intellectual topography may also help us to look anew at some of the leading issues and problems of our own time.

My purpose is to untangle the complex processes of topical engagement, conceptual differentiation, and analytical synthesis that have structured critical inquiry into the character of communication as a determinate social force. Over the last century, as we will see, this claim of social power has been acknowledged in a variety of distinct and even disparate ways. The need, in turn, is to assess this sprawling and unruly intellectual progression across its range. But according to what guiding theoretical principles?

The question itself may be discomfiting. The field's longstanding preoccupation with narrowly instrumental problems has undoubtedly helped to obscure its theoretical affiliations. What intellectual history worthy of the name can attach to such mundane, and frequently manipulative, pursuits as how to develop a more reliable opinion poll, how to measure the extent of TV violence, or how to create a more effective political or marketing campaign? The difficulty of laying claim to a tradition of real significance for social theory would seem to be intrinsic in a curriculum that has contented itself, in Robert K. Merton's celebrated euphemism, with "theories of the middle range."[1] Are we not bound to recount the field's development as a mere parochial progression?

Nor is it obvious how to situate communication study—which became an established scholarly enterprise only during the middle decades of the 20th century—in relation to the inspiring concerns of the 19th century's master disciplines: philosophy, history, and political economy. The work of connecting formal thought about communication to classic lines of inquiry into the nature and forms of social life, the origins of economic value and surplus, and the purposes and character of human thought and action remains largely to be done. What does the historical record show?

I shall argue here that it reveals that the firmament of social theory has *not* been omitted or forsaken by communication study, but only at key points signally displaced. The theorizations which have indeed shaped and guided formal thought about communication lie largely tacit and submerged, and their unrecognizability ironically may owe as much to social theory's own abiding indifference as to communication study's malfeasance.[2] In turn, the challenge is to salvage the infrastructure of theory that underlies inquiry into communication, and to make sense of its historical logic. But again, then, according to what principles?

Much can be learned—as Golding and Murdock[3] suggested some years ago—by seeking to explicate the concepts of society and of social relations which have spiraled through this field. These two cardinal axes of modern social theory will be found also to have played an immanent role in the evolution of communication inquiry. On one hand, then, following a recommendation offered in a different context by Martin Jay,[4] the need is to tease out the field's successive notions of a purported social whole or totality, that we may trace a first subterranean axis of its theoretical identity and development. On the other hand, we must simultaneously seek to comprehend the ascribed linkages between communication and social relations. For my purposes in this book, this can be done best by fastening on how formal thought about communication has continually positioned itself in regard to "labor." A few words on each of these admittedly opaque claims will not be out of place.

Let me begin with the concept of social totality. What, we may ask, have been the schemas through which successive schools have thought to pose the relationship between the communication process and an overarching social field?

There are three formal alternatives; each has been variously pursued over the course of a century of communication study. First, some thinkers have tried to add communication processes or functions to a pre-existing concept of social totality; conceptions of totality are thereby mechanically modified, via one or another new ingredient. The ubiquitous declaration that there is something radically new about this or that communication technology is often made against such a background; so is the observation that mass media should be apprehended as distinctively contemporary agencies of social control. At a certain point, however, we can sense in such claims a second tendency, toward a more thoroughgoing substitution: in this case communication is employed, sometimes quite comprehensively, to supplant or stand in for any pre-existing conception of social totality. To say that "communication is the fundamental social process" is an example. Finally, there have also been synthetic efforts whereby "communication" is brought into "society" even as, in consequence, both ideas are altered. To say that "the system of communication exists interdependently with the political and economic systems" provides a nominal instance of such a synthetic mode of address.

These three conceptual frames—supplementary, substitutive, and synthetic—are not mere abstract or random alternatives. Rather they have succeeded one another in an overarching historical progression, whose significance has gone generally unnoticed. This historical orbit, we will find, has been a function mainly of the way in which seemingly disparate theories of communication, offered within the divergent circumstances of each new watershed in the field's development, have approached the second of our two concepts: labor.

Discomfiture may now give way to disbelief. What, after all, has "communication" to do with "labor"? The answer is Nothing—and therefore everything. This book is, in large part, the story of how their polarization has shaped the fortunes of communication inquiry.

The idea that human activity is always integral in that it comprises both mental and physical dimensions has not managed to predominate—or for long periods even to survive—in social theory. Instead such a unitary framework for comprehending human self-activity has been continually relinquished. Communication study has been an active party to this work of disengagement; at special, vitalizing moments, it has also sponsored attempts at reconciliation.

To be sure, a conceptual schism of such magnitude hardly could be confined to formal thinking about communication; the point is rather that it swallowed up social thought more generally. Because it repeatedly proved decisive for this field's development, however, the history of communication study is perhaps the most promising site we have for excavating the intellectual forms applied, over the last century or so, to the ancient fissure between head and hand.

"Communication" was lodged on the ostensive plane of language, ideology, and meaning only as "labor" came reciprocally to affix to a seemingly remote arena of energy and action. "Communication," that is, became free to demarcate humankind's vast and multifarious potential for symbolic interaction only as "labor" contracted (as it had long since begun to do) around a sharply restricted range of human effort: physical toil or, later, wage work or, most recently, the endeavors that transpire within heavy industry.[5] These two movements of thought were not simply concurrent, however, but intertwined. At the very historical moment that the separation of hand and brain—and more precisely, of conception and execution—was becoming decisive within the social formation,[6] communication study began to expand into the conceptual space bequeathed by the parallel tendency to separate "intellectual" and "manual" labor.

The difficulties seemed increasingly insurmountable for those who would seek to utilize "labor," contrariwise, as the touchstone of a nondualistic position on the nature of human self-activity. The concept appeared to fall far short of capturing the salient features of modernity. How could "labor" be utilized, after all, to take the measure of the cavernous gulf that had apparently come to divide contemporary society from its 19th-century forebears? How could "labor" account for either the new cultural dominants of consumerism and leisure, or the growing economic significance of services and white-collar work, as opposed to manufacturing industry and its allied industrial working class? Yet it is striking that even alternative conceptual bases for a nondualistic framework—and, as we shall see, there have been some—have never been able to constitute a lasting alternative formulation.

Theorizing Communication nevertheless rejects all claims for such a bifurcation of human enterprise, including those that seek to assert dualism as an unchanging and axiomatic ontological condition. Nor are those attempts closer to my own that try to reunite those seemingly disparate categories of language and action—or, to employ the terms used here, communication and labor—via poststructuralist notions of "discourse" or "discursive practice," notions that seek self-consciously to escape the "productivist" bias seemingly inherent in a now-outdated modernism. I will argue in this book that such formulations originate specifically in the same dualism they purport to surmount, and that, consequently, they ironically avoid as much as they transcend.

Leaving substantial discussion of these issues for the chapters that follow, I wish to suggest here only that by reinstating a different concept of labor we may arrive at a very different result. In the perspective offered by intellectual history—that is, of the "historicity of the concepts and categories by which we attempt to understand"[7]—to charge that "labor" is categorically bankrupt or obsolescent is only to say that it has gone out of intellectual fashion. The urgent questions have to do with how and why. To address them, we may begin by embracing that Aristotelean concept of labor—intelligent action—which figured so largely in the thought of both Hegel and Marx.[8] In this tradition, I begin, then, by defining labor not as mere physical production or bodily toil, but as the species-specific capacity for human self-activity to which speaking and thinking, as well as action and energy, are alike integral.[9] Where might such a revisionary assumption—that these twin planes, "communication" and "labor," could not in fact ever really be separated except for schematic purposes—leave us with regard to the history of communication study?

In fact, as I will try to show throughout this book, it casts this entire history in a new light, for it permits us to see that the work of the field has often proceeded as if this dichotomy were real. The first questions for us to address, then, necessarily pertain to when and why this dualism—which led a protean existence and, to repeat, not simply within this one area of endeavor—became significant for students of communication.

Here is my argument: Constituting itself in light of an inclusive and integral conception of human self-activity—productive labor—communication study ironically commenced to develop only in spite of this same formulation. The continuing inability to integrate, or even to encompass, "labor" and "communication" within a single conceptual totality marked a coherent—and fateful—turn in organized thought. Over fully a century-long span, successive theorizations of communication came to revolve around variously reified views of "intellectual" labor, that is, around a partial, but seemingly substantial and autonomous, category of human effort.

Formal study of communication was born and bred of contention over the place of institutionalized communication in American life. As successive inflows of concern about the media washed through academe, scholars' attention and priorities—their intellectual apparatus for apprehending the place of communication in society—underwent repeated metamorphoses. *Theorizing Communication* underlines the continuing significance for inquiry of this contextualist tradition.

In Chapter One I show not only that there was a robust and far-ranging tradition of popular criticism of the institutions of communication, but also that this criticism was embedded within the still-vibrant tradition of "producer republican" thought. Seeking to generalize or at least to elevate the status of handicraft work, in which conception and execution were united, this perspective, which had played a vital role throughout antebellum decades, enjoyed a final efforescence during the 1880s and 1890s, before giving way to increasing inroads being made by "unskilled" factory work and, on the other side, by a growing corps of white-collar employees. Ironically, therefore, even for the radical critics of late 19th-century capitalism and communication—those who sought to imagine a "producer's" republic grounded in "productive labor"—no truly comprehensive and integral category of "production" or "labor" was achieved. As head and hand came to be ever more massively sundered in the world, so they were also polarized within theory.

Such an axial displacement of a unified concept of human self-activity is illustrated by the contradictory position of the first major communication theorist I discuss: John Dewey. Dewey is important not only because other writers on the intellectual history of communication say he is, but also because his pragmatism, or instrumental philosophy, influenced subsequent writers on communication—C. Wright Mills, for example. A member of the first generation of research university-based intellectuals, Dewey is significant for having developed his cardinal concept of "experience" specifically as means of steering round the deepening social (and entrenched philosophical) dualism between head and hand.

Yet already by the 1890s "labor" was eschewed by Dewey in this integrative attempt. Within the alternative framework given by "experience," moreover, "communication," or "organized intelligence," supplied for Dewey—who was himself versed in the radical-reform tradition—a supposedly intrinsic means of reconciling or ameliorating social division. Even a trained philosopher, therefore, whose conscious effort was to transcend dualism, here fell tacitly prey to it. "Organized intelligence" came to the forefront of Dewey's philosophy, finally, exactly as, through an uneven movement, "intellectual" functions were beginning to be systematically reorganized throughout the wider society. One might say that, when considered as a social theory, Deweyan instrumentalism reified, rather than critically appropriated, the profound changes occurring throughout the contemporary social division of labor.

A second phase in the development of U.S. communication study went well beyond this early displacement of an integral notion of human self-activity. During the interwar period analysts looked to communication to effectuate a far-reaching conceptual supplement to existing views of the social process. This was again a complex development, as I show in Chapter Two.

Virtually all across the ideological spectrum, beginning in the later 1930s, communication researchers shared two overarching concerns for a key decade, the decade in which communication study began to be formally institutionalized. First, they agreed that the organization and social implications of propaganda—linked intimately with the "agencies of mass persuasion" such as film, radio, and newspapers—posed worrisome political and moral issues. Second, as I show, they associated these problems and, specifically, the potency of propaganda with the continuing growth of "unaffiliated" white-collar strata. Thus the inability to grasp an increasingly central modality of labor as but another form of human self-activity became profoundly implicated in theorizing about communication.

For Depression- and war-era writers on propaganda, however, these loosely shared concerns about propaganda were also tinged by a third, historically specific recognition: that, in the U.S. of the later 1930s, there existed a glaring gap between popular opinion and media—more precisely, *press*—opinion. The public was squarely behind the New Deal; publishers were almost equally solidly against it. After the Roosevelt landslide in the 1936 election, the existence of this chasm had to be virtually taken for granted by anyone writing about institutionalized communication. Looking to developments occurring across the Atlantic and Pacific Oceans, radicals thus pointed to the growing centralization of the communications industries in the hands of business and political elites, as salient reminders to an actively critical public that—a terrifying portent—"it can happen here." Backed by powerful institutions, mainstream analysts, in contrast, began to develop means of assaying the consequences of this same fissure for political campaign strategy and for overall business leadership of American society. Along the way they developed the notion that persuasion was most effective when it was a multifaceted process, containing both mass-mediated and interpersonal dimensions.

These diverging perspectives broke apart after the onset of the Cold War. Mainstream writers, in keeping with their pluralist premises, reified the gap between press and public opinion and systematically exaggerated "the part played by people" in the communication process, even as, at least in a domestic context, they discounted the social organization and propagandistic potential of the mass media. Radicals, on the other hand, utilizing the theory of mass culture which had begun to be elaborated during the 1930s, reified the gap's closure and turned to formulations that accentuated the newfound role of media manipulation as a means of social control. Onto a presumedly capitalist totality they thus purported to graft an enigmatic and potent new supplement: ideology. Yet again, however, as I detail in the case of C. Wright Mills, the continued growth of theoretically anomalous white-collar occupations lay at the heart of this reformulation; for, by a process of transference, it was the growing preponderance of this new and "unattached" social subject which conferred upon mass culture much of its apparently deadly efficacy. Once again, in sum, the identity of communication study became bound up with the reification of a single vital aspect of human practice.

It was not long before each of these early postwar conceptions—the radical critique of mass culture and the "limited effects" school that formed the mainstream of academic communication study—began to face criticism. The latter emanated from what have since become largely separate projects: British cultural studies and the critique of cultural imperialism. Initially, however, as Chapter Three shows, these were interrelated radical endeavors, linked by their common rejection of behavioral orthodoxy and by their shared concern to develop a revisionary concept of "culture" as a means of reuniting head and hand within an encompassing notion of human self-activity.

The critique of cultural imperialism responded directly to the concerns expressed by leading "Third World" revolutionary intellectuals: Frantz Fanon, Amilcar Cabral, and others. "Culture" it perceived as a newly crucial strategic front within the ongoing reintegration of transnational capitalism, under the aegis mainly of U.S. corporate and state interests. To be sure, the critique continued to express some of the characteristic features of the theory of mass culture, most notably, the latter's willingness to view the media as the prime contemporary means of manipulative social control. But the critique of cultural imperialism also harbored two other aspects, which ultimately—if only momentarily—permitted it to diverge radically from the mass culture thesis: first, it flowed against the mainstream, not only of "administrative" research but also of contemporary Marxism, in attempting to rejoin, if not entirely to reconcile, "culture" and "political economy" in theory. Therefore, second—and above all—the critique sustained, in the form of the movements for national liberation that had developed throughout much of the poor world, a prospectively unified concept of human social agency. In this sense and to this degree, "culture" became for the critique the site at which human practice stood to be reintegrated. The delicacy of this admittedly incomplete theorization, however, was such that when the movements for national liberation began to falter during the 1970s the critique of cultural imperialism fell back on a concept of totality in which capital became the sole significant social actor. It thus became paradoxically vulnerable to those who, lacking sympathy for *any* concept of imperialism, cultural or otherwise, now began to charge the critique with having *neglected* human agency.

In the priority which it momentarily conferred on human social agency the theory of cultural imperialism concorded well with early British cultural studies. The second half of Chapter Three details the striated intellectual history of this latter project, paying attention to the evolving thought of Raymond Williams. I show that Williams sought expressly to use "culture," in the same way Dewey had relied upon "experience," as a synthetic term, a means of unifying the diverse aspects of contemporary society. In particular, "culture" permitted the split between "mental" and "manual" labor to be sidestepped. This formulation, however, despite its powerful challenge to received radical thought, contained its own unbreachable theoretical difficulties.

Williams utilized a complex and sometimes downright contradictory notion of "culture." On one side, in his theorization, his reliance on "culture" to denote an integrative totality of experience often seemed to give way, again recalling Dewey, to "culture" in the more restricted and conventional sense of creatively shared meanings. On the other side, "culture" for the early Williams also seemed to resonate to a single, ineffable principle, endlessly reproducing itself across the social field. A political party, a play, or virtually any other practice or form all might be used to furnish evidence of what he still discerned as a singular and unitary "structure of feeling." Not surprisingly, with the proliferation of the new social movements during the 1960s, this view became—and, I argue, was seen by Williams to have become—increasingly untenable. A different theorization of "culture" and of the totality would be required.

In Chapter Four I offer an overview of three nearly contemporary attempts to address these issues and some of their offshoots. First I survey Althusser's structural Marxism, specifically in reference to the evolving variant of cultural studies practiced by Stuart Hall and the Centre for Contemporary Cultural Studies at Birmingham. Then I turn to the seemingly disparate theory of postindustrial or information society, elaborated by Daniel Bell and others, mainly in the U.S. I show that a reciprocal and tacit attempt to privilege intellectual labor as a separate sphere—via "culture" and "information," respectively—was grounded in each case in a conscious withdrawal from received concepts of labor. This explicit displacement of "labor," which was now conceived almost automatically as denoting simply industrial waged labor, and which was now open to growing feminist attack for this reason, resulted in theory's turn away from any integrated and encompassing concept of human self-activity. It soon was accompanied by a more frontal rejection of "labor," and a far more dramatic and explicit reification of intellectual labor, in a third, influential school of thought, loosely associated with poststructuralism. Forsaken by such writers as Foucault and then Baudrillard was the earlier view shared by theorists of mass culture that the mass media provided a kind of ideological supplement which sustained the basic (but remote) workings of capitalist society. It is not simply that these writers came to reject the primacy of capitalism in the ordering of social relations. It is that they discerned in reified concepts of intellectual labor a thoroughgoing substitutive foundation for the social totality. Soon, and relatedly, the latter was hardly any longer even admitted as a viable concept.

Thus a profound and prolonged fissure in society and in social thought led analysts, who were, after all, overwhelmingly intellectuals themselves, once again back to additive and substitutive modes of animating the "communication/society" couplet. Communication was increasingly portrayed as a separate, and often foundational, sphere. These travails notwithstanding, successive theorizations continued to extend and enlarge the terrain over which significant operative features of a now seemingly separate domain of communication could be traced. That twin process of displacement and creative engagement has led back, however, during our own time, to the submerged conceptual emphasis on unified self-activity that, around the turn of the 20th century, provided a negative origination point for communication study. Based on further investigation of the concept of labor, I think that our own moment of intellectual revision promises to endow the "communication/society" relationship with a new and common basis. This difficult and still unfinished journey portends, in other words, a profound reconfiguration of the relation between the determinate figure of communication and its societal ground.

In my conclusion, I seek such a reformulation by explicating the later thought of Raymond Williams. It is my hope that communication study can eschew its endless reifications of intellectual labor by effecting a return to an integral concept of human self-activity, such as that which was once striven for by the term "labor." On such a basis alone, it seems to me, can established conceptual oppositions—such as those that have long acted to separate analysis of media production from media consumption or reception by audiences, the members of which labor not only at paid and unpaid jobs, but also *as* viewers, listeners, and readers— be supplanted by a focus on the successive twin "moments" of media production. Perhaps it should not go without saying that theory must win to this new position without neglecting the determinative role of capital within contemporary society.

I intend this book, then, to be a means not only of inventorying our collective tool kit but, beyond this, of reckoning the latter's contents. The need for such a study idea announced itself with particular force when, some years ago, I set about to prepare a formal speech to honor my onetime doctoral advisor.[10] It is fair to say that this book had its formal beginning in that occasion; in turn it affords me a new reason to give credit to George Gerbner, who, alongside his colleagues at the (then) Annenberg School of Communications, helped to instill in me a deep interest in this field's fascinating and under-appreciated history.

When I became a graduate student, I fancied that entry into the discipline of communication would afford me a unique license to bind together in an emerging theoretical synthesis my interests in cultural criticism and political economy. I was wrong. Of course I found at once that the study of communication already possessed a freestanding identity, and one that proved resistant to both poles of my interest. From the standpoint of the communication study of this early 1970s vintage, my own prospective enterprise therefore remained tantalizingly opaque. Indeed it has taken me the better part of two decades to understand the historicity of the hoped-for synthesis that motivated my initial entry into communication study, that is, to situate it in the field's own evolution. This book is one result.

Over these years, Marcus B. Rediker has urged me repeatedly to explore this history in public view; through his own example, he has helped me to see the necessity for undertaking what used to be called "history from below." Through most of this same interval, Vincent Mosco has pushed me steadfastly to accept the challenges proffered by problems of communication for social theory. Both of these dear friends have given me repeated lessons in engaged and scrupled scholarship.

Over the entire period of this work's gestation, Susan G. Davis has acted as a sustaining and regenerative force. And through their occasionally uproarious and always enlivening revelry, Lucy H. Schiller and Ethan D. Schiller specifically inspired the integral conception of human self-activity that infuses this work. I thank them.

Zach Schiller has always been a responsive sounding-board; his boundless knowledge of the day-to-day workings of the U.S. political economy makes him an equally invaluable source of ideas. I have also continued to benefit from the learning and example of Anita R. Schiller and Herbert I. Schiller, who have been engaged participants in some of the trends and developments that I try to trace here.

Full of newspaper clippings and questions, Mary Ann Davis graciously allowed me to hold onto the belief that I was making a kind of sense. I will always remember a walk with David G. Davis—one of many, over the years—during which I confided some of my hopes for this project. His unwavering support was characteristic.

My students Meighan Maguire, Dennis Mazzocco, and Lora Taub have helped to inspire and, periodically, to rekindle the excitement I have had for this project. Michael Cole, Susan G. Davis, George Mariscal, Robert McChesney, Vincent Mosco, Herbert I. Schiller, Michael Schudson, and Lora Taub generously read different drafts of the manuscript and proffered invaluable criticisms. Antonia Meltzoff helped me to see that I could and should write this book; conversations over the years with Jeanne Allen, Michael Bernstein, and Robert McChesney—with whom I have had the pleasure of ongoing dialogue on a whole range of issues—energized me to stick with it. When I had the good sense to consult Carlos Blanco Aguinaga, he proved a beacon of unassuming wisdom. Everette E. Dennis did not make possible a year's stay at the then Gannett Center for Media Studies at Columbia University so that I could produce *this* work; but I hope he will not be too dissatisfied by the result.

Acknowledgment must be made to the Speech Communication Association, for permission to use material from my article, "From Culture to Information and Back Again: Commoditization as a Route to Knowledge," in *Critical Studies in Mass Communication* 11 (1) (March 1994): 92-115; and to the International Communication Association, for permission to use material from my article, "Back to the Future: Prospects for Study of Communication as a Social Force," in the *Journal of Communication* 43 (4) (Autumn 1993): 117-124.

Del Mar, California   D. S.
December 1995

Contents

THEORIZING COMMUNICATION

CHAPTER ONE

Communication and Labor in Late 19th-Century America

[I]deas belong to human beings who have bodies, and there is no separation between the structures and processes of the part of the body that entertains the ideas and the part that performs acts.

John Dewey[1]

The separation of hand and brain is the most decisive single step in the division of labor taken by the capitalist mode of production.

Harry Braverman[2]

''. . . what solution, if any, have you found for the labor question? It was the Sphinx's riddle of the nineteenth century. . . .

''As no such thing as the labor question is known nowadays. . . . I suppose we may claim to have solved it. . . .''

Edward Bellamy[3]

In the 19th-century United States, criticism of communication institutions and practices was rife and often sharp. The widest and most significant antipathetic current, during the century's final decades, streamed through labor organizations and oppositional political movements. Lodging repeated protests against the accelerating integration of major media—both the press and the wireline systems of telegraphy and telephony—into the expanding circuits of corporate capital, a broad

3

span of reform groups proposed various collectivist and mutualistic alternatives for the ownership and operation of communications.

This mutualism found its way into the thinking about communication undertaken at century's end, by reform-minded academics associated with emerging research universities and with increasingly bounded scholarly disciplines. Yet we will find that their thought was profoundly marked by an increasingly significant conceptual truncation, or exclusion, from which the most widely available radical traditions likewise suffered. The difficulty lay in comprehending and theorizing the elemental equivalence of productive activity—that is, "labor"—across its range. In particular, it proved impossible, and sometimes uncongenial, to conceptualize so-called "intellectual labor" or "brain work" as existing on a par with skilled tradeswork, factory toil, farming, or domestic labor. John Dewey's notable attempt to provide a philosophical basis for regarding head and hand as an encompassing and inclusive unity proceeded, therefore, only by bypassing the overly restrictive characterizations of "labor" which resulted. The contradictory framework that Dewey created, for all its attractive features, therefore nonetheless also carried a debilitating and, as it turned out, enduring earmark: in Deweyan instrumentalism, "labor" came to be separated from—but also by—formal thought regarding "communication." Dewey's was only the first in what would prove to be a succession of disparate communication theories which displaced this indispensable category.

I

During the 1820s and 1830s, widespread disaffection developed among urban artisans, producers of everything from carriages to shoes to printed business forms, with the growing hold over society exercised by "monopolizing" capitalists. Economically, the independent craft worker was increasingly hard-pressed. Utilizing a coherent system of thought, which historians have come to call "artisan" or "producer republicanism," these tradesmen insisted on their own equal rights, not only to property, but also to political power and knowledge.[4] Widespread antagonism to the elite status and inequitable function of the commercial newspaper was one byproduct of this more encompassing movement. Concerted efforts to establish a more democratic popular press spawned a flock of cheap commercial journals, which energetically cast themselves as an alternative to their pricy rivals: making new room for the concerns of non-elite white men, but themselves still tending to subordinate the interests of women, while often actively denigrating people of color.[5] A related struggle arose in regard to the social purposes and chief beneficiaries of the posts.[6] As against those merchants and elite publishers who were coming to rely on private "express" services to advance their own commercial speculations in two booming commodity markets—cotton and news—antimonopolists admonished that "[i]t should not be permitted that an individual should establish a mode of communication and continue it by which intelligence should be received and acted upon by him before the community at large can have the benefit of it."[7] The Post Office, they insisted, should provide a comprehensive, nondiscriminatory, and exclusive service. Through subsequent decades, Post Office service was indeed extended and diversified. However, the concurrent proliferation of specialized business services, afforded by the new technology of telegraphy, massively subverted any thoroughgoing democratic restructuring of institutionalized communication.

Popular scrutiny of the existing state of communications continued to increase toward a historical zenith, reached during the decades around the turn of the 20th century. In this later period, a shifting array of radicals and reformers sought to dispel or at least mitigate the ravaging conflicts and problems ushered in by the new industrial capitalism. With roots planted not only in different sections of the working class, but also in the farm community and the growing urban middle class, the reformers naturally ranged widely in ideological temper. That they shared a loose commitment to collectivism, and even to "mutualism over competitive individualism" thus did not prevent significant antagonisms from erupting among them.[8] In this fluid intellectual and ideological environment, radical reformers could draw on conceptions as diverse as those offered by Henry George's "single tax,"[9] the moderate socialist Laurence Gronlund's "cooperative commonwealth,"[10] a grassroots agrarian Populism,[11] a militant trade unionism,[12] Marxian socialism, feminism, and a range of ameliorationist schemes stressing Christian uplift, social harmony, and economic efficiency.[13] Proselytizers of a social gospel harmonized relatively well with middle-class proponents of systematic arbitration in disputes between labor and capital, and with some settlement house reformers and evolutionary socialists. But real discord could also flare up between these last-named groups and working-class advocates of vindicative social action grounded in both shop-floor solidarities and the still dominant thought-system of producer republicanism. Animated above all by the practices and concerns of skilled craftsmen and mechanics, producer republicanism bridged over to many industrial workers, small merchants, shopkeepers, farmers, and even clerks.[14]

Folded into this range of rival mutualisms, at a greater or lesser remove from their central doctrines and purposes, were anticompetitive conceptions of communication. The often vital role ascribed to communication by diverse reformers between the 1870s and the 1910s, however, has not been well served by scholars.[15] Several general aspects of these popular critiques of communication need to be teased out because of their underlying relevance to the academic discussion of communication that followed in their train.

Of primary concern, to begin with, were disabling new constraints on the press. Urban commercial and political newspapers had been closely tied, during the 1830s, to class privilege, and their institutional dependencies continued to be debated. In a book-length exposé published on the eve of the American Civil War, Lambert Wilmer had generalized: "Our journalism is both tyrannical and slavish; it succumbs to every powerful influence, and it is bold and independent only when it attacks the weak and defenseless."[16] But by the 1880s, the class bases of commercial journalism began to be criticized quite pointedly in terms of the predisposing and prejudicial effects of capital. Hidden owners—railroad magnates, corporation financiers, and industrial capitalists such as Jay Gould, Henry Villard and John D. Rockefeller—were widely, and validly, suspected of covert attempts to infiltrate the nation's press. Corporate capitalists' attempts to sway public opinion toward private ends were matched by the corporate press's willingness to disguise paid advertisements as news.[17] Far from being free, the newspaper was open only to the ideas of its proprietors and advertisers—the summary verdict rendered by one longtime radical.[18] John Jarrett, president of the Amalgamated Association of Iron and Steel Workers, expanded on this theme:

> Our people are under the impression that the press ought to be the mouthpiece of the sentiments of the people in general, and they are also under the impression that the press is really subsidized by capital, and perhaps by these large corporations. . . . They think it very wrong that the truth is not sent out, not only to the workingmen but to every man in the United States. We believe that the press is largely subsidized by certain corporations, and that it simply works to carry out the ideas of those men whose cause it has espoused, and we do not think that is right.[19]

In 1883, the same year that Joseph Pulitzer purchased the *New York World* in hopes of finding a lucrative means of redirecting the relationship between commercial journalism and the urban working class, Scots-born typefounder and union organizer Edward King reiterated Jarrett's ideas:

> The relation of the press to the labor movement of course is a very bitter one. The laboring classes . . . have great antipathy to the newspapers. . . . It is also a very widespread belief among the working classes that you should not believe anything you read in the newspapers. The want of that faith in the veracity and truthfulness of literary men is one of the phases of the labor movement that I consider very remarkable indeed. The feeling is away beyond what could be accounted for by anything else than very gross cases of misrepresentation, and very exaggerated cases of opposition. . . . The influence of capital upon the fourth estate I regard as most corrupt and fatal, and a thing very much to be regretted, because when you recognize the fact that these influences have not that hold they once had on the formation of the opinions of the people, and when you remember that the press is rapidly

taking the place of what the pulpit once did, I think it is a matter of very grave concern that any large body of people should lose faith in the veracity and justice of a power like the press. . . . it is a most unhealthy state of things that a power such as the press should be believed by the working classes to be warring with them and against their interests.[20]

King went on to speak of "frequent" efforts by "the working classes" to boycott those commercial newspapers which had given particular offense. When questioned about the workings of this early application of the boycott strategy he replied:

> They organize committees in every district of the city, exercise their influence as purchasers upon news stands—the men who own news stands—and they also resolve not to purchase such papers as are boycotted, but resolve to read them without purchasing them. It is believed, I know by the workingmen in this city, that they have brought newspapers to terms once or twice. . . .[21]

King added, as well, that it was now "beyond question that the working class believe they must have papers of their own."[22] Far from being specialized trade union organs, moreover, these journals, he held, should cater to a general interest. King testified, "While the working classes want their trade news, want a labor paper, still they have a burning desire to know what has happened connected with other affairs besides trades affairs, and workingmen cannot be counted upon as willing to throw over their interest in everything else for the sake of a trade paper." But a "want of capital sufficient to advertise a daily labor paper" combined with the difficulty of getting into the Associated Press to rule out such a possibility. The working classes had come, he said, to believe that the only solution was to cooperate. "[T]he tendency now amongst the people," King asserted, "is to believe that all efforts [to start up working-class newspapers] must be failures except co-operative, under a law which prevents the capture of the paper by the shareholders, and prohibits any person from having more than one share, &c."[23]

King's antagonism to the Associated Press news agency was tributary to a wide current of radical criticism.[24] To comprehend this concern, we must know that in the decades after the Mexican-American War (1846–48), newsgathering became profoundly dependent on the telegraph. Telegraphy, in turn, was one of a trio of infrastructural functions (the others were rail transport and banking) whose economic roles attracted increasingly widespread popular antipathy. Many historians agree that railroads, banks, and telegraphs acted as pivots of an emergent corporate capitalism. Before them, no truly interregional capitalist economy could be contemplated. By their means, on the other hand, comparative economic advantages were enlarged and deepened, centralization of industry generative of vast productivity increases became feasible, and corporate decisionmaking on a nationwide scale emerged.

Within this broader matrix, Richard B. Du Boff has detailed the extent to which this transition was predicated on the information advantages conferred on capital by the telegraph.[25] The latter's domination by Western Union seemed, however, to many farmers, workers, and small businesspersons once more to exemplify the growing hold of a predatory and enveloping corporate capitalism. Western Union, whose consolidation of U.S. telegraph networks was complete by 1866, comprised the second corporate monopoly of national scope—the first was the AP, with which the telegraph behemoth became closely interlocked. Western Union confronted government with unprecedented private power, power it did not hesitate to utilize.[26] Its executives evinced a precocious talent for corporate maneuvering, providing free franking privileges to legislators, for example, with an eye to securing their votes should need arise.[27]

In many nations, as the telegraph was assimilated into the Post Office, it came to provide "a vital social link joining families and friends in joy and disaster . . . [and] transferring knowledge, instructions, and human feelings from city, country, suburbs, capital cities, and back again."[28] In the United States, in contrast, more than half a century later such "social uses" of telegraphy were still severely retarded by prohibitive rates. No less than 90 percent of early U.S. telegraph demand has been credited to business and press interests.[29] By the early 1880s, the telegraph was being utilized, according to the president of Western Union—which then controlled perhaps four-fifths of the nation's telegraphs—by at most 500,000 persons, less than 1 percent of the U.S. population; and no more than 5 or 6 percent of the company's total business concerned family or social matters. In contrast, in a small European country such as Belgium in 1880 private dispatches concerning family and social matters amounted to some 55 percent of the whole; in Switzerland, 61 percent.[30]

This pattern of business user domination persisted long into the telephone era. In 1890 Postmaster General Wanamaker characterized the portion of the community that used the telegraph as "infinitesimal."[31] Looking back on his turn-of-the-century Denver childhood, writer Gene Fowler related how "a telegram was a great event in anyone's life, and a fearful one as well. No one other than capitalists . . . ever sent or received telegrams unless there was illness or death in a family."[32] AT&T president Theodore Vail conceded as late as 1911 that "[t]he ratio of the use of the mails to the telegraph is nearly 100 to 1, and less than 5 per cent. of the whole population use the telegraph."[33]

Reformers were not slow to protest the inequity of these constraints on access. "By what gauge or standard shall we undertake to measure the benefit of cheap telegraphy in keeping alive and warm the relations of blood and friendship, and in relieving the anxieties of families, by bringing within the reach of the many that prompt intelligence as to the health and movements of their far-removed members which is now the luxury of the few?" asked Senator Nathaniel Hill in 1884.[34] Sky-high telegraph rates for many critics, however, were only a symptom of Western Union's massively invasive and disequilibrating monopoly over what the Populists generalized as "the transmission of intelligence," or "the means of transmission of information." At the center of the problem, as Charles A. Sumner focused the issue in 1879, was the nation's sorry failure to establish the telegraph as "a common carrier of intelligence."[35]

The historical status of the ensuing campaign to restructure telegraphy has been undervalued, even by sympathetic historians, who tend to subordinate it to the railroad, while also emphasizing the ideological limitations of the reform effort overall. William Appleman Williams, for example, declares that, far from amounting to some sort of agrarian socialism, the Populists' plan to nationalize the railroad, telegraph, and telephone systems was "merely carrying the logic of laissez faire to its classic fulfillment. Given the absolutely essential role of an open and equitable marketplace in the theory and practice of laissez faire, they concluded that the only way to guarantee the cornerstone of the system was by taking it out of the hands of *any* entrepreneur."[36] Leon Fink dissents from Williams's stress on "the limited ideological reach of . . . political demands focusing on 'commercial arteries' of the marketplace" that left "the system of private enterprise otherwise untouched." Fink suggests that a "more convincing explanation for the centrality of transit and communication systems to the radical demands of the period lies in the fact that it was here that public authority appeared most baldly not only to have sanctioned but also to have colluded with private 'monopoly.'"[37]

The popular critique of corporate ownership and control of communications as a site and an agency of class power may have been fiercely pointed, but it was hardly for this reason limited, misguided, or naive. What needs to be underscored is, in fact, its radicalism. The journalist Richard Hinton declared: " . . . as an observer and a student I have long since come to the conclusion that in this country at least the artificial person called a corporation, who is in possession of the public functions of a community, such as the railroad, the telegraph, and the bank, is a person, speaking of him as an artificial person before the law, whose existence is dangerous to the safety of the Republic."[38] The prevailing social purposes of the new telecommunications technology even intermittently provoked forcible responses, such as among Native Americans, who sometimes recognized a strategic need to defend themselves against the U.S. military by burning or ripping down "the singing wire."[39] In eastern Oklahoma as late as August 1917, for example, some 800 to 1000 tenant farmers, militantly opposed to U.S. entry into World War I, staged an armed uprising known as the Green Corn Rebellion, and commenced to cut telegraph wires.[40] Such collectivist destruction was a world removed from efforts by individual financiers, at telegraphy's inception during the late 1840s, to disrupt service as a means of preserving the confidentiality of their foreknowledge of conditions in European commodity markets, and thereby of gaining a speculative edge against the general public.[41]

Opponents of private telegraphy also concertedly embraced formal political action. In 1884, for example, the Anti-Monopoly Party Platform declared that "[t]he great instruments by which [interstate] commerce is carried on are transportation, money, and the transmission of intelligence. They are now mercilessly controlled by giant monopolies, to the impoverishment of labor, and the crushing out of healthful competition, and the destruction of business security. We hold it, therefore, to be the imperative and immediate duty of Congress to pass all needful laws for the control and regulation of those great agents of commerce. . . ."[42] Such a platform could not possibly be accommodated without a far-reaching and potentially explosive societal reorientation. However much reformers may have remained respectful of individual private property rights, therefore, their actions and demands bespeak resistance to, rather than an accommodation with, the ongoing "corporate reconstruction" of social life.

That a vital locus existed between the press and the telegraph, and that it had come to be dominated by another fearsome monopoly—that of the AP news agency—was, by the late 1870s, a chief focus of popular concern. This combined "news-telegraph monopoly" posed unprecedented threats to the polity as well as to the economy. For example, its widely reviled effort to steal the contested Blaine-Cleveland presidential election of 1884 (by delaying announcement of the voting results so as to give Republican politicos time to doctor tallies in key districts of New York State) "drew thousands of New Yorkers to the streets" during two days of demonstrations.[43] Some of the criticisms directed at the AP anticipated the arguments made a century later by poor world states against the role of media, again including the AP itself, in a new style of informal imperialism. They emanated from publishers and journalists in the western states, alongside those elsewhere who found themselves unable to secure an AP franchise. Their protest against the news monopoly encompassed both the AP's economic dominance and its tendency to represent issues from the perspective of capital—and eastern capital, to boot.[44] The radical journalist Richard Hinton thus recounted how, in the wake of Western Union's absorption of a small independent news agency, a subscribing local (Newburg, New York) newspaper had been barred from access to telegraphic news. This story offered, he claimed, an illustration, "which I think every practical journalist will understand," of the corporate pre-emption of "control over great functions of civilization like that of gathering the news and transmitting messages and intelligence."[45]

Antagonism also erupted from within organized labor's ranks. As early as 1869, for example, the National Typographical Union petitioned Congress to approve a bill establishing a government postal telegraph, "thereby increasing the demand for our labor, equalizing the business interests of the country, and destroying one of the worst monopolies in existence." The Typographers' ire was directed chiefly at the contracts which tied the Associated Press to Western Union, because, they asserted, such stipulations effectively decreed "that no more newspapers shall be published in the United States, and that those in existence who do not obtain their news through the Associated Press shall be suppressed, thereby lessening the demand for our labor."[46] The complaint recurred; in 1891 one union typographer declared: "Let the Government take charge of the telegraph and away will go the monopolistic Associated Press, franchises and all. Everybody could get telegraph news at the same price, newspapers could then run without the assistance of Jay Gould and the Western Union Company. . . ."[47] Workers continued to complain that the telegraph was used to their disadvantage in postbellum labor conflicts: private telegraph ownership by Western Union, they charged, denied them the chance to send pro-union messages over the network, while the interlinked AP news monopoly systematically slighted and suppressed news its proprietors deemed inimical to their class interests.[48] On grounds of both constraints on news content and employment practices, union printers led the fight to restructure the communications system with which newspapers were entwined.[49] That newspapers that subscribed to the wire service were barred from speaking out publicly against the Associated Press, by the threat of losing their franchise, only further inflamed antagonism.[50]

Recommendations for reform in turn had to look two ways: toward both the newspaper and the telegraph. Social responsibility and access were alike primary elements in thinking about the first issue, press reform:

> One more suggestion with regard to the newspapers. They are not the expression of the free public opinion of this country. I should suggest that a national law be passed compelling every man who owns a newspaper to leave a blank column to be filled up with the real opinions of the people— my opinion or yours. . . . Some plan of that sort is coming to be more and more essential for the salvation of this Republic.[51]

Something of the same idea appeared as well in the socialist Laurence Gronlund's more formal proposal, itself embedded in his encompassing reform projection. Borrowing from the influential early writings of Herbert Spencer, Gronlund insisted that "the State is a living Organism" whose growing interdependence had come to require "that central regulative system which Spencer says distinguishes all highly organized structures."[52] To establish the "Public Opinion of the practical majority" as the governor of this regulative system, "representative public journals," in addition to "collective control" of "all important instruments of production," would be required.[53]

> There will probably in every community be published an official journal which will contain all announcements of a public nature and all the news, gathered in the most efficient manner by the aid of the national telegraphic service, but no comments.
>
> But we are assured that besides these there will also be published many private journals, true champions of principles and measures. True, the printing press will be a collective institution—but it will be open to every one.[54]

Sixty years before the Hutchins Commission on Freedom of the Press bruited similar ideas, Gronlund proposed to guarantee universal access to the means of public opinion formation by turning the press into a common carrier for hire. What was in some ways a kindred effort to mutualize the nation's system of intelligence, as we shall see, was briefly projected in the following decade by the journalist Franklin Ford, and his associates, including the philosopher John Dewey.

What about the telegraph, the other pole of reform effort? If Western Union defined the negative model of system development, throughout the half-century following the Civil War, the United States Post Office comprised the chief positive model for reconfiguring the institutions of electrical communication. The Post Office probably constituted the most broadly familiar and genuinely popular of any federal agency. Edward Bellamy sought to utilize it as "the prototype" of the state socialism he called "Nationalism,"[55] while Gronlund hailed it for being "already essentially a Socialist institution."[56] The Post Office was seen, moreover, as a triumphant success in discharging its chief mission: to universalize the benefits of postal intercommunication. Gronlund thus sought to clinch an argument for enlarging the scope of the state by asking: "suppose a proposition was submitted to the people to relegate our mail-service back to private corporations, can any sane man doubt, that it would be overwhelmingly defeated . . . ?"[57] Why, as against the rapacity associated with Western Union, should not the Post Office model be generalized?

Not only, therefore, did reformers work to defend the Post Office against what one called "[t]he gold ring, the monopolies, and trusts [which] already control the avenues and agencies of rapid communication and intelligence."[58] Sometimes in unacknowledged alliance with business executives, farmers and laborers and, eventually, suffragettes also actively pressed to enlarge Post Office functions and to extend its territorial and social reach.[59] For half a century, indeed, reformers sought to make the Post Office the foundation for a successively enlarged set of public responsibilities. Second-class mails, rural free delivery, parcel post, postal expresses, postal savings banks—these pyramiding extensions of postal service were some of the results. Extensive debate and theorization of course accompanied this steady augmentation of government responsibility. Protesting that the telegraph had come under the sway of "one overgrown company which has absorbed to itself all other lines, with which no competition is possible, and which can absolutely disregard the rights of the citizen," political economists such as Henry George and Richard Ely thus sought to justify a government takeover by developing the theory that the telegraph, like the railroad, was a "natural monopoly." Said George in the mid-1880s: "Practically, I think the progress of events is toward the extension and enlargement of businesses that are in their nature monopolies, and that the State must add to its functions continually."[60]

This movement in favor of telegraph system restructuring repeatedly attained formal political prominence. Czitrom[61] notes that Congress considered seventy-odd bills designed to reform telegraphy between 1866 and 1900, most of which contemplated either a "postal telegraph"—a government chartered and subsidized private competitor to Western Union—or a government-owned and operated telegraph system. "I do not recognize the necessity of our telegraphic industry . . . being a capital stock concern," was the position of John S. McClelland, telegrapher and trade unionist, testifying before a Senate committee in mid-August 1883.[62] Following the failure that same month of the telegraphers' "Great Strike" against Western Union, as Edwin Gabler has asserted, many telegraph operators rallied to Henry George's United Labor Party and other groups calling for a postal telegraph.[63]

Trade unions continued to bring the issue to the fore during a new round of reform effort after the strike debacle.[64] Postalization, asserted the Cincinnati Typographical Union No. 3, would comply "with the wishes of the great majority of our trades-unionists, agriculturalists, merchants, etc., thus placing all who are compelled to use the telegraph or to rely on the same for their living or any part thereof, on an equal footing."[65] The Knights of Labor claimed to have submitted petitions to the 50th Congress (1887–88) containing no less than 530,000 signatures on behalf of postal telegraphy, and to have spent some $21,000 on public lectures on this subject throughout the country.[66] Unions were not alone in demanding telegraph industry reform. Members of the Farmers' Alliance, as well as a parade of Postmasters General and other government officials, also hoped to enfold telegraphy within the postal service. So too did many leading businesses. In 1890, Postmaster General Wanamaker enumerated the support for a postal telegraph shown by major business users of telegraph services. Memorials in favor of a postalized system had been received, he wrote—"without any effort on

my own part"—from the National Board of Trade and from some two
dozen local boards of trade and chambers of commerce, representing
commercial users in, among other places, Baltimore, Boston, Chicago,
Cincinnati, Detroit, Indianapolis, Milwaukee, Minneapolis, New York,
Philadelphia, and San Francisco.[67] "That man must be willfully blind
who does not see the vast and rising tide of public sentiment against
monopoly," declared Wanamaker, in proposing yet another version of
the postal telegraph, in his 1890 Annual Report.[68] National journals of
opinion, such as the *Arena,* continued to devote substantial space to the
subject, while scholars supplied learned argument and documentation.
The telegraph controversy was perhaps the first media debate in which
academic economists played prominent parts.[69]

Although some reformers were boldly undaunted by the qualitative
changes such steps entailed for the practice and theory of government,[70]
others were acutely mindful that, absent stringent safeguards, a government takeover might only inaugurate new evils. The chief worry was
that a government telegraph system would be incorporated into the
sprawling networks of patronage and political preferment which honey-
combed existing state agencies. "I don't think it should be regarded as
the province of lawyers and doctors and rum-shop politicians to pass
upon the qualifications of a man in telegraphy," declared P. J. Maguire,
the General Secretary of the Brotherhood of Carpenters and Joiners.[71]
Maguire's considered proposal merits our scrutiny:

> . . . first, we want the Brotherhood of Telegraphers legalized as an orga-
> nization by Congress, like any other corporate organization. Then let the
> Government inaugurate a postal telegraph service under its jurisdiction; or
> let it purchase the plant and place that plant in the control of this brother-
> hood, to be paid for by the brotherhood, the Government holding a mortage
> on it, and the brotherhood, at stated periods, making payments on it to the
> Government. But if the Government desires to institute a postal telegraphic
> service under its own direct administration, then I contend that, to avoid the
> evils of Government patronage incident to such a service, we should have a
> provision in the law that will institute a civil service commission composed
> entirely of members of the Brotherhood of Telegraphers to examine and
> pass upon the application of persons desiring positions in the service. My
> reason for that is, that I consider that if the brotherhood be legalized and the
> postal-telegraph service becomes the property of the national Government,
> then under those circumstances it would be to the interest of every employe
> to belong to the brotherhood; and I hold that the power of patronage in the
> corporation known as the State could be offset by the influence of the
> corporation composed of the telegraphers themselves, who, from their
> knowledge of their own profession, must be the people best qualified to pass
> upon the fitness of applicants for positions in the service. . . . There is this
> danger, if the Government takes the postal telegraph without some such
> check, that when, for instance, an employe gives some offense to the Gov-
> ernment officials—perhaps does not vote the ticket of the party in power—

he will lose his situation, and a system of blacklisting could be readily instituted by which he would be followed all over the country and prevented from obtaining employment. That is the case now under the Western Union Company, and the same system might be imitated even by those who administered the business for the Government. . . .[72]

Plans to vest operating control of a government telegraph in the Brotherhood of Telegraphers verged on more direct plans for cooperation via trade unionism. "One of my principal objects in joining" the Brotherhood of Telegraphers, recounted H. W. Orr, one of the union's seven-member executive committee, "was to bring about co-operative telegraphing among the operators themselves." While, Orr conceded, most union members enlisted simply for "protection against their employers," his own ambition was grander: to join in building and operating an independent telegraph system.[73] John S. McClelland, also a member of the Brotherhood, concurred in desiring "a line built by those engaged in the business of telegraphy, without the intervention of any middlemen or third parties. . . . the line-men now in the employ of the telegraph companies could construct the line, and the operators and the managers now in the employ of the telegraph companies could operate it."[74]

But for many, postalization was a stepping-stone in the right direction. As the emergent telephone industry's employment practices, ownership structures, and overall public service obligations in turn became matters of intense and overlapping scrutiny, the demand for postalization of telegraphs quickly came to encompass telephones or, simply, "means of communication." As I show elsewhere,[75] postalization of "the telephone utility" came to be viewed as especially important, as one reformer summed up, because—in this era of dramatically increased immigration—"the telephone is everybody's common means of communication, wherein, more so than with written communication, all tongues, all thought and expressions can be conveyed or transmitted by the persons interested, direct, without resort to writing and really by *personal* conversation."[76] Nationalization, accordingly, was an explicit plank in at least one third-party platform in every presidential election between 1884 and 1924,[77] while campaigns for municipal ownership erupted in many major cities in the decade before World War I. This restructuring initiative came to an end, ironically, only as a result of the dismal experience of actual operation by the Post Office, for one year, following U.S. entry into the Great War.

The demand for postalization even came to dovetail with a projected reform of the patent system. A brief survey of this effort will be useful as a springboard to discussion of what was—for the development of thinking about communication—the most prominent and far-reaching conceptual blockage faced by radical critics and would-be reformers. Henry Palmieri, an inventor, proposed in the 1880s that there be created a

"National Patent Agency, headquarters, Washington; sub-offices at the post-office of each State capital in the United States." The new agency would enforce payment to inventors of a standard 5 percent royalty by manufacturers utilizing their patents.[78] When questioned by a Senator as to why this projected agency could not itself take the form of a corporation, Palmieri responded unequivocally that such "a great monopoly . . . would become more powerful than the Government" and thus would make itself intolerable.[79]

Postbellum decades had seen an unprecedented intellectual and economic enclosure, as a result of the exercise of corporate patent monopoly—a trend associated with the dislodgment of the entrepreneurial inventor by the corporate science and engineering department.[80] Palmieri referenced this experience when he declared that "[t]here are a few inventors who succeed in obtaining payment for their services; there are thousands who spend their substance mentally and physically *pro bono publico* and get starvation for their pains." In an increasingly widespread contest between brains and money, the former were "frozen out"; growing corporate control over invention—Palmieri cited the sewing machine, the telegraph, and numerous railroad improvements—was the unhappy result. "This trick played upon inventors by men of means is so well understood, so frequently witnessed, that its victims cease to inspire a sympathy"; nevertheless, he protested, patent monopolies were tantamount to theft against the entire citizenry. Palmieri's detailed plan for a "national patent agency" thus projected major gains to "consumers" from a standard, low royalty, allowing profits to "go to the people."[81] "Even our patent laws," agreed Gronlund (whose idiosyncratic conception existed at some distance from both producer republicanism and Marxian socialism), "with the general advantage for their primary idea, have become a means of enabling these capitalists, in no sense inventors, to levy heavy tribute upon the community for an indefinite length of time."[82]

Opposing these corporate efforts to enclose creative endeavor allowed some reformers to question the still often delicate status of intellectual property. The telegrapher and trade unionist John S. McClelland, for example, would simply have required the adoption of "legislation that would compel the Western Union company to surrender the right to any instrument that was solely for the public good." No corporation, McClelland explained, "should be allowed to monopolize a thing of that kind."[83] At its most evocative, this critique of intellectual property verged vaguely on the idea of invention as a collective social process embedded in an artisanal or craft labor system: "To whom does the telegraph belong?" asked Gronlund; and he answered: "To Society. Neither Prof. Morse nor any other inventor can lay sole claim to it. It *grew* little by little."[84] Inventors and their advocates not surprisingly had little doubt that, no less than manual or craft or farm work, their labor merited its just reward. The radical journalist John Swinton, supporting this position, took care to urge (though without specifying a workable mechanism for achieving such a goal) "freedom of patents . . . but with a royalty system."[85] And Palmieri proved quick to counter the claim "that although the laborer was worthy of his hire the inventor was not." "In this great bloodless war between labor and capital, and on the labor side of the question," Palmieri unequivocally declared, "we find the inventor, the creator of all improvements in the arts and sciences, the father of progress. . . ."[86] When pressed as to whether he considered himself "a laboring man," however, Palmieri hedged: "Yes, sir; I am essentially a laboring man."[87] His slight hesitation betrayed one important, and quickly fraying, end of the attempt to create an inclusive cooperative commonwealth.

In the twenty years between 1870 and 1890, by one estimate, members of the professions in the U.S. more than doubled—from 342,000 to 876,000; over this same span, moreover, the number of clerical and kindred workers shot up nearly sixfold, from 82,000 to 469,000.[88] If inventors and journalists, like the rest of this growing pyramid of academics and engineers, sales and clerical workers, were to achieve legitimate inclusion within the ranks of the "producing classes"—that expansive, imagined community at the heart of producer republicanism—their efforts had to be widely understood and accepted *as labor*. It is then profoundly significant that such acknowledgment remained, at best, haphazard. The character of so-called "intellectual" labor or "brain" work, into which this whole genus of activity seemed to fall, instead tended to become impenetrably opaque.

During the antebellum era, as Nicholas Bromell has shown, writers and critics had regularly invoked a basic distinction between mind and body, the better to dichotomize "mental" from "manual" labor. Militant craftsmen, such as the shoemaker William Heighton, had regularly proclaimed that the rich were, overall, "unproducers," who with their own hands "*shape* no materials, *erect* no property, *create* no wealth."[89] The artisans who developed this producer republican synthesis were confident that their own labor involved skill—a useful blend of mental and physical activity; bankers and commercial capitalists, by contrast, apparently by relinquishing any bodily investment in toil, transformed themselves into parasites. This distinction, which eventually found its way into Thorstein Veblen's biting analysis of the "leisure class," was useful in differentiating worthy producers—even while a growing proportion of them were becoming, simply, factory "hands"—from others, such as lawyers, who continued to be widely reviled for their occupational attachment to the use of state power against the working class.

But by the late 19th century, this theory's purchase on social reality was being placed under intense strain. Clerks and salespersons struggled to distinguish themselves from the unskilled, by identifying themselves as laborers on a par with the skilled trades, or on the other hand with middle-class professionals.[90] While lawyers were pridefully prohibited from membership in the Farmers' Alliance, and in the deliberately inclusive national union the Knights of Labor, local organizations of retail clerks did sometimes successfully affiliate.[91] Distinctions drawn between the salutary endeavors of the inventor and the predatory machinations of the great capitalist likewise grew troublesomely elusive.

The distinction that tended to be employed between "productive" and "unproductive" labor was anything but clearly drawn. "[I]n our Commonwealth," declared Gronlund, *"there will be a demand for the labor* of *every citizen. . . .* Mark! We speak of *productive* labor, and mean thereby labor that creates anything which men desire," be its products "physical, artistic or intellectual."[92] Such an encompassing category, however enticing and however much needed, was not easy to ground conceptually, nor even to demarcate. Indicative were the difficulties faced in this regard by a leading German-American socialist, at a congressional hearing:

> Q. Where do you limit the line of labor? Who is a laboring man and who is not a laboring man, according to your idea? A. Useful labor, I have already explained, is the only labor. All the rest is wasteful labor.
> Q. What is useful labor? A. That which produces wealth, directly or indirectly.
> Q. Take Mr. Vanderbilt, for instance. I do not know Mr. Vanderbilt, and I merely mention him as an example; nor have I any connection with men of such large wealth; but take him as a representative of his class, does not the man that directs the great influences that control industry become a working man?
> A. *He* does not direct anything. He pays directors, who do the work.
> Q. Is not his brain worth anything? A. No, not at all, since it is not exercised for the advantage of the country.
>
>   . . .
>
> Q. I should like you to tell me where is the line of distinction between useful labor and labor that is not useful. Is it in industrial employment—manual labor—or is it in all the exercises of the brain, just such as you have shown us to day?
> A. I have not for a moment denied that intellectual labor is labor; but this intellectual labor that is exercised to the damage of the whole society and country is not useful labor. Every labor must be useful in order to be true labor. That is the first distinction of political economy.[93]

Was it then labor's broadly "useful" contributions to society or its strictly economic role in "producing wealth" which was primary? How could a unitary category of productive labor be contrived, so as both to accommodate a host of different types of work, blending "manual" and "mental" work in innumerable ways, while still excluding other species of activity? In fact, quite disparate criteria continued here as elsewhere to confound analysis; and the result was that no clear-cut category of productive labor could be made to encompass so-called "intellectual" endeavor.

Historians have stressed that, during the 1880s, the Knights of Labor briefly stood for an inclusionary concept of labor, which gave a prospective common basis to the toil that animated workshop, field, factory and even household.[94] However, cracks shivered through the Knights' grand but somewhat rickety house of labor. Uncertainty about how to comprehend the growing raft of intellectual employments thus symptomatized a multifaceted problem: that producer republicans' dominant concept of labor ironically hindered them from theorizing "the producing classes" in the expansive way projected by their own rhetoric. Nor, in this crucial respect, did Marxian socialists or Bellamyite Nationalists do signally better. Disparagement of "brain" work alternated with its exhaltation; each took its place beside a concurrent tendency to devalue women's domestic labor and to accept that a "family wage" ideally should be paid to male "breadwinners"; and beside widespread acceptance of race- and gender-segmented labor markets and occupational structures. Indeed, the questions were intertwined; as Kocka emphasizes, the burgeoning white-collar occupations were often simultaneously coded by ethnicity, region and especially gender, which may have worked against the achievement of a shared working-class social consciousness.[95]

It was, however, the difficulty experienced in making a clear conceptual space for "intellectual" labor within the idea of productive activity that was specifically—and profoundly—relevant for thinking about communication, and this difficulty sprang, in turn, from a wide range of factors: the unfinished dislodgment of the craft worker from the center of the labor process, during the ongoing transition to an industrial capitalism that was itself soon to become increasingly beholden to ideas of "scientific management";[96] the related incomplete erosion of apprenticeship as a means of imparting craft skills; classical political economy's own persistent difficulties with the concept of labor;[97] and producer republicanism's inherited allegiance to the doctrine—in which the distinction between "manual" and "mental" labor became so generally and deeply ingrained as to become virtually a surrogate for an ontological distinction between body and mind—that nonmanual employments were, at best, "of lesser functional importance" for society.[98] As against all this, mutualist reformers now also had to confront the sudden and unprecedented growth, beginning during the antebellum decades but reaching explosive proportions nearer the turn of the century, of an industrial working class on one side and, on the other, of new social strata peopled by white-collar academics, secretaries, sales persons, and engineers as well as managers, whose relationship to production was indirect and mediated, and often seemed not only indefinite but actively parasitic.[99]

In this context, what is interesting is that the challenge mounted by

producer republicans and other mutualists to corporate capital and to
the wage relation, as putative intruders on a pre-existing totality, could
prove so energetic. During the 1880s, hundreds of thousands of workers
joined the Knights of Labor, the nation's first encompassing industrial
union, in the belief that a common identity provided a bond between
"producers," whose acknowledgment would be the first step toward
needed economic and political reforms. Included, in principle and in the
practice of some of the Knights' local assemblies, were at least some
"intellectual" vocations. Into the 1890s, the same inclusive spirit persisted within portions of the Farmers' Alliance, the group out of which
formed the People's (Populist) Party. With a suddenness that matched its
spectacular efflorescence during the previous decade, however, the capacity to imagine and attempt to organize "grand coalitions of producers" then gave way. In the face of a concerted employers' offensive,
state coercion, and effective cooptation by an entrenched two-party system, the inability to theorize productive activity across its extended and
seemingly disparate range evidently began to foreclose any hope of
viewing labor per se as constitutive of the social totality. Privileged segments of the labor force in turn beat a symptomatic retreat into protec-
tive craft unions and, it might be added, professional associations.[100]

Through the 1880s, in contrast, even though it was never effectively
answered, the question of "intellectual labor" still remained open to
creative address. Forty-five years before the Italian Communist Antonio
Gramsci launched his unsurpassed discussion of intellectuals by declaring that "in any physical work, even the most degraded and mechanical,
there exists a minimum of . . . creative intellectual activity,"[101] Baptist Hubert—a machinist—sought to neutralize the animus "intellectual
people" so regularly harbored against so-called unskilled laborers:

> The great mistake of intellectual people, I think, is that they believe me-
> chanics and workmen are working without brains. It is not so. Every man
> has brains, perhaps not highly cultivated, but, so far as his brains go, he uses
> them in his work. This is true not only of intellectual labor, as it is called, but
> it is true of all kinds of labor. Even the most humble worker uses his brains.
> The street-sweeper, although occupied in a very humble, and, to some a
> very disgusting work, cannot afford to do without his brains. If he does not
> use his brains to direct him you will find the place where he sweeps to be
> poorly swept. Neither, again, can a man leave his body behind. His body
> must move with his brain.[102]

Hubert's was not, like Gramsci's, a sustained attempt to grapple with
the theoretical status of intellectuals, but a more defensive effort to insist
that neither democratic rights nor economic well-being should be reserved for favored segments of the division of labor. His insistent point—
that all labor, even the lowliest of manual pursuits, required brains, and
that therefore the apparent leading difference between "intellectual"
and "manual" work served only to provide a spurious means of social

distinction—was timely and acute. Through the chapters that follow we shall find that, right on down to our own time, the full implications of Hubert's argument have persistently eluded communication study.

The other side of this same argument of course concerned "intellectual people" themselves. Not surprisingly, given his attempt to ward off a long-accustomed disparagement, Hubert did not speak directly to the question of whether "brain" workers should be classed as productive laborers. But we do not lack for equally incisive contemporary comment on this related—and likewise, portentous—issue. In 1869 the German tanner, socialist, and autodidact Joseph Dietzgen (whose writing was hailed by Marx and Engels and later utilized by the Dutch revolutionary Anton Pannekoek, and who himself, after moving to the U.S., served as a radical editor in Chicago during the 1880s), declared unequivocally, "Thinking is a physical process and . . . [a] process of labor."[103] However, his independent derivation of knowledge as a sensuous practice proved to be almost altogether beyond reach, not only of producer republicans, but also of most of their contemporaries whose allegiance lay with Marxism. In Europe, where the latter was being assimilated under the auspices of freshly organized Social Democratic parties, "labor" was equated increasingly instead with the physical capacity for manual toil,[104] while the status of "brain" work—akin to another type of downgraded activity, unpaid domestic labor—again became a source of crippling incomprehension and internecine conflict.

In view of the essential relevance of this point for my own later argument, I will emphasize here that I do not regard this truncation of "labor" as an inherent or even as an originating feature of Marxist theory. Quite the contrary; Marxism should be credited for *ever* seeking, as it unquestionably did—initially to distinguish itself from idealist philosophy—to establish thoughtful labor as *the* distinctive trait of human species being. Evidences may be found in Marx's mature writings that this youthful insight never became altogether remote or inhospitable to him, but the dominant tendency within the organized socialist movement was, equally surely, by the later 19th century to devalue "intellectual" labor. As Walter Adamson, Anson Rabinbach, Marshall Shatz, and other scholars have noted,[105] this truncation of "labor"—however understandable it may have been—inevitably carried punishing implications for socialist theory and practice. The status of intellectuals within the European Social Democratic parties (and for their successors within what was to become actually existing socialism) indeed became well-nigh schizophrenic. On one hand, intellectuals often purported to function as the wellspring of "scientific" Marxian socialism. On the other, while awaiting their own said-to-be incipient proletarianization, they were asked to attach themselves to the proletarian cause as mere adherents, rather than true protagonists. As we will find in the next chapter, it was to become a fact of some moment for communication study that these confused and collisive impulses left numerous radical intellectuals bereft of a comfortable home within the European "labor movement."

In the U.S., meanwhile, the academic concern with "communication," as we are now in a position to see, emerged as a complex and contradictory response to this self-same inability to retain and think with a comprehensively unified category of labor. The vast expansion and enlargement, during the later 19th century, of a realm where "intellectual" labor held apparent sway—key segments of which were socially organized in ways strikingly distinct from those which governed the deployment of "manual" labor—indeed worked to endow "communication" with a seemingly transcendent autonomy. If formal thought about "communication" found its point of departure in this rapidly hardening social division of labor, finally, it in turn acted to make the place of "labor" within the social totality all but vanish.

II

Around the turn of the 20th century, several fields of organized social scientific inquiry were each successively acquiring distinct and formal disciplinary niches within a reorganized research university.[106] However, the question which now needs to be faced is not simply how to comprehend the origins of communication study considered as an academic enterprise. It is, rather, how to place the migration of thinking about communication into the new research universities in relation to the coeval popular critique on which that thinking demonstrably drew. It is of the utmost importance for comprehending the emergence of an academic communication study, indeed, that we recognize that the latter coincided historically with the apex of popular efforts to restructure institutionalized communication.

"Probably no subject in economics is of more interest in the dawn of the era of the co-operative commonwealth," generalized one trade unionist as late as 1912, "than is the question of communication."[107] With this enigmatic assertion, a handful of intrepid scholars, at least, were in desultory agreement. The sociologist Edward Ross penned an article detailing "The Suppression of Important News."[108] Academic economists such as Frank Parsons and Richard Ely, and the latter's disciple Edward A. Bemis, publicly advocated government ownership of telegraphs and telephones, but their orthodox colleagues drifted away from history and institutional analysis and toward a general equilibrium theory—which took for granted perfect access to information even as telecommunications media were rendering this very assumption fatally problematic.[109]

The iconoclastic economist Thorstein Veblen, most consequentially, took up directly the producer-republican dichotomy between "productive" and "unproductive" labor. Equating productive work by turns with "useful employment," "gainful industry," "manual labor," and the creation of "tangible" or "material products," Veblen found in the "conspicuous consumption" enjoyed by those whom he said determinedly produced nothing of any material consequence—members of what he famously termed the "leisure class"—the "waste" which he identified as contemporary society's distinguishing feature.[110] Product publicity and salesmanship, he went on to hold, which were in themselves directed not to production but merely to "the production of saleable appearances," in turn had "come unequivocally to take the first place in the business of manufacturing and merchandising," and thence had resulted "in what may fairly be called a quantity-production of customers for the purchase of the goods or services in question."[111] But advertising paradoxically was not an economic stimulus, but a primary mode of economic "sabotage." To maximize the profits of their absentee owners, business managers sought—through what Veblen, borrowing an expression he credited to members of the radical syndicalist group the Industrial Workers of the World, memorably called a "conscientious withdrawal of efficiency"—to restrict output, by reducing their utilization of raw materials, equipment, and labor power. Precisely because the "mechanical industry of the new order is inordinately productive," such "retardation and restriction," "delay and obstruction" had become entrenched means of maintaining prices "at a reasonably profitable level and so guard[ing] against business depression."[112]

The flip side of this strategy of keeping actual output well short of productive capacity was for managers to inflate sales costs. This latter function could be admirably performed; it had been well learned via systematic recourse to advertising. Through merciless but fruitful appeals to "Fear and Shame," advertising enabled "a shrewdly limited output of goods to be sold at more profitable prices—at the public cost." In the process, "salesmanship" became "the most conspicuous, and perhaps the gravest," of a congeries of "wasteful and industrially futile practices"; Veblen insisted, according to Daniel Bell, "that the elimination of salesmanship and all its voluminous apparatus and traffic would cut down the capitalized income of the business community by half."[113] In a later chapter we shall have additional reason to return to Veblen, whose keen preoccupation with the apparent inability of the contemporary industrial capitalist economy to deliver the goods—that is, to produce at the level made feasible by technology and demanded by human welfare—established vital and enduring terms of reference.

Such critical sentiments did little to further an academic career. Like other too-ardent academic reformers, as a direct result of their radical convictions Ely learned to moderate his sentiments, while Bemis suffered significant damage; and Veblen himself was far less venerated than marginalized. In a series of well-documented collisions with university presidents and trustees and, significantly, also with colleagues bent, despite the cost for academic freedom, on legitimating their own professional autonomy, radical propensities within academic social science were effectively disciplined.[114] "In case after case of university pressure brought against social scientists in the 1880s and 1890s, the conservative and moderate professional leaders carefully parceled out their support, making clear the limited range of academic freedom and the limited range of political dissent they were willing to defend."[115] This response was concordant with the virtual exclusion, within the emergent research university, of nonwhites and (to a lesser extent) of women, and the rampant prejudices that greeted Jews and Catholics.[116] In this denatured milieu, academic interest in "communication"—and in anything else—not surprisingly tended to eschew any direct evidence of rough-hewn radicalism.

Yet this again is not to say that, beyond a few mavericks, an academic concern with "communication" was absent. Far from it; during the Progressive era scholarly concerns about this subject diffused broadly throughout the social sciences. Between the early 1890s and the 1910s, an increasingly prominent group of academics—above all, John Dewey, his onetime students Robert Park and Charles H. Cooley, and his colleague George Herbert Mead—came to be overtly and sustainedly concerned with "communication." What may be said, then, about the relationship of Deweyan instrumentalism, or pragmatism, to the adjacent radical attempts to forward more mutualistic communication systems?

Biographers will no doubt continue to debate how much of the spirit and substance of pragmatism may be attributed—as regards Dewey and Mead—to the outward-directed religiosity which so clearly infused them, akin to many other leading Progressives, and how much to other factors, including their early training in philosophical idealism, and their perhaps equally schooled innocence of direct social exploitation and domination. However, it is pertinent to emphasize that, in the case of Dewey—a vital figure in the gestation of academic communication study—there were also significant lines of descent linking him with the concurrent radical critique. Dewey indeed evinced close and sustained involvement with a broad range of contemporary reform projects. Think, for example, of his participation, at the University of Michigan, in an emerging "social gospel" movement during the 1880s. The latter carried forward into his intimate association, beginning in the next decade, with the Chicago settlement houses, where he learned from and disputed disparate radicals and reformers. Then, too, there is his (and Mead's) alliance with Chicago trade unionists during the early 1900s, in a convulsive struggle over the character of public education. Not least, finally, Dewey enjoyed a set of personal contacts that included such reformers as the economist Henry Carter Adams, Florence Kelley, Jane Addams, and his own formidable wife, Alice Chipman Dewey.[117] Late in life, as he came publicly to affirm a variant of socialist doctrine, Dewey was moved to declare his abiding admiration for two paragons of 19th-century radical reform: Henry George and Edward Bellamy.[118] That Dewey could tap the general currents of contemporary reform thought therefore may not be doubted; we will see momentarily that he also can be tied specifically to concurrent criticism of institutionalized communication practices.

The manner in which this latter linkage was drawn betrayed an extraordinary, and defining, displacement of the key concept around which the producer republican synthesis pivoted: Deweyan instrumentalism's concept of communication eliminated all direct association with "labor" or "production." To explicate Dewey's alternately compelling and contradictory reformulation of the producer republican tradition, we may turn to his well-acknowledged association, during the early 1890s, with the futurist visionary and erstwhile business journalist Franklin Ford.

Scholars concur that Ford exercised over Dewey a profound and lasting influence.[119] Ford was, in truth, an extraordinary individual; there is no question that he had the ability to impress thoughtful men of power. Thus he later came to know AT&T president Theodore Vail—an intriguing assocation, which Ford mentioned in one of the frequent letters he exchanged during the 1910s with another such man, the renowned jurist Oliver Wendell Holmes, Jr. That, between 1888 and 1892, Ford "got to John Dewey" is, therefore, perhaps a sign less of Dewey's gullibility—as is usually suggested—than of Ford's credibility.[120] Prior to meeting Dewey, Ford had edited a premier business journal of the period, Bradstreet's *Journal of Trade, Finance and Economy.* As he came to tell the story, he had clashed with his publisher over his ambitious plans to enlarge this periodical's scope and purpose, and upon quitting Bradstreet's he tried to interest a series of prospective backers in what became a lifelong project: what Ford called "organized intelligence." Robert B. Westbrook's description of the idea, which Ford and Dewey went on to work up together, is apt:

> This trust—an organization of intellectuals and journalists—would create a giant central clearinghouse of information and analysis, and through its own publications and the material it sold to newspapers throughout the country it would provide the public with the knowledge it needed to free itself from slavery. By making the truth its business, the Intelligence Trust would put publications serving narrow class interests out of business. "In place of discussing 'socialism,'" Ford said, "we put out in the rightful sense of the word, the socialistic newspaper—the organ of the whole."[121]

This project, predictably, failed before getting off the ground, leaving Ford in subsequent years to speculate—in both senses of that word—regarding the organization of the nation's system of "intelligence."[122]

The attraction of Ford's ideas, for all their undoubted extravagance and idiosyncracy, should not be underestimated. His ultimate purpose—to overcome what he depicted as a fratricidal social conflict—placed his venture squarely within the multifaceted reform tradition at the American fin de siècle, and this notwithstanding Ford's desultory disavowal of any utopian ambition:

> This nation is at its mental crisis. Secession lurks in our statutes and stalks in our courts. Our whole body of jurisprudence is built upon the supposed antagonism of the individual and the common good. This must persist until the functioning, the getting there of the man of letters the great accounting can be made. The man who sells truth reveals the identity of the individual and the common interest. It is the union of the whole with the part. Perceiving all this we also see that to avoid a fatal issue, or at least a period of dire confusion in the life of the State, the division must be fought out in the "still and mental" field; otherwise, there is a return of physical conflict. Unless intelligence be unified here, unless a single mind can be secured from Maine to California, the nation in the moral sense must go to pieces. The solution of this great problem is the new Gettysburg.
>
> The war cry of a false socialism is heard on every hand. Through this and that mechanical change, by some hocus-pocus in the fiscal region, or by some other device, it is thought to heal the division in the State. But the road to social union lies through the organization, the socializing, of intelligence. . . . Violence is opposed to violence, and only through the incoming of the Intelligence Trust can the breach be healed.[123]

Ford positively reveled in his discovery of "intelligence as a commodity," exclaiming that it offered up nothing less than a "new reading of life." "With truth and commerce at one," he heralded, "the organizing and controlling principle of society is revealed." This quasi-religious stance became explicit in the title of what Ford projected to be the inaugural work in a companion twelve-volume book series: "The Day of Judgment."[124] Given these ambitions, it was beside the point that Ford's venture, had it succeeded, would necessarily far exceed the reach and power of any monopoly made of human clay, notably including that of the AP. "Organized intelligence" was a *response* to crisis, not—albeit only in virtue of eminently questionable "nationalist" assumptions, probably garnered from Edward Bellamy's recently published utopian novel—its cause. Like other middle-class reform schemes building from the work of Gronlund and Bellamy, Ford's was marked by its apocalyptic tone and by its concerted effort to supplant class antagonism with an ostensibly unitary and organic social basis for the realization of an industrial utopia.[125]

After some wandering in the wilderness, Ford brought his idea to the University of Michigan, where for a time it thrived through his ongoing association with Dewey, and with the younger men George

Herbert Mead and Robert E. Park. Park, conceding Ford's influence, later reminisced:

> He had reported Wall Street and had gained a conception of the function of the press by observing the way the market responded to news. The market price was, from his point of view, a kind of public opinion and, being a man of philosophic temperament, he drew from this analogy far-reaching inferences. I cannot go into that. Suffice it to say he came to believe, and I did too, that with more accurate and adequate reporting of current events the historical process would be appreciably stepped up, and progress would go forward steadily, without the interruption and disorder of depression or violence, and at a rapid pace.[126]

"Ford pointed Park in the direction of writing about the newspaper and public opinion,"[127] writes one biographer, and, declares another, "crystallized his interest in the social significance of news";[128] he furnished a bridge, that is to say, between Park's early journalism and the scholarship that followed. Much empirically useful research on communications media was produced by the group of sociologists whom Park went on to lead at the University of Chicago; Park, however, distilled out of Ford's scheme for profitable reform virtually all utopic traces.[129]

Mead, at the moment of his involvement, had been still more grandiose in praising Ford. In 1892 he confided to a close friend that Franklin Ford's scheme "is only the greatest that the world has ever seen. It is the sudden conscious recognition in an integral unit of society that he and all exist only as the expression of the universal self."[130] Mead's typification of society as "an integral unit" expressive of a "universal self" is again worthy of particular emphasis. Like Dewey, Mead was drawn expressly by the anticompetitive ethos that Ford shared with different variants of the reform movement. Possibly, as John Peters argues, both men specifically detected in Ford's ideas the makings of an attractive conceptual counterweight to the individualistic philosophy of the later Herbert Spencer.[131] Yet Dewey's own contemporaneous sketch of Ford's project situates it not so much in this context as more directly within the context of prevailing producer republican anxieties regarding the place and function of communication institutions. Ford, suggested Dewey in 1891 to William James, "had been led by his newspaper experience to study as a practical question the social bearings of intelligence and its distribution. . . ."

> He identified the question of inquiry with, in philosophical terms, the question of the relation of intelligence to the objective world—is the former free to move in relation to the latter or not? So he studied out the following questions: (1) The conditions and effects of the distribution of intelligence especially with reference to inquiry or the selling of truth as a business; (2) the present (or past) hindrances to its free play, in the way of class interests; or (3) the present conditions, in the railway, telegraphy, etc., for effectively

securing the freedom of intelligence, that is, its movement in the world of social fact; and (4) the resulting social organization. This is, with inquiry as a business, the selling of truth for money, the whole would have a representative as well as the various classes,—a representative whose belly interest, moreover, is identical with its truth interest.[132]

Dewey's interest in Ford's project centered foursquare on this beckoning notion of "organized intelligence." Decades later, Dewey's onetime student Sidney Hook was to observe that "the central emphasis Dewey places on 'the methods of intelligence' in all areas of human experience . . . suggests that 'intelligence' functions as the only absolute value in Dewey's ethical and educational philosophy. . . ." Democracy itself, wrote Hook, was for Dewey based on his "faith that intelligence could discover or create shared interests sufficient to preserve civilized society."[133] Ford thus seems to have provided a specific platform for Dewey's growing and much-cherished conviction that, as another authoritative commentator puts it, "[e]ffective distribution of knowledge" was "essential to the development of the 'social sensorium,' and democracy rested as much if not more on the egalitarian distribution of knowledge as it did on the egalitarian distribution of wealth."[134] What, we must therefore ask, were the lineage and vital features of this key word?

On one hand, "intelligence" figured directly in efforts by Dewey, and subsequently Mead, to identify means of working toward a socially configured psychology, whose most arresting feature was its restoration of mind to an immanent role within experience including, above all, individual experience. Dewey's breakthrough into the philosophical psychology which he called "instrumentalism" can be conveniently indexed by recalling his insight, in 1896, into the need to reject the "reflex arc" concept that then ruled over psychology. Refusing the idea that mind and body were separate, and thus that individual experience could be grasped through a model—the reflex arc—that confined itself to studying cycles of purported stimulus and response between the two seemingly skewed planes, Dewey insisted instead on the organismic nature of experience. Thinking had, for Dewey, the same ontological status as action; together they encompassed, in this famous attack on dualism, a ceaseless oscillation. Intrinsically intertwined functions, thinking learned from and tried to correct action within a single unfolding creative—but perhaps, as one critic pointed out long ago, overly biologistic—process[135] which Dewey, in a term that is redolent of his recently concluded association with Ford, here called "organized coordination." "[W]hat is wanted," he asserted, "is that sensory stimulus, central connections and motor responses shall be viewed, not as separate and complete entities in themselves, but as divisions of labor, functioning factors, within the single concrete whole. . . ."[136] Where uncertainty disrupted habitual activity, conscious purpose—thought—was prompted to intervene, establishing its own role in the cycles of coordinative action which progressively ensued. The active construction, the human meaning, of experience came therefore, as Feffer writes, to be "guided by the principle that mind is a self-active, creative force."[137]

But "mind," or "intelligence," in turn was not to be located within the individual in any simple or assumed physical sense. "If mind is socially constituted," wrote Mead subsequently, "then the field or locus of any given individual mind must extend as far as the social activity or apparatus of social relations which constitutes it extends; and hence that field cannot be bounded by the skin of the individual organism to which it belongs."[138] What then happened, as Dewey's salutary effort to transcend dualism, by impelling "organized co-ordination" to assume an active creative role within individual experience, was transposed onto this societal level? Here, in brief, "intelligence" was endowed with an equally intrinsic, but far more problematic role.

The problem was that Dewey's admirable effort to configure mind as a social form was confusingly intercut with a disparate emphasis on the assumed role of "organized intelligence" within society. For who, at the level of the social field, was to organize intelligence? What identifiable social agency could function as the knower, whose goal was to press ahead toward social reconstruction? For Dewey, this eventually emerged as the problem of the "public,"[139] where "communication" augured not a return to religious faith, but a regeneration of democracy —a search, in his terms, for "the great community."[140] On one hand, validly enough, this became a matter of "discovering the means by which a scattered, mobile and manifold public may so recognize itself as to define and express its interests." On the other hand, Dewey severely limited his ability to address this all-important question by continuing to rely on a fatally problematic assumption: "The problem of a democratically organized public is primarily and essentially an intellectual problem. . . ."[141] It hardly needs to be stressed how much this declaration, by the "mature" Dewey (he was in his mid-sixties at the time), resurrected the edicts of Franklin Ford. In Ford's earlier, less considered, and indeed inflammatory discussion of the character of "organized intelligence," there lies already a clear hint of what would emerge as the definitive ambiguity within Dewey's public philosophy—the respective roles to be played in it by capital and labor. Ford, in a typical burst of Bellamyite evolutionary doctrine, hailed his idea alternately as both a "socialistic newpaper" and an "intelligence trust."[142] "Organized intelligence," akin to the trusts that for Bellamyites formed the nuclei of socialism, purported to transcend ensconced antagonisms between capital and labor by positing a category of activity—knowing—whose very function, as we have already seen, was for Ford inherently, indeed by definition, to efface the division on which that conflict was based.

"No paper," Dewey had told Henry Carter Adams in 1889, "can

afford to tell the truth about the actual conduct of the city's business."
But, he quickly added, "have a newspaper whose business, i.e. whose
livelihood, was to sell intelligence, and it couldn't afford to do anything
else. . . ."[143] In this mystifying formulation, the "hindrances" posed by
"class interests" to the "free play" of intelligence—to which Dewey
himself briefly alluded, as we saw, in his sketch of Ford's thought—
vanished altogether. Evidently he believed not only that "belly interest"
and "truth interest" could be reconciled, but also that the "intelligence
trust" could escape or, perhaps, overpower, any lingering effects of class
interest or social division. This optimism could be warranted only because the conception of class that Dewey employed spoke not to the
social relations of production but, in contrast, to any and all particular
group interests—be they regional, occupational, or ideological—that
worked to undermine social union. Exactly here, Dewey's reach for
shared knowledge was transposed into a spiritual movement to effect
what Josiah Royce had taught his colleague Mead must be "the substitution of the social and universal for the private and particular."[144]

It takes nothing away from Dewey's achievement to suggest that
much of the conceptual basis of his theorization was prefigured in the
historically adjacent producer republican synthesis. Producer republicans held that both mental and physical aspects were incarnated in an
integral category of skillful labor, and that this same category of labor
could be generalized, to supply a crucial common bond allying disparate
occupations in their opposition to the prevailing order. These ideas
metamorphosized, in Dewey's hands, into a rebuttal both of the reflex
arc and of the ontological distinctions which were so often drawn between different ranks of human activity. Utilizing what Feffer calls "a
radically democratic philosophy of self-activity . . . that reintegrated
the manual with the mental,"[145] Dewey carried forward into theory as a
general premise the producers' dream of a social totality peopled solely
by laboring folk. While producer republicans often failed on the horns of
a dualist dilemma, therefore, and found themselves powerless to prevent
a defensive lapse onto the body's physical labor as the apparent paramount criterion of productive activity, Dewey refashioned their ideas to
mount an adamant attack against dualism in all its forms: not only
subject versus object and body versus mind, but also action versus
thought, work versus play, and labor versus leisure. In a work that he
himself long considered to be the fullest exposition of his philosophical
stance, Dewey blasted away at all such divisions, arguing that
education—with philosophy itself, the form of "organized intelligence"
to which he was most committed personally—should work to efface
them, both in itself and within the larger society. "What has been termed
active occupation includes both play and work," declared Dewey. "In
their intrinsic meaning, play and industry are by no means so antitheti-
cal to one another as is often assumed, any sharp contrast being due to

undesirable social conditions."[146] And, he continued, the "social distinction between those whose pursuits involve a minimum of self-directive thought and aesthetic appreciation, and those who are concerned more directly with things of the intelligence and with the control of the activities of others" was itself largely responsible for the reproduction of this same dualism within the prevailing system of educational provision. "The problem of education in a democratic society," however, "is to do away with the dualism and to construct a course of studies which makes thought a guide of free practice for all and which makes leisure a reward of accepting responsibility for service, rather than a state of exemption from it."[147]

Yet where, then, within this determined and admirable attack on dualism, was "production" or "labor"? A recent proponent of Dewey has utilized the concept of production effectively, as a heuristic device for trenchantly explicating the full range of Dewey's thought.[148] But Dewey himself, despite occasional experiments with the idea,[149] did not; perhaps even could not. The category of labor evidently was not free to fill the encompassing and multifaceted function on which Dewey tried so scrupulously to insist. "That a certain amount of labor must be engaged in goes without saying,"[150] he suggested, signaling that he had acceded to the prevailing equation of "labor" solely with necessary toil.

In place of "labor," Dewey fell back on a seemingly more inclusive and elastic category, "experience," as his preferred alternative. "Experience," he emphasized in 1916, included "an active and a passive element peculiarly combined"—*"trying"* and *"undergoing."* In itself, it was "not primarily cognitive." However, to "'learn from experience' is to make a backward and forward connection between what we do to things and what we enjoy or suffer from things in consequence." What Dewey termed "the *measure of the value* of an experience" established, moreover, a uniquely cognitive function: "Thinking," that is, "is the accurate and deliberate instituting of connections between what is done and its consequences."[151] Upon "inquiry" or "intelligence" was plainly conferred the lead role, in making "experience" the basis for continuing action in the world. As a result, in turn, the problems of an industrializing capitalism were refocused through the lens of what was too often presumed to be a conciliatory and inherently progressive communication function.[152]

According to Andrew Feffer, conservative capital, which for Dewey as well as Mead was a chief source and site of social "habit," and radical labor, an equally important site of what they called "impulse," coexisted in a "functional evolutionary relation": "the two sides psychologically and socially needed each other, and needed to resolve social conflict through reconciliation." "Communication"—a process equated with reciprocity and cooperation—became synonymous with this functional bond;[153] put differently, "communication" became for Dewey the means of assuring the transmission of "intelligence" harmoniously across and throughout the social field. It is in this sense that we must understand this well-known passage from Dewey's *Democracy and Education* (1916): "Society not only continues to exist *by* transmission, *by* communication, but it may fairly be said to exist *in* transmission, *in* communication. There is more than a verbal tie between the words common, community, and communication. Men live in a community in virtue of the things they have in common; and communication is the way in which they come to possess things in common."[154] In considering individual experience, Dewey successfully reinstated mind as the abiding coadjutant of action; by contrast, in considering society, he abstracted toward a substitutive idea of "communication"—what he himself at one point called an elemental "prerequisite."[155]

Agencies of what Dewey, in the 1920s, still referred to explicitly as "organized intelligence" would conciliate "habit" and "impulse," thereby mitigating conflicts between individuals, groups, and classes.[156] Despite appearances, then, Dewey's psychology of self-activity was not on the same par with his societal application of "organized intelligence." The former comprised a restitutive effort, as against all kinds of dualism, to place consciousness and action together; especially in the context of Dewey's Progressive education, it was premised on the reunification of head and hand. The latter, on the contrary, aimed to differentiate "communication" from present-day society and, in particular, from the lived experience of definite social relations of production. Even as the unsuccessful producer republican effort to speak for the full range of mental and manual activity was taken up, therefore, its prime means for doing so—"production" or "labor"—was relinquished.

Dewey believed, with good reason, that in the United States at the turn of the century "labor" had become a prime locus of a pervasively disabling dissociation of means and ends.[157] A reformed educational process might remediate this failing, he argued—in yet another attempt to reinstate concord between thought and action—by reuniting head and hand. Yet even Dewey's attractive hope of making good through "progressive education" what was being systematically stripped away through massive economic and organizational changes evinced pragmatism's parallel displacement of the adjacent world of social labor. To be sure, Dewey's isolated criticisms could be suggestive; forty years after Baptist Hubert, for example, he wrote that "[t]he notion that intelligence is a personal endowment or personal attainment is the great conceit of the intellectual class, as that of the commercial class is that wealth is something which they personally have wrought and possess."[158] Puncturing the pretensions of what was already aspiring to become a new mandarinate, Dewey still could only plead again that a unitary "organized intelligence" should effect a transcendent rectification of existing social relations.

Until late in his long life, in turn, Dewey transmuted the mutualism of the concurrent popular critique of communication—with its necessary emphasis on the distortive organization of the agencies of intelligence under current social conditions—into an assumedly ameliorative precursor of ideal social relations. Working both from and back toward the idea of democracy, of aiding the "common good," Dewey fell back on an ideal of service[159] to bolster his assumption that "the current has set steadily in one direction: toward democratic forms."[160] On this optimistic but unsatisfactory premise, once again, he long convinced himself that organized intelligence was well-nigh immanent within the social-historical process. "We have every reason to think that whatever changes may take place in existing democratic machinery," he extolled in 1926, "they will be of a sort to make the interest of the public a more supreme guide and criterion of governmental activity, and to enable the public to form and manifest its purposes still more authoritatively."[161] Mead's project was even more pointedly to ground communication systematically in a stabilizing psychology of cooperative sociability.[162] Sustaining Ford's quasi-religious overtones, this shared approach allowed Dewey to call communication a "wonder" beside which "transubstantiation pales."[163] There were significant intimations, finally, that "communication" comprised an anomaly, even an ineffable agency. When Dewey wrote of the role of communication in societal reproduction ("transmission"), he went on at once to mandate that for people "to form a community" they must have

> aims, beliefs, aspirations, knowledge—a common understanding—like-mindedness as the sociologists say. Such things cannot be passed physically from one to another, like bricks; they cannot be shared as persons would share a pie by dividing it into physical pieces. . . .

And again:

> Things can be physically transported in space; they may be bodily conveyed. Beliefs and aspirations cannot be physically extracted and inserted.[164]

To make "communication" a propellant of social consensus, Dewey himself here lapsed into an unqualified dualism, in an appeal to apparently exceptional, spiritual or ideal features. This was not to be the last time that exceptionalist arguments of this kind made their way into communication study.

The idea of "organized intelligence" thus became free to seek opportunistic validation elsewhere, perhaps pre-eminently in an abstracted idea of technology. A portent of such notions can be detected in Ford, who had heaped praise on Postmaster General Wanamaker, for the latter's idea of tying together "the newest telegraphic inventions" within a unitary complex of more efficient Post Office facilities.[165] What Ford characterized as "the completion of the machine for gathering and distributing news," a machine, he specified, "consisting of the printing press, the locomotive, [and] the telegraph," however, meant that now "nothing stood in the way of centralizing intelligence." The grand result, he concluded with customary definitude, was that "class interest could be ignored, and for the first time."[166] Dewey was, to be sure, generally more circumspect. Yet his optimism regarding communication technology remained considerable. Thirty-five years after his collaboration with Ford he would write that "the physical and external means of collecting information . . . have far outrun the intellectual phase of inquiry and organization of its results."[167]

Both Dewey and Mead committed themselves to conceptions in which the category of labor was replaced by turns by ideals of shared citizenship and rewarding self-activity. To admit "labor" as a defining feature would be to open the way to consideration of the sources of the dissension and structural conflict which, at the turn of the century, so obviously pervaded and disfigured the commonwealth. Such an engagement with "labor" might even have allowed Dewey to become a philosopher of socialism. But this was something that he would never do. "It would be a mistake," Dewey explicitly declared as late as 1926, "to identify the conditions which limit free communication and circulation of facts and ideas . . . merely with overt forces which are obstructive" —notably including "those who have ability to manipulate social relations for their own advantage." Not class power nor—hinting at the concerns with propaganda and mass culture that, as we will soon see, were beginning to act as new intellectual beacons—government "by hired promoters of opinion called publicity agents" were the underlying issues.[168] The most Dewey would do was to call attention to "hidden entrenchments." A whole host of conditions supposedly forestalled "habit" and "impulse" from achieving their customary progressive union. Importing into his thinking the influential theory of "cultural lag" which had been recently propounded by the sociologist William Ogburn,[169] Dewey emphasized the pronounced "lag" of political and legal practices in the face of "industrial transformation." He also mentioned the commandering of decisionmaking by specialists and experts; the "powerful diversion from political concern" triggered unwittingly by the "increase in the number, variety and cheapness of amusements"; and, above all, the immense social complexity purportedly produced by "the machine age." These, he claimed, were the underlying sources of public apathy and bewilderment.[170]

To such problems, "organized intelligence" could continue to be relied upon as a preferred answer. To their credit, the pragmatists tolerated and often even sought the expression of genuine political difference; it is fair to say, with Feffer, that they "committed themselves to the enhancement of democratic participation in modern industrial societies." However, from Dewey's association with Franklin Ford onward, even as they thrust themselves into the flux, their commitment to democratic reconstruction was premised on an uncompromising belief that the chief task was to identify and thence to activate neutral agencies of social reconciliation.[171] That such neutrality was itself not only desirable, but also feasible, they scarcely doubted—and this article of faith pervaded their related conceptions of society and communication. To the Chicago pragmatists even a mild cleavage of what Mead, remember, had called the "integral unit of society"[172] was neither necessary nor even tolerable. Attempting precisely to overcome what they variously identified as "force," "desire," or "the unregenerate element in human nature," they sought—in language that again transported Dewey's earlier critique of the reflex arc unproblematically onto the social field—"the perfecting of the means and ways of communication . . . so that genuinely shared interest in the consequences of interdependent activities may inform desire and effort and thereby direct action."[173]

Such usages led at times to unconscionable concessions. Dewey's and Mead's support for U.S. involvement in World War I is the most widely cited demonstration that the prewar pragmatists turned consistently "to the state as the source of cooperative authority," while seeking to chastise and exclude as "utopians" all who did not meet their liberal standards of "responsibility."[174] But the same potential also may be detected elsewhere, in a wide series of historical resonances established by Ford's originating recipe for social "union." Finally, in this vital sense as well, "organized intelligence" was not unique or even especially unusual; rather, once again it embodied what historians since Richard Hofstadter have shown was a common aspiration of middle-class reform schemes at the fin de siècle: that the educated, native-born, "new" middle class in general, and intellectual experts in particular, should play a "directive role" in society's regeneration—and, not coincidentally, act along the way to institutionalize their own newfound role. Within Dewey's academic cohort, related ideas were frequently voiced. Among economists, John Bates Clark, for example, categorized social classes by their degree of "cephalization," denoting the extent to which the brain purportedly controlled the body's animality; Richard Ely called for reform to be directed by "men of superior intelligence"; Simon Patten declared that society was undergoing "the transition from anarchic and puny individualism to the group acting as a powerful, intelligent organism." Directly within the ambit of reform, Henry George insisted in 1883 that "the great work of the present for every man and every organization who would improve social conditions, is the work of education—the propagation of ideas." Edward Bellamy's utopia not only left entrenched the profound social distinction between mental and manual labor, but also ensured that an elite of brain workers, rather than any organized movement of the working class, would direct society.[175]

The effort to "socialize intelligence" by means of a for-profit "Intelligence Trust," finally, introduced a polarity strikingly similar to that which also structured Gronlund's exposition of the cooperative commonwealth: between the need to introduce cooperation throughout all of society, and the fact that only a small but "respectable minority"— Gronlund wrote of perhaps 10,000 persons "representing the most advanced intelligence . . . [and] containing sincere and energetic representatives from all classes," while Ford emphasized the contributions of journalists and "men of letters," and made room as well for "merchants and professional experts"—were to prepare for and guide the coming revolution.[176]

At this level, Ford's benign understanding of the proposed "intelligence trust" comported well enough with an ascending academic social science, which in turn found lodgings in the emergent elite research university. Gronlund had hoped to "raise up" a "competent and qualified body of educators" in which to intrust "the whole function of education . . . and all scientific investigations." "There is not the smallest reason to fear that this will result in any spiritual tyranny," he exclaimed in 1884,

> for the influence of this theoretic body of men is sure to be counteracted by that Public Opinion of the practical majority which we saw will be of extraordinary force in the Coming Commonwealth. We ought rather to hail such a strong and independent organization of a class, devoted to the cultivation of knowledge, as a healthy counterpoise to that Public Opinion.[177]

Notwithstanding such safeguards, whose optimism was somewhat greater than Ford's in 1892,[178] and certainly greater than Dewey's, by the 1910s academic pretensions to privileged knowledge were in fact gaining wide certification and authority. What sociologists were hailing as a new science of "social control"—whose secrets they insisted that they themselves could best discern—was an important locus of this change. Even as American capitalism shifted from a competitive to a corporate basis, according to Dorothy Ross, the social control concept served to focus inquiry "on the distinctively social processes by which individuals were bound together in society":

> Abandoning the polarized ideological conflict of the Gilded Age, with its concern for the fundamental economic basis of society, sociologists turned toward examination of how the existing society—its economic institutions accepted as given—socialized its members. The action of the capitalist market, the loci of power in society, and structural changes over time tended to disappear from view in the search for harmonizing processes imbedded in society itself.[179]

The thesis was both liberal and technocratic.[180] "It accepted as inevitable the inequality and conflict generated by capitalism, and sought to counter them with an enlarged version of social control." Modern society, in this view, might be most happily—and perhaps more important, predictably—administered in accordance with the findings of experts. Prominent among this new class, of course, were social scientists. Conflicts between the individual and society, declared the sociologists, were inescapably modulated by a whole range of agencies, whose secrets they themselves were best placed to discern. Joining a panoply of pre-existing modes—custom, law, religion, morality, and so forth—newspapers and other media thus began to be counted for their contributions to a necessary and overarching process of cohesion.

Not a few remained anxious, to be sure, about the fate of individuals in a world whose guiding institutions were dedicated explicitly to molding and shaping behavior, and some, such as Dewey himself, chafed at the implications of control by experts for the spirit of collective democracy.[181] The period's overarching tendency, nonetheless—and not only within academe—was to forge ahead in the creation of just such overarching systems of regulation. Yet another leading manifestation of this selfsame attempt to reach into the social division of labor, and to readjust its balance in favor of "mental" over "manual" activity—as Robert Wiebe suggested nearly three decades ago[182] and Harry Braverman documented in 1974—may be seen in the practice of "scientific management," which burgeoned throughout industry at exactly the same moment, and which sought—with varying success, as we now know—to centralize the "intelligence" required for production under the organizational control of capital and its delegates.

A final consequential foray in this same direction was pioneered by Dewey's sometime intellectual adversary, the journalist Walter Lippmann. Lippmann's successful effort to adapt "organized intelligence" arose, in a savage irony, around journalism itself. Born thirty years after Dewey, in 1889, Lippmann dallied with socialism first at Harvard around 1910 and then as a mayoral assistant in "socialist" Schenectady. Yet Lippmann soon went on to explicate what became the mainstream liberal rationale for the systematic manipulation of public opinion on behalf of putatively democratic objectives. His prime objective was to cater to the growing need within the political-economic establishment— a need expressed above all during preparations for World War I—for supple and creative agencies of public opinion management. In practice Lippmann labored, amply recompensed, in behalf of an informal apparatus of mass persuasion from World War I until his dissent over Vietnam.[183]

Often at odds with these different elitist expressions of "organized intelligence," Dewey's vision, despite its undoubted real merits, could not supply an effective and thoroughgoing refutation. While Lippmann unabashedly lodged modern-day needs for communication in professional expertise, Dewey could only ground them in a supposedly universal identity framed by intelligent inquiry. At such a level of abstraction there was little—too little—need for examination of how the agencies of communication functioned as workaday tools of an antidemocratic social order, let alone for systematic scrutiny of the forms of domination more generally. "One looks vainly to Dewey," Czitrom aptly concludes, "for a plain sense, or even hints, as to just how we might transform privately owned media of communication into truly common carriers."[184]

Mutualism thus had been retained, but also transmuted: What producer republicans developed in direct opposition to the ongoing corporate reconstruction of the U.S. political economy came through in instrumentalism as an a priori assumption, of the very kind that Dewey otherwise tended to abjure. Not for the last time, "communication" passed into abstraction even as it was rendered into a supposed palliative of strained social relations. For of course "society" tugged, as it tugs today, in contrary ways. Property, like mind, may be "social" in character without being equal in society. Likewise, to consecrate shared meaning is merely to declare for an inspiring ideal. Not all meanings *are* shared, and those that are may take innumerable social shadings, ranging from the thoroughgoing informed cooperation favored by the pragmatists all the way to coercive indoctrination. Ignorance of an idea, as well as indifference and active opposition to it, must also be accounted for somehow. What is shared in "communication," and on what terms, are deeply problematic issues. How, then, to reconcile an idea of communication limited to an undoubted but systematically exaggerated capacity for shared meaning, with a concept of society capable of bearing the twin realities of structural conflict and domination, not least, into the sphere of communication itself? The pragmatists did not pose this problem; not surprisingly, therefore, they did not surmount it. Instead they subsumed social relations in a putatively transcendent and anterior ethos of cooperative communication.

Faced with the dual catastrophe of economic depression and fascist mobilization, however, instrumentalism's ineffable optimism became strained to the breaking point. In the 1930s, Dewey himself publicly claimed that the free use of the method of intelligence "is incompatible with every social and political philosophy and with every economic system which accepts the class organization and vested class interest of present society."[185] The contemporary devaluation of labor, he now argued in a discussion of art, could be changed only through "a radical social alteration, which effects the degree and kind of participation the worker has in the production and social disposition of the wares he produces."[186] In this altered social context, as the next chapter details, "organized intelligence" was recast so as to make "communication" the agency no longer of a presumed informed consensus, but rather of what now appeared to be a newly anomalous variant of social domination.

CHAPTER TWO

The Anomaly
of Domination

During the interwar period, all hope of preserving "manual" and "mental" activities as a complex theoretical unity—even under another name, as Deweyan instrumentalism had attempted—was forsworn. This more definitive categorial displacement of "labor," however, did not prevent thinking about communication from evincing that singularly direct and repeated absorption with great historical processes and controversies which has ineluctably marked it throughout each successive era. Nowhere, indeed, has communication study's capacity to organize a substantial knowledge of reality been more evident than in its interwar engagement with "propaganda."[1] Here it became increasingly plain that the cooperative construct favored by the pragmatists—"organized intelligence"—was vulnerable to routine and unprecedentedly systematic media attacks staged by powerful corporate and governmental actors. Hard on the heels of this revelatory shift in the terms of thought, the discussion of communication also began to lose its restricted reference to news and public affairs, and to be redirected—in a portent of later developments—toward "culture" more generally. In this chapter, after first canvassing the fierce interwar debate which broke out over the social import of propaganda, I then sketch briefly the reactive sequence of changes through which an academic communication study successfully cast itself as the legitimate heir to inquiry in this quickly changing field, principally by attempting to isolate a communicative dimension of interpersonal influence.

39

In the second portion of this chapter, I turn to assess the radical critique of "mass culture," or, alternatively, "culture industry," which accompanied this process of disciplinary institutionalization and, as the latter developed, substantially offset and disrupted it. Here too, however, the knowledge which began to be won during the interwar era began to be arrayed on a skewed "ideological" plane, to emphasize an apparently anomalous function: to persuade people to acquiesce to the authoritarian impulse supposedly inherent within mass culture. Within the social totality's pre-existing armature, therefore, theorists now claimed to have identified a distinctive and perhaps superordinate new dimension: a culturally based hegemony.

"Hegemony" had originated at a remove from the critique of mass culture, as a theoretical means of addressing the political and doctrinal impasse which arose from the failure of European revolutions after World War I. In its modern sense, elaborated by Antonio Gramsci, hegemony was to be attained "through the myriad ways in which the institutions of civil society operate to shape, directly or indirectly, the cognitive and affective structures whereby men perceive and evaluate problematic social reality."[2] "[T]he institutions of civil society," in another account,"—schools, families, churches, media and the rest— now play a more central role in the processes of social control."[3] "Hegemony," then, purports to pinpoint a decisive shift within capitalist society, in the ratio between coercion and consent required for the continuation of class rule. It spotlights the role of consciousness, and of subjective rather than objective conditions in predisposing people to acquiesce, to go along. It is then an easy step to view power as operative predominantly, or even exclusively, within this selfsame sphere of "culture"— which in turn becomes the all-important, quasi-ideological domain in which consent is either secured or lost. Such a conception will be inadequate, however; it neglects what Perry Anderson, for one, reminds us has been "the 'fundamental' or determinant role of violence within the power structure of contemporary capitalism . . . ." We must not forget, therefore, to qualify claims made for a seemingly isolable cultural hegemony by posing the question: "What is the *inter-relation* or *connection* between consent and coercion in the structure of bourgeois class power in metropolitan capitalism?"[4]

Before the onset of the Cold War, significantly, the theorists of mass culture were not blind to this historical ratio between force and acquiescence. Yet as the postwar world unfolded, they progressively tipped the scale further in favor of quintessentially ideological modes of social domination. I hope to show that resurgent conceptual difficulties with the category of labor and, above all, with the particular status of "intellectual" labor, played a part—particularly after around 1948—in this trend. Already during the interwar period, the question of "intellectual" labor had attained a fateful, and agonizing, historical acuteness: the indeterminate class identity borne by the growing throngs of white-collar workers in Germany offered a specific, and widely remarked, social basis for fascist authoritarianism. This anomalous stratum of "intellectual" laborers in fact constituted the social subject in whose presence mass culture, above all in the context of the Cold War clamp-down, became a similarly enigmatic and portentous object.

I

The initial sources of an emergent conceptual synthesis around propaganda were multiple and complex. The muckrake journalism of the Progressive era, which made the health of the press a significant concern,[5] also forged an important bond with the earlier traditions of popular criticism; a second tide of negative sentiment accompanied widespread awareness that extensive media manipulation had occurred during World War I. Throughout the initial postwar decade, however, it should be emphasized that one might meet as well with unabashed appeals to the new media's efficiency at performing what also might be called "mass persuasion." "It was, of course, the astounding success of propaganda during the war that opened the ideas of the intelligent few in all departments of life to the possibilities of regimenting the public mind," wrote Edward L. Bernays in 1928. "The conscious and intelligent manipulation of the organized habits and opinions of the masses," declared Bernays, himself a pioneer of U.S. public relations and an aggressive advocate of the legitimacy of such practices,

> is an important element in democratic society. . . . Vast numbers of human beings must cooperate in this manner if they are to live together as a smoothly functioning society. . . . To avoid . . . confusion, society consents to have its choice narrowed to ideas and objects brought to its attention through propaganda of all kinds. . . . Whatever of social importance is done to-day, whether in politics, finance, manufacture, agriculture, charity, education, or other fields, must be done with the help of propaganda. Propaganda is the executive arm of the invisible government.[6]

With not a little melancholy, Lippmann had installed this argument in the immediate postwar milieu, and now Bernays turned it into a brazen celebration of communication as a mechanism of social control. But those who detected in propaganda a salutary means of making private ends appear to concord with social needs were soon to be joined by others, who—though for quite disparate reasons—viewed propaganda as a deeply worrisome problem.

To comprehend this striated and swift intellectual reorientation, we must first erase the prevailing monochromatic portrait of propaganda analysis. The sources of this caricature[7] are themselves of interest, and I shall touch on them further below. For now it is enough to mention the canonical construction that was fashioned during the 1950s, most notably by Elihu Katz and Paul F. Lazarsfeld, to justify the research approach of which their own work, *Personal Influence*, became the signal instance: that Depression-era analysts had been captivated by crude theories—"hypodermic needle" and "magic bullet" are the capsule terms of disparagement—which overstated, out of prescientific ignorance, the nature and extent of media influence. Systematic scholarly rejection of propaganda analysis, in this view, in turn "set the definitional stance" of a newly elevated field of scientific communication research.[8]

It is true enough that during the 1930s analysts of mass persuasion often attributed to media messages a commanding role. Their stress, however, was neither necessarily nor even generally on the onetime effects of individual messages on essentially passive audiences. A recent authoritative survey of 20th-century research on media and children emphasizes that "the pre-1940 period included study of cognitive concepts, attention to developmental differences in children's use of media, and a focus on children's knowledge of the world, their attitudes and values, and their own moral conduct. Although the commentators felt that media effects could be powerful, they also recognized that other factors, such as the child's developmental level or social class, could modify the media's impact."[9] Perhaps more important, the synthesis around propaganda pivoted neither on messages nor on audience cognition but, as Sproule has insisted, rather on the ongoing institutionalization of publicity and censorship in the hands of powerful social actors pursuing self-interested objectives.[10] A focus on propaganda permitted the great contours of power within American society to be traced into the nation's public culture—as, indeed, it still does today.[11]

The convergence of international fascism, severe economic depression, and domestic political ferment could not but qualitatively transform the intellectual climate. The 1930s were characterized by compounding anxiety over the place and functions of the media and by a broad left-liberal recoil against "the propaganda menace."[12] "Nations have seized upon communication as a prime instrument of social control under modern conditions," summarized O. W. Riegel in 1934. "They are assuring themselves of the control of transmission facilities and of news, as well as mobilizing accessory forms of propaganda, with the purposes of forging an obedient and patriotic mentality in the population, and of spreading advantageous propaganda outside of the state as an instrument of national policy."[13] For decades to come, anxieties about strong media would carry an implied reference, at least, to systematic exploitation of propaganda by authoritarian regimes.

Such worries were inspired by more than foreign dictators. Critics and reformers indeed began to turn the established idea of social control into what Sproule calls an "ethical issue," through which the present status of democracy was continually problematized "by situations where public opinion was manipulated."[14] The critical potential of propaganda analysis accordingly now began to reach beyond its immediate postwar rationale. After all, Walter Lippmann had then utilized the same sort of insight—that routinely effective efforts to shape the "pictures in our heads" had superceded the traditional mechanisms of democracy—to rationalize an antidemocratic argument for institutionalizing elite intervention in public opinion formation. During the 1930s, in contrast, the study of propaganda became a prime means of exposing the structural biases of purportedly benign or, at least, neutral social agencies. Analysts "probed institutions, media and messages" in order to address—and deliberately intervene in—"the basic social problem of powerful social forces laboring to control public opinion."[15] Discussions of mass persuasion thus fused with fundamental issues of politics and social organization.

Concentration of press ownership and the growing general recourse by corporations and allied institutions to advertising and publicity programs,[16] in particular, prompted spiraling concern over the status of techniques and channels of mass persuasion within the commonweal. What is most impressive is the range of this concern, which—despite fierce disagreement on how to diagnose and prescribe for the problem— loosely spanned the New Deal's liberal-left alliance. Thus turn-of-the-century ideas and criticisms resurfaced, albeit often with a new veneer, even within academe. Already by 1933 eminent social scientists were beginning to move from generalization—that growing "concentration" of "agencies of mass impression" was strengthening the ability to control individual behavior—to criticism: not "social desirability," the authors stressed, but "competitive forces" had cumulated in "an all pervasive system of communication from which it is difficult to escape."[17] Even as, with Lippmann, he assumed that propaganda was an efficacious and largely salutary means of organizing public opinion within democracies, Harold Lasswell nonetheless also clinically depicted "the propagandist's bid for power," not only in Germany but also in the United States, and in the service of not only national socialism but also corporate advertising.[18] Lasswell likewise held that a comprehensive assessment of the role of propaganda necessitated historical inquiry. "Thus from the French to the Russian Revolution," he suggested, "the net effect of propaganda upon the emergence or the retardation of the 'proletarian revolution' could be appraised."[19] Acknowledgment that the implications of "mass persuasion" were, at the very least, ambiguous, continued to be made by mainstream researchers through World War II. "[N]ever before the present day has the quick persuasion of masses of people occurred on such a vast scale," Robert K. Merton— another pioneer of the new administrative research in communication— observed as late as 1946. Neither the practitioner nor the academic student of social psychology, he declared flatly, could "escape the moral issues which permeate propaganda as a means of social control." Mass persuasion, Merton concluded in a study of Kate Smith's marathon sale of war bonds over CBS radio during World War II, gave cause for serious concern over the prospects for "democratic values" and "the dignity of the individual."[20]

What prompted this discussion to grow urgent, as the Depression decade wore on, was, above all, intensifying social struggle.[21] On one side, the flare-up of mass working-class militance in and around the Congress of Industrial Organizations and the growth of radical politics at municipal and national levels could hardly be disputed; on the other side a business class, some of whose members openly flirted with fascism, and many more of whom were intransigently hostile to the New Deal, looked with fear and loathing at economic and social programs which invaded the sacred ground of entrepreneurial freedom.

On the left, renewed interest in the social purposes and political-economic control structures of the communications industry, and the condition of a quickly changing popular culture, came through in several ways, above all during the middle and late '30s—the years of the "Popular Front," during which the Communist Party sought to build an anti-fascist alliance with the liberal New Deal.[22] James Rorty's *Our Master's Voice: Advertising* (1934), rooted in Veblen's economics and contemporary socialist theory, is perhaps the outstanding example of informed and biting contemporary media analysis. In offering a fully realized—though still crucially qualified—early expression of the mass culture thesis, as we shall see, Rorty at points achieved an almost poetic quality of observation.

There were, however, many allied contributions of different kinds. Film and radio, for example, were increasingly pivotal to any coherent discussion of the condition of the artist in contemporary society. The Writers' Congresses of the mid-1930s, which brought together a wide range of novelists, playwrights, poets, and screenwriters, were in turn largely animated by what has been called a "radical reversal in the conception of art": from "the principle of artistic autonomy, even independence, to the principle of social representation and responsibility."[23] Such a significant shift of course gave rise to fierce disagreements over aesthetic theory and the nature of artistic commitment; the journals *Partisan Review* and *New Masses*—which had been delving into mass culture regularly since the late 1920s—participated in these debates and, in light of their opposing affinities, generated significant and innovative media criticism. "New levels of sophistication," concludes Paul Buhle of *New Masses*, "were apparent in analyses of 'anonymous' culture, the pulp magazines and the teenage musical culture beneath the contempt of serious art critics."[24] Attention was further awakened by struggles for collective bargaining rights and redress of working conditions, which were breaking out all across the communication industry—in telephone and telegraph service provision and electrical manufacturing, as well as throughout its film, radio, music and newspaper segments.[25]

The upper-crust *New Yorker,* in which A. J. Liebling would pursue his justly famed press criticism, was joined by other periodicals, such as *Harpers,* the *Nation,* the *New Republic,* and, beginning in mid-1940, the advertiser-free newspaper *PM,* in conveying some of these same themes into the mainstream of a politically dominant liberalism.[26]

From directly within the New Deal, finally, came important contributing initiatives: the Federal Writers Project; an unparalleled investigation of telephone industry practices by the newly chartered Federal Communications Commission;[27] and the U.S. Senate Temporary National Economic Committee, whose equally unprecedented general study of the "concentration of economic power" devoted significant attention to telecommunications and radio.[28] Propaganda initiatives undertaken by the National Association of Manufacturers even garnered scrutiny from the Senate Committee on Education and Labor, chaired by Robert LaFollette.[29]

While New Dealers and those to the left of the administration cast the press as a vital public service, now fatally jeopardized by concentrated economic power, ironically, many business leaders found reason to worry that the influence of the commercial press—*their* press—was on the wane. During the process of passage of the National Labor Relations and Social Security Acts (both 1935), the commercial newspaper, still the core of the apparatus of public opinion formation, became solidly anti-New Deal.[30] The press led big business in agitating against Roosevelt, not least by its relentless exposés of the President's own efforts to manipulate and channel public opinion. "Is there a system of propaganda operated by the present Administration for the purpose of misrepresenting governmental activities? Is there a deliberate attempt to distort true conditions and, through a planned system of propaganda, make manufactured fictions appear as facts?" asked one antagonist. He concluded that Roosevelt and his coterie were indeed scheming "to end the free press guaranteed by the Constitution."[31] His book-length survey synchronized with Representative Martin Dies's hopes of sponsoring a congressional investigation into this supposed menace. Thus the vital point: Theorizing about mass persuasion, far from being confined to disaffected radicals or even to liberal groups, likewise became a staple of right-wing criticism of the New Deal, where it frequently merged with preferences for isolationism and appeasement in U.S. foreign policy. Roosevelt's administration returned the favor some time later, by directing the U.S. Justice Department to carry out a content analysis of editorials and news articles, in a search for proof that pro-fascist propaganda was being produced by McCormick's Tribune group and by the Hearst press.[32]

For communication study, the most significant result of this friction attended the business community's hope that the 1936 presidential election would deliver the country from the evils of presidential meddling. In the run-up to that contest, some executives undoubtedly believed, as two contemporaries wrote, that the press—whose hostility to Roosevelt could now virtually be taken for granted—was "an infallible and almost automatic mechanism for directing public opinion, needing only to be properly financed."[33] A week before the election, nevertheless, cautionary notes began to be sounded. A poll of the 68 correspondents who covered the campaign from aboard the two major candidates' trains predicted an "overwhelming victory" for Roosevelt; while, according to one mainstream source, "[m]ajor industries have decided that the Administration stands better than an even chance of another four years in office. . . ."[34] Despite the overall anti-Roosevelt tone of the press, perhaps most bitterly expressed by the press magnates Robert McCormick and William Randolph Hearst, the latter of whom had recently turned against the New Deal, the Republican candidate, Alf Landon, was handed a defeat that shattered all expectations.[35] In the debacle's aftermath, Harry Chandler, publisher of the diehard anti-New Deal *Los Angeles Times,* could only declare lamely that the Republican Party "is by no means moribund."[36] Roosevelt's landslide re-election "was so overwhelming an expression of public opinion," recounted two contemporaries, "that it gravely shocked business men all over the country."[37] The 1936 debacle brought home to big business as nothing else had the severity of the political crisis; and as the economy again sagged into the trough of depression in 1937–38, hopes were dashed that a recovery would ease social polarization anytime soon.

Between 1936 and U.S. entry into World War II, conditions grew increasingly unstable. Even if it did not augur a true hegemonic crisis—a point of debate because opposition continued to be largely contained within the two-party system[38]—from the perspective of the business class, the challenge from below was becoming uncomfortably acute. In a major article of August 1939, one key to the deteriorating situation was spelled out starkly by Henry Luce's *Fortune* magazine, which had, significantly, forecast the Roosevelt landslide with relative accuracy: The press, *Fortune* now starkly underscored, "had lost even the illusion of leadership of public opinion."[39] This ominous fact was widely recognized: Only days after the election, the journalist William Allen White had declared, "I am not sure the press ever had any political influence; but I am sure that it has none now"[40]—even as a liberal journal, the *New York Post,* warned in an editorial headlined "The People vs. the Press" that the President's resounding victory was a serious matter, "because it bespeaks a sharp decline in public confidence in the nation's major channels of information, the newspapers."[41] This disparity was further entrenched through the success of militant organizing drives by the CIO in the face of unabating general press hostility to trade unions. What C. Wright Mills as late as 1950 could take for granted—"the unpredictability of public opinion"— was closely related to the growth of the trade union movement, above all in the decade after 1937, when its membership increased no less than fivefold, to 15 million.[42]

Thus a new and vitally significant conventional wisdom came into being. This was, as Mills was to express it in 1950, that "no view of American public life can be realistic that assumes public opinion to be wholly controlled and entirely manipulated by the mass media."[43] Indeed there were real grounds for taking what Mills termed the primary public, comprised of individuals in their everyday social networks, as "a resistor of media": "If there is any socially organized intelligence which is free to answer back and to give support to those who might answer back, it must somehow be this primary public," Mills observed.[44] His formulation showed that the gap between press and public opinion held vital implications for this customary locus of pragmatist concern. Indeed, we will find that this same polarization underlay the development both of an emergent academic orthodoxy and of its chief contemporary radical antagonist: the critique of mass culture. Before turning to the latter, we must first examine the import of this arresting slippage between press and public opinion for the problems which came more immediately to preoccupy academic communication researchers.

What were the immediate origins of the loss of press leadership? How could the gap be closed? These strategic questions were crucial and, Luce was convinced, becoming more so, because—he was coming to believe—the restoration of national unity was an indispensable prerequisite of the urgent action needed to pre-empt the growing fascist threat to U.S. elites' ambitions. What Luce deemed a socially responsible mass media, really a euphemism for what historian James L. Baughman calls "a middle ground between the New Deal and reaction," would be required to counter the forces that Luce believed were "undermining liberal thought and institutions."[45] Luce would shortly sponsor a commission on freedom of the press to launch a full-scale investigation of such issues; for the moment, however, he sought to clarify the immediate nature of the crisis in public opinion by commissioning and then publicizing the results of a nationwide Roper poll.

The results were, from his perspective, unhappy. Only three-fifths of poll respondents felt that newspaper headlines usually gave "an accurate idea of what really happened," while nearly half thought that newspapers did not furnish fair and unprejudiced news about politics and politicians. Fully two-thirds believed that newspapers were generally given to "soft-pedal news that is unfavorable" to friends of the publisher, while almost as many concurred that favoritism also extended to big advertisers; half of all respondents thought that newspapers tuned the news to serve the interests of "business in general." On the West

Coast, where arch-conservative publishers dominated big-city newspaper markets, negative feeling about the press ran significantly higher.
Echoing this continuing conviction that "the press has failed to gain
broad acceptance as a disseminator of accurate, complete, and unbiased
news and as an instrument of social leadership," public relations impre-
sario Edward Bernays found a receptive audience among editors and
publishers, as late as 1944–45, for his assertion that the press needed to
concentrate on enhancing its own tarnished image.[46]

Was press credibility undergoing dilution in part owing to competition from the robust new mass medium of radio broadcasting? At
least some business leaders must have pondered the question with more
than a trace of anxiety. The unpredictability of public opinion could
be connected in different ways to the spectacular popularity to which
radio had catapulted: By a wide margin, *Fortune* glumly reported,
Roper's respondents considered radio to be more believable and dispassionate than the printed press.[47] No less than 80 percent of the nation's
households possessed a receiver in 1939—more than double the proportion of a decade before. Radio, furthermore, was by the late 1930s cut-
ting into newspaper advertising revenues. If you wanted to hear what
was going on, sang Huddie Ledbetter, "Turn yo' radio on."[48] Publishers
responded by investing ever more heavily in their newfound competitor,
but they could not prevent radio—forced to strive for commercial
success and popular identity amidst the hardship and strife of this
Depression decade—from becoming the medium through which Franklin Roosevelt was enabled "to go over the heads of a largely hostile
press."[49] Leaving aside the hundreds of non-network stations, whose
political instincts might prove even less reliable, network radio itself
clearly enjoyed sufficient autonomy from the print media—an independence that New Dealers, including Roosevelt himself, tried to protect
by repeated attacks on press-radio cross-ownership[50]—to permit the
new medium to develop a relative and largely self-interested accessibility
to the New Deal.[51] Such accessibility in turn further destabilized
the newspapers' hitherto unchallenged role within the news media system, as did the growing competitiveness of radio as a source of spot
news.

In spirit and substance, of course, network radio was far from insur-
rectionary; during the presidential campaign of 1944, for example, the
CIO's Leila A. Sussmann—who was soon to become a media analyst for
the Hutchins Commission on Freedom of the Press—amply documented
her contention that radio network news reporting of labor news "is
biased and unfair."[52] The point meriting emphasis is rather that, at a
moment of gathering social conflict, the media system was itself in flux.
The "press-radio war" which broke out during the mid-1930s[53] thus
discloses an importance far beyond the particular interests of the con-
tending media, for it cannot but have complicated attempts by the na-

tion's already divided business and political leadership to consolidate their response to the social crisis.

What, then, could be done to unify and restore business's grip over public opinion? As war drew nearer, Luce and like-minded peers struggled to come to grips with this paramount issue even as, on the other hand, critical propaganda analysts continued to fan the flames of popular antagonism to big business's routine pre-emption of a democratic press. "What would a careful and thoroughgoing analysis of the ownership structure of American dailies reveal?" prodded sociologist Alfred M. Lee; he added portentously, "The Federal Trade Commission may one day find out."[54] Such premonitions were not without grounds. Two years before Orson Welles barbecued William Randolph Hearst in *Citizen Kane* (1941), no less a personage than Harold L. Ickes took time from his duties as a member of Roosevelt's cabinet to produce a book-length "inquiry into the freedom of the press." A high point in what one scholar calls Ickes's "two-year debate with newspaper editors over the advertising and financial bias of the news,"[55] Ickes's title displayed his colors: *America's House of Lords*. Both here and in a remarkable prefatory passage, the Interior Secretary tacitly acknowledged a debt to *Lords of the Press*—a crusading work published the previous year by the independent journalist George Seldes. "I am encouraged to believe," declared Ickes, "that the people of the United States

> . . . will not much longer submit, at least not without vigorous and open protest, to misrepresentation of individuals and propaganda directed against the public welfare in the interest of the further enrichment and enhancement of the power of our economic royalists, among whom our Lords of the Press occupy a preferred status. Unless the people are aroused to the danger that lies in a subverting press and move to check it, they are likely soon to find themselves no longer free men, but pawns in the hands of a preferred class, the core of whose ideology is a well-filled purse. . . . there can be no greater threat to our hard-won freedom than the threat implicit in an insolent, unscrupulous, and untruthful press.[56]

Some months after the United States entered World War II, similar perspectives echoed from Archibald MacLeish, Roosevelt's Librarian of Congress: "The man who attempts, through his ownership of a powerful newspaper, to dictate the opinions of millions of Americans—the man who employs all the tricks and dodges of a paid propagandist to undermine the people's confidence in their leaders in a war, to infect their minds with suspicion of their desperately needed allies, to break their will to fight, is the enemy, not of the government of this country, but of its people."[57] That such views could find authorized expression among high-ranking members of the administration is, by present standards, signally remarkable. Again, however, what was to be done?

A vital answer came from the Rockefeller Foundation, operating, as William Buxton relates, "as a *de facto* arm of the American state,"[58] as it sought to respond to business's evident loss of leadership over public opinion by sponsoring a systematic program of sophisticated audience research. The latter in turn came to furnish an orthodox foundation for postwar academic communication study. A guiding ambition of the Rockefeller endeavor was to document and verify the relative claims on audience attention of different segments of the nation's swiftly changing media system, including, in particular, the newspaper press and radio broadcasting. This emphasis, to be sure, bespoke a series of intertwined institutional concerns: Perceived needs to place radio audience ratings on a more scientific basis on behalf of radio broadcasters and advertisers and—ostensibly on behalf of the public per se—to elevate popular taste should not be minimized. All this was also combined within the Rocke- feller initiative with the need to get a new and improved handle on public opinion formation—to diagnose and repair the press's evident loss of "leadership" over public opinion. "It becomes of increasingly grave importance, then, how the media of communication are used and misused, and what can and cannot be done with their help is a most vital topic for social investigation."[59] The studied ambiguity of Paul La- zarsfeld's prefatory rationale for *Radio and the Printed Page*—an enter- prise which commenced in the fall of 1937, with Rockefeller Foundation funding—made room for any and all of these anxieties. The turn to empirical study of audience response, therefore, hardly expressed an unattached academic fixation on radio. Rather it was an offshoot of the environing concern to comprehend the new medium's suddenly fraught political significance.

There ensued an energetic search for means of exerting a shaping influence not just over the media, but also over what two contemporar- ies now identified as "personal and social pressures on the community level." "[T]he significant 'selling' that is being done," charged critics of this expanded form of business pressure, "is no longer altogether verbal and pictorial; it is organizational, concrete":

> It is felt that whereas a man may read an advertisement about the "Ameri- can Way" and laugh at it, or draw from it a conclusion opposite to the one its author intended, he will find great difficulty in acting contrary to the beliefs of the organizations to which he belongs or of the social-pressure groups within whose range he lives. To generalize, it is felt that if a man belongs to the "right" groups his thinking will be "right," and that other- wise the "right" ideas cannot be sold to him.[60]

The earlier technocratic emphasis on "social control" comported well with this multifaceted approach to public opinion management. Lasswell declared as early as 1935, for example, that, to achieve its effect, propaganda needed to be coordinated with "all other means of social control," and the public relations expert Edward Bernays specified that control over mass behavior could be achieved best when media appeals "are based on dominant motives and have the support of group leaders."[61]

An increasingly formidable academic enterprise found its basis here. Within business's overall need to find improved means of monitoring, and intervening in, public opinion formation, the specific efforts were to find means of making radio harmonize more sonorously with the printed press and to underwrite more systematic and reliable polling.[62] Among the first fruits of this emergent institutional response before U.S. entry into World War II was Lazarsfeld, Berelson, and Gaudet's classic study of voting decisions in the 1940 presidential election. This work, which guided academic interest toward the mechanisms and networks of "personal influence," constituted another of Lazarsfeld's canny responses to the prevailing climate of business anxiety. In *The People's Choice,* moreover, the leading institutional exponents of a science of audience response made common cause: The study was financed not only by the Rockefeller Foundation, but also by "special contributions" from *Life* magazine, a Luce publication, and Elmo Roper, the pollster whose results Luce had used in the 1939 *Fortune* article on the crisis of public opinion.[63] "We do not know how the budget of the political parties is distributed among different channels of propaganda," the study's authors concluded, "but we suspect that the largest part of any propaganda budget is spent on pamphlets, radio time, etc. But our findings suggest the task of finding the best ratio between money spent on formal media and money spent on organizing the face-to-face influences, the local 'molecular pressures' which vitalize the formal media by more personal interpretation and the full richness of personal relationships into the promotion of the causes which are decided upon in the course of an election."[64]

Opinion leaders, Lazarsfeld's group stressed, were "not identical with the socially prominent people in the community or the richest people or the civic leaders. They are found in all occupational groups."[65] The authors attached special significance to this finding: Was it not indeed a key insight, at once confirming and further specifying the nature of the obstructions which impeded effective control over public opinion? The thesis clearly spoke to—and crucially modified—cruder extant formulations of the process of interpersonal influence. The National Association of Manufacturers, for example, had been targeting its propaganda at what public relations experts called "group leaders" whose influence had been taken for granted: "persons whose word the public will accept: educators, clergymen, columnists, writers on public affairs, political leaders. . . ."[66] In the gap between such "group leaders" and the "opinion leaders" identified by Lazarsfeld lay an eminently serviceable and unmistakably instrumental rationale—and agenda—for an ascending "empirical" communication research. The rise of the mislabeled "limited effects" approach, in turn, occurred not so much as a liberal response to the radical critique of propaganda but, rather, as the result of a dialog between academics and anxious executives at philanthropic foundations and major corporations. The latter were, in the first instance, seeking less to pump up the sales effort—though this was far from a negligible concern—than to renew the legitimacy of the U.S. business system, and they knew they needed to mobilize not only mass media but also interpersonal channels. Intentionally or not, then, the thesis of opinion leadership, so germinal to the further evolution of communication research, originated within this effort to identify and isolate the continuous range of channels that needed to be brought within a single focus for persuasion to be effective.

As the U.S. prepared to enter another world war, attempts to bring the various modes of persuasion into unison of course became more concerted. Again, it was not government but, as Brett J. Gary has persuasively argued,[67] the Rockefeller Foundation which—in the context of an isolationist lobby that effectively barred official government preparation for a national communication system fitted to war needs—organized and superintended the ambitious response that seemed to be needed. "'In a period of emergency such as I believe we now face,'" wrote John Marshall, Rockefeller's point man in communications, in May 1940, "'the manipulation of public opinion to meet emergency needs has to be taken for granted.'" The "'means of molding opinion,'" he continued, had improved to the point that "'any real emergency in this country would be characterized by the manipulation of opinion beyond anything we saw during the last war.'"[68] Anticipating and promoting U.S. intervention, and continuing its crucial funding support even into the early war years, Rockefeller provided the auspices under which the study of persuasion across its range—what Lasswell famously codified in the all-embracing question, "Who says what in which channel to whom with what effect?"[69]—could attain scientific legitimacy in a climate of unexampled national urgency.

Marshall's urgent effort to elevate analysis of mass persuasion harbored twin objectives, both of which Gary details: first, to contrive a "prophylaxis" against the inroads of fascist propaganda; second, to help cultivate a national consensus over U.S. war aims and measures. Within a broad spectrum of Rockefeller-supported private academic and cultural organizations—at Princeton, Chicago, and Columbia, the New School, the Museum of Modern Art—and, even more important once war commenced, at a spate of new state agencies within the Department of Justice, the Library of Congress, the FCC, and the State Department, Rockefeller spearheaded the study of Nazi propaganda and "the development of content analysis as a national security intelligence tool."[70] The first hub of this covert effort was the Library of Congress, which housed Harold Lasswell's "Experimental Division for the Study of Wartime Communications." With funding entirely from Rockefeller, the

Library's director Archibald MacLeish—himself previously a top editor at Luce's *Fortune*—was able to place the Lasswell group at the service of the government's unfolding activities in communications intelligence.[71] "[N]ot only did the Foundation set up and support a host of pre-war extra-governmental propaganda analysis projects," Gary sums up, "it also paid for the organizations and propaganda analysis training of many wartime government employees."[72]

Widespread social debate over political and social ends was suddenly curtailed, in the alphabet soup of wartime propaganda workshops and experimental social science units, and replaced by a series of concerted efforts to exploit means. As early as 1940 Paul Lazarsfeld sensed that "[t]he role of radio as a tool of propaganda has receded to the background because not what to do but how to do it has become the problem of the day."[73] It was this extraordinary fusion of public and private coordinative action that gave rise to the hypodermic needle or magic bullet theory of media effects. A facet of measures taken by the Justice Department prosecutors against "Fifth Columnists"—those who allegedly bored from within to sap Americans' determination to win the war—the magic bullet conception arose as a tactical adjunct of departmental mobilization against domestic fascism. As "the propaganda menace came to be seen as part of a worldwide Nazi conspiracy to undermine democracy and pave the way for the triumph of fascism," Gary shows, the Department turned to the legal system for relief. A discrete legal function needed to be discharged: A finding of seditious intent by a given periodical hinged legally on a successful showing that it posed a "clear and present danger" to the state. Just here the bullet theory was called upon to work its magic: "'[N]o one who has been exposed to such a campaign can escape being affected by it, consciously or unconsciously,'" argued Justice Department lawyers: "'. . . If a military weapon such as propaganda is employed, there is a clear and present danger to loyalty, morale and discipline.'" Nazi propagandizing in Europe, the Justice Department charged, offered a "bitter lesson" that "'proved beyond question the logic of this reasoning.'"[74] Once the assumption was made that the effectiveness of Nazi propaganda in Europe had been already proven, the only thing that mattered was whether a given periodical was indeed plying the Nazi line. Lasswell's content analyses then could be called on to provide an ostensibly authoritative judgment on this issue. Yet Lasswell's scientific standard derived from a portentous capitulation to commercial media; at times it was based on nothing more than indices of deviation from the ideological perspectives evident in *Reader's Digest* and the *Saturday Evening Post!*[75]

This concerted attempt to mobilize all the channels of communication for global war was accompanied, for a ragged moment which continued on for a few years even following that conflagration, by a whole series of ameliorative efforts—yet to find their historian—to rebalance the media, the better to reflect the New Deal orientation which still prevailed in public opinion. One thinks here of the FCC's attempt, in 1946, to codify the public service responsibilities of broadcasters by issuing a general programming policy, and, ironically—given its funding by Luce—of the release in the same year of the Hutchins Commission Report on Freedom of the Press.[76] But there were additional, like initiatives: the FCC's earlier Report on Chain Broadcasting, for example, and the agency's desultory investigation of co-ownership of newspapers and broadcast stations, as well as the Justice Department's subsequent Paramount Decree, which sundered ownership of film theaters from the major production-distribution complexes. Even the still inadequately explained 1949 antitrust case brought against AT&T by the Justice Department might be placed in this same context. Cumulatively, these interventions amounted to a resounding declaration that unrestricted laissez-faire in institutionalized communication was no longer tolerable. The isolationist right wing in American business and politics would neither forgive nor forget this tectonic shift in the media's ideological placement; forty years later, the so-called "New Right" was able to promote its own revanchist objectives by mercilessly exploiting the notion that the "liberal media" had become a prime instigator of social decay.[77]

Though the postwar accent on the "social responsibility" of the press is incomprehensible outside the framework of Depression-decade social conflict, even as World War II's end drew near, it came through most resoundingly only as rhetoric. Practical measures for media reform were soon contained. Certainly nothing as radical as the producer cooperatives sought by late 19th-century working-class reformers was ever contemplated (although hints of this idea were, interestingly, retained by Ickes[78]), while government media ownership was peremptorily dismissed. And the Hutchins Commission's advocacy of a common carrier role for the press was explicitly severed from any prospective change in the latter's substantive legal status: Voluntary restraint and self-imposed responsibility instead served as its watchwords. Even so, its report was greeted with suspicion and antagonism by media owners—notably including Luce himself—for whom any deviation from market freedom now posed a threat to the vaunted "free flow of information," the policy with which they, joining the dominant wing of transnational business, sought to assure the ascension of a U.S. global paramountcy.[79] The public service obligations sought by the FCC, in turn, were viciously rejected by commercial broadcasters.[80] Even as the New Deal was left behind in the ensuing Cold War, finally, what soon became the dominant bloc within academic communication study pried itself loose from the synthesis that had governed inquiry into mass persuasion, and—as we are about to see—codified into a pluralistic dogma the chief lesson learnt from the 1930s: that public opinion and propaganda did not always coincide.

After the 1948 election, a sweeping societal mobilization—at once military,[81] economic,[82] and cultural[83]—quickly resulted in the formation of a national security state. Communication was institutionalized as a scholarly discipline during this period of brutal intellectual constraint.[84] In a process combining opportunism with Cold War allegiance, critical concerns about the far-flung implications of mass persuasion in America were driven to the margins.

To support and bolster a global order maximally conducive to U.S. big business, the propaganda machine created during World War II was refurbished and placed at the service of a generation of class-conscious, interventionist policymakers. Even as mass persuasion was actually becoming an ever more significant domestic and international staple of U.S. policy, however, it was increasingly cast as a defining feature of "totalitarian" states alone. By fiat, propaganda did not exist in liberal democracies, and the issues that had clustered around mass persuasion were thus comparably distanced from mainstream study of American society. Propaganda analysis in turn now denoted not engagement with the ever more central forms and agencies of modern-day mass persuasion, but a narrow fixation on the typical products of state-controlled foreign media and a well-indulged commitment to psychological warfare.[85] It thrived, that is, by being telescoped onto what Allen Ginsberg objectified as "the Russia" and its real and purported satellites around the globe. As Christopher Simpson has recently revealed, leading academic communication researchers made indispensable, if often covert, contributions to this Cold War propaganda effort. Battening on a stream of military and quasi-military contracts, and drawing on the personal and scientific networks they had found during the war,[86] their practical study of propaganda flourished. At the same time, as postwar recovery was succeeded by unprecedented, seemingly unremitting economic boom, communication study was recruited as a prime instrument of a ubiquitous corporate marketing and promotion apparatus.[87] Dispassionate analysis of mass persuasion in such a world required a daunting critical engagement with the very institutions which, while depending increasingly routinely on propaganda's practical exercise, had also come to be staffed and serviced by social scientists themselves.[88] University-based social scientists now found themselves within a thickening web of philanthropic foundations, government agencies, corporate sponsors, and, of course, the media industries, willing and able to contribute individual research grants, program endowments, student recruitment prospects, and even access to attractive research sites. Small wonder that many in the new crop of scholarly communication experts became positively committed to dispelling popular criticisms of dominant communication media.[89]

Far-ranging shifts were signaled in the tone and content of social study. As mainstream researchers toiled to demarcate the purview of a "respectable" scholarship, they emphasized that "science" was an exclusionary enterprise. Mainstream social science came to renew its earlier embrace of American exceptionalism,[90] all but replacing "class"— which, though never especially well developed, had claimed adherents during the Depression[91]—with "status" and "stratification," concepts far more congenial to the succeeding epoch's mechanistic functionalism. Depression-era emphases on "social control"—which, during that tumultuous time, could not be quarantined entirely from class power— ballooned into more euphonious theorizations, as researchers once again became free to concentrate on an apparently stable liberal consensus.[92] As institutionally focused propaganda analysts were placed on the defensive,[93] an individual unit of analysis was codified into orthodoxy within communication study.

It needs to be re-emphasized that the successful effort to reinvent communication study as a formalized social science, setting itself the challenge of understanding an isolable object of inquiry—"communication"—transpired only within the context of what had become an enduring gap between press and public opinion. Two decades of trade union growth and of Democratic electoral victories in the face of an overwhelmingly anti-union and Republican press had clearly underscored, as Mills stated in 1950, the desirability of keeping under "continual observation" the primary public, whose hidden channels of persuasive communication his colleague Lazarsfeld's panel research designs were designed to disclose.[94] Only by recognizing this context will we make sense of the ostensible move to shed concern with the multifaceted processes of mass persuasion, leaving a residue of ever-more focused concern with "intervening variables" "between media and mass."[95] An extraordinary essay published in 1948 can be used to date this shift in conceptual priorities.

In "Mass Communication, Popular Taste and Organized Social Action," Paul F. Lazarsfeld and Robert K. Merton conceded at the outset that, although the "peculiar dread" with which many Americans seemed to view the mass media was unfounded, a more "realistic basis" for concern indeed might be found in "the changing types of social control exercised by powerful interest groups in society." Likewise, there was "substantial ground for concern" regarding the effects of media "upon popular culture and the esthetic tastes of their audiences." But Lazarsfeld and Merton went well beyond such general acknowledgments that mass persuasion possessed continuing relevance for understanding of the social process. Here is their suggestive formulation of the first set of issues:

Increasingly, the chief power groups, among which organized business oc-
cupies the most spectacular place, have come to adopt techniques for ma-
nipulating mass publics through propaganda in place of more direct means
of control. Industrial organizations no longer compel eight year old children
to attend the machine for fourteen hours a day; they engage in elaborate
programs of "public relations." They place large and impressive advertisements in the newspapers of the nation; they sponsor numerous radio programs; on the advice of public relations counsellors they organize prize
contests, establish welfare foundations, and support worthy causes. Economic power seems to have reduced direct exploitation and turned to a
subtler type of psychological exploitation, achieved largely by disseminating
propaganda through the mass media of communication.

   This change in the structure of social control merits thorough examination.[96]

This argument placed Lazarsfeld and Merton beyond the pale of the
"administrative" research perspective of which they were soon to be
taken as exemplars.[97] The authors went further still, however, by isolating three highly significant social functions with which, they argued,
mass media could be prominently identified: status conferral, enforce-
ment of social norms, and the so-called "narcotizing dysfunction,"
through which—via an "unplanned mechanism"—"large masses of the
population" nonetheless became "politically apathetic and inert."[98]
Next admitting "the structure of ownership and operation" into their
argument, Lazarsfeld and Merton proceeded to explain that because, in
the United States, "the mass media are supported by great business
concerns geared into the current social and economic system," it was
only to be expected that "the media contribute to the maintenance of
that system," specifically by "restrain[ing] the cogent development of a
genuinely critical outlook," or, in other words, cultivating "conform-
ism."[99]

   They next led into a revealing discussion of "propaganda for social
objectives": "the promotion, let us say, of non-discriminatory race relations, or of educational reforms, or of positive attitudes toward organized labor."[100] One or more of three conditions, wrote Lazarsfeld and
Merton, needed to be satisfied for such propaganda to "prove effective."
These conditions were: the uniformity of message content that could be
achieved by "monopolization" of mass media, a focus on "canalization
rather than change of basic values," and supplementation of media
messages through the use of face-to-face contacts.[101] Herein the full
range of interpersonal and mediated channels that could be—and were
being—systematically exploited by leading institutional actors, achieved
a true measure of theoretical recognition:

> Students of mass movements have come to repudiate the view that mass
> propaganda in and of itself creates or maintains the movement. Nazism did
> not attain its brief moment of hegemony by capturing the mass media of

communication. The media played an ancillary role, supplementing the use of organized violence, organized distribution of rewards for conformity and organized centers of local indoctrination. . . . the machinery of mass persuasion included face to face contact in local organizations as an adjunct to the mass media. . . . In a society such as our own, where the pattern of bureaucratization has not yet become so pervasive or, at least, not so clearly crystallized, it has likewise been found that mass media prove most effective in conjunction with local centers of organized face to face contact.[102]

On one hand, then, Lazarsfeld and Merton concluded, "these three conditions are rarely satisfied conjointly in propaganda for social objectives."[103] On the other, however,

organized business does approach a virtual "psychological monopoly" of the mass media. Radio commercials and newspaper advertisements are, of course, premised on a system which has been termed free enterprise. Moreover, this world of commerce is primarily concerned with canalizing rather than radically changing basic attitudes; it seeks only to create preferences for one rather than another brand of product. Face to face contacts with those who have been socialized in our culture primarily reinforce the prevailing culture patterns.

Thus, the very conditions which make for the maximum effectiveness of the mass media of communication operate toward the maintenance of the going social and cultural structure rather than its change.[104]

The contrast could not be more compelling between this—a balanced view of the ratio of coercion and consent which, as we will see, was also evident within the early critique of mass culture—and the agenda for research which immediately succeeded and supplanted it. While Merton turned to other concerns, Lazarsfeld and his protégés, Joseph Klapper and Elihu Katz, perversely proceeded to develop a rationale for analysis of personal influence, abstracted, exactly as Lazarsfeld and Merton in 1948 had proposed it should *not* be, from the social and historical processes of media monopolization, canalization, and supplementation. What Lazarsfeld and Merton had synthesized as "the conditions for effective propaganda" were, therefore, now denied the visas they required to remain resident within mainstream communication study.

It was Joseph Klapper, whose work was underwritten by CBS, who first codified this quickly evolving new position. Klapper argued in an influential book, first released as a publication of the Columbia Bureau of Applied Social Research in 1949, that the media acted as agents of reinforcement and that audiences actively sought gratifications to satisfy pre-existing needs. What those needs were and how they had been socially shaped and situated became conceptually irrelevant and methodologically untouchable.[105] As the field of communication became a substantial academic enterprise, boasting full-fledged departments and programs of graduate study, discussions of media effects domestically began to generate ever-thicker hedgerows of qualifications, caveats, abridgments.

The purportedly "limited effects" of the mass media were elevated by mainstream research only as the structural underpinnings of institutionalized communication were willed off-limits. But Klapper's early attempt, again in 1948, to smooth the way for this transition still betrayed a clumsy frankness which, in later years, would rarely recur: "[P]ropaganda—or, if you will, the engineering of consent—is nothing new, nor is its use confined to persons of sinister intent. Whoever seeks in any way to change another's mind, or to have him think in a certain way, is attempting, whether ill or well, to engineer consent. The artist who records his interpretation of a tree is suggesting an attitude, and so laying the foundation of consent. And a notable portion of every person's daily converse is directed toward propagandistic ends. . . . Propaganda, in short, appears whenever there are two unidentical minds and a means of communication."[106] After this distracting discussion, which served to conflate rather than to integrate mass media and interpersonal communication, Klapper went on to suggest that "the limitations upon the influence of the mass media . . . are considerable, and . . . these limitations are partly due to the very aspects of mass media which inspire the greatest concern: commercial sponsorship and the resultant necessity of pleasing as many people as possible."[107] Delimiting the scientist in his laboratory sharply from the society that surrounded him, Klapper sought, by keeping social relations at arm's length, also to keep them at bay. In elevating the need for "cool and careful" scientific study, he went on in his book some years later likewise to abstract with precision from two of the cardinal points of the earlier propaganda synthesis, both of which, if anything, in the intervening years had only come to acquire greater salience. His book, he wrote, would make "little mention" of "the effects of mass communication in international psychological warfare." Nor was any attempt made "to deal with the effects of the media as instruments of consumer advertising." These prodigal exceptions once made, the fundamental social purpose and institutional structure of the contemporary mass media could be nimbly skirted.

The antihistorical character of the kind of social science Klapper preferred made its own contribution to this result. Klapper's admitted emphasis was on "campaign effects"—"short term opinion and attitude effects"—rather than on "the role played by mass communication in long term attitude change."[108] In the conclusion, paradoxically, Klapper tried to have it both ways, as he warned readers against "the tendency to go overboard in blindly minimizing the effects and potentialities of mass communications."[109] It was not, then, that history per se was inadmissible; only that it was not—or not yet, in the optimists' view—scientific. Historians' accustomed methods, in the characteristic charge of yet another leading psychological researcher, David McClelland, were "simply not adequate" for rendering valid scientific judgments.[110]

But it was unquestionably only with what Katz and Lazarsfeld called "the rediscovery of the primary group" that this resurgent individualism definitively supplanted any larger social framework within mainstream communication study.[111] In *Personal Influence* Katz and Lazarsfeld ironically criticized their precursors for supposedly relying on a concept of society "characterized by an amorphous social organization and a paucity of interpersonal relations."[112] But it was, by comparison, their own model of society—from which processes of social relationality were all but absent—which suffered such attenuation. *Personal Influence*, like the scores of researches that followed in its mold, drew on narrowly selective and mechanistic conceptions of the social process. The "primary group" which its authors did so much to resurrect was a concept whose animating ideals had been lodged by its originator, Charles H. Cooley, in the Teutonic village communities which he believed had furnished America with its institutional and racial inheritance.[113]

If Katz and Lazarsfeld did retain a nominal sense of "the primarily social character of ostensibly individual opinions, attitudes and actions,"[114] the environing importance of social relations beyond the workings of the primary group was all but obliterated. Thus they retained only a formal shell of the concept that had germinated out of popular opposition to big business and established state institutions during the New Deal. As an intense focus developed on a separable plane of individually communicated attitudes and behaviors, the social process began quite consciously to be chopped and split into kindling wood. "We shaped insights into hypotheses and eagerly set up research designs in quest of additional variables which we were sure would bring order out of chaos and enable us to describe the process of effect with sufficient precision to diagnose and predict," fretted Klapper in 1960 about the past decade of study of the effects of mass communication: "But the variables emerged in such a cataract that we almost drowned."[115] His wry comment affirmed the successful internalization of an outstanding norm: that research procedure in what many now preferred to call not the social but the "behavioral" sciences had been endowed with seeming methodological rigor.

Despite, but also because of this burgeoning methodological fixation, obvious conceptual deficiencies sprung up. That processes of personal influence at work in the whole society might be read back unproblematically from a sample composed entirely of women was not even questioned by the authors of, for example, the Decatur study (as it is sometimes known). This lacuna, arguably, was no mere result of the instrumental dictates of sponsorship—in this case by Macfadden Publications, whose romance magazines were directed mainly at women. Apart from narrow commentaries on influences between the individuals comprising the family unit (mainly husbands and wives), rather, it was a byproduct of the more encompassing fact that gender relations remained essentially unproblematized.[116] Indeed the authors defined "girls" as "single women under 35 years of age." Still without comment, insult now passed into injury: "Those single women who are older than 35 years are usually outside the marriage market and probably differ from the younger single women in their several activities and interests," Katz and Lazarsfeld explained, concerning their decision simply to omit this group of individuals from their now invalidated category of "girls."[117] Race was similarly excluded from consideration, by the simple but profoundly far-reaching decision—originating as a self-conscious strategy in the Muncie study that had been conducted by Lazarsfeld's senior colleague, Robert S. Lynd, and reappearing thereafter in Lazarsfeld's own work, *The People's Choice*—to study a mid-sized midwestern community, with a high proportion of native-born whites, and relatively free of what Katz and Lazarsfeld termed "sectional peculiarities."[118] In attempting to isolate and map the flow of interpersonal influence, finally, the authors relied on the by-now formulaic tripartite distinction (high, middle, low) for transmuting "class" into "socioeconomic status." The latter, assigned through a mechanical transcription of each sample member's rent and education, took the form of a series of seemingly objective individual attributes.[119] How, in such a conceptual setting, could engagement ever occur with the concept of social class as a relational category? Instead, in Katz and Lazarsfeld's work, and in a slew of similar efforts, consciousness and experience became, at best, thoroughly fragmented correlates of abstract and largely unspecified social locations. The shaping effects of class, gender, and race were rendered all but invisible, even as a purportedly isolable and infinitely graded communication process was highlighted.

For confirmation that these changes indeed did bespeak a general conceptual alteration of the earlier set of governing research objectives—rather than a mere individual turning point—let me turn, finally, to another earlier article by Robert K. Merton. As late, once again, as 1948, Merton had thought to pose the very same issue, "patterns of influence" in an interpersonal context, in a strikingly different way. "The generic problem," Merton had declared, "can be stated simply enough: to what extent and in which situations does interpersonal influence operate largely *within* one's own social group or stratum or category (age, sex, class-power-stratum, prestige-stratum, etc.) and when does it operate largely *between* groups, strata, or social categories?" Although, taking due note of Lazarsfeld's previous research, Merton emphasized that "location within various social hierarchies of wealth, power, and class does not predetermine location within a local structure of interpersonal influence," the search to establish and interrelate such social locations remained for him vitally relevant for the study of interpersonal influence.

Or, as he himself put it, "[t]he sociological problem here is manifestly to explore the interrelations between the several hierarchies, and not to blur the problem by *assuming* that they can be merged into a composite system of rankings."[120]

Notwithstanding Merton's admonishments, for the next generation, domestic research priorities were to be ruled—exactly as Katz and Lazarsfeld sought in *Personal Influence*—by a singularly dessicated interpretation of "the part played by people in the flow of mass communication."[121] Persons whom they continued to call "opinion leaders," following the practice established by Lazarsfeld in the voting study of 1940, were assigned decisive roles within the complex chains of interpersonal influence through which mass media messages selectively filtered and diffused. The authors' blandly affirmative characterization of their study's central ambition, however, gives hardly a hint of its most important conceptual features. First, although "people," after all, certainly also *produced* media messages, the dominant research approach now systematically ignored the structure of media production. Then too, as Todd Gitlin underscored in a subsequent critique, the authors of the Decatur study construed "influence" so much in terms of purchasing decisions that "the part played by people" came to revolve only around consumption. Conceptualizing "people" as individual consumers may have concorded with the needs of the study's sponsors, but as we have seen it was freighted with problematic implications. Above all it obscured any view of "people" as laborers, residing in communities alongside others who owned the factories and offices in which they worked, and in households with others whom their own unpaid labor helped to sustain.

It is illuminating to turn to C. Wright Mills's later judgment on this research. Mills, the sociologist who himself directed the fieldwork for the Decatur study, and whom I will discuss in greater detail below,[122] linked the work as it finally appeared to the dominant trend in communication study. Agreeing with Lazarsfeld and Merton that the organization of interpersonal communication channels (or what Lazarsfeld and Merton had called "supplementation" in their classic 1948 essay) was indeed a vital component of the overall flow of influence, Mills nonetheless averred that attempts to chart this flow were byproducts of an increasingly insistent effort to manipulate human behavior in pursuit of private and self-interested ends. "To change opinion and activity," he wrote caustically of advertisers and other "opinion managers," had come to require paying "close attention to the full context and lives of the people to be managed:"

> Along with mass persuasion, we must somehow use personal influence; we must reach people in their life context and through other people, their daily associates, those whom they trust: we must get at them by some kind of "personal" persuasion.

Although, again in concert with Lazarsfeld and Merton, Mills assigned substantial importance to the monopolization of control over the agencies of mass persuasion, he differed dramatically from his colleagues in his ability to point out during the postwar era that "the primary public" remained "the great unsolved problem of the opinion-makers."[123] It was this vital insight that allowed Mills unblinkingly to identify—and criticize—the manipulative rationale which was working its way, among other things through the Decatur study itself, into mainstream communication research.

The social psychological study of communication processes, for which *Personal Influence* comprised the most hallowed text, developed at a distance from a second, concurrent, conceptual tradition, known as "information theory." But information theory acted only to reinforce the field's newfound detachment from the study of social relations. Imperially inclusive, "information" was said by proponents of this latter theory to cover messages, pattern, "the ability of a goal-seeking system to decide or control,"[124] and, as Krippendorff[125] later cogently specified, a potential for organizational work—at levels of analysis ranging from the psychological to the social to the biological. Endowing a lingering conviction that there existed a transcendent, "informational" dimension of disparate "systems"[126] (which we will see in Chapter Four eventually found its way into the theory of postindustrial society), information theory helped in the meantime to accredit an academic communication study as a Cold War social science fit for institutional accreditation.

"We have every reason to suspect," declared Wilbur Schramm, arguably the latter's foremost spokesman, in 1955, ". . . that a mathematical theory for studying electronic communication systems ought to have some carry-over to human communication systems."[127] Lazarsfeld, too, played a role in importing information theory into social science.[128] Even mainstream opinion has recently come to accept that this comprised a largely facile transposition. As Ritchie emphasizes, Claude Shannon's concept of information, of which the intended reference was to a specialized theory of signal transmission, was extended only invalidly to questions of meaning. In this mechanistic reduction, "the statistical characteristics of a code" were widely and enduringly confounded "with the cognitive and social processes of communication." In contrast, Ritchie concedes, "even the most routine forms of human communication can be understood only in the context of the social relationships in which they take place."[129] But we should remember that this is a judgment post hoc: For the two decades following 1950, the considered comment by Wilbur Schramm was more apt: "We felt that Shannon's information theory was a brilliant analogue which might illuminate many dark areas of our own field." And Schramm likewise gave definitive voice to the sentiment with which leading analysts undertook to institutionalize their new conceptual concerns: "Communication is the fundamental social process."[130] On the most general, explicit, and apparently decisive level, information theory thus conferred legitimacy on the proposition under which academic communication study now sought to operate: that communication processes could and indeed should be studied in relative isolation from environing social relations.

There remained dissenters. However, their terms of reference as well were undergoing a dramatic inversion. This metamorphosis owed above all to the radicals' sudden perception that the disparity between press and public opinion, which had so shaped thinking about communication during the New Deal period, had been rendered obsolete. No longer clinging to instrumentalism's benign view of "organized intelligence," nor blind, as the latter's philosophical advocate had been, to the class structure of U.S. society, a full-blown radical critique of what now began to be called "mass culture" associated a specifically ideological mode of social domination with the anomalous growth of a gigantic white-collar labor force.

<h1 style="text-align:center">II</h1>

In *Personal Influence,* Katz and Lazarsfeld had sought to inflate the status of "interpersonal relations" by deprecating the idea that media power depended largely on the existence of an "atomistic mass of millions of readers, listeners and movie-goers," comprising at best only an "amorphous social organization."[131] Yet, even as they attempted to dispatch it to a bygone era, this selfsame idea of "mass society" was reaching its apogee in social thought.

The "mass" had gravitated through earlier centuries into the repertoire of European intellectuals; "mass" was initially but an extension of "mob," which had been in use among English elites since the late 17th century. In 19th-century England, "masses" became an object of intellectual contestation.[132] During the decades between the Paris Commune and the Russian Revolution, the concept attained pan-European currency, and in this context its conservative connotations grew more pronounced. As German graduate seminars were a frequent destination for late 19th-century U.S. aspirants to a career in social science, "the mass" was also quickly imported into U.S. academic nomenclature. Transplanted to American soil, however, the concept shed none of its fearsome aspects for social analysts.[133] The declining ability of U.S. protestantism to equip public taste with what it deemed to be exemplary genteel standards, radical agitation before World War I, followed by the Russian Revolution and an unprecedented postwar strike wave in the United States all contributed to aggravating sensibilities about society's restive potential.[134] As what sociologists began to identify as a typological shift from "community" to "society" proceeded, many analysts portrayed a slide into a state of anomie, in which there existed—as an influential sociology text put it—"no social organization, no body of custom and tradition, no established set of rules or rituals, no organized group or sentiments, no structure of status roles and no established leadership."[135] By the immediate postwar period the concept of mass society was already beginning to function as an intellectual centerpiece, as, for instance, it did in Louis Wirth's 1947 presidential address before the American Sociological Society.[136] What had been only one distinctive collective grouping thenceforth became a well-recognized synonym for a purported American condition. Marxism apart, the idea of mass society, by the mid-1950s, had transited toward becoming what Daniel Bell—no friend of either conception—called "probably the most influential social theory in the Western world."[137]

The latter plainly resonated even within some of the contemporary culture industry's own products. Vance Packard's[138] bestseller *The Hidden Persuaders* (1957) purported to expose the machinations of the advertising industry, while Elia Kazan's film *A Face in the Crowd* (1957) underscored (in an eerie premonition of presidential politics during the 1980s and 1990s) the demagogic political potential of television. Readers of a popular children's story imported from Britain were likewise treated to sermonizing about mass culture: "The most important thing we've learned,/So far as children are concerned," sang Roald Dahl's Oompa-Loompas about Mike Teavee, as the boy was bodily transported via television in *Charlie and the Chocolate Factory* (1964), "Is never, Never, NEVER let/Them near your television set—/Or better still, just don't install/The idiotic thing at all. . . ."[139] Dwight Macdonald, one of the theory's U.S. originators, became a pundit, regularly publishing acerbic exposés of mass culture in the pages of such periodicals as the *New Yorker* and *Esquire*.

The idea that processes of historical eventuation had become subject to mass culture thus itself became a force to be reckoned with. Macdonald had referred in 1944 to "the deadening and warping effect of long exposure to movies, pulp magazines and radio" which, he asserted, "can hardly be overestimated."[140] By 1953, however, he had sharply globalized this idea: "Like nineteenth-century capitalism," Macdonald now intoned, "Mass Culture is a dynamic, revolutionary force, breaking down the old barriers of class, tradition, taste, and dissolving all cultural distinctions."[141] "[N]ext to the H Bomb," declared a less strident critic, Gilbert Seldes, "no force on earth is as dangerous as television."[142] For many writers who shared a commitment to "serious" intellectual forms and practices, "culture for the millions" continued to comprise an agency destructive at once of aesthetic sensibilities and established social bonds. The new scientists of communication were themselves never able, in these circumstances, to lift their field of study free and clear of a widespread attribution (at least among members of the educated middle class) of corrosively debilitating media effects. Instead, continuing popular concerns about the effects of mass culture achieved at least a limited standing in their own pronouncements.[143] Even some of those who simultaneously pooh-poohed the domestic significance of mass persuasion were moved to wonder vaguely with Macdonald—as did Paul Lazarsfeld—whether there was not "an inherent threat to highbrow culture in mass society."[144]

Again, however, only the extent of such hyperbole was novel. Throughout the early decades of the 20th century, the idea of mass society had been sown with negative references to the agencies of mass persuasion—behind which, through such newly visible media as film and tabloid newspapers, there often lurked a hostile image of the U.S. working class. Even in the heartlands of native white America, close observers soon detected disruptive evidence of the media's presence. During the late 1920s, Robert and Helen Lynd had charted the explosive growth and disruptive impacts of "inventions remaking leisure," notably including radio and film, in Muncie, Indiana.[145] Their often acute, pioneering study of the conditions of contemporary community— heavily influenced by the pragmatism Lynd had accepted directly from John Dewey at Columbia[146]—quickly became a benchmark. In Cambridge, England, it offered grist for the mill of the critic F. R. Leavis, who deemed *Middletown* an unusually sensitive portrayal of the disabling innovations wrought by the machine in the service of "mass civilization."[147] Dwight Macdonald, late to become the doyen of U.S. "mass culture" critics, also cut his teeth on *Middletown* (as well as on Leavis, and Ortega—a leading conservative voice in the chorus of earlier denunciations of "the revolt of the masses").[148] Not least, James Rorty, whose 1934 book provides an early and substantial instance of what we may identify as a full-fledged *radical* critique of mass culture, acknowledged a major debt to Lynd and borrowed the idea of a "pseudoculture" from Leavis.[149]

A disparaging nomenclature resulted, bequeathing terms of reference which remain in wide currency to this day.[150] Through commercialization, it was asserted, contemporary cultural production was being "cheapened," "devalued," "debased," "homogenized"; while, it was often protested, through the operations of what Macdonald was to call "Gresham's Law in Culture," discriminating standards were being routed by values which aimed only at "the lowest common denominator."[151] Not the least revealing of the effects putatively associated with such values was that, as Macdonald put it in 1953, "the upper classes . . . find their own culture attacked and even threatened with destruction. . . ."[152]

Originating during the interwar period, however, and quite remarkably jumbled together with this already entrenched conservative response, might be found as well a series of incongruous radical tenets.

In this emergent usage, mass culture (or as Macdonald initially called it, "popular culture") was "imposed from above," "manufactured by technicians hired by the ruling class," a manipulative "instrument of social domination" which worked simultaneously to "integrate" the masses into "the official culture-structure" and "to make a profit for their rulers."[153] Even during the 1950s, radical concerns about mass persuasion managed to subsist by taking refuge under the borrowed shell of conservative apprehension regarding commercial, market-based cultural production. Whence came this distinctive hybrid, which resists reduction either to a primordial conservativism or to some equally pristine radicalism?

This revision of the concept of mass society, which endowed the idea of "mass culture"—or, alternatively, of "culture industry"—with momentous import, was not altogether of one piece. During the later 1930s, one group of peculiarly alienated intellectuals promulgated tenets regarding the organizational structure, aesthetic character, and social purpose of market-based communication mainly so as to suggest an explicit convergence between the United States and the Soviet Union.[154] This originating sectarian perspective, which quickly transformed, during the first postwar decade, into a mainstream Cold War liberalism, identified parallels which convinced Clement Greenberg, Dwight Macdonald, and like-minded anti-Communists that they could discern in "kitsch" or "popular culture" a leading symptom of totalitarian potential.[155]

In a second and more sophisticated version, the concept of "culture industry" was developed by intellectual refugees who—even before they fled west in the 1930s to the United States, rather than (like their peer, the philosopher and aesthetician Georg Lukacs) east to the Soviet Union—had been repelled, and only secondarily fascinated, by the sweep and character of organized capitalism's institutions of cultural production.[156] Their critique of the culture industry, however, again betrayed, in characteristic combination, both a mandarin mistrust of the new popular forms of film and broadcasting and a politically charged insight into the repressive historical complex stretching "from Caligari to Hitler" and, indeed, across all of capitalist modernity. In this intellectual context, "culture industry" sought an oxymoron effect. Perhaps, as Horkheimer and Adorno had not been especially impressed by Soviet silent film experiments, "culture industry" did not seek to carry the shock of an effective montage, but, still, it did attempt to perplex—to insist that the apparent widespread regimentation characteristic of contemporary society be brought up to a level of solitary critical awareness. Within this framework, the accent was on the "ruthless unity in the culture industry," as Adorno and Horkheimer had termed it, as a defining symptom of an encompassing domination.[157] Adorno stated in 1967 that,

although the culture industry undeniably speculates on the conscious and
unconscious state of the millions towards which it is directed, the masses are
not primary, but secondary, they are an object of calculation; an appendage
of the machinery. The customer is not king, as the culture industry would
like to have us believe, not its subject but its object. . . . The culture industry misuses its concern for the masses in order to duplicate, reinforce, and
strengthen their mentality, which it presumes is given and unchangeable.
How this mentality might be changed is excluded throughout. . . . It can
be assumed without hesitation that steady drops hollow the stone, especially since the system of the culture industry that surrounds the masses
tolerates hardly any deviation and incessantly drills the same formulas of
behavior. Only their deep unconscious mistrust . . . explains why they
have not, to a person, long since perceived and accepted the world as it is
constructed for them by the culture industry.[158]

Did not contemporary culture at once affirm and exemplify an increasingly general form of "mass deception"? The latter could hardly be
a matter, then, of democratic expression. Theodor Adorno, who coined
the phrase "the culture industry," is said by one of his longtime colleagues to have "intensely disliked" the rival term "mass culture." Decades later, Adorno expressly attempted to clarify the distinction:

The term culture industry was perhaps used for the first time in the book
Dialectic of Enlightenment, which Horkheimer and I published in Amsterdam in 1947. In our drafts we spoke of "mass culture." We replaced that
expression with "culture industry" in order to exclude from the outset the
interpretation agreeable to its advocates: that it is a matter of something like
a culture that arises spontaneously from the masses themselves, the contemporary form of popular art. From the latter the culture industry must be
distinguished in the extreme.[159]

When Macdonald made free reference to Horkheimer, Lowenthal,
and Adorno in a 1953 revision of his fiery wartime essay, these two
variants of the radical critique of mass culture became intertwined.[160]
And when, shortly thereafter, C. Wright Mills—who had cultivated associations with both Macdonald and the Frankfurt theorists—also entered the lists, there was established a third variant of the critique of mass
culture, whose deepest affinities, as we will see, lay still elsewhere: in
Deweyan instrumentalism.

These uncompromisingly pessimistic, radical versions of the critique
of mass culture, however, are best seen as common historical outcomes
of what had originated, only recently, in a decidedly more open-ended
assessment. During the late 1920s and 1930s, as Rita Barnard has
shown, radical critics of mass culture—despite their worries regarding
the increasing commoditization of culture and ideological manipulation—never ceased to stress the possibility of historical agency and,
indeed, the need for oppositional politics. Quite the contrary; by imag-
inatively assimilating the shapes and forms of mass culture, the poet

Kenneth Fearing and the novelist Nathanael West were among those who sought to clinch the argument for a revolutionary transformation.[161] The system's economic failure had become only too obvious during the Depression. Yet to the argument that capitalism evinced a glaring inability to deliver the goods now could be added a potent supplement. The antic reifications of mass culture provided fresh evidences, of patent import, perhaps, for those who gained a living through "intellectual" labor, of a way of life that had become intolerable. Thus it was a profound irony that this break with mass culture, when it came, transpired not by way of a social revolution, but only via a headlong leap to accommodate a forbidding modernist aesthetic—in decided preference to any prospectively more common culture—by many erstwhile radicals themselves. Again, however, through the mid-1930s at least, radical criticism of mass culture did not preclude, but rather aimed to motivate, a more thoroughgoing redress. An unduly neglected work by James Rorty can be utilized to develop the point:

> If one wishes to discover America, all one has to do is to forget all the solemn and reasonable things that solemn and reasonable people have spoken and written, and then go listening and pondering into cheap restaurants, movie palaces, radio studios, pulp magazine offices, police stations, five- and ten-cent stores, advertising agencies. Out of this atomic, pulverized life, the anarchic voices rise. They are shameless, these voices, and truthful, and wise with a kind of bleak factual wisdom. Each atom speaks for itself, to comfort itself, to assert itself against the overwhelming nothingness of all the other atoms. . . .[162]

These rather robust "atoms" constituted, for Rorty, a not unsympathetic social subject, which in turn emblematized his own ambivalence regarding the advertiser-based "pseudoculture." On one hand, Rorty's account was not one whit less keenly pointed than those to follow, in assaying a radical explanation of the political and economic functions of the "pseudoculture." The apparatus of advertising Rorty held comprised a "machinery of . . . super-government" which he repeatedly called an "instrument of rule," and whose economic function "in a profit economy"—"the production of customers"—he deemed (after Veblen) "no less essential than the production of coal or steel."[163] The adman himself in turn was only the latest in a long and rather pathetic succession of "middle-class" "crowd heroes."[164] On the other hand, looking to Leavis, Rorty depicted the "pseudoculture" as locked in a "perpetual conflict" with "the older, more organic American culture." The "new, hard, arid culture of acquisitive emulation" he identified with consumer magazines and other sites of the "pseudoculture," while, in what may be judged a vital, if wishful, qualification, "the older more human culture is what the reader wistfully desires." Subsequently, Rorty became explicit about this epochal "battle of the cultures." His precocious content analysis of a wide range of popular magazines showed, he said, "beyond the possibility of a doubt that the acquisitive culture cannot stand on its own feet, that it does not satisfy, that it is, in fact, merely a pseudoculture":

> The magazines live by the promotion of acquisitive and emulative motivations but in order to make the enterprise in the least tolerable or acceptable to their readers it is necessary to mix with this emulative culture, the ingredients, in varying proportions, of the older American culture in which sex, sophistication, sentiment, the arts, sciences, etc., play major roles. . . .
>
> In other words the business of publishing commercial magazines is a parasitic industry. The ad-man's pseudoculture parasites on the older, more organic culture, just as the advertising business is itself a form of economic parasitism. . . .
>
> But the American people do not like this pseudoculture, cannot live by it, and, indeed, have never lived by it. The magazines analyzed, which were published during this the fifth year of a depression, show that fiction writers, sensitive to public opinion, often definitely repudiate this culture. Americans tend, at the moment, if the magazine culture can be considered to mirror popular feeling, to look, not forward into the future, but backward into the past. They are trying to discover by what virtues, by what patterns of life, the Americans of earlier days succeeded in being admirable people, and in sustaining a life, which, if it did not have ease and luxury, did seem to have dignity and charm. Although the main drift of desire is toward the past, there are other drifts. Some editors and readers even envision revolution and the substitution of a new culture for the acquisitive and traditional American culture.[165]

Rorty's overall conclusion was grave, but substantially lacked the totalizing hopelessness which later came to afflict the radical critique of mass culture:

> Examination of this magazine literature reveals clearly that the democratic dogma is dying if not already dead; that the emulative culture is not accessible to the poor and to the lower middle-class; that the poor are oriented toward crime, and potentially at least, toward revolution; that the middle classes are oriented toward fascism. . . .
>
> We must therefore conclude that this culture, or pseudoculture, is not viable, hence cannot be rehabilitated. This conclusion will be regarded as optimistic, or pessimistic, depending upon the point of view of the reader.[166]

In this context, his book's final prediction—"when a formidable Fascist movement develops in America, the ad-men will be right up in front"[167]—was offered, above all, as a warning.

A warning to whom? The answer may be divined by insisting on a linkage which was, as Rorty wrote, quite suddenly becoming commonplace. Radical anxieties about the role of media and mass culture in reproducing a dominated social totality were a product of their indelible association with a vagrant stratum of white-collar workers. Would this expanding group, already construed as parasitic in Rorty's Veblenian comparison with the past's putatively "more organic culture" of production, now lend its energy to socialist reconstruction—or to reaction? For socialists, the question itself was not new; at the turn of the century, concern over the role of intellectuals and other white-collar workers had been at the center of the "revisionist" controversy within German Social Democracy. After 1933, however, the issue attained a new and stark significance. As a host of writers were quick to note, white-collar workers seemed to have provided a necessary basis for Hitlerism.[168] Studies of the German context, conducted by Wilhelm Reich, Hans Speier, and the Frankfurt Institute for Social Research (under the supervision of Erich Fromm) paid particularly close attention to the circumstances which could place "personality structure" in an apparent contradiction with class position and even with overt political ideology. If, even among a goodly proportion of radical workers, the ability to "be relied upon in critical situations" could be vitiated, the wayward white-collar strata—"value parasites," Speier called them—seemed positively eager to accept manipulation from above.[169]

In the United States, one hardly needed to be a radical to follow Lewis Corey, a heterodox and soon a disenchanted Marxist, in connecting Hitlerism with a "crisis of the new middle class," whose mainly white-collar workers had furnished "the shock troops of fascism."[170] Harold Lasswell, as early as 1933, found in the ascent of Nazism "a desperation reaction of the lower middle classes" whose need for differentiation "from the manual worker," Hitler, a "self-made semi-intellectual" backed by "influential elements of the upper bourgeoisie," had successfully exploited through nationalist and anti-Semitic symbols. In this context, Lasswell's portentous suggestion (following Veblen) that "the intellectual class" might be seen as "a potent social formation with objective interests of its own"[171] was not generally taken up. Instead, with Corey, most observers agreed that this "new middle class" was bereft of any overarching and independent identity or consciousness. The question of its political allegiance accordingly edged toward becoming, as Corey noted, "mainly ideological."[172] What required explanation, correspondingly—as a book by Robert A. Brady sought to establish—was no less the "spirit" than the "structure" of German fascism. For the Nazis to accede to power, in this incipient dichotomy, they had to divert the masses "from material to 'spiritual things.'"[173]

The nexus of issues at stake soon attained a horrific palpability. Confirmation that adaptation (what Stanley Milgram later focused experimentally as "obedience to authority") knew no bounds came when, in 1943, Bruno Bettelheim reported with clinical detachment on his own experience in Dachau and Buchenwald, where he had observed fellow concentration camp inmates managing to survive their ordeals by making a series of ghastly attempts at adjustment. Mimicking the games, the uniforms, even the beliefs of guards, long-term prisoners outdid their captors at learning—and internalizing—the rules of the game. Social structure survived, Bettelheim pointed out, but it seemed almost an irrelevancy; and the concentration camp, he summarized, in an explicit attempt at generalization,

> is the Gestapo's laboratory where it develops methods for changing free and upright citizens not only into grumbling slaves, but into serfs who in many respects accept their masters' values. They still think that they are following their own life goals and values, whereas in reality they have accepted the Nazis' values as their own.
>
> *It seems that what happens in an extreme fashion to the prisoners who spend several years in the concentration camp happens in less exaggerated form to the inhabitants of the big concentration camp called greater Germany.*[174]

Bettelheim's essay was reprinted by Dwight Macdonald's journal *Politics,* while Bettelheim himself briefly assisted Horkheimer and Adorno's group in their continuing studies of anti-Semitism.[175]

The impact of this understanding of fascism proved to be as abiding as it was explosive. Far from constituting a reliable emancipatory agency, consciousness now was taken to be unceasingly plastic. Once more it was not that social relations no longer existed but, rather, that they appeared not to make sufficient room for the distinctive contemporary conditions of which a massively enlarged white-collar middle class comprised a leading augury. Mass psychology, ricocheting outward through the social order from its white-collar host, was apparently malleable beyond any previous estimate; thus it allowed for transformative societal change to be wrought on the plane of subjective experience. A steady diet of propaganda, still closely coupled with "rationally" applied violence and everyday terror, seemed more than sufficient to interdict theoretical reasoning—and to override all associated historical projections—which sought a basis in "objective" social relations, most notably including class relations. Or, in reference to the instrumentalist perspective, "organized intelligence" not only contained no inherently ameliorative *telos;* it lent itself, with terrifying ease, to domination.

This awful thesis remained compelling. The postwar critique of mass culture never ceased to be suffused by the perception that entire societies could be, had been, and, perhaps above all, were being so worked over. As C. Wright Mills put it in 1950—in continuing concord with Lazarsfeld and Merton's 1948 thesis that mass media and interpersonal communication needed to be treated within a single analytical context—"without Himmler's powerful grip, Goebbel's manipulations of opinion would have quickly failed."[176] In a memorable sentence which starkly overwhelmed the hint of romanticism still present in Rorty's depiction of human "atoms," Mills captured the essence of this totalitarian complex:

"By terrorization and by rules enforced by threats and use of violence, he tries to fragment the public, in order that each individual stands naked of social relations before the media of the authoritative propagandists."[177] It was not, then, powerful media taken alone but, jointly, a pliant populace, terrorized and cast ever further adrift by virtue of its increasingly predominant white-collar status, which endowed mass culture with what was generally taken—on the left—to be its forbidding authoritarian potential. Each of the major variants of the thesis was an explicit party to this dual orientation.[178]

This shared concern created significant, and usually neglected, common ground between the Frankfurt School's critique of culture industry[179] and Lazarsfeld's mainstream brand of "mass communication" research prior to 1948—for which, as we found, the entire tissue of social life had to be joined to the study of media propaganda in any valid appraisal of mass persuasion's potential. Siegfried Kracauer, for example, asserted in 1947 that sustained study of film and other mass media would disclose that "deep psychological dispositions" had contributed to the rise of German fascism.[180] And then there was Adorno, who worried that ingrained authoritarian proclivities might lead to home-grown fascism in the United States. Far from being a simple product of propagandistic manipulation, anti-Semitism, in particular, in Adorno's view, was deeply entrenched in popular consciousness as a result of longstanding and complex historical processes. In terms which resonated harmoniously with those favored by Lazarsfeld and Merton before 1948—by emphasizing the significance of human predisposition for media power—Adorno's research group stressed as early as 1941 that "as long as anti-Semitism exists as a constant undercurrent in social life, it can always be rekindled by suitable propaganda." Anti-Semitism was thus, as Adorno's colleague Franz Neumann concurrently put it, one of "the soft spots in the social body" of which Nazi propaganda took deadly advantage. In a remarkable passage from his magisterial work on the structure and practice of National Socialism, Neumann wrote that

> [p]ropaganda is violence committed against the soul. Propaganda is not a substitute for violence, but one of its aspects. The two have the identical purposes of making men amenable to control from above. Terror and its display in propaganda go hand in hand. . . .
>
> By itself, propaganda can never change social and political conditions; it acts in conjunction with other and far more important factors. National Socialist propaganda did not destroy the Weimar democracy. . . . National Socialist propaganda, we must not forget, went hand in hand with terror by the S.A. and by the S.S., tolerated by the German judiciary and by many of the non-Prussian states. . . . That the republican leaders did not succeed in inducing the state machine to stop National Socialist terror will remain the mot severe indictment of Weimar.[181]

The same concern for the subjective predispositions of the populace continued to be a well-established theme among still other members of the Frankfurt School. In 1964, for example, in a discussion marred by gender and racial stereotypes, Herbert Marcuse expressed it directly, in *One-Dimensional Man:*

> Our insistence on the depth and efficacy of these controls is open to the objection that we overrate greatly the indoctrinating power of "the media," and that by themselves the people would feel and satisfy the needs which are now imposed upon them. The objection misses the point. The preconditioning does not start with the mass production of radio and television and with the centralization of their control. The people enter this stage as preconditioned receptacles of long standing; the decisive difference is in the flattening out of the contrast (or conflict) between the given and the possible, between the satisfied and the unsatisfied needs. Here, the so-called equalization of class distinctions reveals its ideological function. If the worker and his boss enjoy the same television program and visit the same resort places, if the typist is as attractively made up as the daughter of her employer, if the Negro owns a Cadillac, if they all read the same newspaper, then this assimilation indicates not the disappearance of classes, but the extent to which the needs and satisfactions that serve the preservation of the Establishment are shared by the underlying population.[182]

Once again, therefore—to return to the major point—social relations were attenuated not merely by strong media, but by an encompassing and longstanding "preconditioning"[183] of the populace. The latter, in turn, was no longer associated only with an abstract turning-point from community to society (as Bell was to suggest),[184] but rather found its leading feature in the all-too-apparent "amorphous" consciousness of the key white-collar strata.

But, after the fascist enemy had been laid to rest, what could inspire such ominous parallels between Nazi Germany and the United States? What turned the premonitions observed during the interwar period into a full-fledged scourge? The work of Robert Lynd's younger colleague, the sociologist C. Wright Mills, allows us to trace this deeply felt development.

In a study of labor leaders performed at Lazarsfeld's Bureau of Applied Social Research and published in 1948, Mills projected a fraught, but still relatively sanguine, future. "[T]he labor leaders," he wrote at the very outset of this work, "are the strategic actors: they lead the only organizations capable of stopping the main drift toward war and slump." And again, although Mills conceded that "the number of the politically alert is only a minute fraction of the U.S. population," he quickly added this vital qualification: "That the great bulk of people are politically passive does not mean that they do not at given times and on certain occasions play the leading role in political change. They may not be politically assertive, but it would be short-sighted to assume that they cannot move, on surprisingly short order, into the zones of political alertness." Labor leaders comprised a strategic elite for Mills, therefore, because—in what he, akin to many others, and by no means only on the left—assumed would be an immediate recurrence of protracted economic depression, "[t]hey are the only men who lead mass organizations which in the slump could organize the people and come out with the beginnings of a society more in line with the image of freedom and security common to left traditions."[185] As late as 1950, as I have already underlined, Mills viewed the independent organization of the primary public as the single most important basis for "resistance" against the manipulative effectivity of mass persuasion. A large, if not entirely unbridgeable gap therefore still could be seen as separating contemporary conditions in the United States from Nazi Germany, the archetypal "society of masses."

This gap summarily narrowed, however, as Mills completed the second and third panels of his triptych portrait of American society, turning along the way from labor leaders to the white-collar strata, and finally to the interlocking military, corporate, and political leadership structure that he dubbed *The Power Elite* (1956). "In our time," he asserted in the latter work, " . . . the influence of autonomous collectivities within political life is in fact diminishing."

> Furthermore, such influence as they do have is guided; they must now be seen not as publics acting autonomously, but as masses manipulated at focal points. . . . In all modern societies, the autonomous associations standing between the various classes and the state tend to lose their effectiveness as vehicles of reasoned opinion and instruments for the rational exertion of political will. Such associations can be deliberately broken up and thus turned into passive instruments of rule, or they can more slowly wither away from lack of use in the face of centralized means of power. But whether they are destroyed in a week, or within a generation, such associations are replaced in virtually every sphere of life by centralized organizations, and it is such organizations with all their new means of power that take charge of the terrorized or—as the case may be—merely intimidated, society of masses.[186]

It was not just the successful institutionalization of a "permanent war economy" which inspired this pessimism. Deeply implicated in Mills's newfound despondence was an equally determinative conceptual legacy. His own terms of perception, in a word, continued to be caught up within the unresolved dilemma regarding "intellectual" labor.

Mills neither conceived of social class in the strict Marxian sense of relationship to the means of production nor sought to depict a social totality strictly in class terms: Status and, above all, power comprised equally important aspects of his mature conceptualization.[187] On one hand, therefore, he could categorically specify that, "[i]n terms of property, the white-collar people are *not* 'in between Capital and Labor'; they

are in exactly the same property-class position as the wage-workers."
Yet on the other hand —following Speier, with whose work he was well
acquainted[188]—this equivalence served only to underline what seemed
to Mills to be a more essential non-identity: "[I]f bookkeepers and coal
miners, insurance agents and farm laborers, doctors in a clinic and crane
operators in an open pit have this condition in common, certainly their
class positions are not the same." Some part of this overarching difference he credited to a putatively overarching shift in function. Over previous decades, more and more workers were coming to "handle *people*
and *symbols*" rather than *"things,"* Mills stressed, reviving John
Dewey's inapt typification: "The one thing they do not do is live by
making things; rather, they live off the social machineries that organize
and coordinate the people who do make things."[189] As a consequence of
this apparently mysterious organizational function[190]—and its concomitant, a rising standard of living—white-collar workers were said to have
suffered a loss of independence, which in turn vitiated any prospect that
a common class experience might be forged, either with the established
working class or the old middle class.

Arching back to prior explanations of the Nazi rise to power, it was
the apparent susceptibility to—even predilection for—manipulation
evinced by this increasingly distended white-collar stratum which sustained Mills's newfound acceptance of the idea of mass society in reference to the United States. Between 1900 and 1950, in one estimate, the
number of white-collar workers in the United States had increased to 22
million, doubling as a proportion of the total labor force (to 36.6%).[191]
Mills's first widely read book declared, in this context, that white-collar
identity furnished clues to "the shape and meaning of modern society as
a whole."[192] "In modern society," he wrote in 1951,

> coercion, monopolized by the democratic state, is rarely needed in any
> continuous way. But those who hold power have often come to exercise it
> in hidden ways: they have moved and they are moving from authority to
> manipulation. Not only the great bureaucratic structures of modern society,
> themselves means of manipulation as well as authority, but also the means
> of mass communication are involved in this shift. . . . The formal aim,
> implemented by the latest psychological equipment, is to have men inter-
> nalize what the managerial cadres would have them do, without their
> knowing their own motives, but nevertheless having them. Many whips are
> inside men, who do not know how they got there, or indeed that they are
> there. In the movement from authority to manipulation, power shifts from
> the visible to the invisible, from the known to the anonymous. And with
> rising material standards, exploitation becomes less material and more psy-
> chological.[193]

Mills therefore amplified the "ideological" line of argument introduced during the interwar period. Rather than being connected, however, overtly to the historical ascent of Nazism, the experience of the

social stratum which apparently incarnated "intellectual" labor became the basis for a totalizing indictment of "organized intelligence" under contemporary conditions. Mills interposed his own distinctive pragmatist rendition of the mass culture thesis in protest, that is, against not so much a dominant ideology as a massive and increasingly systemic failure of "organized intelligence" to carry through its still-beckoning promise. Where many of his peers simply acquiesced to the relativistic inclination of a philosophy that would judge truth only by its consequences, Mills focused instead on an increasingly cohesive and manipulative "cultural apparatus," which alone afforded the power elite its capacity for systematic processing and redirection of what passed for truth. A nearly absolute negation of the original instrumentalist program had become, it seemed, an all-too-functional operating mechanism: far from acting to regenerate democracy, "organized intelligence" was construed as having been comprehensively perverted.[194]

In Cold War America, it must always be stressed, sharp-witted observers *could* find actual evidence aplenty that "organized intelligence" was being systematically corrupted and debased. Processes of opinion formation *were* being comprehensively, often blatantly, restructured. But this fearsomely coordinated effort ironically conformed, not to the theory of ideology, but to the criteria for successful mass persuasion that had been laid down before around 1948 by Lazarsfeld, Merton, and, not least, Mills himself. Not only mass media but also schools, trade unions, universities, churches, the professions, political parties, and the civil service were alike attuned, by means of smaller or larger doses of coercion, to the Cold War mobilization.[195] Radicals' anxieties that fascism was an organic outgrowth of monopoly capitalism thus also carried over into the postwar period. The Nazi regime, Robert A. Brady had written in 1937, could be fairly described "as a *dictatorship of monopoly capitalism. Its 'fascism' is that of business enterprise organized on a monopoly basis, and in full command of all the military, police, legal, and propaganda power of the state.*" Horkheimer, in 1939, concurred, declaring that anyone "who does not wish to speak of capitalism should be silent about fascism." This linkage had played a compelling role before the Second World War, in the cultivation of a distinctive radical rationale to make the fight against fascism the most urgent of struggles: "It can't happen here" expressed, simultaneously, a substantial fear and an injunction to organize a political opposition. Not surprisingly, therefore, those who, like Bell, came to revel over the apparent postwar "exhaustion" of left-wing ideology, likewise came to regard the radical critique of mass culture with keenly personal antagonism. Radicals themselves, on the other hand, found in postwar mass culture the gleaming surfaces of an ascendant totalizing fascism.[196] Nevertheless, the striking fact is that, within the radical critique of mass culture, "ideology" itself was now called to bear the lion's share of the task of social domination. The balance be-

tween coercion and consent seemed, accordingly, to have tipped decisively toward the latter.

There can be no doubt that the mass culture critique dramatically
stretched the scope of debate over communication as a contemporary
social force. Under its aegis, academic "communication" began to expand beyond any narrower concern with news and documentary genres
and, certainly, beyond the individualistic psychology of *Personal Influence*, to encompass—in perhaps the leading compilation of the period—
bestsellers, paperback books, detective novels, cartoons, comic strips,
magazines, motion pictures, television, radio, popular music, and advertising.[197] What was significant was that, across this whole vast range,
radicals theorized the popular arts in terms of their role within an implicit cultural hegemony. This sense that institutionalized communication comprised a powerful form of modern-day domination was extended from news to "culture" in part through the unlikely vehicle of
content analysis. Through content analysis, critical researchers extended
to a growing series of systems of representation the older and more
confined radical argument about propaganda as a form of ideological
control exerted through news media. This shift was evident in the ear-
liest formulations of "mass culture" and "culture industry,"[198] but was
given systematic expression during the 1950s and 1960s. Across an
increasingly broad range of media forms and genres, a stress on the
textual incarnation of ideology not only survived but prospered; the
assumption was that the most essential keys to the understanding of
media influence often lay in hidden or latent images and patterns. At the
same time, the study of textual meaning was placed on a plane seemingly better adapted to the increasingly industrial scale of cultural
production: the attempt was to study not only individual texts but entire "message systems"—a week's prime-time television programming,
for example. Both ideas powerfully extended the purview of critical
inquiry.

George Gerbner's continuing content-analytic research offers what
is arguably the most important instance of this extension of the mass
culture argument. While mass culture critics like Macdonald sought
mainly, during the 1950s and 1960s, to expose successive evidences of
cultural debasement, Gerbner turned to media content for specific textual proofs of the "symbolic functions" performed on behalf of the ruling
order by romance magazines, television serial dramas, and journalistic
news accounts. While most humanities (let alone social science!) professors did not yet deign to allow such genres even provisional admission
into their seminars, Gerbner and a few like-minded communication
analysts insisted that "what an entire national community absorbs" in
the way of symbolic forms indeed did deserve serious and sustained
inquiry.[199] In particular, what he came to call the "symbolic environ-

ment" merited attention in light of the changing American class structure.

Thus in one 1950s study, Gerbner observed of the women who comprised the primary readership for confession magazines (quoting an executive of one of the magazines): "These new women from the homes of labor find the white collar world strange, uncomfortable. Uncertain, often bewildered in their new roles, they have a burning interest in 'reading how other women—like themselves—solved *their* problems.'" The purveyors of *True Story* and other confession magazines were of course only too happy to tell them, but the underlying message of these stories actually functioned, wrote Gerbner, to resign the reader to society's inviolable "code."[200]

This line of inquiry naturally came to include television as its sine qua non. "Television," Gerbner went on to declare, "is a prime cultivator of common images and patterns of information among large and heterogeneous publics that have little else in common. These images and patterns form a major part of our symbolic environment. They help socialize members of society to the prevailing institutional and moral order." Gerbner was at pains, furthermore, to locate the "basic structure" that "determines the process of program control and development and shapes symbolic content" in the concentrated power relations that existed "between major national advertisers and the managements of the three national [TV] networks."[201]

But this broadened ability to approach culture as the site and agency of an ascribed ideological domination also harbored a tendency to indulge in overgeneralization. Mills observed, for example, that values and standards and tastes were now increasingly "subject to official management":

> the terms of debate, the terms in which the world may be seen, the standards and lack of standards by which men judge of their accomplishments, of themselves or of other men—these terms are officially or commercially determined, inculcated, enforced.[202]

What evidence supported such a flat assertion about the American people's purported self-understanding? Only everything, and, as Daniel Bell was quick to point out, therefore nothing. Despite its pluralistic accent, this criticism—that "the *theory* of the mass society affords us no view of the relations of the parts of the society to each other that would enable us to locate the sources of change," and that it barely managed to "reflect or relate to the complex, richly striated social relations of the real world"[203]—was largely warranted. It is indeed unfortunately characteristic that, under cover of the critique of mass culture, specific practices harboring substantial oppositional impulses (for example, rhythm and blues and rock music) were overlooked. Radical scholars, moreover, did

not seek to counterpose a systematic alternative to the highly problematic notion that television programming sought out "the lowest common
denominator," but instead largely acceded to the dominative aesthetic
standards in which the mass culture thesis was awash.

Such slippages testify chiefly to a suddenly arisen limit on the radicals' terms of perception: a sharply restricted view of human social
agency. As earlier social relationships became progressively attenuated,
Mills declared, mass culture had metamorphosized into one of "the most
important of those increased means of power now at the disposal of
elites of wealth and power."[204] Yet, as the first lines of *The Power Elite*
make clear, significant social action and organization he reserved, virtually by fiat, for a small minority of people in society's topmost ranks:

> The powers of ordinary men are circumscribed by the everyday worlds in
> which they live, yet even in these rounds of job, family, and neighborhood
> they often seem driven by forces they can neither understand nor govern.
> "Great changes" are beyond their control, but affect their conduct and
> outlook none the less. The very framework of modern society confines them
> to projects not their own, but from every side, such changes now press upon
> the men and women of the mass society, who accordingly feel that they are
> without purpose in an epoch in which they are without power.
>
> But not all men are in this sense ordinary. As the means of informa-
> tion and of power are centralized, some men come to occupy positions in
> American society from which they can look down upon, so to speak, and by
> their decisions mightily affect, the everyday worlds of ordinary men and
> women. . . . What Jacob Burckhardt said of "great men," most Ameri-
> cans might well say of their elite: "They are all that we are not."[205]

While "[t]he top of American society is increasingly unified, and
often seems willfully co-ordinated," Mills concluded in his discussion of
the mass media, "[t]he bottom of this society is politically fragmented,
and even as a passive fact, increasingly powerless. . . ." The media, "as
now organized and operated," he declared, had become "a major cause
of the transformation of America into a mass society."[206] In marked
contrast with Rorty's pioneering foray into the radical theory of mass
culture, for Mills, twenty years later, the culture industry's ability to
disorient, manipulate, and deflect the lower social orders came close to
becoming both cause and consequence of the latters' ostensible lack of
social agency. The frightening and dismal revels of mass culture seemed
in turn to be disencumbered of any need to offer a substantial account of
their own ascendance. Thus not only the past *history* of the culture
industry but also its future could hardly be imagined, let alone adequately analyzed: The concept was utilized to typify what appeared at
times to verge on a frozen—dominated—ethos.

"Human beings," declared Dwight Macdonald, "have been caught
up in the inexorable workings of a mechanism that forces them, with a
pressure only heroes can resist . . . into its own pattern."[207] "What

has happened is that the terms of acceptance of American life have been made bleak and superficial at the same time that the terms of revolt have been made vulgar and irrelevant," concurred Mills, his onetime friend.[208] Herbert Marcuse's reflections on a purported "one-dimensional society," though keeping barely alive in theory the idea "that forces and tendencies exist which may break this containment and explode the society," circled similarly around its recurrent theme, "that advanced industrial society is capable of containing qualitative change for the foreseeable future." Social classes in particular, Marcuse argued, had been altered in structure and function "in such a way that they no longer appear to be agents of historical transformation." "Domination," he bleakly forecast, "in the guise of affluence and liberty—extends to all spheres of private and public existence, integrates all authentic opposition, absorbs all alternatives."[209]

Even toward the rowdy end of the 1960s, the identification of social agents capable of challenging prevailing structures of power remained meekly tentative: The "resistant" public opinion of the New Deal period was a distant memory. University students and, especially, the African American social movement, it is true, were now sometimes hesitantly singled out.[210] Ceasing to be the prerogative solely of the power elite, therefore, agency now at least could begin to be glimpsed in what came to be called (inadequately) "the new social movements." Even in radical writing, however, social agency remained enigmatically disconnected from U.S. capitalism's largest, theoretically vital, collectivity: the domestic working class. This was, in part, because such a prospect had been pre-empted, for a generation, by the anomalous status assigned by observers to a growing plurality of the labor force. It was only *outside* the United States, characteristically, in the "national liberation movements" erupting across the world, that overarching and powerful forms of human social agency could be credited with an unassailable importance, with profound intellectual consequences (to be scrutinized in the next chapter). In the meantime, however, radical critics of mass culture found themselves unable to shake off a series of intrusive and obfuscatory tenets, introduced with the cryptic social subject which they saw as the prime bearer of mass culture's stigma: the white-collar or "intellectual" laborers who preponderated within the U.S. occupational structure.

Thus was disclosed a defining limit on the radical usage of "mass culture." As the capacity for organized self-activity continued to be identified overwhelmingly with the capitalist class and its deputies in and around the giant corporation, historically unfolding class *relationships* between capital and labor tended to be conspicuous chiefly by their absence. Raymond Williams's comment, offered in a different context, catches this limitation precisely: "[w]here only one class is seen, no classes are seen."[211] For all its merits, the tendency to concentrate on the tight directorate which rules "the culture industry" simply cannot substitute for analysis which foregrounds the social relations of production. The medium of historical eventuation is mutually determining social relationships, rather than unalloyed class power, let alone decisions taken autonomously within and by one or another of society's chief institutional complexes. It was in the context of society and social labor that the culture industry became institutionalized and embedded; it is thus also to the relational and formative social aspects of productive activity that questions of communication in society have to be referred.[212]

This slippage created an ironic parallel to mainstream communication research, which itself began, sometime after 1948, to conceive of opinion formation as occurring on a largely autonomous plane. Exactly against their own earlier injunction against dichotomizing "personal influence" and "mass persuasion," orthodox analysts simply deflected their gaze away from the national security state's ongoing deployment of a comprehensive range of persuasive modes and circuits. Instead they did what they could, in Stuart Hall's subsequent criticism, to contribute to the "installation of pluralism as *the* model of modern industrial social order."[213] For such researchers, the media, as Hall continued, were held by fiat "to be largely reflective or expressive of an achieved consensus. The finding that, after all, the media were not very influential was predicated on the belief that, in its wider cultural sense, the media largely reinforced those values and norms which had already achieved a wide consensual foundation."[214] Dissenting from this basic premise, a handful of radicals continued to insist, in the face of witchhunts and blacklists, that the ascendance of pluralist theorizing itself constituted one small reminder that American society remained dominative. Yet the continuing absence of the social class relation—let alone of social labor more generally—constituted a powerful and enduring drag on the radicals' own thought.

Its obstructive potential is amply evident, for example, in what was *excluded* from Todd Gitlin's otherwise incisive critique of Katz and Lazarsfeld's discipline-demarcating work. Gitlin's major criticisms—that *Personal Influence* invalidly truncated and downplayed the reality of media power over consciousness and experience and that, relatedly, its authors chose to chart "influence" almost exclusively in terms of people's activity as consumers—were both elegantly expressed and perfectly well justified. However, Gitlin remained almost entirely within the bounds of the still ensconced, and still only incompletely differentiated, radical critique. That Katz and Lazarsfeld, as we found, had systematically substituted networks of abstracted individuals for the encompassing and constitutive modalities of social organization—pre-eminently social class but also race and gender relations—remained largely unremarked. Gitlin instead criticized Katz and Lazarsfeld for conceptualizing "the audience as a tissue of interrelated individuals rather than as isolated point-targets in a mass society."[215] His own theorization remained lodged within this familiar, Millsian framework, which still obscured how the extension and enlargement of capitalist social relations continued to be both incomplete and contested. Questions of ideological construction in turn tended, at least tacitly, to be localized within the putatively universalized institutions of the culture industry, rather than interwoven with the dynamic, conflicted, and generative social process embedded in but also around it.[216]

Dissenting researchers apparently could not but slight the defining contours of social experience. Beneath the power elite, and crucially disconnected from "the drifting set of stalemated, balancing forces" at society's middle levels, wrote Mills, "at the bottom there is emerging a mass society."[217] Even in the rare cases where a more formative and relational social process did remain, the results seemed to portend only minor conceptual revision. Stanley Aronowitz in 1973 purported, true, to grapple with the emergent culture of the "new" working class in the United States. Aronowitz's familiar theme, however, was that long-standing working-class institutions—in particular, the family, but also the church and the school—had been undermined. "[T]raditional forms of proletarian culture," he asserted, had been supplanted—replaced, in a direct reprise of Mills, by "a new, manipulated consumer culture." The latter, moreover, again was discerned in terms of the service it was presumed to offer in integrating "the working masses into a bureaucratic consumer capitalism."[218] Aronowitz's central concern with social class, therefore, despite its helpful focus on some potentially important changes in the character of labor, could only begin to chip away at—rather than directly confront—the cardinal assumption on which both orthodox communication study and the radical critique of culture industry alike continued to rest: that a social order dominated by capital had come to achieve an essential equipoise. "What distinguishes culture under capitalism?" asked two other radical critics as late as 1978: "Certainly not class divisions."[219] It is a savage and telling irony that even radicals remained unable to detect more than desultory social agency apart from capitalists and their managerial stewards. It might be argued—as we will see, Raymond Williams did begin to argue[220]—that "culture" could be set free to achieve an altogether different dynamism and analytical thrust only because "society" seemed set and static.

That such a profound displacement could occur shows that radical scholars could not resist the gigantic tides which, for a generation, overwhelmed public opposition—with the noteworthy exception of the struggle for African American civil rights—within the U.S. In the 1950s, a newly acclaimed "age of affluence," longstanding social scientific preferences for interest groups, and social control, rather than class conflicts, combined with the effects of Cold War repression, business unionism, a recharged cult of domesticity, racism, and ascending U.S. global hegemony to subvert the possibility of identifying any robust, let alone genuinely oppositional, working-class social agency. At the highwater mark of the American Century, the assumption that capitalism had at last attained stability—overwhelmingly dominant in mainstream political science, economics, history, and sociology—could not be effectively undercut.

Radicals trained their attention instead on the underlying sources of what was for them a profoundly troubling quiescence. Historians who disdained to join the chorus proclaiming the purported glories of an achieved liberal consensus, for instance, overwhelmingly stressed "the incorporation of working class challenge and the easy destruction of radical movements."[221] Marxian economists emphasized not class struggle but the vast increases in government military spending that had combined with ever-accelerating consumer debt to ameliorate and postpone the debilitating cycles of boom and bust. Despite their oddly hopeful assertions that the tendency to economic stagnation could only be deflected and delayed, rather than permanently averted, they too granted little room to human social agency.[222] So too, as I have argued, arose conceptions of an omnipresent and dominating culture industry, crucial to the mysterious consolidation of the postwar Pax Americana. This development, seemingly unique to 20th-century society, retained a cryptic quality that I have attributed to a continuing incapacity to grapple effectively with the theoretical status of "intellectual" labor.

Marcuse, in 1967, came as close as anyone to confronting some of these questions, employing the language of an apparently invigorated Marxism:[223]

> Political propaganda and commercial advertisements coincide. The political economy of advanced capitalism is also a "psychological economy": it produces and administers the needs demanded by the system—even the instinctive needs. It is this introjection of domination combined with the increasing satisfaction of needs that casts doubt on concepts like alienation, reification and exploitation. Is the beneficiary of the "affluent society" not in fact fulfilling himself in his alienated being? Does he not, in fact, find himself again in his gadgets, his car and his television set? But on the other hand, does false subjectivity dispose of the objective state of affairs?[224]

Marcuse's merit was to pose these directly as questions worthy of consideration. But the dilemma to which they pointed was all but unbreachable, because its main means of address lay in the entrenched belief that to speak of propaganda was to leave behind the domain of bodily labor, and to enter the enigmatic domain of mind or thought, or even spirit. For Adorno, indeed, "culture's" only protection perversely lay in the critic's ability to insist on such a dualism. "[C]ulture," Adorno observed in 1967, both originated and, under contemporary conditions, drew whatever remaining strength it could summon from "the radical separation of mental and physical work." "As long as even the least part of the mind remains engaged in the reproduction of life, it is its sworn bondsman."[225]

Horkheimer and Adorno had been predisposed, as far back as the late 1930s, to assail the primary status accorded by Marxism to labor; they had rejected efforts to elevate labor to a defining theoretical position for exhibiting what Jay calls "an ascetic ideology inherited . . . from the bourgeois apotheosis of the work ethic."[226] Ideology, like Adorno's preferred type of cultural criticism, thus had nothing to do with labor, but existed on a willfully disparate plane. In turn the need was forever to find means of explicating the seemingly decisive contemporary mutation, through which, as Wilhelm Reich had put it as far back as 1933, ideology was enabled to act "as a material force."[227] Ideology's effectivity appeared to be not only terrifyingly self-evident but, equally, anomalous; its usage therefore seemed only to escalate the demand for theoretical reorientation. Mills, steeped in a pragmatism whose notion of "organized intelligence" was a product of the same dualism, was hardly in a position to remedy this default.

The characteristic effects of this all-or-nothing version of the thesis of cultural hegemony appear to warrant an easy dismissal. And indeed, the radical critique of mass culture, beginning in its own heyday, has been repeatedly pilloried for constituting nothing more than "an ideology of romantic protest against contemporary life."[228] But, if we know people by the company they keep, then perhaps theory can be situated by looking at the enemies that it earns. We know that the critique drew the notice of such vigilant academic top guns as Daniel Bell and Edward Shils; what prompted their censure? The answer must by now be plain: For those radicals who managed to survive it with their convictions more or less intact, both the sudden consumer spending boom and McCarthyism appeared only to provide a jarringly powerful joint confirmation for their view, that strong linkages bound the agencies of mass communication and pre-existing mass psychology into a tight and repressive unity: the unity of an "administered society." By insisting that social domination remained the defining feature of American life, in turn, Mills and other mass culture critics garnered the enduring enmity of cold warriors hostile to all such "unpatriotic" incursions.

The story, however, of course does not end here. The radical critique of mass culture remained and, in some respects, remains today, a durably accessible and compelling critical rhetoric. Its most recent revision holds that, through its very sweep and scale, contemporary mass culture makes it necessary—as against the prescriptions assayed by older traditions of criticism—to search for oppositional and utopian, as well as dominative, elements *within*, rather than apart from, it. This view carries with it the virtue of refusing to accept, by sheer assumption, that mass culture comprises a domain free of significant internal conflicts. Through a corollary tenet, mass culture may no longer impose, virtually by definition, a unitary understanding or consciousness, either on its practitioners or its audiences; at its best, this new view takes seriously Bell's early injunction, and restores to human agency its substantial and variegated historical role. It would seem, therefore, that the open-ended approach to mass culture of the early 1930s has been at least nominally reinvented. But this gain is offset by a different and damaging assumption. The warrant for searching for opposition and resistance *within* mass culture stems from a conviction that commercialized cultural production has become more or less coextensive with human culture per se: Jameson simply accedes to what he deems to be "universal commodification," while Denning, hedging slightly, declares, "There is now very little cultural production outside the commodity form."[229]

This totalization of mass culture can easily blind inquiry to the fact that commoditization—of "culture" or, indeed, anything else—is, from the perspective of capital, a forever unfinished and incomplete project. Mass culture, in this fundamental sense, can never sweep the field. Some forty years after the thesis was elaborated, current frontiers of "mass culture," if one wished to identify them as such, are hardly lacking: I think, for example, of the ongoing extrusion of enterprise into "virtual reality" software, explicitly market-based school curricula and "courseware," and, perhaps, even genetic engineering ("designer genes"). How are these dynamic outposts of accumulation to be apprehended, let alone resisted, by a theory whose inclination is to fix primarily on mass culture's purported intrinsic impulses to reification and utopia, domination and resistance? How can such a revision account for mass culture's historical, and still continuing, growth?

We will see in a later chapter that this myopia regarding the ongoing commoditization of cultural production discloses its own substantial significance as a theoretical development. Anticipating that discussion, it is worth stressing here that the trend to reopen mass culture to contestation, by fixing the nature of that challenge primarily at a discursive or textual level, itself acts to truncate, and even to omit, what had been a second crucial component of the originating critique. From James Rorty and *New Masses* onward, an emerging political economy of communication worked within the radical critique of mass culture, in an attempt to specify the pressures and limits set by capital within mass culture's active process—its commercializing instinct. Exploiting a potential overlap with more conventional institutional economists, to take a pioneering example, Dallas Smythe sought to explicate the structures of resource allocation and policy decision in media and telecommunications.[230] Smythe suggested that "as our culture has developed it has built into itself increasing concentrations of authority and nowhere is this more evident than in our communications activities."[231] By emphasizing that mass culture indeed *had* its political economy, the tradition of research that he championed emphasized the increasingly centralized command structure that prevailed over this vital field of capitalist development. Evidence was sought of trends that served to annex communication institutions to what still appeared to be the pre-existing heartland of productive economic activity: manufacturing and extractive industry, and agriculture. Such overarching tendencies were identified, for example, in growing economic concentration in communications and various forms of cross-media ownership. Attention was quickly drawn as well to the forms and policies of all-too-pliant agencies of governmental oversight and regulation.

But the emergent political economy of communication was important beyond its capacity to direct attention to the continuing perils of monopoly capitalism, on one side, and, on the other, to what lay beyond the unit of analysis—individual attitudes—favored overwhelmingly by mainstream researchers: that is, to a social level of organization, whose structure and function in turn comprised apparent new indices of capitalist ownership and control. By the late 1960s, as radical scholars began to shift their attention outward, toward the so-called Third World, the scattered individuals who had persevered in developing the political-economic aspects of the mass culture thesis now threw themselves spiritedly into what soon became a full-scale critique of supranational corporate culture industry. Almost without recognizing it, those who developed this critique of "cultural imperialism" exchanged the doubtful social subject that had animated the mass culture thesis—the white-collar strata of the United States and Europe—for a social agent seemingly possessed of a far more sympathetic and determined revolutionary will: the movements for decolonization and national liberation. As they embarked on this new trajectory, moreover, metropolitan radicals were joined by other analysts, mainly from Britain, who sought to develop terms of reference capable of granting a new and crucial cultural presence to the working class within developed capitalism itself. Suddenly, therefore, as we are about to find, human social agency became the centerpiece of an inclusive and restorative radical heterodoxy within communication study.

CHAPTER THREE

The Opening
Toward Culture

By the 1960s, extra-academic circumstances were again infusing communication study with a critical edge, and a multifaceted but common-spirited intellectual heterodoxy was beginning to crystallize around the concept of "culture." On one hand, the need became to understand and challenge modern-day neocolonialism, a concern shaped and intensified by the spread of militant movements for decolonization and national self-determination throughout what now was being called the Third World. The humanities and social sciences in general were convulsed, most vocally around the U.S. war on Vietnam; a series of related domestic agitations, notably including the struggle for African American civil rights, increased the pressure.[1] On the other hand, a surging revisionism, originating in Britain but powering across the Atlantic, was freshly problematizing the status of "culture" in the metropoles of developed capitalism. Full-fledged radical opposition to the behavioral orthodoxy which continued to dominate communication study was accompanied by a deepening critical engagement with received political economy.

This complex movement activated not one but two revisionary theorizations, which became known, respectively, as a critique of "cultural imperialism" and a "cultural studies." Yet we will see that these two positions were developed in light of a single shared concern. Their common basis lay in a mutual effort to restore human social agency— inclusive of "mental" as well as "physical" aspects—to a pre-eminent place within analysis. This synthetic orientation was, however, precariously balanced. It did not survive unscathed, therefore, from the sharpening social and intellectual conflicts which, during the late 1960s and early 1970s, had helped bring it into being.

I

The critique of cultural imperialism is, today, surrounded by almost as many misconceptions as those that cling to the earlier synthesis around propaganda. The thesis remained admittedly provisional and incomplete; it was the subject of developing argument rather than established doctrine. The need remains, however, to specify this intellectual position, whose very terms of reference now threaten to become impermeably opaque. Ignorance has played a considerable role here; but scholars often unfriendly to any idea of imperialism, cultural or otherwise, have also effectively transmuted the basic issues at stake into quite other—and misleading—terms. In order to situate the initial theorization, therefore, it is useful to begin by considering briefly the argument brought against it by subsequent detractors.

Mainstream analysts tried to utilize their finding that wide and continuing variations in the interpretation of media content differentiated members of different cultures as proof that cultural imperialism itself was a chimera. "Theorists of cultural imperialism," wrote two leading researchers in 1990, "assume that hegemony is prepackaged in Los Angeles, shipped out to the global village, and unwrapped in innocent minds." Where, they inquired, is the evidence?

> To prove that *Dallas* is an imperialistic imposition, one would have to show (1) that there is a message incorporated in the program that is designed to profit American interests overseas, (2) that the message is decoded by the receiver in the way it was encoded by the sender, and (3) that it is accepted uncritically by the viewers and allowed to seep into their culture.[2]

Despite this seemingly careful concern for procedure, however, such studies of differential audience interpretations systematically misstate the premises of the critique of cultural imperialism; not surprisingly, therefore, they also misconstrue the significance of their own attempts at rebuttal. The critique was not only, nor even principally, about the purported homogenization of interpretation, nor even about cultural consumption more generally. Rather, it centered on how structural inequality in international cultural production and distribution embodied, pervaded, and reinforced a new style of supranational domination. To put a point on it, the analytical center of gravity of the critique lay not in the purported export of meaning from core to periphery, but in the demonstrably changing forms and processes of an emergent global capitalism. Thus the seemingly scientific procedure utilized in the example above to refute cultural imperialism betrays an essential spurious-

ness. It creates a straw man: It is not *Dallas* per se that was "an imperi-
alistic imposition," as this metonymic substitution invalidly holds, but
the system of social relationships in which the program was embedded,
and within which responses to the program, in any truly critical method,
themselves also have to be situated.[3]

Elementary methodological reflection would suggest, moreover,
that even at the level of cultural consumption this revisionary account
has been anything but exacting. The relevant comparison is not—as Katz
and Liebes assumed—between viewers in today's Los Angeles (or
Amsterdam[4]), and their counterparts in today's Tel Aviv (or even Lagos
or Mexico City or Manila). Such a rigid focus on abstracted acts of
television viewing is but a poor substitute for a process that was grasped,
by the initial critique, as essentially historical. There can be no surrogate
for concrete study of the cultural practices and preferences of inhabitants
of whichever specific location is selected, *before* and *after* the introduction of a Western commercial media system. It is not overly intemperate
to suggest that such facile procedures testify to an intellectual, and ideo-
logically inflected, regression; for, long before the critique of cultural
imperialism took root, orthodox communication researchers themselves
took a Western-dominated "world culture" to be an unobjectionable
commonplace.

Radicals of the 1960s were not, by a long shot, the first metropolitan
analysts to perceive that members of each of the ninety-odd mainly poor
states that had gained formal political independence since 1945 were on
the receiving end of the global system of marketed cultural production
and distribution. Such insight was feasible even before the process of
decolonization attained irresistible worldwide momentum. Already by
1934, an early critic of mass culture wrote of the motion-picture industry
as "emulative promotion machinery, used as such both at home, and as
an 'ideological export,' to further the conquests of American imperialism
in 'backward' countries."[5] A second critic of mass culture observed in
1939 that such "kitsch" "had shown little regard" for geographical and
national-cultural boundaries:

> Another product of Western industrialism, it has gone on a triumphal tour
> of the world, crowding out and defacing native cultures in one colonial
> country after another, so that it is now by way of becoming a universal
> culture, the first universal culture ever beheld. Today the Chinaman, no less
> than the South American Indian, the Hindu, no less than the Polynesian,
> have come to prefer to the products of their native art magazine covers,
> rotogravure sections and calendar girls.[6]

During the first postwar decades, direct and explicit claims of a
closely related kind became an indispensable staple even of orthodox
studies of communication in national development. Daniel Lerner, for
example, wrote in 1958 that the media comprised a "mobility multi-

plier," acting as "both index and agent of change" within "the Western model of modernization [which] is operating on a global scale."[7] It was not Michel Foucault but again Lerner—whose research in Turkey proceeded in tandem with the domestic initiatives undertaken by Lazarsfeld's Bureau of Applied Social Research at Columbia University—who wrote, making free use of Mead's conception of the social self, that the mass media "have been great teachers of interior manipulation. They disciplined Western man in those empathic skills which spell modernity. . . . Their continuing spread in our century is performing a similar function on a world scale."[8] A few years later, Lucien W. Pye referred matter-of-factly to the "leveling qualities" of the new "world culture."[9] Leonard Doob, in a study of communications in Africa, concurred: As Africans "accept more and more practices and values from the West, they come to be intimately dependent upon the . . . mass media of the culture they absorb."[10]

Once again, the real issue concerned not media potency but the preferred conceptual framework in which media effects were to be sought. Mainstream analysts thus could portray international communication as a powerful force principally because they also freighted the mass media with unique and benign significance. Typified by "primitive" agriculture-based economies, underdeveloped nations—said these researchers—needed to pass through a sequence of developmental stages before landing in the nirvana of consumer capitalism. Prominent in prodding them along to this familiar endpoint was a series of interrelated institutions and agencies, the more unsavory of which usually went unmentioned: foreign aid projects and bank credits, CIA "advisors" mounting counterinsurgency operations, direct foreign investment by transnational corporations, and, finally, communications media. As Pye put it, albeit with considerable indirection, the need was for "the coordinated and reinforcing use of both the impersonal mass media and the more personal, face-to-face pattern of social communication."[11] In a direct reprise of the 1948 argument made by Lazarsfeld and Merton, mass media were enlisted within a multitiered campaign to redress the purported human deficits that supposedly crippled prospects for economic development. The media would consolidate and multiply the individual drive for achievement or, alternately, the empathic personality structure, absent which, underdeveloped nations would continue to lack an essential prerequisite of the so-called "take-off" into sustained economic growth.[12]

Through these dubious and self-serving arguments had been introduced a not-so-innocent discrepancy. Strong media effects among nonwhite peoples in "undeveloped" countries continued to be emphasized by some of the same researchers who scoffed at the very idea of media power when studying Main Street, USA. But a deeper congruence appeared in the essential support for American capitalism offered by both

faces of the pluralist social-psychological research tradition. Citizens of
purportedly civilized societies, on one hand, could supposedly continue
to rely on sound judgment and good sense, even in the face of an ever-
escalating commercial and ideological blitz. Backward folk, on the other,
could only benefit from modernization, which itself turned on the supposed "multiplier effects" of mass media.

As against such claims, some radical scholars sought to document
the systemic barriers to national self-determination that were being
thrown up by the workaday structures and practices of contemporary
international communications. The latter harshly invalidated the supposed "new era" of equal cultural exchange between independent peoples, which was being touted by diplomats and policymakers eager to
consolidate a U.S. international paramountcy.[13] The first signal achievement of the critique was to link these inequalities and blockages in
communications to the historical rise—then still undergoing consolidation—of a globally significant species of informal domination. This
stance served to place the proponents of the critique at a substantial,
though perhaps deliberately understated, distance from received Marxian political economy. In an article entitled "Colonialism (c. 1450–
c. 1970)," written for the 1974 *Encyclopaedia Britannica* and dropped
summarily from subsequent editions, the Marxian political economist
Harry Magdoff observed:

> The rapid decline in colonialism stimulated the rise of alternative means of
> domination by the more powerful nations. Control and infuence by means
> other than outright colonial possession is hardly a new phenomenon.
> . . . But the spread of informal empire as a substitute for formal colonial
> rule and the introduction of new mechanisms of control have been so
> pervasive since World War II as to give rise to the term neocolonialism. The
> term and the ideas underlying it are of course highly controversial. While
> conventional thought in the United States and western Europe generally
> rejects the validity of the term, in the former colonial world the existence of
> the phenomenon of neocolonialism is commonly recognized and discussed.
>   What is usually meant by neocolonialism is the existence of consider-
> able foreign direction over a nominally independent nation. In its narrowest
> sense, this means a high degree of influence over a country's economic
> affairs and economic policy by an outside nation or by foreign business
> interests, usually entailing influence over political and military policy as
> well. In addition, the term is used to suggest the predominance of the
> culture and values of the former colonial powers.[14]

Later, the critique of cultural imperialism would be widely faulted
for not "specifying 'the cultural'" as an irreducible moment in its own
right, and for purportedly tugging back to a "wider context of political/
economic domination."[15] This charge (which will be assessed on its own
terms in the following chapter) is profoundly ironic. The critique *itself*
was animated by a conviction that radical political economy had de-

voted too *little* attention to the sphere of culture; that, for example in Magdoff's characterization, "culture" should have been characterized as something more than a residual appendage. The critique of cultural imperialism swam against the stream of established doctrine, including established Marxian doctrine, by insisting at once that "culture" be restored to front-rank importance, and that such an elevation required more, rather than less, analytical engagement with political-economy. Far from being disparate elements, it seemed to those who would develop this critique that "mass communications and American empire" were fusing into a single generative process.

Amidst an unquenchable postwar world trend toward decolonization and formal freedom, substantively inegalitarian and exploitive political-economic structures nonetheless threatened to become widely re-established. But it was not only the endurance of colonialist values, as Magdoff conceded, that demanded attention. For those who sought to comprehend the dynamics of this newly expansive but informal imperialism, prominent room needed to be made for communications, alongside the conventional forms of military and political-economic power. "The communications apparatus," therefore, in one early and influential account, was taken as an Archimedean point, "without which the new imperial surge would be ineffective, coming as it does on the heels of political liberation in so many former colonial territories."[16]

In contrast to mainstream researchers, on the other hand, the radicals asserted that the appropriate unit of analysis for the study of communication and culture had to be supranational. This choice underwrote their empirically documented attack on the dominant conceptual framework. Orthodox scholarly conceptions, with their simplistic equation of modern personality-types with economic growth,[17] not to mention their Pollyanna-ish optimism about the prospects for national economic development itself, were vulnerable to an approach which carefully traced the substantive features of a political economy dominated by transnational corporations and extraterritorial state agencies. No less than for international agricultural commodity flows, the structural relations shaping international communications also gave the lie to nominal notions of national sovereignty, which combined credulity with opportunism in about equal proportion. Because of the cardinal role assigned to communications by influential analysts of the development process, moreover, the radicals were able to challenge some of the vital assumptions governing the entire discussion. In particular they showed that the emergent "world culture" was inequitable because, and inasmuch as, it was dominated to an ever-increasing degree by U.S. capital. Their critique of cultural imperialism thus exposed, as well as opposed, an emergent political-economic enclosure which, in the absence of permanent colonial occupation—though not, it should be emphasized, of the repeated projection of armed force—could rely on the real and prospective extensions of this transnationalizing culture industry as an unprecedented agency of reintegrative power.

No valid argument against this critique can be based—as unfriendly commentators would have it—on its own supposed overestimation of the "cultural" depth and range of impact of this renascent, if informal, imperialism. The latter in fact continues to be the bearer of crude and pervasive damage to indigenous cultures.[18] It was reported in 1993, for example, that between 20 and 50 percent of the world's 6000-odd languages are no longer being spoken by children. "That doesn't mean they're endangered," linguistics professor Michael Krauss emphasizes: "It means they're doomed." The anthropologist Clifford Geertz blandly generalizes the point, conceding the "rapid softening" of global cultural "variety" into what he calls, with apparent innocence, "a paler, and narrower, spectrum."[19]

But what did transnational culture industry portend for consciousness and experience in the ex-colonial territories? With this question we reach the core of the controversy over the critique. "It is the imagery and cultural perspectives of [the] ruling sector in the center," wrote Herbert I. Schiller, "that shape and structure consciousness throughout the system at large."[20] A process of "cultural leveling" was therefore initially assigned a significant role. Such a formulation, to be sure, introduced troublesome ambiguities. Did "leveling" refer (as in "the leveling of the city by mortars") to transnational culture industry's pounding impact on indigenous culture? Or (as in "leveling down all distinctions") did the term denote the growth of a global common culture—a culture of "the lowest common denominator," whose negative feature was that it transgressed established social and territorial boundaries? Frequent reference, within the critique, to both "cultural invasion" and "cultural homogenization" showed that each of these established positions had been carried over. Transferred into a new setting, this radical variant of the mass culture thesis retained the latter's ambiguous perspective.

Just how significant, however, was the critique's undoubted indebtedness to the vexed idea of mass culture? To get at this issue we must try to set the critique astride the emerging theory of informal imperialism to which it made regular reference. For it needs to be emphasized that, on the left, "imperialism" itself had again begun to occasion deep-seated debate. In the period around World War I, "imperialism" had chiefly denoted a policy of outright conquest pursued by rival capitalist powers, each of which had now developed economically to the point that it was forced to compete on a world stage for resources and markets. Military invasion and direct colonial administration were the obvious hallmarks of this global battle for capitalist supremacy. In the aftermath of the Second World War, in contrast, a quite distinct usage of "imperialism" gained widespread favor. The postwar period witnessed the decline of formal empires, and the accelerating export of capital by the United

States, acting as the capitalist world's momentarily unchallenged hegemon. Great power rivalries, accordingly, began to take a back seat, while attention shifted to the role being played by a "neocolonial" or "neoimperial" United States.

Perhaps inescapably, the great postwar boom, which brought unprecedented levels of wealth and consumer abundance to the "metropolitan" capitalist nations, likewise deeply colored perceptions of the troubled economic status of the colonial and post-colonial "periphery." The apparent "economic retrogression" of the Third World indeed now positively cried out for explanation. What was the source of this chronic stagnation? Was the powerful developmental lag that afflicted wide segments of the globe intrinsic to exchange relations within a "capitalist world economy"? Alternatively, did it attach to the globalization of a monopoly stage of capitalist development, in which a tendency to stagnation was again inherent? In either case, if the impoverished countries of the Third World were indeed enmired in a permanent state of economic "dependence" on the metropolitan centers of capitalist modernity, then it seemed necessary to inquire above all into how the formers' economic surplus came to be systematically expropriated by transnational companies, and how local elites were induced to collaborate with foreign capitalists to suppress their own countries' prospects of economic development.[21]

Preserving the notion of imperialism's overwhelming presence, ideas of "cultural invasion" and of "leveling" emerged within this analytical framework. Notions of "cultural dependence," however, bespoke not a simple extension of the mass culture thesis but, rather, adherence to a theory of imperialism which stressed the stagnationist tendencies that were generated by the contemporary capitalist world economy.

This theorization itself was—and remains—highly debatable. A competing interpretation, growing in visibility through the economic turbulence of the 1970s, emphasized that the transnationalization of corporate capital had to be interpreted not in terms of the creation and distribution of an economic surplus, but rather with the social relations of production that prevailed within particular societies—India or Zimbabwe (Rhodesia) or Congo-Brazzaville.[22] This rival theorization never attained extended expression within the critique of cultural imperialism; but, as we shall see, it could find tacit accommodation in the critique's evolving emphasis on the role played by domestic elites in a process of "cultural domination" that was spearheaded by transnational capital.

The critique's adherence to stagnationist views of imperialism, however, did bear directly on its theorization of media effects on social consciousness. The formalism of the critique's approach to media effects is noteworthy: Why, we may ask, did the critique tend simply to posit a

threat posed by dominative forces to a putative "national cultural identity"? Why, that is, did it stop short of any more comprehensive and
substantive engagement with what we, today, have come to identify as a
continuing interaction rather than a summary end point? Is all this to be
attributed to sheer thoughtlessness or indifference? Is it, more damn-
ingly, because the discourse of cultural imperialism "is inescapably
lodged in the culture of the developed West," and therefore betrays its
own naively ethnocentric preoccupation with metropolitan notions of
nationalism?[23] Once again, the answer lies elsewhere. It is more apt to
view the critique as having aligned itself with a corollary thesis of the
stagnationists': That the way out of underdevelopment could be found
not within any further process of capitalist "development," since the
latter only blocked and limited economic growth, but rather only in
social revolution.

The radicals' apparent inability to reckon with national cultures
stemmed in significant part from their hopeful demand that *the character
and ultimate object of the decolonization process should remain substantively
open*. Successive militant movements for national liberation across colonial and backward capitalist zones, notably in Algeria, Cuba, and above
all, Vietnam, seemed to offer powerful proofs that just such an assumption was warranted. Besides, above all in Africa, were not national bor-
ders themselves often merely settlements between rival imperialisms,
lines scrawled on maps, whose relation to indigenous languages, eth-
nicities, cultures and societies was profoundly arbitrary? The very term
"Third World" removes a large majority of the world's people from any
ascertainable relations of production, be they either capitalist or socialist.
Today this may be criticized as residualizing;[24] during the 1960s and into
the 1970s, in contrast, it underscored a profound social and political
question mark.

For radicals, national culture was a thing of the future. Necessarily,
as well, it was an emergent site—perhaps even *the* emergent site—of
struggle. Only arduous and deliberate processes of social and cultural
construction, they believed, could offer an effective challenge to a dying
colonialism, on one side, and an emergent neocolonial encirclement, on
the other. Disengagement from extant national culture aimed above all
to make adequate analytical room for what radicals dared hope would
come to be a thoroughgoing metamorphosis of established social relations.

The critique of cultural imperialism looked not toward academic
advancement, in turn, but toward an increasingly acute and overarching
social struggle. In conception it projected not only inward, as is usually
argued,[25] toward the imperializing culture industry, but also, and crucially (and this has not been enough acknowledged), outward, into the
imperialized territories. In 1979, in an argument concerning "culture in
the process of dependent development," Salinas and Paldan wrote that

"national culture appears to possess an inherently contradictory nature. On the one hand, it is an expression of the basic relations of domination as they exist in the cultural sphere, the representative of the dominant culture itself, imposed upon and inculcated in the subordinated social groups. Basically, therefore, national culture cannot escape its class character. On the other hand, national culture provides the site for the subordinated social groups to struggle against the dominant culture."[26] Therefore, the internal features of "dependent" societies required further elaboration. Similarly, in 1981, Fejes declared that the theory of cultural imperialism needed to make a greater effort "to place the development and function of the various communications media in the context of the class and power dynamics that operate within a nation and in the context of that nation's status as a dependent society."[27] The same issue had been addressed pointedly as early as 1976: "[T]he development and protection of the people's culture *came in the process of struggle*. It was not embalmed and revered. It was hammered out in the daily confrontations and battles against dominators, foreign and domestic."[28]

By the mid-1970s, therefore, at least some of the indeterminacies attaching to "cultural leveling" had become objects of intensifying scrutiny *within* the critique. Early efforts to single out the emergent structures of international cultural relationships had retained the mainstream theorists' nominal emphasis on nations. While, in the radical critique, the latter were counterposed to more powerful transnational political-economic actors, little social or cultural differentiation within the nation was conceded. As Tomlinson points out, this elision of national with cultural identity continued to be common in UNESCO debates on the subject and elsewhere: In reference to "culture," "inauthentic" and "foreign" (i.e., U.S.) became virtual synonyms.[29] At the same time, however, for some radicals, who also moved to accept the capitalist "world system" as their explicit framework, the critique of cultural imperialism came to permit a more considered concern for social differentiation and, in particular, social class. Particularly after the fall of electoral socialism in 1973 in Chile—which, though aided by the U.S. corporate and governmental intervention, was widely seen to be inexplicable without significant reference to domestic social relations—the radicals became increasingly mindful of the role of ruling elites, within as well as outside the newly independent countries:

> . . . The world system is the theater, and the action moves from the center to the edge. It is undertaken with the mutual consent, even solicitation, of the indigenous rulers, either in the core, the semiperiphery, or the periphery. These rulers strive eagerly to push their people and their nations into the world capitalist economy.
>
> It is for this reason that it may be inappropriate to describe the contemporary mechanics of cultural control as the outcome of "invasion," though I, too, have used this term in the past. Dagnino writes:

". . . the effects of cultural dependence on the lives of Latin Americans are not a consequence of an 'invasion' led by a foreign 'enemy,' but of choices made by their own ruling class, in the name of national development. Through this choice, national life and national culture are subordinated to the dynamics of the international capitalist system, submitting national cultures to a form of homogenization that is considered a requirement for the maintenance of an international system."

What is happening is that "the cultural and ideological homogenization of the world is being pursued not by a single nation but by an integrated system of different national sectors, committed to a specific form of socioeconomic organization."[30]

"[N]ew communication technology, rather than diminishing, [widens] the communication gaps in the poorer nations and [accentuates] economic disparities" within them.[31] The term "cultural domination" captured and generalized this emphasis on the multifaceted dimensions of class rule, while the latter also became prominent in a revised definition of cultural imperialism. It was in the social separation of domestic elites, and their incorporation into the structures of transnational capitalism, that the threat of culture industry was, literally, localized. Cultural imperialism therefore now comprehended *"the sum of the processes by which a society is brought into the modern world system and how its dominating stratum is attracted, pressured, forced, and sometimes bribed into shaping social institutions to correspond to, or even promote, the values and structures of the dominating center of the system."*[32]

It bears emphasizing that such revisions only reconveyed into metropolitan thinking the hard-won learning of contemporary anti-colonial resistance. By 1970, to take a notable example, Amilcar Cabral, the revolutionary who led the successful war for independence against the Portuguese in Guinea-Cape Verde, could insist that "it is vital not to lose sight of the decisive significance of the class character of culture in development of the liberation struggle. . . ."[33] "[N]o culture is a perfect, finished whole," Cabral asserted: "Culture, like history, is necessarily an expanding and developing phenomenon." "[I]f imperialist domination has the vital need to practise cultural oppression," moreover, Cabral declared in a famous phrase, "national liberation is necessarily an *act of culture.*"[34] Cabral had come to view armed struggle as a crucible in which the "weaknesses" and "defects" of existing culture could be identified and cast off in the process of forging a new national cultural identity.[35] The process thus evinced both positive and negative elements. Construction of a new national cultural identity, on one hand, rested in profound ways on existing indigenous cultural resources. Cabral was a strong proponent of the view that

the main potential for national liberation and revolution lay precisely in the fact that the vast majority of the colonised people had been affected only marginally, if at all, by colonial culture. Cultural homogeneity and identity among the villagers, he argued, formed the only possible basis for the development of a nationalist consciousness. . . . strategy for political mobilisation was based on a respect for and utilisation of local traditional culture.[36]

On the other hand, Cabral also singled out for rejection "social and religious rules and taboos contrary to development of the struggle," among which he specified "gerontocracy, nepotism, social inferiority of women, rites and practices which are incompatible with the rational and national character of the struggle."[37]

Some of Cabral's ideas were anticipated by the psychiatrist and revolutionary activist and theorist Frantz Fanon. Born in Martinique in 1925, Fanon died at age 36 after a long, firsthand involvement with the Algerian Revolution. "It is a question of the Third World starting a new history," Fanon summed up; in this struggle, he suggested, "the demand for a national culture and the affirmation of such a culture represent a special battlefield."

> To fight for national culture means in the first place to fight for the liberation of the nation, that material keystone which makes the building of a culture possible. There is no other fight for culture which can develop apart from the popular struggle. . . . The national Algerian culture is taking on form and content as the battles are being fought out, in prisons, under the guillotine, and in every French outpost which is captured or destroyed. . . . A national culture is the whole body of efforts made by a people in the sphere of thought to describe, justify, and praise the action through which that people has created itself and keeps itself in existence. A national culture in underdeveloped countries should therefore take its place at the very heart of the struggle for freedom which these countries are carrying on.[38]

Neither Fanon nor Cabral would have had any difficulty at all in assimilating Raymond Williams's insight (explicated later) that culture is ordinary, in the sense of persons partaking of a common realm of vernacular creativity and experience; yet, for them, culture was perhaps more saliently extraordinary, because the people's experience was only now in the process of being created and defined. To be precise, it was being actively created through an open-ended anticolonial struggle:

> We believe that the conscious and organized undertaking by a colonized people to re-establish the sovereignty of that nation constitutes the most complete and obvious cultural manifestation that exists. It is not alone the success of the struggle which afterward gives validity and vigor to culture; culture is not put into cold storage during the conflict. The struggle itself in its development and in its internal progression sends culture along different paths and traces out entirely new ones for it. The struggle for freedom does not give back to the national culture its former values and shapes; this struggle which aims at a fundamentally different set of relations between men cannot leave intact either the form or the content of the people's culture. After the conflict there is not only the disappearance of colonialism but also the disappearance of the colonized man.[39]

Exactly the same overall emphasis is made in the critique of cultural imperialism, which insisted, from the beginning, that "the opportunity to freshly mould a new nation's outlook and social behavior is historically unique and merits the most careful deliberation."[40] While the theory of mass culture certainly continued to muddy the waters of that process, far more important is that the critique of cultural imperialism sought to confer attention on what Williams elsewhere called "the nature and origin of the shaping process."[41]

In a variety of ways, this open concern for "the shaping process" elicited a crucial freedom to bypass the stale and crippling dichotomy between "intellectual" and "manual" labor. Especially but never only in the Latin American nations (many of which, of course, had already achieved formal state sovereignty in the nineteenth century), the critique of cultural imperialism *itself* comprised what Armand and Michelle Mattelart remember as "a mobilizing notion . . . helping to open new fronts of resistance by artists and intellectuals. . . ."[42] From the Africa of the late 1950s, Fanon agreed. "Instead of according the people's lethargy an honored place in his esteem," declared Fanon of the revolutionary native intellectual, "he turns himself into an awakener of the people," so as to become "the mouthpiece of a new reality in action."[43]

For national cultural identity was necessarily not only a matter of cultural invasion, but also of what the critique itself acknowledged— again following Fanon—as continuing forms of often repressive, "reactionary traditionalism."[44] What the radicals sought, above anything else, was room for this process of cultural struggle and transformation to occur, free of neocolonial intervention.[45] What they most feared, in contrast, was the blockage or diversion of the massive and sustained popular projects through which alone a thoroughgoing transformation of national culture—and society—might succeed.

The locus of this fear was transnational capital—"imperialism"— but its local affiliate was the national bourgeoisie. For, as Edward Said has lately emphasized, in Fanon we are hardly in the presence of any simpleminded nationalism.[46] Not only did Fanon, for example, acknowledge the continental scope of the African rebellion against colonialism. Not only did he make regular reference to the experience of Latin American and Arab resistance against imperialism. In his later writings, he also reserved some of his most biting comment for the "national bourgeoisie" ("that company of profiteers impatient for their returns"), then newly ascendant within many African countries. "The bourgeois phase in underdeveloped countries can only justify itself," Fanon declared, "in so far as the national bourgeoisie has sufficient economic and technical strength to build up a bourgeois society, to create the conditions necessary for the development of a large-scale proletariat, to mechanize agriculture, and finally to make possible the existence of an authentic bourgeois culture." Current reality was vastly different than this. Content to serve as "the Western bourgeoisie's business agent," the national bourgeoisie's mission, Fanon wrote, "has nothing to do with transforming the nation"; "it consists, prosaically, of being the transmission line between the nation and a capitalism, rampant though camouflaged, which today puts on the mask of neo-colonialism." "It is absolutely necessary," he insisted, "to oppose vigorously and definitively the birth of a national bourgeoisie and a privileged caste."[47]

It is in this connection, crucially, that the critique of cultural imperialism verged upon—though in truth it never fully became—a theory of transnational class struggle. Time and again the preference of this national bourgeoisie was, as we now know, to append itself to imperialism. This, as Ngugi wa Thiong'o reminds us, was already obvious in Fanon's scathing comments in *The Wretched of the Earth* (1961). The process "of creating a colonial elite in the image of the Western bourgeois," Ngugi declared, in a paper he wrote for UNESCO in 1982, comprised "an achievement . . . which is now proving so fatal to real development in Africa."[48]

The remaking of the culture of decolonized states, finally, although often certainly a process of forging new national traditions out of disparate elements, took as its chief priority the need to claim the nation for its own inhabitants, rather than for transnational capital:

> On the cultural level, in the colonies and neocolonies there grew two cultures in mortal conflict: foreign imperialist; national and patriotic. And so, out of the different nationalities often inhabiting one geographic state, there emerged a people's literature, music, dance, theater, art in fierce struggle against foreign imperialist literature, music, dance, theater, art imposed on colonies, semicolonies, and neocolonies. Thus the major contradiction in the third world is between national identity and imperialist domination.[49]

Ngugi goes on to recount how in his own country, Kenya, "the national tries to find its roots in the traditions mostly kept alive by the peasantry in the forms of their songs, poems, theater and dances"; how, even in the cities, "a fighting culture" took shape; and, critically, how, in response, domestic state authorities continued the policy of the previous settler regime in suppressing vernacular cultural initiatives.[50]

It is telling that mainstream analysts, who often made a point of charging that the critique of cultural imperialism was neglectful of national culture, should prove so utterly indifferent to these enduring expressions of cultural resistance. The reorganizations attending the growth of a transnational capitalist culture industry have not been simply a matter of introducing Western cultural commodities. Where a national bourgeoisie has claimed state power, they have also continually involved domestic repression of oppositional and potentially oppositional vernacular cultural practice. "We"—scholars in the United States and Europe—are woefully ignorant of this history.[51] Across much of the Third World, however, cultural production outside or on the periphery of the culture industry of course continues. Not in Kenya only, but also in South Africa and throughout much of Asia, for example, a "theater of liberation" has been often in evidence—and, almost as often, put down.[52] This theater constitutes just one of the ongoing traditions of vernacular cultural production, whose very existence goes unacknowledged in mainstream discussions of how national cultural variation purportedly offsets cultural imperialism. Its existence also supplies a necessary reason for us, today, to take up anew the question of culture and social consciousness in the ex-colonial territories.

For the critique of cultural imperialism, itself, the baseline for judgment of national culture was this: What could communications media contribute to revolutionary social transformation? Anything other—anything less—than such a commitment was at best an irrelevancy; and the best was rarely to be found. After the establishment of the Voice of Free Algiers (a radio service instigated by Algerians in their war against the French), Fanon wrote—in a passage from his extraordinary essay, "This Is the Voice of Algeria," first published in 1959 and quoted by Herbert Schiller a decade later—"the purchase of a radio in Algeria has meant . . . the obtaining of access to the only means of entering into comunication with the revolution."[53] What other yardstick should there be?

In attending to the nature and origin of the "shaping process" the critique not only placed its hopes with the vernacular practices of cultural production which combined "mental" and "manual" elements, and which could be extended and literally amplified through the utilization of electronic and other media technologies. It also identified and rejected a range of structures, agencies, and practices which appeared to comprise pre-emptive agents of transnational business and state power. And were they not? Among these forms, critics noted, were the following: the undermining of domestic media production, above all throughout emergent and poor nations, via dumping of U.S. telefilms, which in turn reinforced one-way information flows rather than mutual interchange of indigenously produced news and entertainment; cultivation, through the introduction of commercial Western media systems, of consumerism—whose insidious effects Fanon, for one, had singled out—in place of development priorities that would favor production of universally adequate access to food, medical care, education, and other basic necessities; systematic violation of sovereignty via new, supranational communication technologies (especially satellites) controlled largely by U.S.-based political elites and transnational corporations; mass distribution for global audiences of false or systematically distorted images of poor nations and peoples; and schooling of foreign students to U.S. or U.S.-style media practices, with their built-in assumption that private, advertiser-supported media should dominate.[54]

The concern, again, was that such practices carried punishing opportunity costs. Opportunity costs: I mean that they signified, at best, that a wide range of all-too-scarce social resources would be channeled into affiliation with the transnational culture industry, rather than directed toward a thoroughgoing democratic cultural transformation. What, for instance, could the media do, as Fanon put it, to teach about "the experiments carried out by the Argentinians and the Burmese in their efforts to overcome illiteracy or dictatorial tendencies of their leaders"?[55] Normally, affiliations with an expansionary culture industry helped rather to propel the newly independent states back into the emergent capitalist world system, or to deter their departure from it in the first place. Unfriendly researchers, in contrast, worked from the ill-founded idea that evidence of cultural imperialism had to be sought outside and apart from the very changes that comprised its primary axis. They sought to employ each evidence of continuing difference as a refutation of the reality of cultural domination.

The critique's own elemental claim was that national self-determination mandated that far more stringent attention be accorded to the fact that cultural production *has* its political economy. Not individual artistic inspiration, nor putative standards of taste and morality, both of which continued to captivate those committed to conventional elitist conceptions of culture, but ownership and control of means of communication were seen as determining, increasingly on a transnational scale, of a widening range of contemporary cultural practice. This, together with its allied insight into the necessity for national cultural reconstruction, brought communication study nearer than it had come in many decades to the idea of culture as a domain or type of production. To be sure, no such link as yet managed to become explicit and theoretically productive. But it was soon to rise to a prominent place in the agenda. On the other hand, a telling indicator of the impact of this critique on the academic field of communication came through even at the time, in what Everett Rogers—a pioneer of the academic canon to which he referred—styled "the passing of the dominant paradigm."[56] Rogers acknowledged that the established orthodoxies had been effectively delegitimated by a decade of radical pressure on the abstracted patterns of national development and personal influence favored by mainstream scholars. Although radical positions, especially those relating to the critique of neocolonialism, remained secondary, they were no longer marginal.

The critique itself, to be sure, never assimilated into a formal theory all of the insights that it generated. Even as neocolonialism made unprecedented use of the culture industry in the service of capitalist reintegration, however, the critique tried to show how it likewise was eliciting a new front of contestation and resistance around culture and consciousness. "[T]he preservation of cultural options to peoples and nations only now becoming aware of their potential," wrote Herbert I.

Schiller in 1969, was of commanding importance. "If there is a prospect that cultural diversity will survive anywhere on this planet," he continued, however, "it depends largely on the willingness and ability of scores of weak countries to forego the cellophane-wrapped articles of the West's entertainment industries and persistently to develop, however much time it takes, their own broadcast material."[57] Closely connected to the Non-Aligned Movement, a loose but ongoing effort to achieve what began to be called, significantly, a "New International Information Order," seemed, even as late as the end of the 1970s, to offer further evidence that, henceforward, the struggle to remedy cultural imbalances and inequalities would only intensify.[58]

It was, therefore, in the critique of cultural imperialism that human social agency finally tore free of the constraints that had, for a generation, overwhelmed it in U.S. communication study. The analytical core of the critique did not lie—as critics unfriendly to the theory mistakenly asserted—in a one-note insistence that the political economic structure of the transnationalizing culture industry comprised a newfound source of domination. Quite the contrary, its truly radical impulse stemmed equally, and from the beginning, from the primacy it sought to accord to a multifaceted human social agency. Through a critique of cultural imperialism, the political economy of international communication itself helped to lay the basis for a more thoroughgoing engagement with—and, it hoped, transformation of—lived experience. In the postwar conception of U.S. mass culture, recall, the social process had been truncated and static; while culture industry itself had appeared as the dynamic element. The critics of cultural imperialism nominally retained this emphasis. On one side was their exposure of the culture industry's unprecedented transnationalizing sprawl—its political-economic chokehold on cultural production. Insistently opposing the juggernaut of transnational culture industry, however, on the other side, was a newfound transformative agent: popular movements, whose stance against imperialism and whose increasingly focused concern with national culture appeared to leave their ultimate societal destinations open, and whose resources included the full range of "mental" and "manual" activity evinced in oppositional vernacular practice.

This very openness underlay an act of intellectual allegiance whose fortunes were now linked indissolubly to its referent and intended agent: the movements striving to effect a forcible social abstraction from an unjust reality. Extrapolating hopefully from present-day national cultures, at least some of the radicals proposed forms of human agency precisely in order to counter the concrete and enduring relations of domination that predominated within the territories of backward capitalism—and more generally.[59] This bold *political* alignment, however, established what would become a subsequent point of vulnerability. This soft spot became apparent as the upsurge of anti-colonial and anti-imperialist opposition was checked, transnational capitalist reintegration proceeded, and the whole matrix of affinities and concepts likewise began to shift.

Aijaz Ahmad writes of the era that succeeded these heady years—the period in which we now live—that it saw "the consolidation of the national-bourgeois state in the majority of the Asian and African states that had been newly constituted as sovereign nations, where the expanding dynamic of global capitalism was bringing unprecedented growth and wealth to the newly dominant classes."[60] In Western Europe, Japan, and North America this succeeding period is best characterized, again, as one of massing reaction. Over large parts of the world, very distinctly after the mid-1970s, the prospects for democratic social transformation receded: Both the domestic class basis of the national state and the latter's articulation toward transnational capitalism grew stronger and more overt. The critique of cultural imperialism, whose aim was precisely to contribute what it could to challenging these developments, was not well situated of itself to address—that is, to investigate and theorize—their consequences. The critique's originating concern, simultaneously situated in the structures of domination and the capacity for active opposition to them, contracted increasingly around a single pole. As various national agents of social transformation became increasingly isolated and beleaguered—some time around UNESCO's Mass Media Declaration in 1978—the critique responded by emphasizing an austere and apparently unbridgeable political economy of transnational capitalist domination.[61] "Culture" in turn lost much of the open potential with which the critique initially sought to invest it.

But by this time—the 1980s and on into the present—a wide range of crosscutting issues had come to bedevil the discussion. Before turning to appraise this complex passage of thought, we must complete our assessment of the inclusive radical heterodoxy of which the critique of cultural imperialism comprised one aspect. Let us turn, therefore, to the other chief site of revisionary effort, which was Britain. Here, what Raymond Williams sought to conceptualize as "the shaping process"[62] again appealed to human social agency to suspend the problematic dichotomy between "intellectual" and "manual" labor, and indeed to inaugurate a direct challenge to its dualistic legacy.

II

By the 1960s, a fresh and vital revision was developing in and through a British project that was beginning to be known as "cultural studies." As this new thinking percolated into communication study in the United States, many graduate students and some professors—including some of those open to the critique of neocolonialism and/or to the 1960s "counterculture"—began to find the ethnocentric codes of inquiry man-

dated by mainstream social science increasingly inadequate and, in an
increasing number of instances, fatally flawed. Narrow fixations on individual attitudes, opinions, and behaviors—which conventional scholars
were beginning to abstract as media "uses and gratifications"—began to
be supplemented by a concern for "meaning" generated in and through
collectivities. Far from developing in pristine separation from the critique of cultural imperialism, a deepening concern for metropolitan
"culture" overlapped it at an increasing number of points. In the context
of the then-reigning behavioral science, this tentative, ramifying, and
largely untheorized interchange seemed, for a pregnant moment, to portend an expansive heterodoxy, whose second point of critical reference
was social theory. How did this come about?

The traditions of historical and critical scholarship that would unite
within cultural studies—and which, almost simultaneously, began to
infuse a growing segment of communication research—directly drew
upon both the personnel and the political orientation of Britain's "first"
New Left. Although, as Raymond Williams has stressed, changing conceptions of "culture" emanating from extra-academic thinking had
already begun to develop even before this, the pivotal concerns for human agency and lived experience broke through in wider public discourse only during the mid-1950s. Both intellectual and political divergences, however, were amply evident and, at key points, sharply
pronounced, in the works of the four most-cited progenitors of cultural
studies: Stuart Hall, Richard Hoggart, Edward Thompson, and Raymond
Williams.[63] Each was in broad agreement that the often perplexing
changes occurring in postwar Britain required that far more attention be
paid to lived experience and, thus, to what could be called "culture."
Beyond this, the terms of their respective reorientations splintered. To
assess adequately the still-unfinished assimilation of "culture" that followed from this complex effort, we need to take care in reckoning these
formative differences.

All four writers, crucially, were working not in academe but in adult
or extramural education; as Williams later insisted, moreover, this was
not simply a random result, but a considered *"choice."*[64] Their work as
teachers made them intermediaries between the polished traditions of
academic criticism and historical scholarship, and the rudely pertinent
questions of their students—removed by background and self-understanding from the formal habits of elite culture. Such a position also
surely nourished the conviction that social experience—that admittedly
"imperfect" but nonetheless "indispensable" category, as Thompson
would come to call it[65]—could not be referred back, as a reflex, to any
isolable analytical domain ("the economy") or prefabricated model. The
process of historical eventuation, these writers believed, instead needed
to be cut free from static theories of social control, such as those favored
by mainstream sociology, or—signaling a break, which the New Left

claimed to be one of its own primary sources of self-definition—from preponderant Marxist orthodoxy. For Hoggart and for Williams, both of whom came from working-class families, the emergent emphasis was at once social and deeply personal. Williams acknowledged: "Getting the tradition right was getting myself right, and that meant changing both myself and the usual version of the tradition."[66]

Experience, then, just as it had been for Dewey, was an intended solvent of mechanism. This fresh effort to inspect the changing ratio of what Dewey had called "trying" and "undergoing"—what Thompson now reinvented as "desire" and "necessity"—would permit the forerunners of British cultural studies both to suspend the conventional dichotomy between "intellectual" and "manual" labor and to establish a congruence with the subsequent political-economic critique of cultural imperialism. "What a socialist society needs to do," Williams declared in 1957, in a formulation which could make room for both emphases, "is not to define its culture in advance, but to clear the channels, so that instead of guesses at a formula there is opportunity for a full response of the human spirit to a life continually unfolding, in all its concrete richness and variety."[67]

The same need to make room for the full "variety" of human response was evident in the New Left's commitment, as Stuart Hall recalled it, to the idea "that ordinary people could and should organize where they were, around issues of immediate experience":

> racial oppression, housing, property deterioration and short-sighted urban planning alongside the more traditional themes of poverty and unemployment. . . . Questions of alienation, the breakdown of community, the weakness of democracy in civil society and what the early American New Left, in its Port Huron statement, called "quality of life" issues, constituted for us as significant an indictment of the present regime of capital as any other—an indictment we thought irremediable within an unreformed and untransformed society and culture.[68]

Yet here, at once, there entered an important source of contention. Without altogether demurring, Edward Thompson sought, in contrast, to sustain a more pointed direction than that evinced by Hall's disparate groups and settings. Thompson had no doubt that "working people" and "the Labour Movement" should remain the constitutive axis of politics:

> What will distinguish the New Left will be its rupture with the tradition of inner party factionalism, and its renewal of the tradition of open association, socialist education, and activity, directed towards the people as a whole. . . . It will insist that the Labour Movement is not a thing but an association of men and women; that working people are not passive recipients of economic and cultural conditioning, but are intellectual and moral beings. . . . It will counter the philistine materialism and anti-intellectualism of the Old Left by appealing to the totality of human interests and poten-

tialities, and by constructing new channels of communication between industrial workers and experts in the sciences and arts.[69]

In the tradition of William Morris, the English artist-craftsman, writer, and socialist who formed the subject of his own first major work, Thompson thus issued a passionate call to reintegrate "manual" and "mental" labor. But this was by no means the sole, or even a generally recognized, focus of early cultural studies. Those who purport to find in "culturalism" a common wellspring, as Thompson himself later reprimanded, widely ignore the fact that, from the start, the revision around "culture" occasioned deep-seated disagreements. Involved here were, in the first place, disputes regarding the respective analytical placement of "culture" and "class," and such conflicts could not fail to register pragmatic political divergences.[70]

Hoggart, briefly, accorded pride of place to the media in his survey of continuities and discontinuities in the felt experience of the working class; his chief work, *The Uses of Literacy*, was subtitled "aspects of working-class life with special reference to publications and entertainments." As against those who simply hailed the "embourgeoisement" of the working class, however, Hoggart insisted that an older and "more genuine class culture," which he recalled and vividly rendered across an anthropologized register of urban lifeways, faced the threat of severe erosion at the hands of a new and significantly "less healthy" "mass culture."[71] Conspicuously secondary, in his account of encroachment by this "candy-floss world" on the experience of the working class, were politics and ideology. A chasm thus separated the culture of the working-class majority, in Hoggart's depiction, from the politics of an "earnest minority." Stuart Hall's views find more detailed exposition in Chapter Four, but it is worth underlining that his early thought substantially overlapped that of Hoggart—who, in 1964, helped him obtain a post as Research Fellow in Cultural Studies at Birmingham University. Hoggart's stress was on what Hall consistently agreed could be seen as "the break-up of traditional culture, especially traditional class cultures," under "the impact of the new forms of affluence and consumer society."[72]

The Uses of Literacy in turn was recognized by Raymond Williams as a "welcome" and "natural successor and complement" to the cultural criticism that had begun to cohere in the early 1930s around F. R. Leavis and the journal *Scrutiny*.[73] In extending the range of criticism beyond the characteristic procedures of the *Scrutiny* group—from documents to the anthropology of everyday life, or what Williams now called "the reading public as people"—*The Uses of Literacy* succeeded, he declared, in raising problems of "exceptional contemporary interest." Hoggart's answers, however, he found far from conclusive. Hoggart had "taken over too many of the formulas" and, in particular, Williams charged, essentially "conservative ideas of the decay of politics in the working-class"; relatedly, Hoggart had admitted "the extremely damaging and quite untrue identification of 'popular culture' . . . with 'working-class culture.'"[74] Williams, as we will see, explicitly rejected the notion "that the working class was becoming 'deproletarianized.'" It was, he thoroughly agreed, "of the utmost importance that we should try to understand the complex social and cultural changes" under way.[75] About these, however, Williams harbored an optimistic reformism. Changes apparent in and around communication hinged, he believed, on what he implied was a potentially decisive process of democratization—again, of "clearing the channels" along which art, learning and education could flow.[76]

In turn, and equally summarily, for Thompson, Williams's strivings on behalf of a democratic or common culture, though admirable in intent, smacked of gradualism and lent themselves to an impermissible over-reliance upon "the collective 'we.'" A shared culture, Thompson argued, seemed to be at once the aim *and* the basis of Williams's purported "long revolution." But then, he wondered, what was the nature of the problem to which a "common culture" was the answer? What was it that disrupted or blocked the progress of "culture" as a society-wide form of shared experience? What, in short, was Williams's long revolution *against?*

Thompson could be forgiven if he chafed at the attention showered on Williams for his pair of books, *Culture and Society* and *The Long Revolution*. It was, perhaps, a question of timing. Having had the misfortune to appear just before the crystallization of the first New Left and the parallel rout of British Communism, Thompson's commanding study of William Morris placed itself within the latter's intellectual force field. Yet *William Morris* not only covered some of the same ground trod by Williams in *Culture and Society*, but also began to establish a prospective rival basis for situating these complex key words within the received tradition of English thought.[77] Thompson had cast Morris as a late avatar of Romanticism, emphasizing that the moral basis for Morris's turn to socialism had been his felt need to find means of rejecting and transcending the growing split under capitalism between the work of art, in both senses, and "manual" toil.

The monumental study that followed, Thompson's *The Making of the English Working Class*, placed on the agenda for a whole generation of historians the specific mode of social labor—handicraft production, in which artisans who relied upon their own hand tools characteristically labored to execute their own conceptions of diverse products—which Morris had celebrated, and which in the U.S. context had begotten the producer republican tradition that was to be of such consequence for communication study itself. In *The Making of the English Working Class*, Thompson proceeded back to the moment when, during the early decades of the 19th century, these craft producers had helped to mount an epochal challenge to the ascent of a more fully articulated industrial capitalism and, he suggested, in that process had gone far to constitute the early British working class. Thompson thus tacitly insisted that capitalism's own progressive historical bifurcation of "manual" and "mental" labor comprised a fundamental historical turning point. In the process, he not only developed the idea of "culture" as a means of throwing new light on the history of social class, but also identified conscious class struggle as the prime motor of historical eventuation; his review of Williams's *Long Revolution,* no less stinging than solidary, turns repeatedly on the latter of these points.[78]

We can do no better in glossing Thompson's perspective than to attend to his often-quoted admonition:

> By class I understand a historical phenomenon, unifying a number of disparate and seemingly unconnected events, both in the raw material of experience and in consciousness. I emphasize that it is a historical phenomenon. I do not see class as a "structure," nor even as a "category," but as something which in fact happens (and can be shown to have happened) in human relationships.
>
> . . . The class experience is largely determined by the productive relations into which men are born—or enter involuntarily. Class-consciousness is the way in which these experiences are handled in cultural terms: embodied in traditions, value-systems, ideas, and institutional forms. If the experience appears as determined, class-consciousness does not. . . . Class is defined by men as they live their own history, and, in the end, this is its only definition.[79]

This was in 1963. Around the same time Thompson also suggested that class—"a social and cultural formation"—referred to "a very loosely defined body of people who share the same categories of interests, social experiences, traditions and value-system, who have a *disposition* to *behave* as a class . . . ."[80] In this context, the chief burden of "culture" was, patently, to sustain the reorientation of social class toward experience; class or perhaps even class consciousness never relinquished its unifying thematic and conceptual role.[81] There remained for Thompson a fruitful tension over whether "class experience" was "determined" by "productive relations" or more loosely rendered via subjective "interests, social experiences, traditions and value-systems." For Williams, on the other hand, this tension was almost entirely suspended; "culture" in its own right for him comprised—though in an awkward, plural sense—the basic and enveloping category. Further explication of Williams's curiously authoritative, complex application of the culture concept constitutes the most useful benchmark against which to chart that pivotal idea's subsequent declension.

After sweeping the Conservative Party out of office, the Labour government had successfully undertaken to launch a progressive welfare

state during the immediate postwar years. Nationalization of key industries took place, and social security measures and income-redistribution
efforts also proceeded. But, as the Cold War cranked up, any will the
leaders of the Labour Party might have had to continue to restructure
British society was subdued. The 1951 General Election conferred on a
now-refurbished Conservative Party, who as a group had acquiesced to a
"modernizing" welfare state, a new lease on power. A Labour recon-
quest languished through two subsequent elections, occurring only with
the Wilson victory of 1964.

This unseasonable Conservative enthronement appeared to many
on the left to comprise the most visible, but perhaps not the most formidable, of the novel blockages associated with the postwar settlement.
During the first half of the 1950s, despite unprecedented material abundance, Britain seemed to those who would come together to form a New
Left "a society in which creative, popular and intellectual initiative was
at low ebb."[82] Were the two conditions—abundance and apathy—
connected? "Effective Conservatism," wrote Williams in 1964, "in
theory and practice, has idolized the super-administrator, the salesman,
the speculator; the institutions it will leave as a legacy are the super-
market, the betting shop, commercial television and the motorway beside the closed railway."[83] However, was not the accompanying state of
political debility perversely and, perhaps, definitively, compounded by
Labour's collaboration—even as the party's own leaders and theorists
heralded "Welfare Britain" as the very realization of socialism?[84]

This last question got down to the core of the controversy in which
"culture" was to figure so prominently. "In place of its own order of
priorities," Stuart Hall declared, "Labour has followed along the trail
which consumer capitalism opened up. . . . The new aspirations of a
skilled working class have been diverted into the satisfaction of personal
wants. . . ."[85] Again, Hall's view of this formative period explicitly
emphasized the apparent "undermining impact of the mass media and
of an emerging mass society on this old European class society."[86]
Williams, in 1964, could agree that Labour might be characterized as
"not the party of the working majority, but the party of the latest wave of
the rising commercial and technical middle class."[87] But he wanted no
part of an explanation of the impasse that rested on a familiar appeal to
mass culture's corrosive impact. Williams later looked back on this moment, with its "probability" that "the stylish consumer society . . .
would be the new form of capitalism," in deeply revealing personal
terms: "[B]ecause I saw the process as options under pressure, and
knew where the pressure was coming from, I could not move" to accept
the mass culture position, which he characterized as being founded on
"contempt of people, of their hopelessly corrupted state, of their vul-
garity and credulity by comparison with an educated minority . . . ."
Such a position, Williams was to suggest during the 1970s, "was the

staple of cultural criticism of a non-Marxist kind and . . . seems to
have survived intact, through the appropriate alterations of vocabulary,
into a formalist Marxism which makes the whole people, including the
whole working class, mere carriers of the structures of a corrupt ideology."[88]

At the time, he had been no less combative. "The most popular and
also the silliest" version of the idea that the working class was losing its
identity was, Williams emphasized in 1960, "that which proves the
'deproletarianization' of the British working class" by reference to its
apparent flagging support for the Labour Party—a shift then said to be
explained "by the increasing availability of modern houses, television,
washing machines, and cars to the better paid workers."[89] There were in
fact several million more Labour voters during the 1950s, Williams
pointed out, than there had been during the 1930s—as many as there
had been in the watershed election of 1945.[90] An analysis which sought
to lodge Labour's misfortunes in the new mass culture was not only
mistaken in fact, he declared, but also simpleminded: "The working
class does not become bourgeois by owning the new products, any more
than the bourgeois ceases to be bourgeois as the objects he owns change
in kind." It was, flatly, "not bourgeois . . . to enjoy a high material
standard of living."[91]

Williams's views on this issue were, surely, too little qualified; after
all, "a high material standard of living" need not countenance annual
model changes nor, indeed, the waste that is arguably the most reliable
product of consumer capitalism. And Williams's corrective statistics detailing the size of the Labour vote could not allay even his own sense of
the scope and depth of contemporary social change, as regards both class
structure and self-understanding. But these shortcomings hardly vitiated
his argument, which was broadly conditioned by what he himself called
an "almost prepolitical" and class-embedded commitment to Labour: "I
had grown up in the belief, which was in practice assumed by most of
the left in Britain, that a Labour government with a strong majority
would be able to overcome the limitations of social-democratic parlia-
mentarianism," he would later recall.[92] Williams was undeterred, therefore, by what he saw as only an interval of transitory, if frustrating,
adversity. On one hand, then, despite deep and substantive differences
with the leadership of the Labour Party, he still found it possible to work
on Labour's behalf full-time during the run-up to the 1955 General
Election. (Indeed he resigned from the party only in 1966.[93]) On the
other hand, however, he also found it necessary, joining many who had
been galvanized in 1956 by the Suez Crisis and the Soviet invasion of
Hungary, to seek independent means—a New Left—to prise the Labour
Party from its willfully lackadaisical course. "Labour's forward march,"
as Raphael Samuel put it dispassionately some thirty years later, had
"transformed living conditions within a generation"; "[m]ore perti-

nently," however, "it still seemed to have a whole reformist programme to fulfill."⁹⁴

What was involved, Williams believed, was an effort to redefine "what politics should be, and the remobilization, at every level, of the forces necessary for it." Swiftly changing patterns of lived experience were making hash of ensconced traditions of radical analysis, forged during the Depression, which continued to argue the case against capitalism in terms of its failure to produce—its inherent stagnationist tendency. If, therefore, on one hand, the right wing of the Labour Party "seemed to be capitulating completely to consumer capitalism," then, on the other, like the Communist Party's, the Labour left's bearings "were predicated on the existence of general poverty and the old kind of class structure." A reinvigorated radicalism therefore now required sustained analytical engagement with what Williams referred to as "a new phase of capitalism."⁹⁵ This process of unremitting and public critical reflection would have to be nondogmatic without becoming undisciplined, relying both on fresh categories and, once more, unremitting attention to a changing lived experience.

The approach that resulted, wrote a searching critic, could seem "almost too civilised for a rough world." Williams's injunction that "[t]here are in fact no masses; there are only ways of seeing people as masses" in this view comprised more an ideal than a historical truth: Was not the Tory Mob—"drilled in our improving age into an S.S. Division"—a hatefully "authentic" feature of the historical record?⁹⁶ Williams's recurrent terms of reference to an environing common culture—"sharing," "community," "expansion," "growth"—radiated something more, however, than a relentless commitment to being reasonable: his dogged belief in the possibility of social betterment under contemporary conditions. Consider this discussion from 1961, where no diminution of everyday commitment is contemplated, despite a harshly realistic assessment of the present status of cooperatives, trade unions, the Labour Party, and other initiatives by the working class:

> the point has been reached when each of these institutions is discovering that the place in existing society proposed for it, if it agrees to limit its aims, is essentially subordinate: the wide challenge has been drained out, and what is left can be absorbed within existing terms. For many reasons this has sapped the morale of the institutions, but also, fortunately, led to crisis and argument within them. The choice as it presents itself is between qualified acceptance in a subordinate capacity or the renewal of an apparently hopeless challenge. The practical benefits of the former have to be balanced against the profound loss of inspiration in the absence of the latter. If I seem eccentric in continuing to look to these institutions for effective alternative patterns, while seeing all too clearly their present limitations, I can only repeat that they can go either way, and their crisis is not yet permanently resolved.⁹⁷

Exactly at this point, as we will see, through his revision of "culture" Williams intended to provide a means of pressing beyond the postwar plateau. "Culture," that is, remained obstinately and consciously anchored in what he characterized as "a slow reach again for control" and, now explicitly, a "struggle for social democracy."[98]

Thompson, honing in on this apparent reformism,[99] understandably did not stress that the common culture Williams sought to project was in fact also openly aligned—albeit only some of the time—within the force field of social class relations. Williams's revision turned on a sharp cultural divergence between the working class and the bourgeoisie, one that elsewhere he explicitly avowed was "the most important cultural distinction of our time."[100] "The crucial distinguishing element in English life since the Industrial Revolution is not language, nor dress, nor leisure—for those indeed will tend to uniformity. The crucial distinction is between alternative ideas of the nature of social relationship."[101] As against the individualism of the bourgeoisie, the working class's "major cultural contribution" was "the collective democratic institution, formed to achieve a general social benefit":

> It is indeed characteristic of working-class culture that the emphasis it has chosen is the emphasis of extending relationships. The primary affections and allegiances, first to family, then to neighbourhood, can in fact be directly extended into social relationships as a whole. . . . the working class sees no reason, in experience . . . why these primary values should not be made the values of society as a whole. . . . the mainstream of working-class life continues, in its own directions, offering . . . an idea of society under which we all can again unite.[102]

Let us make no mistake; Williams sought a thoroughgoing overhaul of established property relations. "The demand for redistribution of the industrial product and for industrial democracy from the board room to the shop floor, is not a sectional demand; it is an expression of principles and objectives for the whole society."[103] But at this stage the supervening class distinction he posited was never grounded directly, let alone exclusively, in the social relations of production. Williams's framework was rather based mainly in the expressive intersubjectivity which, he wished to hold, was constituted by "culture." His abiding commitment to a transformed "culture" in turn comprised both the fount of his radical revisionism and, ironically, an intellectual constraint against which his own thinking had ceaselessly to struggle.[104]

The "new phase of capitalism" that Britain had entered, Williams believed, to be sure could and should be associated with "qualitatively new kinds of magazines, advertisements, television programmes, political campaigning."[105] But, where Hoggart and Hall connected these new forms with a "mass culture" corrosive of social class, Williams, in contrast, even when disheartened by Labour's third successive electoral defeat, sought to recruit "culture" for an entirely different role:

The central problem, as I see it, is cultural. The society of individual consumers which is now being propagandized by all the weight of mass advertising and mass publications, needs a new kind of socialist analysis and alternative. We are full of confectionery and short of hospitals; loaded with cars and ludicrously short of decent roads; facing an educational challenge of major proportions, yet continuing a limited class system of schools. These are incidental examples of a crisis which needs different analysis and different programs from those appropriate to poverty and depression. That such analysis and such programs must be socialist seems more clear than ever before. Only in projecting a new kind of community, a new kind of social consciousness, can the Labour Party offer anything distinctive and positive. It may take a long time, and some may be impatient for power and therefore restive. But, short of ruin or folly, this is the only way in which the Labour Party can now ever win, and it is not after all anything out of the tradition that is being offered: Labour came into existence, not as an alternative party to run this society, but as a means of making a different society.[106]

"Culture's" cardinal import bespoke "the Labour Party's permanent task of creating a new kind of social consciousness."[107] "[I]n contemporary Britain," Williams wrote in 1957, "many of the questions which most radically affect the working-class movement are quite clearly cultural questions."[108] To speak of "culture" indeed was to work toward nothing less than an "effort at total qualitative assessment" of "the conditions of our common life."[109] It was, once more, to clear the way for a sustained opening of theory to the gathering revisionary energies of a changing, and newly unfamiliar, social experience. Here we get very close indeed, needless to say, to the tenor of the subsequent critique of cultural imperialism.

The power of Williams's revisionary attempt is, however, more difficult to recapture. His belief that postwar Britain could effect a transit by degrees toward a common culture was soon overtaken by events. Nonetheless, Williams's dogged reworking of "culture" carried explosive possibilities for "the Tradition," as he called it, still with enough respect to raise Edward Thompson's hackles.[110] In particular, his intransigent claim that "art and culture are ordinary"[111] directly confronted and, backed by the whole range of accumulating anthropological and psychological findings, effectively counterweighed the disabling and self-serving elitism which dominated formal cultural criticism. "We speak of a cultural revolution," he declared in 1961, "and we must certainly see the aspiration to extend the active process of learning, with the skills of literacy and other advanced communication, to all people rather than to limited groups, as comparable in importance to the growth of democracy and the rise of scientific industry."[112] Thus did this longtime lecturer for the Workers Education Association seek to enfranchise those who had been locked out by reigning standards of criticism and, indeed, of education in general.[113] In a sharply critical book review, Thompson went out of his way to credit Williams on this point: "With a compromised tradi-

tion at his back, and with a broken vocabulary in his hands, he did the
only thing that was left to him: he took over the vocabulary of his
opponents, followed them into the heart of their own arguments, and
fought them to a standstill in their own terms. He held the roads open for
the young, and now they are moving down them once again." But
Thompson went on to explicate his major point, that Williams "has not
yet succeeded in developing an adequate *general* theory of culture."[114]

The latter's arguments about "culture" indeed did pivot around not
just one analytical pole, but two. Though not mutually exclusive, each
not only carried a different intellectual spin, but was also itself a site of
active and incomplete theorization. Coexisting problematically within
Williams's work, but also giving the latter its authority and force, this
difficult conception has offered a complex inheritance for scholarship
right on down into the present.

At one pole, Williams was revising an established anthropological
conception:

> If the art is part of the society, there is no solid whole, outside it, to which, by
> the form of our question, we concede priority. The art is there, as an activity,
> with the production, the trading, the politics, the raising of families. To
> study the relations adequately we must study them actively, seeing all the
> activities as particular and contemporary forms of human energy. If we take
> any one of these activities, we can see how many of the others are reflected
> in it, in various ways according to the nature of the whole organization. It
> seems likely, also, that the very fact that we can distinguish any particular
> activity, as serving certain specific ends, suggests that without this activity
> the whole of the human organization at that place and time could not have
> been realized. . . . I would then define the theory of culture as the study of
> relationships between elements in a whole way of life.[115]

This synthetic impulse was thus deliberately shorn of a priori notions of the primacy of the economy. Williams, that is to say, effectively
held in abeyance the Marxian tenet of "economic determination," from
"base" to "superstructure."[116] All domains of experience, all "active
relations," Williams asserted, had to be "seen in a genuine parity"; none
could be isolated and then shown to determine the features of any other.
Indeed "any concession of priority" to a given activity was invalid: "If
we find, as often, that a particular activity came radically to change the
whole organization, we can still not say that it is to this activity that all
the others must be related; we can only study the varying ways in which,
within the changing organization, the particular activities and their in-
terrrelations were affected."[117] The point was that notions of determination had been too often utilized in abstract and ahistorical ways, so that
analysts (and not solely Marxists) presented themselves with what then
appeared to be an autonomous category, "the economy," seemingly
capable on its own of controlling or predicting developments occurring
elsewhere in a society.

At the second pole, revising away from the received Arnoldian emphasis on "culture" as the best that has been thought and known, Williams declared that "culture" instead denoted a universal human capacity for creative endeavor. This capacity was, for him, evident not only in classic literary texts and paintings but, above all, in the series of collective working-class institutions underscored above. Despite its overt effort to batter away at the dominant traditions of criticism and education, Williams's projection of "culture" was designed, in its very universality, to disable mechanical appeals to a concept of social class which divorced "manual" from "intellectual" effort. Williams, for example, took considerable care (doubtless looking over his shoulder to prewar aesthetic debates) to emphasize that "[t]he body of intellectual and imaginative work which each generation receives as its traditional culture is always, and necessarily, something more than the product of a single class."[118] Rather than seeking, with Thompson, to refer "culture" to conscious class conflict, however, Williams instead over-optimistically permitted it to become synonymous with an apparent general process of human communication:

> The emphasis that matters is that there are, essentially, no "ordinary" activities, if by "ordinary" we mean the absence of creative interpretation and effort. . . . Since our way of seeing things is literally our way of living, the process of communication is in fact the process of community: the sharing of common meanings, and thence common activities and purposes: the offering, reception and comparison of new meanings, leading to the tensions and achievements of growth and change.[119]

At such moments, the tension established by Williams's twin uses of "culture" became overpowering: For his revision appeared to sanction just such an apparently autonomous plane of cultural expression as he himself was to deliberately reject. Absenting any notion of determination, while simultaneously stressing the universal human capacity for creative expression, "culture" then grew slack and appeared to lapse into an idealist concept, redolent of Dewey's "organized intelligence":

> Everything we see and do, the whole structure of our relationships and institutions, depends, finally, on an effort of learning, description and communication. . . . all activity depends on responses learned by the sharing of descriptions. . . . [120]

"Culture," in this reformulation—whose unitary and unconflicted appearance drew Thompson's sharpest criticisms—became society's animating, propulsively meaningful aspect.

Williams intended his synthetic, dual usage of "culture," which so clearly sought to suspend the dichotomy between "intellectual" and "manual" labor, to bridge toward what he took to be most necessary: an empirically accessible and historically specific synthesis around lived experience.[121] "Culture" thus referred to a "community of process," "a whole world of active and interacting relationships, which is our common associative life."¹²² And again: "[W]e cannot understand the process of change in which we are involved if we limit ourselves to thinking of the democratic, industrial, and cultural revolutions as separate processes."¹²³ The search for such interrelationships constitutes the guiding axis of Williams's method throughout the succession of case studies which comprises the central section of *The Long Revolution* and, indeed, his overall quest. Their significance even led him to caution, undoubtedly with an eye to formalist criticism, against a possible inversion of economic determinism—against, that is, "a new abstraction" in cultural theory: "The pattern of meanings and values through which people conduct their whole lives can be seen for a time as autonomous, and as evolving within its own terms, but it is quite unreal, ultimately, to separate this pattern from a precise political and economic system, which can extend its influence into the most unexpected regions of feeling and behavior. To isolate the system of learning and communication, as the key to change, is unrealistic."¹²⁴ Williams therefore attached a vital caveat to each of his two usages of "culture": respectively, first, to avoid economic reduction, and, second, to avoid any "new abstraction" toward an autonomized plane of expression.

For in Williams's formulation, "culture" was ultimately intended to be something qualitatively other than would be allowed by either of his two distinct uses, taken by itself—more, that is, than what might be conveyed by the accustomed anthropological sense, of an analytical site of study of the interrelationships binding together diverse human practices and activities; and, again, more than an ordinary, already given capacity for shared expression, meaning, and experience. Williams indeed deliberately sought to erase the distinction between these two poles. The theoretical bridge that he tried to build between analytical synthesis and expressive ethos he called the "structure of feeling." A coinage destined to achieve a lasting but opaque currency, the "structure of feeling" originated in Williams's criticism of the drama. "What I am seeking to describe," Williams wrote, in a passage worth quoting in its entirety,

> is the continuity of experience from a particular work, through its particular form, to its recognition as a general form, and then the relation of this general form to a period. We can look at this continuity, first, in the most general way. All that is lived and made, by a given community in a given period, is, we now commonly believe, essentially related, although in practice, and in detail, this is not always easy to see. In the study of a period, we may be able to reconstruct, with more or less accuracy, the material life, the general social organization, and, to a large extent, the dominant ideas. It is often difficult to decide which, if any, of these aspects is, in the whole complex determining; their separation is, in a way, arbitrary, and an important institution like the drama will, in all probability, take its colour in

varying degrees from them all. But, while we may, in the study of a past period, separate out particular aspects of life, and treat them as if they were self-contained, it is obvious that this is only how they may be studied, not how they were experienced. We examine each element as a precipitate, but in the living experience of the time every element was in solution, an inseparable part of a complex whole. And it seems to be true, from the nature of art, that it is from such a totality that the artist draws; it is in art, primarily, that the effect of a whole lived experience is expressed and embodied. To relate a work of art to any part of that whole may, in varying degrees, by useful; but it is a common experience, in analysis, to realize that when one has measured the work against the separable parts, there yet remains some element for which their is no external counterpart. It is this, in the first instance, that I mean by the structure of feeling. It is as firm and definite as "structure" suggests, yet it is based in the deepest and often least tangible elements of our experience. It is a way of responding to a particular world which in practice is not felt as one way among others—a conscious "way"—but is, in experience, the only way possible. Its means, its elements, are not propositions or techniques; they are embodied, related feelings. In the same sense, it is accessible to others—not by formal argument or by professional skills, on their own, but by direct experience—a form and a meaning, a feeling and a rhythm—in the work of art, the play, as a whole.[125]

As Martin Jay has shown, the idea of social totality—of a coherent social whole whose parts may be shown somehow to fit together—offers an indispensable means of distinguishing the theories propounded by different Western Marxists, for whom the concept comprised a subterranean but no less central preoccupation. Now we may see that the idea of social totality also provides a necessary heuristic tool for comprehending Williams's notion of culture, for which the structure of feeling acted as a kind of index.[126]

We have it on the authority of Williams himself that he was working consciously in light of just such a notion. "I did not want to give up my sense of the commanding importance of economic activity and history," he reminisced in 1971: "My inquiry in *Culture and Society* had begun from just that sense of a transforming change. But in theory and practice I came to believe that I had to give up, or at least to leave aside, what I knew as the Marxist tradition."

[T]o attempt to develop a theory of social totality; to see the study of culture as the study of relations between elements in a whole way of life; to find ways of studying structure, in particular works and periods, which could stay in touch with and illuminate particular art works and forms, but also forms and relations of more general social life; to replace the formula of base and superstructure with the more active idea of a field of mutually if also unevenly determining forces. This was the project of *The Long Revolution*, and it seems to me extraordinary, looking back, that I did not then know the work of Lukacs. . . .[127]

Williams's mention of Georg Lukacs—whose major works, like those of other Continental Marxist theorists, were just now being recognized and translated into English—was signally appropriate. In the founding text of what became called "Western Marxism"—*History and Class Consciousness* (1922)—the revolutionary Lukacs had famously written: "It is not the primacy of economic motives in historical explanation that constitutes the decisive difference between Marxism and bourgeois thought, but the point of view of totality. The category of totality, the all-pervasive supremacy of the whole over the parts is the essence of the method which Marx took over from Hegel and brilliantly transformed into the foundations of a wholly new science."[128]

Still, Williams's totality was not that of Lukacs. The latter had sought to ground the characteristic "antinomies of bourgeois thought" in a pervasive "reification" of consciousness. "Reification," which he utilized to characterize what he took to be the defining experience of life under capitalism, meant, in Jay's felicitous phrase, "the petrifaction of living processes into dead things."[129] It was to be identified, Lukacs asserted, with the "self-objectification" that was implicit in, and indeed emanated from, the commodity relation, which Lukacs significantly referred to as the "unified economic process" of contemporary capitalism. This totalizing conception of capitalist class relations was borne up by subsequent critics of mass culture, even as they ultimately sought to assay a more strictly ideological domination, associated more with the institutions of the culture industry than directly with the social relations of production.[130] Yet Williams, who rejected the mass culture argument, nevertheless claimed to find in Lukacs's concept of reification a "real advance": "For here," he declared in 1971, "the dominance of economic activity over all other forms of human activity, the dominance of its values over all other values, was given a precise historical explanation: that this dominance, this deformation, was the specific characteristic of capitalist society, and that in modern organized capitalism this dominance—as indeed one can observe—was increasing, so that this reification, this false objectivity, was more thoroughly penetrating every other kind of life and consciousness."[131]

The explanation is that Williams had already, in 1971, embarked on a revision of his own early conception; he was modifying Lukacs's more severe strictures so as to edge toward what has been called (in the concurrent context of French existential Marxism) an open totality.[132] But, in a different dimension, the writing of Lukacs unquestionably remained productive of a direct revisionary affinity. Marx had declared, in what became a standard orthodoxy regarding revolutionary epochs which subject "the whole immense superstructure" to thoroughgoing upheaval, that ". . . one cannot judge such a period of transformation by its consciousness, but, on the contrary, this consciousness must be explained from the contradictions of material life. . . . new superior relations of production never replace older ones before the material conditions for their existence have matured within the framework of the old society. Mankind thus inevitably sets itself only such tasks as it is able to solve. . . ."[133] As against this particular tenet, there was Lukacs's heterodox declaration in *History and Class Consciousness:* "[*T*]*he strength of every society is in the last resort a spiritual strength.* And from this we can only be liberated by knowledge. This knowledge cannot be of the abstract kind that remains in one's head. . . . It must be knowledge that has become flesh of one's flesh and blood of one's blood; to use Marx's phrase, it must be 'practical critical activity.'"[134] Was there not, from the perspective of the late 1960s, an unlikely bond between Lukacs, who attempted, through revolutionary will, to insist that mind and body should once more achieve an integral unity, and Williams, who had written, in *Culture and Society*, "The human crisis is always a crisis of understanding: what we genuinely understand we can do"?[135]

At such points, nevertheless, Williams's complex revision of "culture," which intended a conceptual reintegration of disparate areas of social experience, still indisputably gave pride of place to the sharing of meaning. A more or less conventional search for the codes and languages of expressive culture was thus almost invited to pre-empt the integrative and synthetic study of a purported general culture. Thompson complained that Williams's effort to push against the damaging limits of an exclusive dominant canon hereby ironically reproduced the latter's proclivity for an isolated plane of expressive form as a privileged vantage point on the historical process. His summary objection was not to be avoided: "[I]f Williams by 'the whole way of life' really means the *whole* way of life he is making a claim, not for cultural history, but for history."[136] Absent this needful enlargement, Thompson warned, there might succeed very unfortunate consequences. "[I]f others accept his vocabulary and his conceptual framework, without sharing his allegiances," he observed, "they may come up with very different results."[137] The merit of Thompson's criticism is best judged in light of Williams's own eventual admission: "No full account of a particular formation or kind of formation can be given without extending description and analysis into general history, where the whole social order and all its classes and formations can be taken properly into account."[138]

Williams's quest was likewise remote from the conscious class struggle for which Thompson bore such warm and intellectually productive sympathies. In *Culture and Society*, for example, Williams declared once more that "[t]he area of a culture, it would seem, is usually proportionate to the area of a language rather than to the area of a class."[139] This preference became even more evident, paradoxically, when "culture" was explicitly emended to make room for an extra-communicative dimension: "Reality, in our terms," Williams enjoined at one point, "is that which human beings make common, by work or language."[140] The addition of "work" (as well as Williams's regular reference, throughout the concrete historical chapters of *The Long Revolution*, to changing economic relations and practices) served only to point up the difficulties inherent in the task of binding and interconnecting humanity in a shared project: For where, anyway, in a conception which repeatedly returned to this theme of a common culture, was the place of labor? The question mattered, in the first place, because the latter comprised an obvious taproot of social division. A restorative emphasis on culture as a whole way of life, in turn, for all its equilibrating power, could not take anywhere near adequate account—despite Williams's own tenacious socialism—of continuing exploitation and social struggle.

Williams's initial formulation found its genetic basis, rather, in the active interrelationships which were said to emanate a unitary general culture. In this crucial sense, Williams's initial conception of culture constituted a variant of what has been labeled a Hegelian or expressive totality, in which particular aspects and articulations are seen as expressions of one "simple principle."[141] Yet for Williams this guiding unitary logic issued not so much from the contradiction between the classes as, rather, from "culture" itself. Thus, he declared of "the culture of a period: it is the particular living result of all the elements in the general organization."[142] Even as, in one place, "the structure of feeling" in turn could be used in reference to the status of the British Labour Party, it was also said to be most tellingly evinced and most uniquely accessible in a nation's art and literature—which might, Williams asserted, in the case of Greek drama at least, touch the culture "at every point."[143]

Neither, however, were social class relations unequivocally displaced. Far from it; the expressive subjectivity on which art drew, and on which it afforded a purportedly privileged window, in contemporary Britain also bespoke Williams's conscious projection of universalized working-class solidarities. "[I]t is only in terms of working-class culture as a whole that we have the opportunity for any valuable transformation of society," declared Williams in the late 1950s: "There are no masses to capture, but only the mainstream to join. May it be here that the two major senses of culture—on the one hand the arts, the sciences and learning, on the other hand the whole way of life—are valuably drawn together, in a common effort at maturity."[144] All of Williams's staunch commitment was gathered up in this last formulation; his invocation of an expressive totality propelled by "culture" was anchored by his hope of generalizing working-class values and ideas of social relationship.

Just how closely integrated these two quite disparate aspects of Williams's integrative revision had been was to become apparent only during the shattering social conflagration of the late 1960s. Through the more open struggles that then commenced, Williams could not, finally, sustain the balancing act which had produced his stress on a "common

effort at maturity": a synthesis around "culture" which sought its revisionary effect not only in the universalization of working-class values
but, simultaneously, through the superordinate importance it sought to
confer on an apparent human universal, the ordinary capacity for creative expression. Williams's expressive totality then became a casualty,
both of a sharpening sense of capitalist domination and, paradoxically,
of the heightened opposition which the latter simultaneously provoked.

III

The year 1966 demonstrated, finally and decisively, that what Williams
still called "the most plausible formation for intermediate reform"—the
Labour Party—had "not only defaulted on its own best purposes but at
the level of government has shown itself, unmistakably, to be an active
part of the very system which it has appeared to oppose."[145] With an
unprecedented majority of 100 in Parliament following the 1966
election—surely more than enough, at last, to pursue an autonomous
course dictated by an opposing social vision—Wilson's Labour government instead accepted cuts in social services to keep up the pound's
exchange rate. Believing that a fateful juncture had been reached,
Williams swiftly resigned from the party. He placed himself instead in
the thick of the New Left, a movement to reconstitute an effective political opposition around workers and students; supercharged by the May-
June days in France and student activism throughout Europe and the
United States, this effort peaked between 1968 and 1970.

Amidst the left's continuing differences of political perspective and
strategy around the 1970 election, however, the Conservatives, led by
Edward Heath, returned to power. The upshot was what Williams
termed a "whole series of battles up to the miners' strike of 1973/4,"
signifying what he hailed, evidently with relief, as "a return to real class
politics." The National Union of Miners brought down the Heath government, in what Perry Anderson has termed, despite its severe and all
too evident limitations, "the most spectacular single victory of labour
over capital since the beginnings of working-class organization in Britain."[146] The Labour government which formed after the March 1974
election, however, offered an all-too-predictable reprise of its dispiriting
role during the mid-'60s, by swinging left and then, upon election,
working to contain and defuse "[t]he very considerable crisis to which
British society had been brought by the conflicts of Conservative
rule."[147] It thus effectively prepared the way for its own demise, and for
the postwar period's second protracted Conservative ascendancy, beginning late in 1978: "Thatcherism."

The first intellectual fruit of this wrenching history was, paradoxically, to cement a unified heterodoxy around "culture," now explicitly inclusive both of cultural studies and of the critique of cultural

imperialism. This was not altogether unanticipated. It should be recalled, for example, that Edward Thompson had already linked his epochal history of English class formation during the industrial revolution
to the movement for contemporary decolonization: "Causes which were
lost in England might, in Asia or Africa, yet be won."[148] This comment
may be read as a riposte to Frantz Fanon's declaration, two years earlier:
"The Third World today faces Europe like a colossal mass whose aim
should be to try to resolve the problems to which Europe has not been
able to find the answers."[149] Raymond Williams too had made a similar
association, in 1961, in introducing the need to scrutinize a third, cultural revolution, alongside the industrial revolution and "the democratic
revolution": "[I]n any general view it is impossible to mistake the rising
determination, almost everywhere, that people should govern themselves, and make their own decisions, without concession of this right to
any particular group, nationality or class. In sixty years of this century
the politics of the world have already been changed beyond recognition
in any earlier terms. Whether in popular revolution, in the liberation
movements of colonial peoples, or in the extension of parliamentary
suffrage, the same basic demand is evident. . . . If we take the criterion
that people should govern themselves (the methods by which they do so
being less important than this central fact) it is evident that the democratic revolution is still at a very early stage."[150] And, a few years later,
with greater pungency: "What are still, obtusely, called 'local up-
heavals,' or even 'brushfires,' put all our lives in question, again and
again. Korea, Suez, the Congo, Cuba, Vietnam, are names of our own
crisis."[151] Hall too would insist that "[t]he goals, interests, structures
and ideological drives of a society are nowhere so clearly expressed as in
the imperial, neo-imperial and colonising context." Citing Fanon directly, he was to suggest that, "in the context of Latin America and
Vietnam . . . the slogans of 'Afro-Americanism' and 'Black Power' can
be seen as *international* revolutionary slogans."[152]

For a fraught few years toward the end of the 1960s, then, these
three progenitors of cultural studies achieved a delicate, politically
charged unity, in the practical work of editing *May Day Manifesto*, a
touchstone work of the period. The *Manifesto* was conceived, during the
summer of 1966, as "a bringing together of existing socialist positions
and analysis, as a counter-statement to the Labour government's policies
and explanations." From the process of intellectual revision which necessarily followed, there emerged a work of kaleidoscopic scope covering,
in fifty pointed segments, everything from poverty, work, and unemployment; housing, health, and education; communications and advertising; to the transnational corporation, imperialism, and foreign aid;
U.S. foreign policy and the cold war; and the British state. *May Day
Manifesto*'s editors had no hesitation, moreover, in identifying the operative mechanism of this changing capitalism in the "economic drive

outwards"—from the United States to Europe, Africa, and Asia—on behalf of giant transnational corporations. Spearheaded by advertising, by an overarching effort to create demand, the system that was taking shape was recognized as informal by any recognized historical comparison. European elites, declared the *Manifesto,* had begun to understand "what the United States had already learned in the American continent, that powers other than direct political control were quite sufficient to direct the broad framework of development." And, most strikingly: "[I]n the free play of the cultural market, we inevitably get the products of a sophisticated American market-oriented cultural industry."[153]

Thus the *Manifesto* overlapped, in many of its themes and insights, the concurrent critique of cultural imperialism. Williams's favorable prospectus regarding the status of "communications studies in education," as late as 1976, bore continuing testimony to this momentarily inclusive understanding—undertaken by a new kind of "critical work," in which the procedures associated with the *Scrutiny* group could be combined with "analysis of the institutions, of the kind pioneered by the New Left, and by new kinds of work, in a more closely shared orientation, on popular culture."[154] Mutually approving cross-references provide a final evidence of the bridge which emerged during the late 1960s between cultural studies and what soon would be viewed as a divergent tradition of "political economy."[155] But this connection was, even at the time, already becoming subject to a series of destabilizing centrifugal forces.

The attempt of *May Day Manifesto* was to consolidate "into a general position . . . the many kinds of new political and social response and analysis" which had begun to proliferate. "What we need is a description of the crisis as a whole," the book proclaimed, seemingly in a ringing reassertion of Williams's integrative thematic:

> Our own first position is that all the issues—industrial and political, international and domestic, economic and cultural, humanitarian and radical—are deeply connected; that what we oppose is a political, economic and social system; that what we work for is a different whole society.[156]

Despite this manifest echo of Williams's earlier synthesis, a watershed had been reached.[157] The point stands out, with sudden definitude: felt *opposition* to an existing state of domination precedes mention of "a different whole society." This was a sharp break, and it provoked a specific recognition that the process of communication could not be looked to as the vehicle of reform. Far from it: "[W]e can see in the communications system the effective priority of the institutions and interests of a new capitalism," declared the *Manifesto* unequivocally. This pivotal change would also endure. Williams was arriving at an implacable conviction that, as he would put it a few years later, Britain's communications institutions, rather than acting as means of extension and cultural growth, had proved to be "central agencies" in a "systematic evasion" of the society's longstanding "structural problems."[158] Just how deeply this new oppositional posture undercut Williams's earlier synthesis, with its stress on a "long, slow reach for control," was only beginning to be apparent.

May Day Manifesto in fact overlooked the increasingly sharp debates which were fastening on Williams's kindred notions of a "common culture" and a "long revolution," and which—as may now be emphasized—were already beginning to prompt Williams to set about revising his concept of totality. Even as the *Manifesto* was getting started, Hall was underlining a "duty now to take these concepts further," as he himself tried to do "by counterposing" to them—in an extended essay on "the growing radical and resistance movement among American students and youth, black and white," significantly entitled "The New Revolutionaries"—"the 'short' revolution and the politics of cultural conflict." For Hall, in sum, "[e]ither race, poverty and war are *not* the pivotal issues in American political life"—a proposition which could have virtually no credibility within the New Left, either in Britain or the United States—"or the role of the coalition of 'outsiders' in rupturing the consensus on these critical issues must penetrate further than it has into our theoretical structures."[159]

This resumption on new grounds of Thompson's earlier criticism again stung Williams. "[W]hen what I have called the long revolution is defined, by someone else, as if it meant slow evolution, something has obviously been changed in the original idea."[160] As, earlier, he had taken great care *not* to do, Williams now sharply asserted that it was simply "class society," in which "a solid social structure of private property," involving domination "by capital or state power," against which the revolution needed to be waged.[161] The idea of the long revolution, he asserted,

> was never intended to suggest that society would evolve, of itself, towards a culture in which all people were in a position, through changing their institutions, to participate in a common determination of meanings. This, quite clearly, will not happen: there are groups which oppose this participation in principle and practice, and the long revolution . . . is being opposed, now as in the past, by violence and fraud.[162]

Williams likewise now countered Hall by claiming that he had always intended the term "common culture" "as a way of criticising that divided and fragmented culture we actually have":

> If it is at all true that the creation of meanings is an activity which engages all men, then one is bound to be shocked by any society which, in its most explicit culture, either suppresses the meanings and values of whole groups, or which fails to extend to these groups the possibility of articulating and communicating those meanings. This, precisely, was what one wanted to

assert about contemporary Britain. . . . It was . . . perfectly clear that the majority of the people, while living *as* people, creating their own values, were both shut out by the nature of the educational system from access to the full range of meanings of their predecessors in that place, and excluded by the whole structure of communications—the character of its material ownership, its limiting social assumptions—from any adequate participation in the process of changing and developing meanings which was in any case going on.[163]

"If a common culture is taken," he emphasized, "by some sleight of argument, to mean the existing balance of interests and forces, the existing institutions which are said to be common but which in fact compose the structure of a class-society, then of course revolutionary politics will oppose it." Perhaps a terminological confusion, he suggested, had allowed some people "to suppose that it is this balance of interests and forces which one has in mind when speaking of a common culture." And then, in an extraordinary passage, Williams continued:

> The whole point of the definition as *common* was to suggest active community of access and participation; in this sense, clearly, the existing society is not a common culture, and it is in the name of a common culture that one opposes it. To talk of revolutionary politics as a kind of counter-common culture is then a verbal confusion. I don't want simply to "outleft" Stuart Hall, but the idea of the proletarian cultural revolution in China (subject as it must be, for those of us without immediate contact with it, to possible misunderstandings, and recognising the fact that it may be the terms in which a struggle of a quite different kind is being fought out) seems to me a definition very close to my own. There is, in this revolution, an insistence on the continual participation of what Mao calls, in marxist terms, the masses, in the determination of common meanings: an insistence that this can be done for them by no group—not even by the party vanguard—and that this is a continuous process because it cannot be achieved in any final sense. Nobody can inherit a common culture—it has always to be made, and re-made, by people themselves—and the perspective which Mao is now opening up, of a socialist struggle which includes the continual, common re-making of values and the most active conflict, seems to me wholly compatible with the idea of a common culture as I have argued it.[164]

Williams then turned to the question of whether "the definition of culture as a whole way of life should be replaced by its definition as a way of struggle." His answer remained clear:

> No; because though struggle will always be there—intense in periods of oppression and deprivation; still active in a more equal society—it is still only part of the process by which meanings and values are determined. It is not only that, by this altered definition, we would be excluding love and comradeship and any possible agreement; it is also that the isolation of struggle, where this is not merely a rhetorical device, would be empty and even, in certain circumstances, malign. The need for conflict is now absolute, because of the issues involved; but we lose too wide a range of the

process in which meanings and values are determined if we do not also include, even in periods of intense struggle, the seriousness and responsibility of work, and the recognition and care of each other, that must continue and be extended. We cannot properly call culture anything less than this range of active life, which is what the struggle is for.[165]

Therefore, he concluded, straining to its outermost bounds the conception that had underlain his earlier work, the notion of a common culture might be equated increasingly with "the detailed practice of revolution."[166] For if there now existed an "absolute" need to struggle, to universalize throughout capitalist society that same mutualistic idea of social relationship with which, as we have seen, Williams credited the British working class, then it was exactly the status of this social subject and this hoped-for historical operation which were now coming in question.

Williams had not yet fully responded to Hall's proposed alternatives: race, poverty, and war on one side; theoretical revision to accommodate "outsiders" on the other. Or, rather, he assumed that such a response involved "merely" the prospective transformation of the proletariat into a universal class. The unity that animated *May Day Manifesto* disguised this underlying fracture; but the latter still harbored profound, though often inchoate, implications both for the theorization of class relations and, therefore, for the interlocked theorization of culture. Although of course feminism and anti-racism enjoy longer histories than this, the challenge proffered by the "new social movements" to traditional Marxism indeed was to become inexorable. It took a further decade for this vital issue to be met head-on; but, in 1978, Hall and his collaborators would write:

> [W]ithout question, the most important feature of this level of the crisis . . . is the role of "labourism"—specifically that of the Labour Party, but also the labourist cast of the organised institutions of the working class. Labourism has emerged as an alternative party of capital, and thus an alternative manager of the capitalist crisis. At the most fundamental political level—and shaping every feature of the political culture before it—the crisis of British capitalism for the working class has thus been, also, a crisis of the organised working class and the labour movement.[167]

The question was, what inference should be drawn from this dismally valid generalization? Williams, in the late 1960s, was tacking back and forth between "class society" and a still-to-be-demarcated open totality. While he did so, he resolutely consulted his accustomed compass: "[W]ith a majority of English people (though not of Scots or Welsh) opting for consumer capitalism," he later reminisced about the experience of the British working class during the 1950s, "it was hard to hang on, but it was still not true that the existing resources of the people were so depleted or corrupted that there was no option but to retreat to a residual minority or a futurist vanguard."[168] There is little reason to believe that his sense of the available options differed in regard to the then present, the mid-1970s. Hall, in contrast, struck a quite different note, retrospectively typifying the "patient" wait of "[t]he Left . . . for the old rhythms of 'the class struggle' to be resumed" as an entirely vain and fruitless enterprise.[169]

The concurrent abandonment of the synthetic impulse which had suffused the left's revisionary effort around "culture" in turn occurred alongside, and indeed interwined with, the slippage of the British working class from its ascribed position as an essential theoretical subject and social agency. It was a central result of the New Left's rejection, already beginning to be evident within the bounded polemic between Hall and Williams in 1967, of the idea "that capitalism is riven by one, simple master contradiction which determines all else."[170] This typifying rejection emanated, finally, from three unavoidable historical facts: that, first, movements for national liberation during the postwar period were far and away more visible in "peasant" societies than in the European and North American heartlands of a "developed" industrial capitalism; that, second, such movements for revolutionary change as had come to the forefront in the latter context claimed students and, in the United States, racial and ethnic minorities as their "vanguard"; and that, third, some response needed to be made to the increasingly vocal feminist claim that class relations alone could not be taken as coextensive with social domination, and that "productionist" schemes needed to be more or less drastically overhauled to make room for reproduction, sexuality, "women's sphere." Juliet Mitchell tartly commented on the existence of this protracted silence in socialist theory in the very title of her 1966 article for *New Left Review:* "Women—The Longest Revolution."[171]

Complicating this already very complex picture was a fourth eventuality. Toward the end of the 1970s, the political scene in Britain lurched sharply to the right, and "culture" as a form of pressure brought by popular experience on "the Tradition" in turn gave way at key points to "culture" as a means of winning consent for increasingly iron-fisted forms of rule. The *Manifesto's* opposition to the dominant media was now extended. "Culture" had now as well to be seen, in other words, in relation to the sources of social containment and of acquiescence to a ruling order which seemed palpably more unjust and inequitable: what Hall, recognizing a debt to Ernesto Laclau, began to call "authoritarian populism."[172] The need grew commensurately to theorize and to redress a rampant sexism, as well as the rapid re-entry of a hard and active racism into the "accepted" mainstream of British and U.S. political and social life.

In at least one crucial respect, however, no blanket rejection of early cultural studies transpired. The reorientation toward subjectivity and lived experience, which so stimulated the latter's formative engagement with social class, was simply turned to other uses, now that the way could be opened to the assumption of a rough equivalence between any and all experiences, identities, subjectivities. This preoccupation with subjective experience had and continues to have useful and even desirable consequences, not least because it preserved intact Williams's vision of culture—or, at least, of cultural studies—as a battering ram aimed at the socially exclusive and constrained forms of the ensconced canon, that is, as a means of broadening the franchise for a regenerative "new social consciousness." Analysts, in other words, remained free to search across the social field for sources of opposition and resistance, as well as of social containment and ideological subjection. As Hall came later to emphasize, in turn, not gender oppression alone, but the feminist movement as well, forced "a major rethink in every substantive area of work" being undertaken by the Centre for Contemporary Cultural Studies.[173] In the wake of the postwar decades' experience of decolonization and anti-imperial struggle, furthermore—to mention the other leading site of redefinition—"race" could be seen as a defining factor in the head-on collision in Britain between "authoritarian populism" and the vindicative energies of people of color hailing from different outposts of the erstwhile empire. Hall and his colleagues detailed in a brilliant and wide-ranging work of the later 1970s how "race" offered an efficacious means of reorienting the polity to the right—and, vitally, a means in whose creation Labour had been characteristically complicit. As Hall later came to gloss the shift:

> The problem of racism arises from every single political development which has taken place in Britain since the new right emerged.
> Blacks have themselves, at times, tried to isolate the issue of race from the wider questions of social politics in Britain—as if black people have nothing to do with rates and ratecapping and monetarism and the Falklands factor until they affect the black communities directly. This separation, if it ever existed, has long since departed. In *Policing the Crisis*, a book some of us wrote in the mid-1970s when Thatcherism was still only a tiny gleam in Sir Keith Joseph's eye, we argued that race was deeply and intimately intertwined with every single facet of the gathering social crisis of Britain; and that it was no longer possible for blacks to have a political strategy towards that part of the dynamic which affected them without having a politics for the society as a whole. That argument has immeasurably strengthened over the years. . . .[174]

Implicitly and explicitly gendered and raced conceptions of class also worked, however, to undercut the synthetic impulse which had always animated Williams's idea of "culture." Williams's "common culture" indeed began to appear, to many on the left, to spell out an untenable—and, as events sped onward, a residual—position. If communication and cultural studies were to retain an actively engaged political presence, their axial term would have to undergo fundamental revision.

From the 1970s to the present, this need to work all the way *through*, to a positive theorization with which to replace Williams's version of "culture" as an expressive totality, remained unrelievedly problematic. This rejection or closure ushered in an interval of often confusing effort, in which continued reliance on an unmoored category of "experience," opening helpfully outward to "race" and "gender," vied with attempts to give theory new points of self-conscious reference. It should not be surprising that, as this transition proceeded, the gyroscope with which Williams had contrived to keep in view the mutual constitution of "mental" and "manual" activity would be set off balance. But perhaps it will be less obvious that this metamorphosis itself turned—as we are about to find—on a series of new reifications of "intellectual" activity, justification for which was sought, very precisely, in a repeated rejection of the category of "labor" itself. And it could hardly have been forecast that the medium through which this blowout transpired—or, at least, to which it made sustained reference—was Marxism.

CHAPTER FOUR

The Contraction of Theory

During the late 1960s and 1970s, the category of labor staged a series of profoundly significant, direct appearances within three leading conceptions of culture and communicative activity, clustering respectively around Althusserian structuralism, post-industrial theory, and post-structuralism. This engagement, which rendered "labor" an immediate intellectual touchstone, was predicated on a broad and explicit encounter with orthodox Marxism, in which each school selectively identified a tradition of cardinal importance for its own more or less discrete theorization. Far from being simply reproduced and carried over, however, orthodox Marxism's concept of labor was taken up only so as to be categorically rejected.

In the eyes of its disparate beholders, Marxism's validity hinged on how well—or poorly—its conception of labor fared in accommodating the distinctive features of late 20th-century society. Figuring prominently among the latter, in the cases of structuralism and poststructuralism, were issues cast up by the renewed emphasis on human social agency discussed in the previous chapter, issues which emanated specifically from feminism, anti-racism, and anti-colonialism. But it is less well appreciated that a concern for "intellectual" labor's contemporary status also lay at the very heart of this multifaceted revisionary impulse. To a significant extent, indeed, latter-day theorizations of "culture" and "communication" were rendered possible only by breaking, albeit in disparate ways, with the treatment of "intellectual" labor by a received Marxism.

Entrenched Marxian theorizations of "labor" did indeed continue to betray a long-unresolved dualism. On one hand, Marxists had always reserved a special historical prerogative for the proletariat, whose labor—by definition exploited directly by capital—was for this reason endowed with a unique potential for transcendence. On the other hand, first through its battles with various forms of idealism and then, conversely, through its too-easy accommodation with a physicalistic model of labor power,[1] Marxism privileged "material" production, or "social being," as the supposed medium of historical eventuation. These comprised disjoint impulses; nonetheless, unfortunately, with the formation of the European social democratic parties during the late 19th century, they came to be programmatically equated within Marxist orthodoxy. For several generations, within the major institutionalized variants of Marxism, "material" production then came to grant pride of place to the toil of wage-earners. Slighted, for different reasons, was a great range of activities that did not fall within the contemporary capital-wage relation. An important subset of nonwaged activities was, in addition, consigned to "consciousness" or "ideology" or "the superstructure"—including, most saliently, the "brainwork" of literary artists and intellectuals. "It is a fundamental idea of materialism," one influential British subscriber to this particular commonsense wrote in 1951 (quoting Stalin), "'that the multifold phenomena of the world constitute different forms of matter in motion,' and 'that matter is primary, since it is the source of sensations, ideas, mind, and that mind is secondary, derivative, since it is a reflection of matter, a reflection of being.'"[2] How in turn could the labor performed by intellectuals not seem to evade any material placement or definition? Grounded by turns in the social relationships of production and the mind-body split, "labor" gave rise to ambiguities, which in turn subtended fierce and often destructive debates within Marxism, throughout most of the twentieth century, over the status of intellectuals in the socialist movement.

We have already seen, in the cases of Raymond Williams and Edward Thompson, that Marxism's continuing inability to resolve this ancient dualism between mind and body came to figure in the initiative which comprised early British cultural studies. But even Williams and Thompson only sidestepped the problem; they had not yet solved nor even fully faced it. Likewise more generally: Those who struggled in the West to revivify an active Marxian tradition could not break free from this dualistic legacy.

Western Marxism's efforts to move beyond the immediacy of the capital-labor relation, in a summary recap, were informed by a conviction that the economic nature of that relationship was already known.[3] Cut loose for a panoply of reasons from working-class political movements, Western Marxism, as Perry Anderson has argued, from its outset consistently severed political economy from its continuing appraisal of

"culture" and "ideology,"[4] and remained content with capsule totaliza-
tions: "late capitalism," "state capitalism," "the administered society."[5]
Not despite but because of this loose agreement regarding what could be
and, at points, seemingly had to be taken for granted, Western Marxism's attention was redirected toward a series of seemingly strategic
anomalies: What role was being played in 20th-century society by the
processes of "reification"—again, "the petrifaction of living processes
into dead things, which appeared as an alien second nature"[6]—which
seemed so massively to overreach the capital-labor relation? What was
the theoretical standing of the intermediate social strata, the growing
numbers of white-collar workers whose existence increasingly appeared
to interdict the confrontation projected by classical Marxism between
proletariat and bourgeoisie? What did the cultivation of mass consumerism mean for the self-consciousness of the proletariat and, therefore, for
the prospect of revolutionary social transformation? Lying at the core of
Western Marxism, such questions seemed to require that theory veer
ever further away from "labor," which some of this tradition's leading
representatives contemplated, in any case, with a distinct unease.

On one hand, as we will find in the conclusion, Marx's use of
"labor" as providing the basis of human species-being was intermittently reaffirmed. Even so, this category's unifying ontological promise
remained essentially unrealized, again because contemporary social
conditions appeared to have led beyond the categorial apparatus of classical Marxism, thereby engendering a whole series of unbridgeable im-
passes and contradictions. Adorno and Horkheimer, as I mentioned in
an earlier chapter, remained actively suspicious of "labor" for comprising a recrudescence of an ascetic bourgeois sensibility;[7] while Herbert
Marcuse, conceding "labor's" ontological significance, nonetheless
sought to envision a world where "play" would be free to supercede toil
and its associated reality principle; even Georg Lukacs evidently could
not find means of translating his commitment to a "social ontology"
grounded in labor into a comprehensive theorization, spanning "art" as
well as more familiar "material" realms. Alfred Sohn-Rethell, an isolated representative of the tradition, on this point only accentuated
Western Marxism's overall propensity when he insisted that truly to
understand "the enigmatic 'cognitive faculties' of civilised man" required a "complete methodological separation from any consideration
of . . . the role of human labour."[8] The leading result, as we have seen,
was in this instance a protracted diversion into theories of ideology and
mass culture.

It now may be added that, despite other differences, leading Marxist
political economists paradoxically reproduced this same tendency to
dispense with "labor." This again owed chiefly to the difficulties that
seemed to inhere in any attempt to fit the category to the seeming
mutations of contemporary capitalism. Across a broad range, all the way

through the 1960s and 1970s, and stretching from intellectual affiliates of Communist Parties to a variety of "non-aligned" and academic Marxisms, political economic theorists were generally agreed that the labor of white-collar workers was not productive of surplus value.[9] Concerning this question, the structural Marxist Nicos Poulantzas offered an especially uncompromising certitude: "[W]age-earners in commerce, advertising, marketing, accounting, banking and insurance," he asserted in 1974, regarding those whose toil occurred ostensibly within the realm of circulation rather than production; lawyers, doctors, teachers, and other service workers whose labor was said not to be exchanged directly with capital; "the agents of the state apparatuses, the civil servants"; and even, finally, the scientists whose research was "no more directly involved in the process of material production today than it was in the past"—for Poulantzas these manifold forms of what could be classed as mental labor remained, simply, "unproductive."[10]

Albeit basing themselves on different premises, neo-Ricardian political economists went so far as to assail Marxism on its own high ground, with arguments that the Marxian concepts of value and, indeed, of labor, had been rendered obsolete. And Harry Braverman, whose momentous achievement was to resurrect the thesis of white-collar proletarianization by endowing it with a substantive historical content, via a learned focus on the labor process, generally characterized the work of this stratum as unproductive of surplus value.[11]

No matter how extensive a portion of the waged labor force white-collar workers might come to constitute, and no matter how substantial their manifold contributions to the overall process of accumulation, the character and historical significance of their labor therefore could be registered only obliquely. In the mind's eye of Marxian political economy, this hardly condemned mental laborers to exercising a mere residual influence within modern-day capitalism. What it did mean was that their role could be theorized only in light of classical Marxism's prior commitment to the primacy of industrial waged labor. For a second leading variant of Marxist theory, thus, the swelling numbers of white-collar workers visible in the mid-20th-century United States seemed to portend a political-economic metamorphosis, for which valid account might be made only by positing a discontinuous historical stage of "monopoly capitalism." The latter, on this view, could be distinguished by the massively intensified "sales effort," which had been occasioned by capital's increasingly aggravated need to find means of disposing of wholly unprecedented levels of economic surplus. As this sales effort, centering on a host of marketing, design, advertising, and related functions, "reach[ed] back into the process of production"—via such icons of postwar American life as the automobile industry's annual model change—the "necessary costs of production" in turn grew exponentially. Productive and unproductive labor had become so intertwined, in fact, as to be "virtually indistinguishable." Rather than taking this to mean that the entire category of unproductive labor required systematic rethinking, however, the Veblenian inference was to pre-empt such inquiry by declaring instead "that an economic system in which *such* costs are socially necessary has long ceased to be a socially necessary economic system."[12]

With this conclusion, this second brand of Marxist political economy again effectively consigned the question of mental labor to a state of theoretical limbo. The result, as an authority on Marx and the division of labor wrote in 1982, was that "[s]everal different versions of the differentiation between productive and unproductive labour are available in Marx's texts and contemporary Marxists appear to be hopelessly divided as to the real meaning of the distinction or its analytical value."[13] A profoundly significant concomitant of this frustration was the virtual cession, by Marxian political economy, of an elemental—and potentially generative—category. Harry Braverman—certainly the outstanding, though still only partial, exception to this trend—explained that, as a result of this and related diversions, "Marxism became weakest at the very point where it had originally been strongest"—the analysis of the social relations of production.[14] "Labor" ironically became free, in turn, to act as a means by which rival approaches might try to differentiate themselves, even, should the prospect appeal to them, by mounting out-and-out attacks against Marxism.

These encounters therefore almost at once placed Marxism's own fate as a theory at risk. In this quickly changing context, even as Thompson's insistence on the need to engage explicitly with Marx was resoundingly reaffirmed, a torrent of revisionary scholarship quickly overflowed the already-stricken mandate of *May Day Manifesto*. The promise of the inclusive heterodoxy attained during the late 1960s and early 1970s in turn quickly dissipated, and the delicate circuits which, during this brief interval, had begun to be etched between "culture" and social relations were extensively rerouted. Few of the concepts that had governed the earlier revision around "culture"—"experience," "ideology," "totality," and, not least, "culture" itself—escaped the gale. Even as further issues of moment continued to be brought within the compass of thinking about communication, therefore, the terms on which they were assimilated underwent a startling sea change.

The overriding result of this shift was a new set of substitutive conceptions. On one hand, there crystallized a new general position, even an orthodoxy, which tended to permit otherwise fragmenting theorizations around "culture" to indulge a shared view of signifying or communicative practice. No longer was such discursive production to be seen, with Williams, as a neglected activity whose mutually constitutive interrelationships with the economy and politics then could be taken as the prime subject of "culture" and its study. Instead signification was accorded a self-directed and inward-looking character, often verging on a thoroughly reified autonomy. On the other hand, by means of a further fracture of radical effort, discussion of "culture" was momentarily skewed away from an eruptive center of conceptual development— "information." Yet a powerful bond continued to link this pair of disparate revisions; for "postindustrialism," akin to structural Marxism and poststructuralism, again fashioned its own reified identity only through recourse to a confounded understanding of "labor" in general, and of "intellectual" labor in particular. Scrutiny of this convoluted topography commences with the further adventures of "culture."

I

We may begin by turning to look in some detail at the evolving thought of Stuart Hall, who, under the aegis of structural Marxism, during the 1970s made a direct, though finally unrealized, attempt to bring "labor" into cultural studies. Hall's intellectual predispositions impinged substantially on this effort, and these early affinities may be traced in his 1958 discussion of the contemporary "interpenetration of base and superstructure," where he noted that "there are periods when cultural alienation and exploitation become so ramified and complex, that they take on an independent life of their own, and need to be seen and analysed as such."[15] This contemplated flight into a detached dimension of culture avowedly originated in Hall's pessimistic assessment of the character and potential of the British working class. Changes in the capitalist economy, Hall observed in the very first issue of a flagship journal of the New Left (which he then coedited)—changes centering above all on the growth of supervisory jobs in industry, often filled, Hall said, by "young men of talent . . . from the lower-middle class"— were working fundamental changes in attitudes and consciousness. Thus, here is Hall, in 1957: "As Alistair Cook observed, at the time of the 1955 General Election, the result would depend on how many working-class men, looking into their mirrors, saw middle-class faces." For Hall then "[t]he Conservative victory was reply enough." He rechristened the period of structural reform over which the Labour Party had presided between 1945 and 1951 "as the focal point in a challenging new-style middle class revolution."[16] In a provocative article published the following year, Hall fleshed out this assessment. Massive rebuilding programs resulting in transformed physical surroundings; the unprecedented availability of consumer goods and the new spending habits that attended them; and changes in the rhythm and nature of industrial work, above all within "the technological industries," now combined to create a general feeling of "class confusion."[17]

George Orwell had noted in 1941 the growth, during the earlier interwar period, of what he—alongside, as we have seen, many others—

identified as a "new indeterminate class of skilled workers, technical
experts, airmen, scientists, architects and journalists, the people who feel
at home in the radio and ferro-concrete age." Supplying a striking portent of Hall's argument, Orwell had further declared that "older class
distinctions [were] beginning to break down" in the presence of this
new stratum's "restless, cultureless life, centring round tinned food,
Picture Post, the radio and the internal combustion engine."[18] But the
disruptive and bewildering "sense of classlessness" emphasized by Hall
was also a correlative of the estrangement that came with the radicals'
recognition that no resurgent economic slump was about to plunge
society back into depression.

In the 1950s context, Hall's argument comprised a direct reprise of
the mass culture thesis. With anchoring references to Riesman, Mills,
and, above all, Hoggart, Hall conferred the accustomed leading role on
"'the mass media[,]' . . . advertising and culture" in preparing members of the working class "for new and more subtle forms of enslave-
ment" by making them accessories to "their own . . . exploitation."
And Hall, unlike Williams during this early phase, directly employed a
Marxian vocabulary to pinpoint once again the growing need to emphasize nonmanual activity:

> Every form of communication which is concerned with altering attitudes,
> which changes or confirms opinions, which instils new images of the self, is
> playing its part. They are not peripheral to the "economic base": they are
> part of it.[19]

"The gap between the rising standard of living of the skilled worker
and the casino holidays of the very rich is bridged not in the real world,
but in dreams," Hall wrote two years later in an article entitled, again
portentously, "The Supply of Demand." The sole concession to
Williams's emphasis on an unabating differential in class subjectivities
was hidden within parentheses: "The Press and the mass media, which
(whenever we are off our guard) shape our consciousness of the society
in which we live, continually feed and nourish these fantasies. . . ."[20]
Hall's penchant for the characteristic arguments proffered by theorists of
mass culture continued, without interruption, into the late 1960s, when
he relied substantially on Herbert Marcuse in a survey of the American
youth movement.[21]

The divide that thereby opened between Hall and Williams notably
did *not* center on whether the mass media were capable of potent effects.
"The existence of immensely powerful media of mass-communication,"
declared Williams already in 1958, was "at the heart" of the problems of
contemporary democracy—for, through these media, "public opinion
has been observably moulded and directed, often by questionable
means, often for questionable ends."[22] The "stylish consumer society"
pulling toward a "new form of capitalism" was, rather—as Williams

later put it—best apprehended as a process of "options under pressure."[23] With this characterization, we reach the heart of the perspectival clash that framed the two writers' early efforts, though without eroding their continuing mutual regard and sustained intellectual and political cooperation.[24] For Hall, as we have already seen, harbored a significant contrasting urge to make the media themselves his analytical fulcrum.

It was, however—and significantly—Hall who initially tried to negotiate this divergence, for Williams's position as yet could be neither dispensed with nor dislodged. After a somewhat strained attempt at incorporating Williams's protest against abuses of the term "masses," therefore, Hall nonetheless emphasized that "consumer capitalism" had become skillful at "producing the consumer" through "persuasive manipulation." Again the overlap with later fashions within cultural studies is already palpable: "When we speak of 'communications' in a consumer society, we have to think . . . of how other people speak *at* us." And, perhaps responding to the critical responses provoked by his earlier assertions about classlessness, Hall now qualified his argument by invoking Hoggart: "[W]hat should be taking our attention is not the smooth shift to middle-class attitudes, but the coarsening and loss of working-class values when faced with the appeals to individualism and selfishness of a revived, status-conscious capitalism." At issue, he said, artfully staking his argument also to Williams, was "the whole notion of community responsibility"; the current crisis was one that existed "in the psychology of the working class itself, and therefore, in extension of that . . . in the Labour Movement."

The bromides being handed round by 1950s Labour leaders provoked Hall, however, to a revealing fury: "Has the Labour Movement come through the fire and brimstone of the last fifty years to lie down and die before the glossy magazines? Has Labour no sense of the capacities, the potential of a society, more various, more skilled, more literate, less cramped and confined, less beaten down and frustrated? So that now, we are going to fade away in front of the telly and the 'frig.?"[25] Such a public show of frustration has no parallel in Williams, and surely symptomatized Hall's continuing attempt to comprehend what appeared to him to be Britain's specifically ideological blockages and deformations via forms of freestanding cultural criticism.

A work Hall coauthored with Paddy Whannel in 1964 originated in a more widespread concern over the impact of popular culture in the schools; its terms of engagement pronounced that "the struggle between what is good and worth while and what is shoddy and debased is not a struggle *against* the modern forms of communication, but a conflict *within* these media."[26] Therefore, they went on, "the distinction which we want to make is based not on the institutions but on the quality of the work done within them."[27] Elaborating:

We often write and speak as if the new media—the cinema, television, radio, record, popular printed matter—had simply extended the means available for communicating between groups of people. Had this been true, their impact on our social life would have been far less direct than it has turned out to be. But when the means of communication are extended on this scale the development cannot be judged in simple quantitative terms. People are brought together in a new relationship as audiences, new kinds of language and expression are developed, independent art forms and conventions arise. The media are not the end-products of a simple technological revolution. They come at the end of a complex historical and social process, they are active agents in a new phase in the life-history of industrial society. Inside these forms and languages, the society is articulating new social experiences for the first time.[28]

This inward turn toward media "forms and languages" was already differentiated by an aversion to any supposed too-thoroughgoing reliance on political economy: "It is a mistake of some left-wing critics of the mass media to suppose that a change in ownership, organization and control will solve all our problems. No doubt such changes are necessary, but unless they are accompanied by some greater concern for the experiences that art and entertainment have to offer we shall find that we have changed the form while the substance remains the same."[29] True, this might be read as an utterly level-headed criticism of the postwar settlement and, specifically, of the terms on which significant segments of British industry had been nationalized. It might be equally well understood as a criticism of the culture of Soviet socialism. In the context of Hall's and Whannel's work, however—which comprised a virtuoso demonstration of the applicability of critical procedures to "the popular arts" in postwar Britain—it is unmistakably dismissive.

Emphasized are not collective social relationships, but individual fulfillment and alienation. While the media's institutional underpinnings receive minimal scrutiny, for example—this, too, exactly as commercial broadcasting was making determined inroads into Britain—a bow in the other direction concedes far more, surely, than was needed to "the Tradition": "No system can guarantee either freedom or cultural health. Ultimately it is our quality as individuals that will count."[30] Hall and Whannel likewise skipped over Williams's arguments about social class, thereby obscuring the basis of his demand to force back what they termed "an exclusive tradition denying people access to what should be part of the common life." Reverting to the very language of "high and low" that Williams was arguing should be jettisoned, they insisted rather that "the radical aims at a common culture based on a community in which the culture at the top is a more refined, more articulated expression of the values shared by all."[31]

As late as 1971, Hall's predilection for "forms and languages" finds a closely equivalent expression in his concern with how, immediately before and during the Second World War, "the conditions were created which enabled a historical experience directly to inform a style" of photojournalism: a "socially-structured 'way of seeing'" that he termed "the social eye." In the British journal touched on by Orwell, *Picture Post,* Hall observed, this "collective social experience and the formation of a distinctive 'social eye' reciprocally informed and determined each other." *Picture Post's* documentarists thus "returned to their readers their own experience, augmented by the resources of popular journalism and photography; augmented—and of course transformed."[32] This subsumption of "experience" or "social consciousness" in "style" *within Picture Post* is both consistent and prefigurative of what shortly was to become a more overtly powerful intellectual current:

> The documentary style, though at one level, a *form* of writing, photographing, filming, recording, was, at another level, an emergent form of social consciousness: it registered, in the formation of a social rhetoric, the emergent structure of feeling in the immediate pre-war, and the war, periods. Here, once again, we encounter that fateful nexus where the subject-matter and content of historical experience, the revolutionary development of the means of reproduction, and—in response—the evolving forms and styles of collective social perception made a striking rendevous.[33]

"Forms and languages" here remained tightly interwoven with Williams's expressive totality, a concept which, as we found, had already been placed under mounting strain. A climactic intellectual "break" was, however, already imminent. Paradoxically underscoring the continuities within Hall's own work, Althusser's Marxist structuralism nevertheless afforded him distinctly new grounds for reasserting his longstanding commitment to the thesis of an overarching social discontinuity—a discontinuity, moreover, whose basis could be lodged with seeming newfound rigor in "culture" or "ideology." Through the prism of structural Marxism, therefore, Hall was enabled to resolve cultural studies' concerted emphasis on social experience, including working-class experience, into what appeared to be its own unique and brilliant hue.

II

Among the "dislocations" in British society identified by Hall's group in its premier collective work of the 1970s, *Policing the Crisis,* there might have been noted a series of dislocations in *theory.*[34] These emanated, in the first place, from the growing reservations which I have noted concerning the category of "experience." Williams's earlier formulations fell too largely, Hall now definitively concluded, within what he characterized as an "empiricist relationship to knowledge," which "assumes that social relations give their own, unambiguous knowledge to perceiving, thinking subjects; that there is a transparent relationship between the situations in which subjects are placed and how subjects come to recognize and know about them."[35] The fissure was, moreover, enduring. Hall noted in 1980 that he "continue[d] to take issue" with Williams on the latter's unrecalcitrant appeal to "experience." An "uninspected notion of 'experience,'" Hall charged, had produced what he now considered to be a "quite unsatisfactory concept": "the structure of feeling" (an idea which, we have seen, Hall himself had utilized as late as 1972). Although Williams had since gone on, as we will see in the conclusion of this work, to reconceive "experience" as "indissoluble elements of a continuous social-material process," this more recent formulation still retained, Hall thought, "disabling theoretical effects":

> I do think that the indissolubility of practices in the ways in which they are experienced and "lived," in any real historical situation, does not in any way pre-empt the *analytic* separations of them, when one is attempting to theorise their different effects. The ways in which everything appears to interconnect in "experience" can only be a starting point for analysis. One has to "produce the concrete in thought"—that is, show, by a series of analytic approximations through abstraction, the concrete historical experience as the "product of many determinations." Analysis must deconstruct the "lived wholeness" in order to be able to think its determinate conditions. I believe this necessary use of abstraction in thought is quite mistakenly confused, in current debates, with a sort of "fetishisation of theory" (theoreticism, of course, exists, and is a plague on all our houses: but so is empiricism). . . . However one attempts to displace the plenitude which the term "experience" confers, and however much one allows for "marked disparities" and "temporal unevenesss," so long as "experience" continues to play this all-embracing role, there will be an inevitable theoretical pull towards reading all structures as if they expressively correlated with one another: simultaneous in effect and determinacy because they are simultaneous in our experience.[36]

In contrast, Hall himself held, "structures can be temporally simultaneous, but they need not thereby be causally equal." A chief virtue of this sharply distinct and formidable new theorization—again, we are now in the mid-1970s—was that it appeared to offer a valid means by which to accommodate within Marxism "the irreducible heterogeneity of the material world."[37] Gaining admittance to high theory via structural Marxism, the manifold contradictions which so evidently laced through contemporary capitalism—above all, those of "race" and "gender"—were now reconstituted so as to pose an explicitly theorized response to the "expressive totality" which we have seen animated Williams's early cultural studies.

Hall's own erstwhile supposition, as we also found, had been that through its encounter with mass culture, the working class was being tamed and reincorporated. His emergent focus, in contrast, not only allowed for marked social class antagonism—which, during the early 1970s in Britain hardly could be denied—but also vested in the latters' encounter a vitally indeterminate ideological potential. Classes, following the architect of structural Marxism, Louis Althusser, were no longer to be seen as "historical givens" whose unity was "already given by their position in the economic structure." Instead, as Hall agreed, they should be understood "only as the complex result of the successful prosecution of different forms of social struggle at all the levels of social practice, including the ideological."[38] In declarations far bolder and more explicit than any Williams chose to offer,[39] Hall now regularly echoed structural Marxism's axiomatic endorsement of economic determination. It was, however, not the least significant aspect of this torturous theory, that such affirmations served mainly to permit the "social formation" to be apprehended increasingly through what it termed the "instance" of "ideology." Hall in turn soon reconciled Althusser's Marxism with what we have seen was his own prior preference for just such a differentiated dimension. The character of "ideology" indeed quickly attained a paramount importance; Hall himself came to hail the concept as "the basis of all our subsequent work" in media studies.[40]

How could this happen? Of what stuff was this "relatively autonomous" ideological medium made? To address this issue requires a further venture into the thickets of structural Marxism.

The latter's strenuous procedure was to fashion a pedigree for its doctrines by tracing them back to a very particular Marx; Althusser and his colleagues boasted self-importantly of the need "to read *Capital* to the letter . . . line by line."[41] The product of this engagement was nowhere more striking than in Althusser's often-quoted dictum concerning "superstructures," which placed the mass media in the company of the state, the family, law, religion, and education:

> . . . the economic dialectic is never active in the pure state; in History, these instances, the superstructures, etc.—are never seen to step respectfully aside when their work is done or, when the Time comes, as his pure phenomena, to scatter before His Majesty the Economy as he strides along the royal road of the Dialectic.[42]

Althusser thus also posited that these "largely . . . autonomous, and therefore irreducible" superstructures possessed their own "specific efficacy."[43] The relative autonomy of each instance or level of the social totality—economic, political, and ideological—in turn meant that each such domain of "practice" could be legitimately considered "as a *partial whole*', and become the object of a relatively independent scientific treatment."[44] Like the kindred economic and political instances, finally, "ideology" was also taken to comprise "an objective reality, indispensable to the existence of a social formation . . . that is, a reality independent of the subjectivity of the individuals who are subject to it. . . ."[45]

"Ideology" was sustained, then, by conscious or unconscious "adherence to an ensemble of representations and beliefs—religious, moral, legal, political, aesthetic, philosophical, etc."[46]

"Ideology" thereby also wrenched away from conceptions, notably the radical variant of mass culture theory, which continued to equate it with an instrumental manipulation, whose intention and effect were to instill acquiescence to social domination. Ideology's role in social reproduction was rather redirected toward "experience," across its great range. It became "a matter of the lived relation between men and their world" or, again, " . . . *the way* they live the relation between them and their conditions of existence":[47]

> The representations of ideology thus consciously or unconsciously accompany all the acts of individuals, all their activity, and all their relations—like so many landmarks and reference points, laden with prohibitions, permissions, obligations, submissions and hopes. If one represents society according to Marx's classic metaphor—as an edifice, a building, where the juridico-political *superstructure* rests upon the infrastructure of economic foundations—ideology must be accorded a very particular place. In order to understand its kind of effectivity, it must be situated in the *superstructure* and assigned a relative autonomy vis-a-vis law and the State; but at the same time, to understand its most general form of presence, ideology must be thought of as sliding into all the parts of the edifice, and considered as a distinctive kind of *cement* that assures the adjustment and cohesion of men in their roles, their functions and their social relations.
>
> In fact, ideology permeates all man's activities, including his economic and political practice; it is present in attitudes towards work, towards the agents of production, towards the constraints of production, in the idea that the worker has of the mechanism of production; it is present in political judgements and attitudes—cynicism, clear conscience, resignation or revolt, etc.; it governs the conduct of individuals in families and their behaviour towards others, their attitude towards nature, their judgement on "the meaning of life" in general, their different cults (God, the prince, the State, etc.). Ideology is so much present in all the acts and deeds of individuals that it is *indistinguishable from their ''lived experience,''* and every unmediated analysis of the "lived" is profoundly marked by the themes of ideological obviousness.[48]

Much has been made of the fact that Althusser's conception pulled in two contrary directions: on one hand, toward consideration of a resisting subjectivity, and, on the other hand, toward a resurgent concern with the ingrained capacity to equip subjects, as Eagleton has put it, "with the forms of consciousness necessary for them to assume their 'posts' or functions within material production."[49] But, while each pole—resistant or oppositional subjectivity, as against a dominated subjection[50]—became a site of heated debate and prolific revision within a refocused cultural studies, the momentous gap that emerged between "ideology" and "economy," via structural Marxism's so-called "relative autonomy" of instances, survived as a ubiquitous intellectual feature.

Structural Marxism's rationale for the abstraction of a separate "ideological"—or, soon thereafter, of a "cultural" or "signifying"— dimension, lay in its promise of a successive moment of synthetic totalization. Seeking to break with the inadequate concept of totality that he justly believed predominated within contemporary Marxism, thereby fatally compromising the latter's validity, Althusser held that the distinct instances—again, "ideological," "political," and "economic"—had to be reunited, without reduction, in a complex totality in which economic practice was "determinant in the last instance" but in which, nonetheless, the ideological level might be structurally "dominant." Hall accepted this pathbreaking revision, and himself sought to ground it in Marx's method and epistemology. By means of a closely reasoned exegesis of a newly translated text, Hall detected convincing proof that Marx himself had, at least in 1857, subscribed to the proposition that four distinct "moments"—comprising production, distribution, exchange, and consumption—remained analytically distinct within a complex totality. Hall was able to reason from this that, "in the examination of any phenomenon or relation, we must comprehend both its internal structure—what it is in its differentiatedness—as well as those other structures to which it is coupled and with which it forms some more inclusive totality. Both the specificities and the connections—the complex unities of structures—have to be demonstrated by the concrete analysis of concrete relations and conjunctions."[51]

How well honored was this crucial stricture, for whose exegesis Hall must indeed be given credit?[52] Its true virtues, we will find, remained too often unrealized and, indeed, even unrecognized; because Althusser's complex social totality continued to harbor a crippling dualism, which effectively prevented the assimilation of all of its own constituent terms within a single coherent system. Yet, paradoxically, structural Marxism's category of "ideology" sought to refute such an imputation of dualism by its seemingly rigorous appeal to the moment of production. Its singular esteem for "intellectual" labor—inherited from structuralism proper, but now often rechristened "theoretical practice"—formed the hub of these difficulties.

The promise of Althusser's complex social totality, for Hall, surely lay also in the prospect it offered of reuniting, or at least not dichotomizing, "labor" and "language." During the mid-1970s, Hall acknowledged an overarching need for "a materialist . . . definition of culture" whose "originating premise" lodged "the foundation of human culture in labour and material production."[53] He even acceded to Engels's famous declaration regarding the primary role of "labour, [and] after it and then with it, speech," in the evolutionary transition from ape to

man.[54] This admirable effort to situate "culture" in reference to a concept of labor[55] was inflected—but not effaced—by Hall's customary
stress on language: "Human culture . . . is not a 'knowledge' which is
abstractly stored in the head. It is materialized in production, embodied
in social organization, advanced through the development of practical as
well as theoretical technique; above all, preserved in and transmitted
through *language.*"[56]

It may be easily forgotten that Hall's was but one of many noteworthy attempts during the late 1960s and 1970s to place "labor" higher up
on the agenda of formal social study. One thinks, for example, of Harry
Braverman's masterpiece, *Labor and Monopoly Capital,* with its sustained
and innovative treatment of the historical separation of conception from
execution within the labor process, and its powerful impact on the field
of sociology; and one recalls as well the plethora of historical studies
guided by David Montgomery's *Workers' Control in America.*[57] And what
of the other proximate attempts to link "labor" directly to communication, Vincent Mosco's programmatic assimilation of the labor process as
a central category for the theorization of communication in contemporary capitalism, for example?[58] Equally promising was a fledgling tradition of sociological analysis of media production processes. In Britain
such work had originated during the late 1960s, with a book-length
study by researchers at Leicester University of press coverage of a major
demonstration against the Vietnam War; for around a decade the work
carried through in a series of revealing analyses, undertaken by Philip
Elliott, Peter Golding, Paul Hartmann, Graham Murdock, Philip Schlesinger, Jeremy Tunstall, and others, of news and documentary production in the press and television.[59] Then, too, we may remember Dallas
Smythe's attempt to join "communication" to "production" by resituat-
ing the process of commercial media audience reception within the category of labor.[60] Disparate revisionary linkages between productive activity and signification were likewise being pursued by poststructuralists
such as Jean Baudrillard[61] and by Raymond Williams; these last two
attempts find further explication in subsequent portions of this book.

Within this larger matrix, the distinctive attempt of the Althusserian
Marxism on which Hall drew was to seek a special warrant for the
scientific enterprise. Althusser viewed science as a determinate social
labor, "distinct from other practices."[62] But the place ascribed by him to
science, or theory, within the totality went well beyond this legitimate
differentiation. Althusser explicitly sought to ground theory in terms of
"intellectual" labor's putative contribution to a revolutionary transformation of society. "For intellectuals, scientists or literary specialists, the
question takes a precise form," he declared in 1967: "What place does
our activity occupy in the world, what role does it play? What are we as
intellectuals in this world?"[63] His answer was to confer on intellectuals a
putatively independent, even a superordinate, function within the revo-

lutionary socialist process: "[T]*he working class cannot, by its own re-sources, radically liberate itself from bourgeois ideology,*" Althusser pro-claimed. "For 'spontaneous' working-class ideology to transform itself to the point of freeing itself from bourgeois ideology it must *receive, from without, the help of science. . . .*"[64] "[E]verything"—and this particular "everything," of course, carried great gravity—"depends on the *transfor-mation of the ideology of the working class, on the transformation which can extricate working-class ideology from the influence of bourgeois ideology and submit it to a new influence—that of the Marxist science of society.*"[65]

No matter how justified by the need to think about the diverse forms of signification as determinate practices in their own right, this scientistic tenet, which reiterated Lenin's dictum that the task of intellectuals was to introduce Marxist science into proletarian practice "from without,"[66] this conception of science *also* introduced into radical social theory a crucial feature drawn from structuralism proper. Implicit within the idea of "theoretical practice"—or, sometimes, "theoretical labour"—was, to be sure, "a material history, [which] includes among its determinant conditions and elements non-theoretical practices (economic, politi-cal and ideological) and their results." Pride of place, nevertheless, Althusser explicitly and repeatedly reserved for thought's own "internal relations" and for the supposedly rigorous "fixing" of theoretical mean-ing "by the relations between theoretical concepts within a conceptual system."[67] Here "theoretical practice" evidently shared a vital common property with what was, for Althusser, its unscientific antagonist—ideological practice:

> Ideology comprises representations, images, signs, etc., but these elements considered in isolation from each other, do not compose ideology. It is their systematicity, their mode of arrangement and combination, that gives them their meaning; it is their structure that determines their meaning and func-tion.[68]

Althusser claimed to have revealed a Marx who, upon comprehend-ing the massive error of his early Hegelian ways, therewith broke irre-versibly with humanism and its categories—chief among which was the "anthropological ideology of labour" which was equated with the es-sence of human species-being, of which we will soon hear more—in order to undertake the astringent "theoretical practice" required by a fully scientific analysis of modes of production:[69]

> . . . we regard what is commonly called theory, in its "purest" forms, those that seem to bring into play the powers of thought alone (e.g., mathe-matics of philosophy), leaving aside any direct relation to "concrete prac-tice," as a practice in the strict sense, as scientific or theoretical practice, itself divisible into several branches (the different sciences, mathematics, philosophy). This practice is theoretical; it is distinguished from the other, nontheoretical practices, by the type of object (raw material) which it trans-

forms; by the type of means of production it sets to work, by the type of object it produces (knowledges).[70]

In short, as Martin Jay summarizes, for Althusser, "theoretical production was carried out within theory itself."[71] Theoretical practice was a process of production whose "product" was ostensibly "knowledges," created and assembled out of a unique "raw material"—facts and concepts.[72]

We have it on the authority of Althusser himself that this theorization was infused with a "most unusual *structuralism.*"[73] It was from structuralism, in turn, that he imported what Frederick Newmayer calls "the autonomous approach to linguistics,"[74] and gave it a seemingly rigorous Marxist warrant. Fredric Jameson drew the proper conclusion over two decades ago: "For Althusser, in a sense, we never really get outside our own minds: both ideology and genuine philosophical investigation, or what he calls 'theoretical practice,' run their course in the sealed chamber of the mind." In this system, as Jameson insightfully adds, "materialism is thus preserved by an insistence on the essentially idealistic character of all thinking."[75] The paradoxical hallmark of Althusser's effort to merge theoretical and ideological practices into the thriving corpus of contemporary thinking about labor was, all protestations notwithstanding,[76] a presumption that cognition subsists within a pristine and self-enclosed zone.

Within Britain, a historian and a historically minded critic took increasingly pointed issue with this formulation. At the far end of the 1970s, Edward Thompson's fiery and often trenchant book-length denunciation of Althusser's "orrery of errors" subjected his structuralist assumptions to a masterful rhetorical decapitation.[77] Less well known, however, is that Raymond Williams found that he could take the measure of his own evolving theorization—a point to which I return in the conclusion—by means of a sharp distinction with Althusser's structural Marxism. Across its putatively extended range, neither "ideology" nor, certainly, "superstructures," Williams asserted, could validly substitute for the sweepingly synthetic totality of experience whose employment in *The Long Revolution,* though it might indeed now require significant revision, remained for him absolute. "[T]he only thing right" about the attempt made by the "theory of Ideology" to link "art" with "mass communication," and other practices, wrote Williams unequivocally in 1976, "is the realization that the theoretically separated 'areas' have to be brought within a single discourse. The main error of this solution is that it substitutes Ideology, with its operative functions in segments, codes and texts, for the complex social relations within which a significant range of activities, in a significant range of situations, were being at once expressed, produced and altered. . . ."[78] Williams's acute and hard-edged reaction to Marxist structuralism—which helped him, as we will see in the conclusion, to drive toward an overarching revision of his own—took direct aim at the latter's truncating effort to substitute "a theory of ideology . . . for both culture and experience."[79] "[I]f ideology is a major reference-point, or even point of origin . . . it is difficult . . . to know what is left for all other social processes."

> To say that all cultural practice is "ideological" need mean no more than that (as in some other current uses) all practice is signifying. For all the difficulties of overlap with other more common uses, this sense is acceptable. But it is very different from describing all cultural production as "ideology," or as "directed by ideology," because what is then omitted, as in the idealist uses of "culture," is the set of complex real processes by which a "culture" or an "ideology" is itself produced. And it is with these productive processes that a full sociology of culture is necessarily concerned.[80]

Yet what became the mainstream of cultural studies programmatically ignored these substantial rebukes. Quoting Althusser, Hall instead took over exactly the same idea of practice, as "any process of transformation of a determinate raw material into a determinate product, a transformation effected by a determinate human labour, using determinate means (of 'production')."[81] It was his acceptance of this pivotal but fatally problematic doctrine—that signification itself comprised a self-enclosed practice—which in turn barred Hall from continuing further with the effort to reconcile "labor" and "language."

"Knowledge, whether ideological or scientific, is the production of a practice," Hall would write, integrating Althusser with the early Roland Barthes: "It is not the reflection of the real in discourse, in language. Social relations have to be 'represented in speech and language' to acquire meaning. Meaning is produced as a result of ideological or theoretical work."[82] Signification, more precisely, again involved nothing other than its own "determinate form of labour, a specific 'work': the work of meaning production. . . ." The latter, in Hall's scheme, did not much lend itself to analysis as a "social practice"; critical researchers who sought to liken the labor of media production to that employed in the production of other sorts of commodities were barking up the wrong tree.[83] Indeed what needed highlighting beyond this, Hall further asserted, was actually "what distinguishes discursive 'production' from other types of production in our society and in modern media systems."[84] Hall even hazarded that the process of meaning construction was not only distinct from but also anterior and superordinate to, for example, motor car production: in this case, at least, "the exchange and use values depend on the symbolic value which the message contains. The symbolic character of the practice is the dominant element although not the only one."[85]

Leave aside for now this assertion (with its nod toward contemporary work by Baudrillard) that "symbolic value" dominates the exchange and use values of cultural commodities. This was merely symptomatic of the more elemental displacement which transpired through the assumption that, despite its standing as a form of "labor," "culture"—and, in a reciprocally defining variant which we must soon examine, "information"—because it has its own "specificity," must be held to exist in self-determining isolation from the rules and practices which structure other kinds of production. Because for Althusser's Marxism they purportedly eventuated in "discursive objects," just as, under the different name of white-collar work they had for C. Wright Mills, signifying practices were to be seen as categorically different from "other modern labour processes."[86] Even years later, after having shed other trappings of Althusserian Marxism, Hall continued to assert flatly that "[i]deology has its own modality, its own ways of working and its own forms of struggle."[87]

What evidence did Hall furnish, what justification, to support this foundational claim that the labor of signification is not only distinct, but categorically self-enclosed and inward-looking, because its product is ostensibly equally sharply differentiated from the products created by other kinds of labor? None—*none*—is offered. Yet both premises—that signifying practice results in a unique species of "discursive object," and that the production of ideology is a unique type of labor—are essentially and aggressively exclusionary. Exactly how far and in what ways are discursive objects "different" from other products? Can such a difference merely be presumed? Why, on the other hand, should the most salient property of the ideological labor process be taken as that which serves, precisely, to detach it from other social relations of production?[88] Perhaps, on the contrary, it is the similarities, overlaps, and correspondences that it evinces with other labor processes which help to mark a distinct ideological labor process as significant. Or perhaps, as Hall himself sometimes allowed, an ideological aspect should be looked for in labor processes in general. Merely because meaning "is not the reflection of the real," in short, patently need not require that it be produced within an independent dimension of signification, over which jurisdiction is exercised by self-determining generative principles.

The terms on which Hall attempted to shore up his argument in the face of the subsequent post-structuralist dismissal of any nondiscursive social field revealed both his own reservations about, and the ultimate damage wrought by, the growing effort to privilege signification, whether as "forms and languages" or as "ideology":

> The designation of ideologies as "systems of representation" acknowledges their essentially discursive and semiotic character. Systems of representation are the systems of meaning through which we represent the world to ourselves and one another. It acknowledges that ideological knowledge is the result of specific practices—the practices involved in the production of

meaning. But since there are no social practices which take place outside the domain of meaning (semiotic), are *all* practices simply discourses?

Here we have to tread very carefully. . . . It does not follow that because all practices are *in* ideology, or inscribed by ideology, all practices are *nothing but* ideology. There is a specificity to those practices whose principal object is to produce ideological representations. They are different from those practices which—meaningfully, intelligibly—produce other commodities. Those people who work in the media are producing, reproducing and transforming the field of ideological representation itself. They stand in a different relationship to ideology in general from those who are producing and reproducing the world of material commodities—which are, nevertheless, also inscribed by ideology. Barthes observed long ago that all things are also significations. The latter forms of practice operate in ideology but they are not ideological in terms of the specificity of their object.[89]

Hall frontally rejected poststructuralism's claim that "there is nothing to social practice *but* discourse."[90] Yet his effort at rebuttal was marred by a profound concession, which had previously escaped overt acknowledgment.[91] Charging that those who subscribed to the idea that discourse was the only social practice were exhibiting a "mechanical materialism," Hall now was forced back on the argument that poststructuralists invalidly sought to "abolish the mental character . . . [and] the real effects—of mental events (i.e., thought)."[92] Notwithstanding its admirable concern to defend the idea of an active and consequential subjectivity, this admission still provided a telling glimpse of just how selective had been Hall's own rendering of the work of "representation." The latter simply threatened to lapse into an artifact of the prevailing—dominative—division of labor. Hall thus specifically ignored the fact that the prime locus of ideological production—"those people who work in the media"—necessarily comprises not only different kinds of storytellers, but also engineers and blue-collar technicians. What better index of Hall's reification of "intellectual" labor could be found? Within his account of the process of "ideological" construction, technical labor is accorded no standing whatever. This can hardly be accidental. For were the contribution of technical labor not to be elided, where could the line between mental and manual labor be drawn? How in turn could the ostensibly "differentiated" character of signification, representation, knowledge as production, be salvaged? Hall's endeavor to privilege what he now called "representation" therefore ultimately fell prey to the same affliction that inhered in Althusser's notion of "theoretical practice." Martin Jay's apt pronouncement regarding Althusser thus may be validly extended to Hall, for in both thinkers the "characteristic bourgeois distinction between mental and manual labor of exchange-oriented societies was thus valorized rather than undermined."[93]

This ascription of supposed inherent singularity to the labor of representation—Hall's unabating exceptionalist premise—meant that, fully a century after the arguments made by Joseph Dietzgen and Baptist Hubert, the theoretical unclarity of "intellectual" labor remained both fundamental and damaging. It is ironic that Hall, who increasingly proclaimed an allegiance to the thinking of Antonio Gramsci, found himself on the wrong side of Gramsci's own famous declaration regarding this very question:

> Can one find a unitary criterion to characterize equally all the diverse and disparate activities of intellectuals and to distinguish these at the same time and in an essential way from the activities of other social groupings? The most widespread error of method seems to me that of having looked for this criterion of distinction in the intrinsic nature of intellectual activities, rather than in the ensemble of the system of relations in which these activities (and therefore the intellectual groups who personify them) have their place within the general complex of social relations.[94]

It would be unfair, however, to assert flatly that Hall sought to reinvent cultural studies around a putatively self-enclosed, reified process of signification. He rather sought to reinforce and extend structuralism's characteristic grant of an unbridgeable autonomy to what cultural studies also increasingly apprehended as proto-linguistic domains. If the "weakness" of earlier relevant perspectives had been "their tendency to *dissolve* the cultural back into society and history," Hall explained in 1980,

> structuralism's main emphasis was on the specificity, the irreducibility, of the cultural. Culture no longer simply reflected other practices in the realm of ideas. It was itself a practice—a *signifying* practice—and had its own determinate product: meaning. To think of the specificity of the cultural was to come to terms with what defined it, in structuralism's view, as a practice: its internal forms and relations, its internal structuration. It was—following Saussure, Jakobsen and the other structural linguists—the way elements were selected, combined and articulated in language which "signified."[95]

Although Hall characteristically insisted on a critical distance from structuralism proper, he never relinquished this seemingly cogent catchphrase, "the specificity of the cultural." What, then, comprised the substantial content of this fundamental term?

In the space developed and occupied by Hall's variant of cultural studies, any claim that the "specificity of the cultural" itself might require scrutiny to be paid to culture's economic status was becoming the sine qua non of a purported "reductionism"—and thus an idea off-limits to aspirants to theoretical knowledge (or, soon thereafter, simply "Theory"). In a striking instance of what had been a right-wing argument passing into left-wing parlance, instrumental and political economic schools of radical thought were often combatively charged with exactly this reduction. But what actually transpired was a rather different, reciprocal process. Thompson wrote, in a 1977 discussion of Christopher Caudwell, "of a phenomenon repeatedly witnessed within bourgeois culture: that is, the repeated generation of idealism and mechanical materialism, not as true antagonists but as pseudo-antitheses, generated as twins in the same moment of conception, or, rather, as positive and negative aspects of the same fractured moment of thought."[96] For communication and cultural studies during the mid-1970s, no conception of social totality, seemingly, could be retained absent a resurgent dualism between "political economy" and its compensatory rival, "signification." The resulting dualism was to remain predominant down to the present, and, in the next section of this chapter, I will have reason to present a further indication of its significance for a separating pole of study around "information."

For the moment, it is more important to trace the significance of this dichotomizing instinct within cultural studies. Here, as Lawrence Grossberg has recently conceded, there was betrayed a heightening tendency to reduce "human reality to the plane of meaning"; "questions about the effects of the materialities which exist 'outside the sphere of the discursive'" were habitually "bracket[ed]."[97] The practical consequence of acquiescence to a self-enclosed domain of "mental" labor was a marked tendency, not least in Hall's efforts to apprehend contemporary Britain through the lens of "Thatcherism,"[98] to exaggerate "ideology's" domain of effectivity. Reference might come to be made to a series of arresting economic changes—as in the eventual assimilation of "Post-Fordism" by the New Times project, to which Hall was a major contributor—but these could not eventuate in a revival of the economic as a category of specific relevance for "culture" itself. Sundered from other processes of production, signification—properly credited with being "a real and positive social force"—veered off as an increasingly self-determining generative principle.[99]

Instead, British cultural studies began to sanction an often bellicose denial of standing to *anything* that could not be apprehended primarily in terms of a seemingly self-sufficient signifying practice. Sometimes this trend was expressed through a forthright insistence on the primacy of forms of communication, alongside an equally explicit refusal to situate meaning within any environing social field. Sometimes it took a milder guise, as in John Fiske's declaration that "meanings are the most important part of our social structure."[100] Either way, the full range of productive activity, which was to remain of vital importance for Williams and others who challenged the classic model of base and superstructure, was severely truncated. Whether economic activities were to be selectively reassimilated or, rather, rhetorically dispatched, seemed increasingly a matter of mere preference.[101] In turn "culture's" growing autonomization countenanced, even invited, attempts to confer upon signification

the axial role in organizing the entire social process, ironically, notwithstanding that such attempts themselves sometimes supplied objects of
animadversion (and even of self-definition) for some of the denizens of
the Centre for Contemporary Cultural Studies. Hall's project, in turn,
defines the limiting case, never sliding over into a full-fledged cultural
autonomism, but portending, as Williams and Thompson had feared,
just such a slippage.

The singular ambivalence that continued to typify British cultural
studies during the 1970s is apparent, for example, in the treatment Hall
accorded to language. During the mid-1970s, theories of language garnered intensive critical scrutiny at the Centre for Contemporary Cultural
Studies. Some members of the group, including Hall himself, tried to
place themselves at a distance from structuralism proper, by seeking to
accredit Volosinov's "Marxist linguistics" as a rival theory, as they put it,
"in opposition to Saussurean linguistics." Relying on Volosinov as well
as Althusser, Hall leveled a battery of cogent criticisms at the near-
hermetic theorizations which were even then being pyramided atop
Saussure by a variety of French thinkers.[102] Yet, although Hall also
cautiously suggested that ideology and language should not be treated as
identical,[103] and even conceded in 1980 that there existed an "immensely powerful pull towards idealism in Cultural Studies,"[104] the
hold exercised over theory by structuralist conceptions of language was
such that Hall could arrive at no thoroughgoing alternative formulation.
Thus Hall never freed his thought from a somewhat contradictory assertion "that the elaboration of ideology found in language (broadly conceived) its proper and privileged sphere of articulation."[105] Instead he
contented himself with carving out within Althusser's complex social
totality an ambivalent space, in which one might remain free to assail
selectively the self-enclosed conceptions of language that began to proliferate, but still without overturning the governing interpretive "problematic" within which they were encased.

Under Hall's direction British cultural studies took its programmatic
warrant from Althusser's theory "of different contradictions, each with
its own specificity, its own tempo of development, internal history, and
its own conditions of existence—at once 'determined and determining':
in short . . . of the relative autonomy and the specific effectivity of the
different levels of a social formation."[106] Through the 1970s, in turn, its
procedures remained broadly congruent with Hall's declaration, that
Marx's method and epistemology implied that "any attempt to construct
'thinking' as wholly autonomous . . . constitutes an idealist problematic, which ultimately derives the world from the movement of the Idea.
No formalist reduction—whether of the Hegelian, positivist, empiricist
or structuralist variety—escapes this stricture."[107] Hall's acceptance of
the matrix of separate and specific Althusserian instances in turn engen-
dered praiseworthy research, in which the pursuit of interrelations

across at least some parts of the social field continued to achieve a genuine evocative significance. Thus the Centre associated the study of media and ideology at different points not only with "family television," but also with a political instance, in the form of a state-centered "control culture," whose "primary definers" encompassed police, judges, and government officials.[108] At such points the members of the Centre for Contemporary Cultural Studies brought the analysis of ideology to a new level of sophisticated elegance and topicality. Through the 1970s Hall's group, often relying on ethnographic technique, traced both domination and resistance to the dominant order, while providing an ostensible check against a purely textual criticism, with its attendant— and acknowledged—dangers of theoreticism.

Paul Willis's remarkable ethnographic study of school lads readying themselves to enter the work force offers a final exemplary instance of the unreconciled tensions within the approach that prevailed within British cultural studies during the 1970s. On one hand, as feminists were to protest, Willis's category "labor" denoted not merely waged labor, but male waged labor—and, it should be appended, male waged labor within a city ("Hammertown") wherein the proportion of industrial manufacturing was atypically high by contemporary British standards. As against this tightly contained idea of "labor," on the other hand, "culture" assumed a tantalizing ambivalence. Glimpsed explicitly as "a material force," "culture" still seemingly remained a separate—and in key respects, a prior—domain of practice within the lads' experience of what was, after all, "learning to labor."[109] "Culture" preceded and, through the relative expectations and self-understandings which it culti- vated, went far to predefine "labor."

This ambivalence becomes further apparent when such works as Willis's are set next to a disparate, though nearly concurrent effort to stage a return to the pragmatists' celebration of the idea of cooperative communication. "Culture," conceded James Carey—here drawing on Clifford Geertz—should be thought of as "an ordered though contradic- tory and heterogeneous system of symbols."[110] But where and why contradiction and heterogeneity were to be introduced remained, as also for Geertz himself, enigmatic questions. And, on the other hand, Carey premised his dedication to communication as a cooperative, even a com- munitarian, enterprise, on an increasingly resolute and explicit effort to marginalize the significance of economic relations. This quest eventually took on a self-consciously exclusionary character:

> Economics is the practice of allocating scarce resources. Communication is the process of producing meaning, a resource which is anything but scarce, indeed is a superabundant, free good. . . . For nothing is more primitive, in the sense of primordial, savage, in the sense of at the root of our hu- manity, and public, in the sense of the common and shared, than communi- cations. . . . Communication is nothing if not a collective activity; indeed,

> it is the process by which the real is created, maintained, celebrated, trans-
> formed and repaired. The product of that activity, meaning, establishes a
> common and shared world. . . . Language is the one collective and shar-
> able phenomenon we have: not something created and then shared but
> only created in the act of sharing.[111]

With this somewhat ironic revival of Wilbur Schramm's dictum that
"communication is the fundamental social process,"[112] we are, once
more, evidently within the purview of an exceptionalist appeal: "Communication" is different, special, incommensurable. Here, however, the
implications of Carey's notion that language is, simply, "shared," can
hardly be masked: How—and how far—is English shared, for example,
and by whom? Is standard English an example of Carey's shared language? If not, what is? Have not class, gender and race relations contributed to the social construction of a striated and contested English?
Although for Hall, for example, questions of linguistic creolization remained supremely a matter of unequal power relations, such a contex-
tualization lay largely outside Carey's warrant.[113] We may even turn to
Hall and his colleagues for a clear rejection (in 1978) of this sweeping
assumption that "[w]e exist as members of one society *because* . . . we
share a common stock of cultural knowledge with our fellow men: we
have access to the same 'maps of meanings'":

> Now, at one level, the existence of a cultural consensus is an obvious truth;
> it is the basis of all social communication. If we were not members of the
> same language community we literally could not communicate with one
> another. On a broader level, if we did not inhabit, to some degree, the same
> classifications of social reality, we could not "make sense of the world
> together." In recent years, however, this basic cultural fact about society has
> been raised to an extreme ideological level. Because we occupy the same
> society and belong to roughly the same "culture," it is assumed that there is,
> basically, only *one* perspective on events: that provided by what is some-
> times called *the* culture, or (by some social scientists), the "central value
> system." This view denies any major structure discrepancies between differ-
> ent groups, or between the very different maps of meaning in a society.[114]

Hall had been at pains, somewhat earlier in the 1970s, to underscore
that—in explicit contrast to the proposal (by Habermas) that "normal
communication" proceeded in accord with rules and meanings which
were "identical for all members of the language community"—language
"competence" was "quite unequally distributed as between different
classes and groups." Such sociolinguistic ideas carried considerable significance for the differentiated processes of audience comprehension, or
what Hall then called "decoding."[115] Under cover of "shared experience," on the other hand "language" offered means through which
others might covertly reinstate conventional liberal ideas of pluralism
and countervailing power.[116] In Carey's conception the idea was determinedly absent that "culture" might be seen—as Edward Thompson

once put it—most fundamentally "as a field of change and contest, an arena in which opposing interests make conflicting claims." Through appeals to shared experience there transpired instead a "cosy invitation to consensus," to continue quoting Thompson, which serves "to distract attention from social and cultural contradictions, from the fractures and oppositions within the whole."[117]

Through the 1970s, on the other hand, Hall's preferred version of cultural studies still seemed to share significant ground with that of Williams.[118] "[I]f I had to pick out one area in which significant development is likely, just because it brings to a head many of the underlying theoretical and practical problems" declared Williams with characteristic optimism in 1976, "it would be the emphasis which I would describe as the *materiality of signs.*"[119] Even as he continued to take note of a vast range of activity beyond elite art and thought, then, Williams himself also still conferred on "culture" a singular status: "[S]pecifically cultural institutions and formations," he wrote in 1981, required new kinds of analysis.[120] It is worth reiterating that this idea might appear to resonate with the Althusserian schema: "[T]he theory of the specific influence of the superstructures," Althusser had declared, remained to be developed; in particular, he looked forward to an "elaboration of the theory of the particular essence of the specific elements of the superstructure."[121] Yet at once it needs to be re-emphasized that, in Williams's eyes, it was the absence of a true "sociology of systems of signs" which comprised "the reason" for what he accurately forecast as "the successes of cultural structuralism, which speaks to such systems but at the price of excluding, as contingent, all other real practice."[122] And it must also be stressed that this exclusionary thrust portended a resurgent idealism, of whose dangers, as we saw, both Williams and Hall himself had warned.

What, we may then ask, created the conditioning architecture of this curious space, in which theory became free to enact, almost as a matter of instinct, the separating-out from society and, in particular, from a reciprocally reified "economic" instance of a putatively independent and self-generating realm, variously fashioned "signification" or "ideology" or "language" or, indeed, "culture"?[123] The pull in this direction may be associated with cultural studies' defensive reinstitutionalization within a primary site of "intellectual" labor—the university. A number of proponents have recently begun to concede that cultural studies indeed has suffered from the deformation that is all too characteristic of academic projects and disciplines. Cultural studies' "unprecedented international boom," declares one analyst, coincides with concerted attacks on its originating political impulses. "The pressure is on," in short, "to produce a less abrasive version of cultural studies."[124] "[C]ultural studies," writes a second, "may be in the process of becoming diluted."[125] Carrots, assuredly, were increasingly on offer. Substantial and concerted efforts to cultivate increased respectibility for cultural studies within and around the academy have not been adequately noted.[126]

But the inward turn toward academe itself may be seen as coincident—nay, concordant—with cultural studies' changed intellectual compass. Hall himself offered two markedly different comments on what he hailed as a structuralist "break." First, in 1980: "From this point onwards, Cultural Studies is no longer a dependent intellectual colony. It has a direction, an object of study, a set of themes and issues, a distinctive problematic of its own."[127] A decade later, having had to bear up under the damage of Thatcherism, he had grown markedly more somber about this pivotal moment, during the 1970s: "The Center for Cultural Studies was the locus to which we retreated when . . . conversation in the open world could no longer be continued."[128] Each of these disparate characterizations conceals a nugget of truth.

Structural Marxism imbued the left with a heady self-awareness whose seeming remoteness from "material" labor comported all too well with cultural studies' migration into the academy. But at the same time that structural Marxism appeared to supply a rigorous means of scrutinizing "forms and languages"—reappearing now as "codes and practices"—it continued to lay claim to a sweeping intellectual territory. Academic security, to say nothing of repute, could be gained only by finding means of surmounting the tensions which not surprisingly sprang up with adjoining disciplines.[129] Faced, in sociology, with a particularly significant rival—for sociology itself was institutionalized as a social science in Britain only during the 1950s—cultural studies successfully staked its future on the unique inheritance to which it could lay claim: the encompassing topical warrant of English literary criticism during the interwar period. This tradition of criticism comprised the best, and perhaps even the only, basis for an academic cultural studies in Britain. For it was not, crucially, sociology, but English literature (alongside anthropology) which, as late as the 1950s, comprised the chief refuge "of the idea of a social totality within English culture."[130]

Hall's characterization of cultural studies as a "retreat," however, also remains suggestive, pre-eminently in the context of what Perry Anderson initially tried to portray not as a general defeat administered to Marxism by a suddenly formidable intellectual adversary, but as a regional intellectual response—largely restricted to the Latin countries of Europe—associated most centrally with the debacle of Eurocommunism.[131] Yet this, after all, was rapidly revealed to be a phenomenon of grosser proportion. We must now see that the ascent of an increasingly academic cultural studies coincided, indeed, with what Ahmad has called a "global offensive of the Right, [and] global retreat of the Left . . . [that] is the essential backdrop for any analysis of the structure of intellectual productions and their reception in our time."[132] Or, as Graham Murdock asserts, "[t]he takeoff of cultural studies to growth is almost exactly conterminous [*sic*] with neoliberalism's dominating economic and social policy and with the gathering crisis in the traditional rhetorics and organizational forms of established politics, and more particularly of socialism."[133]

This context is surely implicated—though the question merits additional scrutiny—in cultural studies' shifting conceptual affinities.[134] Hall again furnishes a ready benchmark. In theorizing "the capacity of the Right . . . to hegemonise [the] defeat" of the working class, Hall's appropriation of Gramsci worked to displace, rather than altogether disengage, a class-based problematic.[135] Gramsci's concepts of "the national popular" and "power bloc" became, for Hall, helpful categories precisely inasmuch as they allowed questions of domination and struggle to be posed at a level one step removed from the immediacies of social class relations. Here is a passage from his remarkable essay of 1981, "Notes on Deconstructing 'The Popular'":

> The term "popular" has very complex relations to the term "class." We know this, but are often at pains to forget it. We speak of particular forms of working-class culture; but we use the more inclusive term, "popular culture" to refer to the general field of inquiry. It's perfectly clear that what I've been saying would make little sense without reference to a class perspective and to class struggle. But it is also clear that there is no one-to-one relationship between a class and a particular cultural form or practice. The terms "class" and "popular" are deeply related but they are not absolutely interchangeable. The reason for that is obvious. There are no wholly separate "cultures" paradigmatically attached, in a relation of historical fixity, to specific "whole" classes—although there are clearly distinct and variable class-cultural formations. Class cultures tend to intersect and overlap in the same field of struggle. The term "popular" indicates this somewhat displaced relationship of culture to classes. More accurately, it refers to that alliance of classes and forces which constitute the "popular classes." The culture of the oppressed, the excluded classes: this is the area to which the term "popular" refers us. And the opposite side to that—the side with the cultural power to decide what belongs and what does not—is, by definition, not another "whole" class, but that other alliance of classes, strata and social forces which constitute what is not "the people" and not the "popular classes": the culture of the power-bloc.[136]

This qualified detachment from class, however, proved to be a stepping-stone to a disengagement which was characteristically to became more concerted and pronounced. Here, to take an especially apt example, is John Fiske, writing twelve years after Hall, ostensibly about the same concept: " 'The people' is not a social category. It can never be. It transects class, it transects the individual, it transects all solid social categories and social structures. . . . It is an alliance of powers, an alliance of social interest formed and reformed around issues strategically. . . ."[137] Whence these purported "powers," themselves, significantly, said to be plural rather than singular? What "social interest," whose "strategic" selection of issues? These indeterminacies offer a measure of the distance that now intervened against the concepts and concerns that had hitherto motivated cultural studies. It is no slight to the hard-won scattering of departments and programs of Ethnic Studies, Women's Studies, Chicano Studies, African American studies, Asian American Studies which developed during the 1970s and 1980s, to note the absence of comparable university programs in "class studies." Perhaps the issues which, a century ago, were generalized as "the social question" were to be left in the custody of their original academic purveyors—sociology, economics, and perhaps history. But the first point to be made, surely, is that "race" and "gender" were not.

True, the affirmations of difference that then cascaded through cultural studies, even as they forced a continuing retreat from reigning concepts of totality, never gainsaid a substantial preoccupation with the character of social relationality. In this churning context, as conceptual lenses were unceasingly ground and reground, it must be agreed that the great gain of the 1950s and 1960s—this actively relational concept of social agency—remained accessible and even compelling in at least some academic work; George Lipsitz's book-length study of Ivory Perry, to take one relatively recent example, powerfully tenders the complex heroism and dignity of everyday resistance in the contemporary world.[138] But the analysis of social subjects and identities was also more generally skewed, despite regional differences in approach, onto a single flattened plane. "If we want to go on believing in categories like social class," enjoined an eminent Marxist critic already in 1979, "then we are going to have to dig for them in the insubstantial bottomless realm of cultural and collective fantasy."[139] It was almost as if, having to make a virtue of the necessary abandonment of received concepts of totality, the elaboration of subjectivities sought familiar bearings by sliding back once more into comfortably reified concepts of "intellectual" labor.

Discussions of "resistance" were one point at which such a procedure became characteristic. "[T]he textual struggle for meaning"—this is again Fiske—"is the precise equivalent of the social struggle for power."[140] Really? Must homeless men, covertly inserting *Hustler* within the covers of *Life* magazine so as to deceive censorious overseers, be reckoned on this count as taking their places in a battle against the dominative social policies that lead to their search for shelter in the first place?[141] A parallel slippage figured in those theories of colonial discourse for which resistance to the power of empire, itself already transmuted into a regularly reified form, "orientalism," likewise occurred pre-eminently via textual strategies—indexed, in one witty formulation, by the phrase "the empire writes back."[142]

Paul Gilroy has cogently criticized both an "essentialism" which celebrates "difference" as an "overintegrated sense of cultural and ethnic particularity" and, on the other hand, an "anti-essentialism" which, in some variants, threatens to cut free subjectivity altogether from the tenacious modalities of "power and subordination."[143] Neither "essentialism" nor "anti-essentialism," as Gilroy aptly notes, exhibits the ability or sometimes even the desire to name the dominative centripetal forces which today continue to obtrude overarchingly on "experience." Think, in this connection, of the increasingly integrated complex of advertisers and marketers that exploits ever-more-sensitive information technologies to target "most needed audiences"[144] in terms of "race," "gender," and "ethnicity" as well as other attributes.[145] Essentialism and anti-essentialism each in its own way misrecognizes and discounts this exploitive complex—which, when seen historically, involves something more than a belated acknowledgment of a pre-existing ethnicity or gender subjectivity, on one side, or, on the other, "the endless play of difference" through which such identities are said to be fashioned. These respective misrecognitions symptomatize a shared tendency invalidly to privilege signifying practice far above its own conditions of existence.

Is all this simply an inescapable exaction, imposed in response to the left's traditional reliance on gendered and sometimes racially exclusionary conceptions of class?[146] I think not; it must be situated as well in terms of cultural studies' increasingly reactionary milieu. Even if we can agree with the inclusionary spirit of Hall's recent directive—that "[t]he capacity to live with difference is . . . the coming question of the twenty-first century"[147]—the latter furnishes little more than a hollow shell in which to tolerate whatever oscillations choose to present themselves. What room is made here for exploitation, still—across a veritable plethora of unhappy shadings—the leading mode of social relationship? What, conversely, beyond mere preference, stands in the way of having to validate the exploitive experience of transnational corporate executives? Does not Hall's admonishment come perilously near to what John Fiske cautions may be "a new liberal pluralist consensus that differs from the old only in that the agreement is to be different"?[148] Is such a pluralism, finally, all that can—and should—be salvaged from the oppositional hopes in which cultural studies originated?

III

Unabashedly justifying and contributing to the same neoliberal upsurge which beset oppositional projects such as cultural studies was a quite different intellectual formation gathering round the concept of "postindustrial society." Postindustrial theory, however, not only once again reified "intellectual" labor, but—in a further parallel with British cultural studies after the structuralist "break"—also claimed a warrant for this operation in the apparently anomalous character of its seemingly disparate newfound object: "information."

Postindustrial theory encapsulated an astonishing conceptual progression. The theory can claim a pedigree going back to Saint-Simon's "prescient vision" of the "society of scientists."[149] Yet it palpably extended the vision of a more direct ancestor. As far back as Bakunin and, in a more fully elaborated theorization, in the anarcho-Marxism of the Pole Jan Machajski at the turn of the 20th century, the proponents of a so-called "new class" of educated managers and scientists had developed their thesis to assail what they projected would become just another species of social domination, ironically presenting itself as socialism, but bereft of any true measure of social equality.[150] During the 1950s, this idea of a "new class" resurfaced as a publicly acclaimed anti-Communist argument—just as the radical critique of mass culture was emphasizing that an apparently anomalous white-collar stratum portended an ominous slide into authoritarianism. In the hands of Daniel Bell,[151] the theory's skillful U.S. interlocutor, postindustrialism inverted the logic of both discussions, and magically effected thereby to kill two birds with one stone. In Bell's formulation, the new class of white-collar workers functioned neither as catalyst nor as ruler of a debased and a dominated polity, but rather as the basis of a new social order, in which knowledge rather than market relations would be primary.

Together, intellectuals and technical workers were putatively amidst the process of actualizing what a later contributor to the discussion termed a "universal class." Even this second, somewhat more muted, variant of postindustrial theory, promulgated by the self-described "left-Hegelian" Alvin Gouldner, portrayed the ascent of this class—however "flawed"—as "the best card that history has presently given us to play." Gouldner did not so much break with Bell's postindustrial theory as recreate it, through a series of parallel formulations.[152] Whether cast as a purported "universal class" or simply as a "principle" of the emerging social order, "intellectual" labor therefore once again came to be rendered in highly circumscribed terms.

As Bell was to note,[153] his theory of postindustrial society hearkened back most directly to the ideas of Thorstein Veblen. Veblen had written in 1919 that economists' conventional reliance on three coordinate "factors of production"—land, labor, and capital—had come to be an antiquated and unreliable basis for analysis. It unjustly omitted any mention, most significantly, of the "productive effect" of "the industrial arts." What were these "industrial arts"? Veblen explained:

> The state of the industrial art is a joint stock of knowledge derived from past experience, and is held and passed on as an indivisible possession of the community at large. It is the indispensable foundation of all productive industry, of course, but except for certain minute fragments covered by patent rights or trade secrets, this joint stock is no man's individual property. For this reason it has not been counted in as a factor in production.[154]

Elsewhere, Veblen was still more explicit. "The foundation and driving force" of the industrial system "is a massive body [of] technological knowledge." It followed "that those gifted, trained, and experienced technicians who now are in possession of the requisite technological information and experience are the first and instantly indispensable factor in the everyday work of carrying on the country's productive industry." What Veblen called the corps of "production engineers" thus constituted—in stark contrast to the claims made by the captains of industry regarding their own indispensability—"the General Staff of the industrial system," whose role it was to ensure the "painstaking and intelligent coordination of the processes at work, and an equally painstaking allocation of mechanical power and materials." However, drawing on a veritable arsenal of weaponry to limit or "sabotage" production, absentee owners and their henchmen, top business managers and financiers, were systematically preventing science and technology from achieving the productivity and material welfare of which they were easily capable if freed from this "commercial bias." Truly optimal allocation and deployment of resources and labor could be maximized, to promote the material well-being of the people, only by allowing unbiased technicians and production engineers to reign directly and comprehensively over production and, as Bell pointed out, over the entire direction of American society. Indeed "any question of a revolutionary overturn, in America or in any other of the advanced industrial countries, resolves itself in practical fact into a question of what the guild of technicians will do."[155]

During the 1930s, Veblen's positive valuation of intellectual work was outshined by an ascending negative theorization, which found its rationale in linkages between fascism, propaganda, and, soon, mass culture. But related portents of Bell's postindustrial theses nevertheless continued to appear. Lewis Corey, who was moving from Communist to anti-Communist militance, and who Daniel Bell in the 1940s befriended and published, declared in much the same terms as Veblen that only socialism could liberate production, and thereby place the fulfillment of human needs on a beneficent scientific basis. "Limitation of production represses the growth of technology and science," wrote Corey, "for their growth under capitalism is conditional on the upward movement and profitability of production. Never fully utilized even during the upswing of capitalism, the utilization of technology and science must steadily decline under the conditions of capitalist decline." On the other hand:

> All the economic elements of a new social order are already in existence: immensely efficient forces of production, an abundance of skilled labor and of raw materials (including the increasing creation of synthetic materials), and a constantly larger mass of scientific knowledge capable of technological application—all united in the collective forms of production which are the objective basis of socialism. It is wholly possible today not only to

abolish poverty but to make plenty available to all; and it is wholly possible to multiply almost indefinitely the professional and cultural services which it is the function of many groups in the middle class to provide.[156]

Harold Lasswell in turn acutely noted, in 1933, in reference to the grip of Nazism on the white-collar strata, that:

[t]he growth of the vast material environment in modern society has been paralleled by the unprecedented expansion of specialized symbolic activity. Medicine, engineering, and physical science have proliferated into a thousand specialities for the control of specific aspects of the material world. Those who master the necessary symbol equipment are part of the intellectual class whose "capital" is knowledge, not muscle. There is a sub-division of the intellectual workers, the "intellectuals" in the narrow sense, who specialize in the symbols connected with political life. The growing complexity of modern civilization has created a vast net of reporters, interpreters, pedagogues, advertisers, agitators, propagandists, legal dialecticians, historians and social scientists who compete among themselves and with all other classes and sub-classes for deference, safety and material income. . . . Lenin dismissed the "intellectuals" as classless prostitutes hired out to the highest bidder. It is evident that a "brain trust"—to use a current American expression employed to describe President Roosevelt's expert advisers—is a useful form of political armament on all sides, but the tremendous growth of symbol specialists within The Great Society suggests that we have to do with the emergence of a potent social formation with objective interests of its own. . . . [157]

Both the ambiguous reference to "intellectual workers," whose "knowledge" comprised a kind of "capital," and the suggestion that they comprised "a potent social formation with objective interests of its own" were to recur directly within postindustrial theory. But the latter awaited the long postwar economic boom, which was so obviously and determinately linked with the systematic exploitation of science and technology, and which brought in its train so many other seemingly palpable signs of the enlarged social importance of "intellectual" labor. White-collar workers in the U.S. practically doubled in number between 1958 and 1980, though their representation in the paid labor force increased at a slower rate—from 43 to 52 percent, in one estimate.[158]

Bell's revival of Veblen comprised the second portion—the first transpired through his earlier work, *The End of Ideology*—of a complex act of rehabilitation: to furnish a new self-justification for a particular stratum which, relinquishing the leftish alienation which had tinged it during the New Deal, during the 1950s acquiesced to an obsequious but instrumental role within the ascendent national security state. Postindustrial theory coincided with a massive upsurge in government support for research and development and, more generally, with the "golden years" of the short American Century. In this context, Cold War intellectuals found it generally agreeable, as Bell's Columbia University colleague

Richard Hofstadter underlined, to seek a rapprochement with their society.[159] Hofstadter found good grounds for charging—with modesty and mellifluous insight—that the cyclical havoc wrought by "anti-intellectualism" over the span of American history had been evidenced most recently during the McCarthyist spasm of the 1950s. He shrewdly observed that "the resentment from which the intellectual has suffered in our time is a manifestation not of a decline in his position but of his increasing prominence."[160]

On one hand, Cold War intellectuals had to find means of passing muster before "anti-Communist pundits, offended by the past heresies of a large segment of the intellectual community."[161] On the other hand, they wished to sustain their newfound preferment. Able to play offense during the comparative ideological relaxation of the Kennedy years, Bell crafted a positive theorization, fully commensurate with the intellectuals' enhanced contemporary social significance. Education, or "human capital," he wrote, figured increasingly clearly "as the basic resource for technological and productive advance in society." Technology, or what Veblen had termed "the industrial arts," indeed comprised "a joint stock of knowledge derived from past experience—a social asset, which is no man's or no firm's individual property, though it is often claimed as such." And, finally, "[i]n the coming decades, as any reading of changes in our occupational structure indicates, we will be moving toward a 'post-industrial society,' in which the scientist, the engineer, and the technician constitute the key functional class in society." For Bell, "this wave of the future," which would establish "the technological rule of society" was, unmistakably and simply, "good."[162]

Bell set Veblen's ideas within an apparently symbiotic, but truly quite disparate, framework. Postindustrial argument indeed cannot be separated from the "information theory" that emerged—as we saw in Chapter Two—as a scientistic capstone in the postwar reformulation of academic communication study, and in which an "informational" aspect or dimension of diverse "systems" was singled out.

Bell[163] was ultimately to concede that, in an important sense, "every human society has always existed on the basis of knowledge." How, then, to identify and distinguish "information societies"? Because message processing is a ubiquitous feature of human social organization, he needed to do more than merely isolate and catalog an unfolding array of contemporary information functions, occupations, and processes. In order to differentiate postindustrial societies, postindustrial theorists also had to associate information with other, apparently distinctive or changed societal features. In *The End of Ideology* (1960), Bell had already argued that a "breakup of the 'ruling class'" that had been grounded in "family capitalism" had stripped that class of any significant political role; that the "independent" managers who now led large corporations had largely eliminated any moral reliance on the "fiction" of private productive property, and instead were motivated chiefly by "'perfor-mance' for its own sake"; that the twin "'silent' revolutions" which were bringing all this about centered on a decline in the importance of property inheritance and on a vital shift in the *"nature of power-hold-ing itself* insofar as technical skill rather than property, and political posi-tion rather than wealth, have become the basis on which power is wielded."[164]

After the convergence with information theory, these tenets—which expanded on the idea of a "managerial revolution," put forward earlier by James Burnham and others—could be associated with other apparent shifts and transitions. Postindustrial analysts accordingly began to stress not only the codification of theoretical knowledge through modern sci-ence and technology, and the growing numbers and reputedly changing status of "knowledge workers," but also the astonishing capacities of microelectronics, the shifting international division of labor, and the vital role of the university. Virtually unanimously, however, they con-curred that the ultimate source of social discontinuity emanated, appar-ently of itself, from the anomalous nature of information.

Those who trumpeted the news of postindustrial society's imminent arrival pivoted their theory on information's apparent inherent singu-larity. Their attempts at historical specificity coexisted, in an uneasy but muted tension, with this anti-historical impulse. The leading variant of the theory pre-empted recognition of this tension, however, by grafting postindustrialism onto the powerful idea that there exist discernible "stages" of economic growth. The latter, recall, had come to the fore in the context of "underdeveloped" countries, to sustain arguments about the proper course of policy for "development." Now, in information society theory, the stages of growth concept was again mobilized, but within a massively altered context. This time, the theory was used to sustain an argument, not about the supposedly necessary and desirable passage of the "underdeveloped" countries toward consumer capital-ism, but, rather, about the purported ongoing historical movement of "advanced" economies into a new and even higher phase of the devel-opment process.

Just here, however, the exceptionalism which underlay postin-dustrial theory also entered as an axiom. In Daniel Bell's *The Coming of Post-Industrial Society*, the *locus classicus* of the theory, the scientific and technological revolution—or what he called "the centrality of theoreti-cal knowledge as the axial principle of social organization"—constituted the new "determining feature of social structure." However, in a striking parallel to Mills's earlier supposition concerning white-collar work, and to Hall's subsequent effort to justify a separate ideological sphere, Bell charged that science "has a distinct character which is different from other modes of activity, including labor; it is this character that sets apart a society based on science from industry."[165] This pair of unsubstantiated assertions was soon taken over by those who wished to emphasize that information's singularity comprised a defining anomaly of the emerging era. "Information," underscored the then executive director of Bell Laboratories, "has properties quite different from those of the substantive goods with which we are used to dealing." He declared that these "important differences" should "form a backdrop for our thinking about . . . the information age."[166] "The information resource," another leading proponent summarized baldly, " . . . is different in kind from other resources." Not subject to the laws of thermodynamics, according to this writer, information is "expandable, compressible, substitutable, transportable, leakable, shareable." These vexingly unique, "inherent characteristics" supplied, he held, the vital clue to information's mounting economic importance.[167] On these twin assumptions—that information production was radically divergent from other forms of production, and that information was qualitatively different from other resources—was borne the idea that information had supplanted capital and labor as the transformative factor of production. Postindustrial theory utilized its exceptionalist premise to invoke a comprehensive but undemonstrable historical rupture, and therefore to draw back decisively from the predominating social relations of production, and into essentially schematic and false models of societal development.

Postindustrial theory might easily have suggested that this presumed liftoff of the social order toward parts unknown should be attended with anxiety, even fear. Instead, in its dominant variant especially, it greeted the future complacently, exhuberantly confident that it would prove congenial. This stance both required and appeared to validate a whole series of abstractions—in direct contrast with British cultural studies—from the defining matrices of contemporary social experience: economic stagnation, the critiques of contemporary society being mounted by the new social movements, and, not least, the crisis of American empire that erupted over Vietnam, with which the critique of cultural imperialism was intertwined. Webster and Robins[168] have emphasized postindustrialism's ideological basis in an incisive appraisal of Bell's "informed anti-Marxism." The theory's ideological work was based, however, on a sleight-of-hand: in place of engagement with lived realities, it offered a sustained abstraction toward information's supposed intrinsic and transcendent universal properties.

That information exceptionalism served this overt ideological purpose is easily confirmed: "The distinction . . . between the industrial society and the post-industrial, or scientific-technological society, means," Bell[169] proclaimed, "that some simplified Marxian categories no longer hold." The latter included the purported "leading role of the working class" in social change and, more generally, the overall conceptions of social development—that is, of history and of social process—promulgated by diverse radicals. Once again, it was labor's revaluation that served as the lynchpin of postindustrialism's project; a purported "knowledge theory of value" thus might be substituted for the labor theory of value. The latter's field of reference was held to be limited to industrial societies and thus not to encompass the ostensibly sharply different social formation then emerging.[170]

"By information," declared Bell,[171] "I mean data processing in the broadest sense; the storage, retrieval, and processing of data becomes the essential resource for all economic and social exchanges. These include: data processing of records . . . data processing for scheduling . . . data bases." Bell's definition invoked the deeply embedded association of "information" with science, and thus, relatedly, with ostensibly factual or documentary material. (These had been evident, for example, in the public policy discussions in the 1950s and 1960s of the growing importance of "STINFO," the acronym for "scientific and technological information."[172]) This scientistic definition separated "data processing" or "information" from the realm of meaning—the same domain to which information theory itself was so often invalidly extended, and in which Hall and other writers were seeking, on the basis of a parallel exceptionalism, to found an autonomous but engaged cultural studies.

Severed by postindustrial theory from its specialized engineering usage, and now viewed as "data processing in the broadest sense," "information" of course might validly have been utilized as a synonym for "culture." But then why would the new term have been needed? Bell's usage, in contrast, worked to distinguish "information" sharply from any identifiable equivalence with "culture" as a potentially serviceable surrogate. "Information" then not only covered, but also covered up, much of what was referenced by the anthropological sense of "culture." Bell could not easily utilize "culture" because, by this time—the late 1960s—its dominant usages were verging on downright antagonism to his endeavor. On one side, "culture's" lingering humanistic echoes certainly could do nothing to amplify the scientism on which postindustrial theory was founded. On the other, far more direct threats were being posed by the concurrent reworking of "culture" to pinpoint the creativity and broad historical salience of ordinary human experience— and not only in the theorizings being propounded by the progenitors of British cultural studies.[173] Indeed "culture" at points appeared to be metamorphosizing, as Edward Thompson preferred, to an all-too-visible way of struggle. In the United States, for example, the civil rights movement and, although its political role may at times have been overblown, the "counterculture," gave at least some indication of the conflicts emerging within "culture." In and around the less-developed countries, Mao's "Cultural Revolution" and the rising chorus of opposition to "cultural imperialism" itself were the most overt of many signals that "culture" no longer translated simply into conceptions that stressed an apparent timeless traditionalism. Such usages moved actively against postindustrialism's ideological current. They made it overwhelmingly difficult for the propagandists of "information" to accept "culture" as their primary field of reference.

"Information's" aura of objectivity instead accommodated a pronounced tendency to economism: the assumption, so prevalent in contemporary public discourse, that something called "the economy" could be diagnosed and prescribed for as if it existed in pristine separation from "politics" or "culture." The absence of any clear-cut difference between the two formulations, "the information society" and "the information economy," was symptomatic. In itself, of course, the attention paid to such matters as the growing trade in information services, the expanding numbers of information workers, the unfolding corporate applications of information technology, the extent of skills training, and "human capital formation" was unobjectionable, even enlightening. But, regularly, consideration of such topics served to shift attention away from the continuing experience of social division, aggravated inequality, and political conflict. "Information" immediately lifted analysis free and clear of "culture's" rich sediment: the long series of productive debates filtering through the terms "high culture," "mass culture," and "popular culture," that is, debates over what culture, *whose* culture, could and should be ordinary. "Information" likewise abstracted altogether away from social life and social process; it took a contextualizing noun— "information society"—to widen its field of reference in this direction. In shifting discussion onto what purported to be wholly new grounds, the ideologists of "information" sought to re-establish a crucial analytical distance from lived, and conflictful, experience. Their theory thus harmonized with Richard M. Nixon's private comment to a onetime political aide, that "[p]olitics would be a helluva good business if it weren't for the goddamned people."[174]

This distance came through in Daniel Bell's dichotomous (actually, trichotomous) thinking. Bell[175] consistently accepted that culture should be identified with "the expressive symbolization of experience." Between "culture" and what he identified as the "techno-economic order" Bell posited a veritable chasm. In a gesture that established a significant, if only partial, parallel with Althusser, he averred that culture, politics, and economy comprised entirely disjunct realms, existing on separate planes and operating on mutually independent and even "contrary" principles. How revealing, then, to learn that Bell ripped out hundreds of pages from what originated as a single bulky manuscript, and ultimately published *The Cultural Contradictions of Capitalism* separately from *The Coming of Postindustrial Society*.[176] From the perspective of postindustrial theory, "culture" remained overtly tied to capitalism—and to struggles within and against it—in ways that "information" apparently did not. Or, more precisely, "information" could be

defended, for the moment successfully, against any full-scale engagement with the radical heterodoxy whose fulcrum was "culture."

Nowhere was this defense more active than in the response to the
movement for a New International Information Order. Despite a decade
of political effort, the latter's advocates proved unable to prise open an
organizational space in which the politicization of "culture" could be
forcefully extended into the new modalities of "information technology."[177] By the 1990s, a crude descendant of Bell's postindustrial
theory—the fruit of an unrelenting agitation by Alvin Toffler (another
ex-staffer at *Fortune*) and others—showed strong signs of having metamorphosized into a hard-shell reactionary futurism, fully capable of encompassing both the diktats of the Republican right wing and the racist
revival of the discredited thesis that "intelligence" is a genetic endowment.[178] But the theory had been vulnerable to such revision from the
first; its most damning feature was always speciously to reserve pride of
place for a mere segment of the social division of labor. Specifically, of
course, it favored professionals, scientists, and managers: the stratum
that the great weight of historical prejudice—as Baptist Hubert had
complained—never ceased to equate with "intellectual" activity itself.

An emergent radical critique of postindustrial theory, thankfully,
also began to develop. Coming through in the work of Herbert I. Schiller
and others, already by the late 1970s, were hints of the transformative
shift from "culture" and the established mass media to what the postin-
dustrialists were purporting to generalize—but also, as we have seen,
covertly to redirect—under the unfamiliar names of "information" and
"information technology." The latter specified a panoply of emerging
instrumentation, whose progressively more manifold and impactful applications, it was becoming clear by the late 1970s, would revolve
around controlling hubs of computer communications. Even a decade
before this, presentiments of this development might be found in the
critique of the ongoing process of cultural imperialism. "[T]he volume,
form, and speed with which current electronic systems transmit intelligence," wrote Herbert I. Schiller in 1969, "have produced a qualitatively new factor in human and group relationships. Telecommunications are today the most dynamic forces affecting not only the ideological
but the material bases of society."[179] "We are now in an epoch of the
most far-reaching changes in technology that man has ever devised,"
emphasized *May Day Manifesto*; among the ramifying effects of this continuing innovation in the "forces of production" was—as John Fekete
separately insisted—that "electronics and computers" might be seen as
"essential new productive forces" within an ongoing "neocapitalist
transformation, reconsolidation and integration."[180] Though still only
suggestive, such comments bespeak a continuing search for alternatives
to the mechanical consignment of the media to something called the
"superstructure."

A decade later, alongside the international ascendence of reaction, the pace and scale of application of information technology, above all by transnational corporations, helped to pull the political economic critique of "culture" and "cultural imperialism" into an entirely new register. The new objects of concern, notably, could not be confined to any traditional inventory of expressive works and practices. Now apparent in the complex of communication and information technology—and moving with seemingly ruthless speed from the horizon into the immediate foreground—was nothing less than a global gale of creative destruction. The character of the U.S. occupational structure *was* shifting; business and other applications of information technology *were* mushrooming. The turn to "information" identified by postindustrial theory thus became central to the introduction of a whole series of agenda items for radical research.

The critique of cultural imperialism had asserted that "communication" contributed in newly vital ways to the contemporary social process. Where postindustrial theorists sought to extricate their vision of a benevolent future society from the social relations of capitalist production, these radicals instead began to fix exactly on "information's" apparently stunning significance within and for a transnationalizing capitalism. "Information" thus now prompted—and to a significant extent rewarded—their ongoing scrutiny of a series of linked economic and institutional trends: the reorganization of work within modern industry, changes in the international division of labor, the history and political economy of office technology. As a consequence, a burst of fruitful research brought a whole range of new issues within the effective scope of communication study. Through an offensive of historic proportions during the 1970s and 1980s, transnational business was shown to be extruding through a completely unprecedented range of activities.

Contributing to this result were: state-guided privatization campaigns, which turned information and information technologies into untrammeled media of corporate profit; corporate reliance on an exploding array of communication and information processing technologies to achieve more thoroughgoing transnationalization of production; utilization of information technologies to monitor and control the labor process across a vastly widened range of the division of labor; and the vital deployment of information technology in military applications to contain and put down threats to transnational capitalism.[181] Thus the architectonic shifts to which the postindustrial analysts were pointing began to be apprehended in dramatically different terms.

However, it remained less than clear that a deeper challenge had been posed by Bell's acute portrayal of contemporary U.S. society. How—and how far—should the key tenets of postindustrialism be accepted by a reinvigorated radical critique? The stage theory of history at the center of postindustrial theory, in particular, was discounted and

transmuted by radical critics, but not forcefully retheorized. From agriculture to manufacturing industry to—what? Where postindustrial
theorists spoke of "information societies," their adversaries tended to
substitute ideas of "informational" or "cybernetic" capitalism. How
much discontinuity was there, and where did it lie? The answers remained vexingly unclear, because "information's" apparently anomalous character continued to go largely unquestioned.[182]

By staking its hopes for social transformation on the numerous real
and apparent agents of national liberation, the critique of cultural imperialism had already abstracted, as we saw, from national culture. It is a
signal fact of our era, however, that capitalism persists, much strength-
ened, in the wake of the radicalizing moment of decolonization. Thus
the onset of political reaction which began to deflect British cultural
studies likewise inflicted damage on the critique of cultural imperialism.
The latter, to be sure, effectively braided "information" into political
economy so as to reinforce its existing concern with the lineaments of an
increasingly full-blown transnational capitalism. As the moment of decolonization and national liberation faded, indeed, political economists
of information technology were enabled to make unique provision for
the forms and modalities of contemporary corporate power. While unrivaled critical insights were thereby attained, however, the formative
idea of "culture" as the practice of an active human agency also became
sidetracked. Mainly implicitly, the concept of social totality was utilized
chiefly as a space into which capital strived, all too efficiently, to make
an epochal new round of incursions. Transnational capital, no longer
countered and conceptually offset by movements for national liberation,
instead became the overwhelmingly preponderant force for social transformation. The portrait radical analysts sought to draw of "information"
thus demonstrated an unrivaled use of line and shape, but its monolithic
use of movement was a testimony to the resurgent dualism which, as we
found, was likewise reciprocally regenerated within cultural studies.

In yet a third variant of theory—poststructuralism—there was often
heralded a sort of rapprochement. Once more, however, as we now may
see, yet another reification of "intellectual" labor intruded on this final
theorization, exactly as this latter project sought to predicate itself on a
direct, and damaging, dismissal of "labor."

IV

Does not the scornful dismissal of binary oppositions, between material
and ideal, action and language, divulge a yearning for a workable rejection of dualism? Did poststructuralism effect such an epochal transcendence? They are, alas, quite different questions. Poststructuralism is a
more more variegated tradition that either Althusserian Marxism or
postindustrial theory, and I hazard no claim here to a comprehensive

assessment of either its beginnings or its chief claims. I wish rather only to emphasize what I take to be one of its characteristic acts of self-definition. For, no matter what else it may claim to do or to be, post-structuralism differentiated itself only through a widely repeated categorial dismissal of "labor."

In itself this is not a novel claim. Mark Poster, for example, showed that the thought of Michel Foucault could be illuminated by sustained reference to Western Marxism's typifying distance from classical Marxism's concern for labor and the mode of production.[183] We shall find, however, that Foucault—like another leading poststructuralist, Jean Baudrillard—defined his project only via negative reference to a very *particular* concept of labor. This theorization in turn sustained a series of overarching reifications of "intellectual" labor, which covertly substituted an abstracted moment—now variously called "representation" or "signification" or "discursive practice"—to act as the theory's center of gravity. How, then, may we apprehend this "labor," whose impact on the elaboration of poststructuralism was to prove simultaneously ubiquitous and elusive?

Poststructuralism was bound, positively and negatively, to the entire forbidding edifice of postwar French social thought. "Labor" was, in this context, a principal—perhaps even the prime—area of conceptual overlap between prospective poststructuralists and a whole succession of other writers—existentialists and phenomenologists, independent Marxists, structuralists, Catholic thinkers. Across this disparate range, "labor" was generally seen as a crude and economistic category, presided over by the French Communist Party, and existing largely within the intellectual force field of orthodox dialectical materialism. It denoted, first and foremost, the exploited work of the industrial proletariat; anything beyond this could be enfolded into the category only with difficulty. Here lay the shared problem; and, as Mark Poster has shown,[184] it was through a recovery of Hegel, as well as the closely associated discovery and translation of previously unknown texts by the young Marx, that half a generation's worth of intellectuals attempted to distance themselves—albeit in divergent ways—from this straitened framework.

"Labor," however, remained at the root of their projected differentiation: For was not "labor" incapable of capturing such vital aspects of the human condition as faith and alienation and, indeed, as the phenomenologists insisted, consciousness? How could the great range of human activity, subjectivity, and desire, be confined in "labor's" procrustean bed? This crucial and multifaceted issue, seething on the French intellectual scene during the first postwar decades, moved accordingly to the forefront of radical inquiry. It did so, paradoxically, during a period when—as a result simultaneously of effortful retheorizings prompted by the new social movements coupled to massing political reaction—the very existence of coherent, willfully active social subjects was itself thrown widely open to question.

The structuralist rejection of "humanism"—which in turn was seen to encompass both Marxist orthodoxy and existentialism—prefigured what soon became a more widespread and specific rejection of "labor." Even by the 1960s no less a figure than Althusser, for example, was calling into question the conceptual status of "labor" within the Communist Party itself. Labor, he declared, comprised only "one of the old forms belonging to the conceptual system of classical political economy and Hegelian philosophy":

> Marx made use of it, but to lead to some new concepts which, in Capital itself, render this form superfluous and constitute its critique. It is extremely important to know this in order to avoid taking this word (labour) for a Marxist concept; otherwise, as many current examples attest, one may be tempted to erect upon it all the idealist and spiritualistic interpretations of Marxism as philosophy of labour, of the "creation of man by man," of humanism, etc.[185]

"Practice," as we saw, was Althusser's preferred, and apparently more rigorous, conceptual substitute. Whatever its other features, however, "practice" still foretold linkages between the disparate dimensions of a complex structural totality. Poststructuralism, as it developed, hazarded no such promises. Seeking to base itself on a wholly discrepant premise, it frontally attacked both the "productivist discourse" in which, its proponents claimed, Marxist theorizations of social totality had long been so adversely embedded, and the idea of social totality. Poststructuralism's uneasy and problematic legacy for communication and cultural studies originates in this dual rejection, which in turn often sustained the reified concepts of "mental" labor that dotted the poststructuralist landscape.

Althusser's erstwhile protégé, Michel Foucault, still betrayed the characteristic structuralist preference for the idea of totality in his *The Order of Things,* published in 1966. "In any given culture and at any given moment," wrote Foucault, "there is always only one *episteme* that defines the conditions of possibility of all knowledge, whether expressed in theory or silently invested in a practice." The internal cohesion evinced by this epistemic set of rules—the "methods, procedures, and classifications" which governed what Foucault would come to call discourse[186]—had heretofore, however, been unglimpsed. "It had seemed rather peculiar to me," Foucault was to recall about *The Order of Things,* "that three distinct fields—natural history, grammar, and political economy—had been constituted in their rules more or less during the same period, around the seventeenth century, and had undergone, in the course of a hundred years, analogous transformations. . . . The problem was . . . of finding points in common that existed between different discursive practices: a comparative analysis of the procedures internal to scientific discourse."[187] "By 'scientific practices,'" Foucault reiterated, "I mean a certain way of regulating and constructing discourses that in their turn define a field of objects, and determine at the same time the ideal subject destined to know them."[188] This characterization, however, did not properly accentuate Foucault's methodical imperative: Endowed with a seemingly unbridgeable remoteness from any forebear, each episteme was said to effect nothing less than a "global modification" in a preceding, similarly cohesive, "regime of truth."[189]

Akin to others within the disparate intellectual moment which comprised French structuralism, Foucault strived to reject any hint of existential Marxism's "theoretical affirmation of the 'primacy of the subject.'"[190] He thus claimed to practice a type of historical inquiry "which can account for the constitution of knowledges, discourses, domains of objects, etc., without having to make reference to a subject which is either transcendental in relation to the field of events or runs in its empty sameness throughout the course of history."[191] Yet he was happy to introduce equally overarching categories of a different sort. The constitutive principles of the unique episteme which supposedly came to cohere around the turn of the 18th century were identified by reference to a trio of what Foucault himself referred to as "quasi-transcendentals"— "labour, life, and language."[192] These overarching categories were hardly selected by caprice. Together, they constituted that very conception of the human subject, of man as a "living, speaking, laboring being,"[193] which Foucault continued to seek to topple from its grand philosophical perch. Again, however, in positing "language" *and* "labor" as independent pivots of discourse, Foucault reproduced at the outset the entrenched analytical separation of these same two categories.

Foucault's portrayal of "labor's" function within the discourse of classical political economy, furthermore, relied specifically on the same familiar dualism to sustain his anti-humanist historico-philosophical project. In his account of "the space of knowledge" of political economy after 1775, the "fundamental figure" is no longer that of exchange or circulation (which is said to have governed political-economic discourse at its constituting moment) but, instead, that of labor and production. In this new episteme, "labor" alone appeared to suffice in providing "means of overcoming the fundamental insufficiency of nature and of triumphing for an instant over death."[194] "Labor's" imputed function is sketched in rapidly, as Foucault aligns the Marxian idea of capitalist class exploitation with the thesis of increasing immiseration:

> . . . the number of those maintained by History at the limit of their conditions of existence ceaselessly grows; and because of this, those conditions become increasingly more precarious until they approach the point where existence itself will be impossible; the accumulation of capital, the growth of enterprises and of their capacities, the constant pressure on wages, the

excess of production, all cause the labour market to shrink, lowering wages and increasing unemployment. Thrust back by poverty to the very brink of death, a whole class of men experience, nakedly, as it were, what need, hunger, and labour are.[195]

Whether of a Marxian or Ricardian (or, though it is left unsaid, of a directly Hegelian) derivation, political economy's ostensible commitment to the liberation of what Foucault disdainfully called man's "material truth"[196] is left to comprise its defining typification.

A year earlier, we may note, Edward Thompson had utilized strikingly similar phrases to get at the very same problem: " . . . the bare forked creature, naked biological man, is not a context which we can ever observe, because the very notion of man . . . is coincident with culture."[197] In general substance if not in name, for Thompson and for Raymond Williams, in direct contrast to Foucault, the needful effort was to enlarge the very basis of the humanist concept of the subject. Only by making "labor" grasp thinking and language, in this prospective view, could there be any return to the idea of sensuous self-objectification which had supplied, for the young Marx, the analytical foundation for "man's act of self-creation."[198] As a harbinger of the theme to be pursued at the conclusion of this book, it may be emphasized that this historically attuned variant of "Marxist humanism" was to remain vitally significant to the progressive reformulation of "labor." But for now we may reiterate that the immediate context for Foucault's concept of the episteme was not humanism but anti-humanism.

In a book published in 1955, in which he sought to pinpoint key linkages between Hegel and Marx, Jean Hyppolite—the Hegel scholar whom Foucault credited with a momentous significance in his own development—had written of "the empirical postulate underlying the whole Marxian edifice, namely, the conception of man's production of his own life through the process of labor."[199] Despite his skepticism regarding Marx's prediction that alienation would end with the transcendence of the reign of capital, Hyppolite accepted the contention (shared as he emphasized by Hegel as well as Marx) that the historical reshaping of the division of labor and the concomitant progressive mechanization of production by capitalism had "transform[ed] intelligent and integral labor into a stupefying and partial labor."[200] This meant, on one hand, that "the proletarian struggle for its liberty" was not useless: "It is never useless to struggle to overcome an alienation that is insupportable once one is conscious of it," concluded Hyppolite.[201] On the other hand, it also meant that Hyppolite had retained Hegel's humanistic conception of the subject, whose "labor," both writers held, had been deformed by capitalism. It was this humanistic dimension at which Foucault took aim.

His rebuttal, ironically, could rely on the selfsame conception of labor in light of which Hyppolite also wrote. However, it is crucial that

Hyppolite's attempt to depict "intelligent and integral labor" as a historical casualty of industrial capitalism (and one, moreover, which can be resisted by subjects newly "conscious" of their condition) is summarily dropped by Foucault. "Labor" instead is presented by Foucault as an elementally physical or "material" activity, apparently denuded at its discursive birth of any symbolic or linguistic dimension. With this drastic truncation, a rigid, though essentially subterranean, dichotomy can be introduced, between a material production purportedly stripped of any thoughtful element and the "episteme"—which, here working through the rhetoric of political economy, is said to instigate "labor" itself. By deftly utilizing this elided concept of labor, Foucault is enabled to unveil political economy's contribution to the human subject as an ostensive "knowledge effect" of a deep "anthropological sleep"—wherein "the precritical analysis of what man is in his essence becomes the analytic of everything that can, in general, be presented to man's experience." It is not going too far to suggest that, in this respect, Foucault's reliance upon the predominant concept of labor is a tactic, a means with which to sidestep or, better, to disrupt, the concurrent effort to rethink this category within the terms of a prospective settlement between Marxism and existentialism, that is, within "humanism." Thus it is Foucault's systematic dislodgment of thought from the body, which here clears the way for his own revision: the "episteme." The "episteme" encapsulates that which Foucault rigorously excludes from political economy's own ostensive domain: "mental" labor.[202] Small wonder to learn that, several years after *The Order of Things* appeared, Foucault conceded just such a dualistic instinct, when he explicitly earmarked the intellectual as "a guy hooked into the system of information rather than into the system of production."[203] Foucault, that is, preserved in the "episteme"—and thence in "discourse"—a reified image of the domination that had seemingly come to be exercised in society by "intellectual" labor.

Of itself, Foucault's reification of "intellectual" labor does not invalidate his endeavor, whose debunking of the human subject proceeds from other bases as well. It does, however, offer a glimpse of the basic congruence that existed between Foucault's ostensibly anomalous project and other concurrent reifications of "intellectual" labor.

In the philosophical *battle royale* against humanism, therefore, the reigning conception of labor, though fiercely assailed by both sides, remained for the moment unbreached by either. Althusser's concurrent shift toward "practice" has already been underscored; but even the tradition of humanistic Marxism, as represented by such eminences as Henri Lefebvre, Jean-Paul Sartre, and Jean Hyppolite, could not yet sustain a thoroughgoing reconceptualization of "labor" such as would be needed to rebut Foucault.[204] A decade later, indeed, another philosopher heir to humanistic Marxism, Jurgen Habermas—this time on disparate evolutionary and ethnological grounds—would assert that a reconstruction of historical materialism would have to begin by recognizing that "the Marxian concept of social labor . . . does not capture the specifically human reproduction of life." Lacking sympathy for Foucault's anti-humanism, Habermas nonetheless again proclaimed a need to turn away from "labor." Thus was the ground prepared for diverting theory in a linguistic direction and, specifically in the case of Habermas, toward symbolic interaction.[205]

It was symptomatic, in Foucault's case, that his own concept of the episteme should retain its totalizing ambition. Perhaps this fleeting propensity appeared as a reflected image of Foucault's immediate analytical object: the means by which had been constructed a deceptively unified human subject. Once his demolition of the subject had been placed on an apparently firm foundation, in any case, Foucault took increasingly open and deliberate exception to notions (and, above all, Marxist notions) of social totality. Assailing what, for Althusser, unquestionably had remained a critique of capitalism, Foucault, like other poststructuralists, hoped to jettison or at least revise this category;[206] and he ultimately tried to position "discourse" as a purported methodological corrective to it.

In Foucault's case, it would not be incorrect to call this manuever opportunistic.[207] Out of a precisely calculated intention, Foucault sought, "apart from any *totalization*—which would be at once *abstract* and *limiting*—to *open up* problems that are as *concrete* and *general* as possible, problems that approach politics from behind. . . ."[208] He hoped thereby to effectuate "a liberation of the act of questioning," which could present itself as nonpartisan, to the degree that it occasioned "a plurality of questions posed to politics rather than the reinscription of the act of questioning in the framework of a political doctrine."[209] To accomplish this objective—whose attack on Marxism was both overarching and, again, deliberate[210]—Foucault notably did not need to suppress the "relations of exteriority" which, he freely admitted, discourses might maintain with nondiscursive practices: "To reveal in all its purity the space in which discursive events are deployed is not to undertake to re-establish it in an isolation that nothing could overcome; it is not to close it upon itself; it is to leave oneself free to describe the interplay of relations within it and outside it."[211] Nor did he have to suffer the adverse conceptual consequences of explicitly insisting, akin to poststructuralists such as Baudrillard, that signification or "symbolic exchange" alone was important.[212] Within the models or rules denoted by the concept of discourse Foucault now made room both for erstwhile "material" and "ideal" practices, for subject as well as object. Foucault purchased this apparent transcendence, however, not only as we have seen by positing discourse itself as a transcendent category, but also by supplanting his erstwhile unitary episteme with an assumption of discursive fracture, as in this well-known declaration: "Discourses must be treated as a discontinuous activity . . . we should not imagine that the world presents us with a legible face, leaving us merely to decipher it. . . ."[213] Thus the earlier totalizing character of the episteme was forsaken, in favor of what Poster would call a "decentered" totality.[214]

At least one true advantage could be associated with this centrifugal theorization. "Discourse" acceded to structuralism's accustomed emphasis on the links between ostensibly disparate forms and practices, activities often lying at a vast remove from conventional notions of text; at a stroke, therefore, a cultural studies endowed with Foucauldian tools might look alike to formal scientific treatises, news reports, architecture, institutional structures, economic practices, and gender relations to create its unique series of optics. In an unexpected continuance of the tradition of early British cultural studies, the varied modalities of labor (art, science, reproduction, and child-rearing, as well as the accustomed range of conventional economic activities) therefore still might be studied with an eye to their concrete interrelations. To the extent that post-structuralism's utilization of "discourse" permitted these varied forms and facets of human activity to be analyzed without abiding slight in one or another direction, scholarly practice may be said to have worked ahead of well-secured principle, in favor of an anti-dualistic concept of "culture."

Yet the price at which this newfound freedom was purchased was steep, because "discourse" never addressed the cleavage within social being of which it was itself a sign. Instead "discourse" merely banished production or labor from its purview, for putatively comprising part of the armature of humanism's phantom subject. Mark Poster stated this very explicitly, in 1979:

> Foucault's accomplishments undercut the privileged place of labour as developed by Marx. Foucault's books analyse spaces outside of labour—asylums, clinics, prisons, schoolrooms, and the arenas of sexuality. In these social loci Foucault finds sources of radicality that are not theorised by Marx and Marxists. Implicit in Foucault's work is an attack on the centrality of labour in emancipatory politics. His thought proceeds from the assumption that the working class, through its place in the process of production, is not the vanguard of social change. Foucault may take this as a fact of life in advanced capitalism, or more interestingly, he may be suggesting that the working class is, in its practice and through its organisations (the Party and the union), an accomplice of capitalism and not its contradiction. Radical change may have come instead from those who are and have been excluded from the system—the insane, criminals, perverts, and women.[215]

I leave for the conclusion further discussion of whether such "spaces" are indeed remote from labor. For now it is enough to add that, via the concept of discourse, there transpired a rejection of totality that was far more rigorous than anything Hall's cultural studies, for instance, had wanted to contemplate.[216] The characteristic results of this rejection are conveniently indexed through a recent discussion by John Fiske:

> Discourse constantly transgresses, if it doesn't actually destroy, the boundary between material and cultural conditions, because discourse, through the specificity of its practices, always has a material dimension. . . . There is a physical reality outside of discourse, but discourse is the only means we have of gaining access to it. It is going too far, though only by a smidgeon, to say that reality is the product of discourse: it is more productive to say that what is accepted as reality in any social formation is the product of discourse. Discourse produces a knowledge of the real which it then presents and represents to us in constant circulation and usage. Events do occur, physical reality does exist, but we can know neither until they are put into discourse. . . . Discourse is never neutral or objective: its work of production and repression is always politically active in specific social conditions, and it is always, then, a terrain of struggle.[217]

Deferring the issue of social struggle, I wish only to stress how Fiske shifts between "physical reality" and "events" and "specific social conditions"—and even "social formations"—as if they were synonyms. Through such loose and multiform usages, the question of "discourse's" relations with what appears still to be some kind of environing social totality is kept at arm's length. What do "specific social conditions" within, or against, a given "social formation" have to do with "discourse's" production of "a knowledge of the real"? The same question might be posed to Hall, when he suggests that subjects "are positioned by the discursive formations of specific social formations."[218] "[R]egimes of power," answers Fiske, change in vague and unpredictable fashion, "when changes in the social conditions mean that the old regime has lost its efficiency."[219] But by what right is "efficiency"—or, to speak to the underlying issue, any principle—accorded a global presence, a priori, in accounting for supposedly disparate discourses? Here we find ourselves in the face, once again, of the problem of incommensurable epistemes. As, echoing Sartre, Fredric Jameson put the issue years ago in reference to Foucault's own writings, "one cannot . . . reduce history to one form of understanding among others, and then expect to understand the links between these forms historically."[220] For Fiske, in turn, "old regime" and "social formation" have become equivocations, serving mainly to mitigate and disguise the disparate stances toward totality that had respectively characterized British cultural studies, either in its expressive or structuralist renditions, and Foucault's concept of discourse.

Let us now briefly attend to a second influential variant of poststructuralism, with its own pronounced bearing on communication study, in which signification became primary by virtue of a rejection of "labor" that was far more thoroughgoing and severe than that attempted by Foucault.

The latter had positioned the category of labor merely as a cut-out, so as to shore up his own anti-humanist conception. It was Jean Baudrillard, in contrast, whose self-conscious and concerted emphasis on the deficiencies of "material production" resulted in a sharp and comprehensive reification of "intellectual" labor. I do not wish so much to draw attention to Baudrillard's own mystifyingly transcendent and totalizing coinage—"the Code"[221]—as, once more, to underline the specific depiction of Marxian "productivist discourse" on which the latter explicitly rested. This much is clearly evident in Baudrillard's still somewhat unresolved rejection of Marxism:

> Against those who, fortified behind their legendary materialism, cry idealism as soon as one speaks of signs, or anything that goes beyond manual, productive labor, against those who have a muscular and energetic vision of exploitation, we saw that if the term "materialist" has a meaning (one that is critical, not religious) it is we who are the materialists. But it does not matter. Happy are those who cast longing eyes at Marx as if he were always there to give them recognition. What we are attempting to see here is to what point Marxist logic can be rescued from the limited context of political economy in which it arose, so as to account for *our* contradictions.[222]

Thus this onetime student of the Marxist philosopher Henri Lefebvre revealed the shipwreck of his own efforts to recast historical materialism to take adequate account of what his tutor had sought to generalize as "everyday life in the modern world."

Did not Marxism's "phantom of production," Baudrillard inquired, act with arbitrary systematicity "to code all human material and every contingency of desire and exchange in terms of value, finality, and production"? Was not production actually "nothing but a code imposing this type of decipherment"? And, most fundamentally, did not the very scope of this imaginary mirror portend that "[i]t is no longer worthwhile to make a radical critique of the order of representation in the name of production. . ."?[223] In the tracks of Foucault, Baudrillard charged with evident glee that a Marxism that merely connived at generalizing "the economic mode of rationality over the entire expanse of human history, as the generic mode of human becoming," only "*assist* [ed] *the cunning of capital.*"[224]

But when we examine the fine print, we may see that, like Foucault but with far more pervasive implications, Baudrillard again overreached his object. Baudrillard grounded his concept of symbolic exchange in a categorical rejection of "labor." He suggested, first, that "[p]erhaps political economy is inseparable from the theory of the determinant instance of material production, in which case the Marxist critique of political economy is not extendable to a generalized theory." Deftly stringing together quotes from both Marx and Herbert Marcuse, Baudrillard then explicitly insisted that for Marxism per se, "The social wealth produced is material; it has nothing to do with *symbolic*

wealth. . . ." And again, when "he brands Nature and himself with the
seal of production, man proscribes every relation of symbolic exchange
between himself and Nature." And yet again, when he neatly skewered
Althusser's unsuccessful effort to wed Marxism and structuralism by
flatly asserting that "[h]istorical materialism . . . is incapable of thinking the process of ideology, of culture, of language, of the symbolic in
general."[225] Such assertions substantiate the view of Baudrillard put
forward by Douglas Kellner, to the effect that he believed "that it is
impossible to combine radically different logics of production and signification."[226] Do they not also provide whatever foundation exists for his
signature claim, that ". . . we must move to a radically different level
that . . . permits the definitive resolution of political economy"? "This
level is that of symbolic exchange and its theory. . . . For lack of a
better term, we call this the critique of the political economy of the
sign."[227]

The fatal flaw in "productivist discourse" lay in its supposed incapacity to grasp "symbolic articulation" (and thereby to account, in reference to "the work of art," "for the moment of its operation and of its
radical difference") specifically with regard to "the strategic configura-
tion of modern societies."[228] "[T]he center of gravity has been displaced," Baudrillard writes; "the epicenter of the contemporary system
is no longer the process of material production."[229] What Baudrillard,
like so many other postwar intellectuals, apprehended as a widely dis-
junctive society of consumption[230] comprised the taproot of his hostility
to productivist discourse.

"[A] revolution has occurred in the capitalist world without our
Marxists having wanted to comprehend it," he asserts. This "decisive
mutation" toward "culture . . . consumption . . . information . . .
ideology . . . sexuality, etc.," attends the historical passage toward
"consumption" as the "strategic element": after 1929, "the people were
henceforth mobilized as consumers; their 'needs' became as essential as
their labor power." To correspond with this widely accepted assumption, the "theoretical basis of the system" also needed to shift, claimed
Baudrillard, from political economy to "the new master disciplines of
structural linguistics, semiology, information theory, and cybernetics."
Only thus might the "new ideological structure," which "plays on the
faculty of producing meaning and difference," be sharply enough distinguished from its predecessor, "which plays on labor power."[231] Baudrillard's entire conceptual edifice was built on this presumed dichotomy, which alone underwrote his reification of "symbolic exchange."
Ironically but fittingly, the infinite and, for some, unrestrained productivity of language turns out to be based—albeit negatively—on the ostensive finitude of "labor."

Via Baudrillard and others, "culture"—during the late 1980s—gave
signs of rejoining what hitherto had remained a largely separate discus-

sion of "information."[232] A century earlier, U.S. Protestant intellectuals had sought to distinguish what they called "culture"—the refinement and inner growth contingent on diligent training—from "mere information."[233] Now, significantly, this relationship between "information" and "culture" began to be reversed. A portent of this metamorphosis appeared in an essay published by the anthropologist Clifford Geertz as early as 1966. Even as postindustrial theory was first being formulated, Geertz linked the two terms, only to focus, at once and apparently exclusively, on "culture" alone:

> What happened to us in the Ice Age is that we were obliged to abandon the regularity and precision of detailed genetic control over our conduct for the flexibility and adaptability of a more generalized, though of course no less real, genetic control over it. To supply the additional information necessary to be able to act, we were forced, in turn, to rely more and more heavily on cultural sources—the accumulated fund of significant symbols. Such symbols are thus not mere expressions, instrumentalities, or correlates of our biological, psychological, and social existence; they are prerequisites of it. Without men, no culture, certainly; but equally, and more significantly, without culture, no men.[234]

Here, even as "culture" and "information" were reified and separated, the former was irredeemably colonized by the latter: the concept of "culture" was endowed by Geertz with the trappings of "information": instructions, programs, "control mechanisms," codes. Prefigured here were attempts to enlarge "information's" presence *within* "culture," via more recent ideas of a supposed "InfoCulture"[235] and, now returning to Baudrillard, a "mode of information." In this latter conception, offered by Mark Poster, the attempt is simultaneously to reject postindustrial theory, while nevertheless reintroducing on new grounds the characteristic exceptionalism on which Bell's project had been based—that science constitutes a distinct enterprise. Poster concedes that the broad reordering of society that postindustrial theorists perceive as dramatically disruptive in fact might be encompassed by the "capital-labor relation" posited by Marx. Yet, evidently, he regards such an explanation as a dead letter,[236] for he goes on to posit peremptorily that "these changes are less important in understanding the quality of social relations than are changes in the structure of communicative experience."[237] The chief difference between Poster and Bell thus once again becomes that, for the former, the purportedly exceptional nature of science is properly seen as a function not of labor at all, but rather of "discourse":

> Science . . . is a form of knowledge, a discourse. As such it cannot be examined, from the perspective of critical social theory, by use of the concepts designed to reveal the structures of the domination of labor. The production, distribution and consumption of science, to employ economic

categories, are governed by a different logic from those of labor. The theoretical step from a notion of the emancipation of the labor act to liberation of scientific discourse is not obvious and requires drastic conceptual reformulation. When the transformation of natural materials into commodities is mediated not simply by manual labor operating on machines but by scientific discourses, discourses that are tied to research institutions, government granting agencies, the apparatuses of journals, and the social ritual of conferences, then the master/slave relation of capital and labor has become unrecognizably changed.[238]

Whether couched in the language of postindustrial theory or of a seemingly disparate poststructuralism, this embrace of Bell's claim that, after all, science is not labor, led only to still another invalid reification. As such, it brings us back to the need to insist that, even as "brainwork" cannot be understood absent the sensuous body, so too does all human activity contain its quotient of thought.

Structural Marxism, postindustrialism, poststructuralism: Each is built from the assumption that an anomalous realm, purportedly above and beyond "labor," may be—indeed, must be—granted outstanding conceptual privileges, and each then constructed this space by developing its own reified concept of "intellectual" labor. "Culture" and "information" therefore were reassimilated by communication study only in virtue of one or another variant of a pervasive exceptionalist premise. For Marxist structuralists, this exceptionalism involved a still-tentative and incomplete turn toward a self-enclosed realm of "ideology," which was, its adherents enjoined, to be enfolded into a more encompassing totality. Postindustrial theorists' more severe exceptionalism sought to warrant the conceptual metastasis of intellectuals into a specious universal class, comprising an enticing but unwarranted vehicle of benign historical transcendence. Similarly, for post-structuralists, exceptionalism sanctioned the bearer or possessor of "intellectual" labor solely as a signifying agent, ensnared in the infinitely productive systems of discourse which alone organized and defined the social world.

Out of what appeared at first to be wholly separate processes of assumption and argument, "culture" and "information" therefore eventually arrived at a mutually defined terminus. As reified conceptions of "intellectual" labor once again turned out to supply the node around which communication and cultural studies formed and reformed, the true range of human practice was correspondingly truncated and recast. A new beginning needs to be made, for we are verging on the same sort of intractable exclusion that gave rise, during the 1950s, to cultural studies itself. With this, we can no longer postpone the question that has silently dogged our inquiry from the start: How are we to move out of reification's shadow?

CHAPTER FIVE

Toward a Unified Conceptual Framework

Labour is blossoming or dancing where
The body is not bruised to pleasure soul,
Nor beauty born out of its own despair,
Nor blear-eyed wisdom out of midnight oil.
O chestnut tree, great rooted blossomer,
Are you the leaf, the blossom or the bole?
O body swayed to music, O brightening glance,
How can we know the dancer from the dance?

W. B. Yeats[1]

[W]hat is in question is . . . the necessary social process through
which the materialist enterprise defines and redefines its procedures,
its findings and its concepts, and in the course of this moves beyond
one after another ''materialism.''

Raymond Williams[2]

Our subject has repeatedly recreated itself in the half-light of its enigmatic object. Rippling across the field of vision of communication study
from generation to generation, the epic question of "intellectual" labor
has been episodically remodulated and reshaped.

In the period before World War I, widespread popular concern focused on a series of social problems that accompanied the rise of corporate monopolies over telegraphy and news. Abstracting from this sharply
pointed criticism, John Dewey gestured toward the mutualistic concepts

of communication which pervaded late 19th-century producer republican thought. Dewey's instrumentalism proved far more successful in isolating the limits and drawbacks of dualistic thinking, however, than in effectuating a positive synthesis with which to override them. Rather than opting to subject the intellectual inheritance of producer republicanism—"labor"—to sympathetic critique and revision, Dewey chose to apprehend human self-activity by means of a free-floating concept of "experience," whose steering mechanism was for him an intrinsically benevolent notion of "organized intelligence." As "labor" was displaced, the first of what proved to be a succession of reifications of "intellectual" labor was launched within communication study.

During the interwar decades, this initial displacement was massively extended, even as concern about communication became freshly energized. While some influential proponents of "organized intelligence" waxed enthusiastic, others began to recoil before the ideological mobilization of established institutions, including both corporations and, above all, the state; the latters' growing reliance on "mass persuasion" gave these institutions a strong and worrisome anti-democratic—for some, "totalitarian"—potential. Even before World War II, as we found, concerns about "mass persuasion" began to extend beyond a restricted set of media of news and information, so as to engage both private life and the encompassing field of "mass culture" or "culture industry." As the massive and conflicted crisis of the Depression era was put behind, and the U.S. assumed the mantle of postwar international supremacy, mass culture was said by radical critics to comprise a vital but enigmatic social supplement. The latter's defining characteristic was the ideological basis which it seemed to give to contemporary domination, a feature rooted not only in manipulation from above, but as well in the anomalous status of the white-collar strata.

As challenges to U.S. international supremacy became pronounced, communication studies again refashioned itself. Coming through in the critique of cultural imperialism, a reintegrative political economy of transnational corporate communication confronted what it took to be a still-to-be-formed national identity. At roughly the same time, the concept of human social agency also began to propel a profound intellectual engagement with the history and present status of the British working class and, soon, with the anti-racist and feminist movements that began once again to burgeon. In both cases, "culture" appeared to satisfy, or at least, to raise the prospect of satisfying, the need for drastic conceptual revision of entrenched Marxian formulations.

But the nature of the needful revision remained far from clear and, out of these direct confrontations with Marxism, there eventuated only a new set of reifications. The concepts of communication that resulted seemed to be coextensive not with a limited set of media, but with thoroughgoing substitutive visions of social totality, themselves or-

dained by acceptance of a purportedly autonomous plane of signification. Brainwork could be credited, and speciously generalized, as the
dominant factor or principle of social organization, only inasmuch as—
through Marxist structuralism, postindustrial theory, and poststructuralism—it shed its identity as "labor."

This history, at the end, discloses a significant new question: How
may we work out from under the sedimented reifications which have so
constrained inquiry? How, that is, may we find means with which to
bypass what we have seen has been the supervening, and repeatedly
damaging, assumption that an isolable category of "intellectual labor"
can be accorded substantial significance?

I suggest that such an attempt requires that we identify a valid
conceptual alternative to any kind of exceptionalism. "Culture" or "information," in short, must not be viewed as expressions of an
anomalous, self-enclosed logic. Rather they need to be situated, in all
their singular specificity, in light of some more general and inclusionary
categorial principle.

Such a generative category, as I have repeatedly urged, can be found
in labor, which must then likewise be made to sustain a "labor theory of
culture."[3] As we have seen, however, it has proven an exceedingly
difficult business to grasp "culture" as *production*. Not the least significant consequence of the reifications which have so preoccupied us has
been to compel a continued reliance on quite inadequate conceptions of
this formative category. We may begin to explicate the prospects for such
a labor theory of culture, I think, by returning to Raymond Williams,
whose historical and theoretical orientation—as now at last may be
emphasized—developed in mounting tension with the substitutive characterizations of "culture" that ascended during the 1970s and 1980s.

A word of clarification before we commence. Williams's work did
not tend to evince the pointed propositional structure with which I have
tried to endow it. Or, rather, it overlaid a scaffolding of active argument
with a series of cross-cutting and sometimes confusing, incompletely
theorized, assertions. "What I would now claim to have reached,"
Williams wrote in 1976, " . . . is a theory of culture as a (social and
material) productive process and of specific practices, of 'arts,' as social
uses of material means of production (from language as material 'practical consciousness' to the specific technologies of writing and forms of
writing, through to mechanical and electronic communications systems)."[4] For all its suggestiveness, this formulation—Williams dubbed it
"cultural materialism"—generated an ambiguous oscillation, for it explicitly assigned to language, communication, and consciousness as such
"a primacy co-equal with other forms of the material social process,
including . . . 'labour' or 'production.'"[5] A vital confusion, in turn,
originated not in the corrective impulse that motivated this assertion, but
rather in the imprecision with which it came to be conveyed: Williams

had reproduced the deeply ingrained tendency, to put "language" (or "consciousness") in one place and "production" (or "being") in another. The terms of discussion, paradoxically, slid back into the very framework against which Williams was, as we will see, seeking to lodge an insuperable objection. With reinstatement of this dualism, how would it be possible, as he had hoped as far back as *The Long Revolution*, to approach "[t]he art . . . the production, the trading, the politics, the raising of families" each and all *as* production?

As late as 1980, therefore, Hall could reasonably claim that, in his ongoing labor of revision, "Williams is still on surer ground when he identifies negatively the positions against which 'cultural materialism' is defined ('a totally spiritualised cultural production' on the one hand; on the other, its 'relegation to a secondary status') than he is on clarifying the positive content of his thesis."[6] Within an increasingly expansive and confident cultural studies, in turn, Williams's acquiescence to the "materiality of language and forms of writing" perversely came through as a preferred emphasis in its own right. Those who sought to do so could read Williams as if he were concerned with an encompassing and exclusionary labor of signification rather than, now as always, with extending and, where necessary, challenging and redirecting the more multifaceted "culture and society" tradition.[7] Let us turn, therefore, directly to this ongoing and incomplete revision.

Williams came to believe that he had been wrong in assuming "that a cultural and educational programme alone could revitalize the left or alter areas of popular opinion sufficiently to change the traditional institutions of the labour movement."[8] He now held that the New Left's early orientation toward cultural change had exacted a prohibitive price—in the shape of its prolonged and dramatic "underestimate of everything that had not changed in contemporary capitalism," including, in particular, "the political power of the capitalist state."[9] Whatever pain might have been created by the attempt to rework "traditional Marxist arguments"—rather than jettisoning such discussion, as he himself had done during the 1950s, in favor of "exploring current changes in cultural experience"—remained, simply, "necessary." That such work had been neglected in turn constituted "a weakness which was heavily paid for later."[10] Thus Williams, too, turned directly to Marx, and his thinking on "culture" and "society" accordingly underwent extended scrutiny and modification.

"Cultural" forms and activities, to begin with, needed to be comprehended as taking their places within what Williams now generally identified as a *more* encompassing, and always dynamic, "social process." What he began to term a "sociology of culture" thereby inherited the synthetic impulse that he had previously vested in "culture" per se. "Society," in this later formulation, is then never only the "dead husk" which limits social and individual fulfillment. It is always also a constitutive process with very powerful pressures which are both expressed in political, economic, and cultural formations and, to take the full weight of "constitutive," are internalized and become "individual wills." Determination of this whole kind—a complex and interrelated process of limits and pressures—is in the whole social process itself and nowhere else. . . .[11]

"Society," rather than "culture," was now identifiably and, despite occasional lapses, remained the inclusive—indeed, totalizing—term. Indeed it has been too little noticed that, in his unfolding "sociology of culture," Williams correspondingly began, quite deliberately, to *contract* the scope of reference of this once all-important keyword. He downplayed the idea of "culture" as "a whole way of life," again in order to emphasize "all forms of signification . . . within the actual means and conditions of their production,"[12] and later, more precisely, so as to "specify and reinforce the concept of culture as a *realized signifying system.*"[13] Such a limitation was needed, Williams came to assert, in order to exercise greater intellectual control in developing "an adequate theoretical account of the *conditions of a practice,*" an account that would *simultaneously* affirm that particular practice's determinate specificity, while still also continuing to sustain exploration of "the inevitable relations between different practices."[14]

Unlike the main body of cultural studies, Williams took this injunction with the utmost seriousness. His guarded acceptance of the Marxist concept of "determination" nonetheless still stubbornly resisted granting any greater primacy to "the economy" than he had been willing to accord it in *The Long Revolution*. Utilizing what Hall aptly called a "radically interactionist conception,"[15] Williams instead continued to stress the need for "the whole difficult process of discovering and describing relations" between "practices" which crisscrossed what had previously been reified into a separate "base" and "superstructure."[16] Because, however, he was only beginning to formulate a set of theoretical terms to guide this search for social relationality—for of course "pressures" and "limits" could not be expected simply to announce themselves as such— Williams's conception of "determination" could be seen, as Hall preferred in 1980, as "nothing more than a holding operation."[17] Yet this judgment must not becloud recognition of the further breakthroughs toward which Williams was working.

Although his emerging synthesis was predicated on an irrevocable rejection of social democratic consensus, "a whole way of life," still, as we saw, the latter never quite gave way to Thompson's earlier express preference—"a way of struggle."[18] Appropriating Gramsci's vital concept, instead, Williams came to assert that within the class-defined "hegemony" that structured contemporary capitalist society, both domination and continuing struggles could claim constitutive roles. But Williams did not ascribe to "culture" (let alone to "ideology") a superordinate role in the achievement of such a hegemony (here finding nominal agreement from Hall, who ironically criticized Williams himself for this same shortcoming).[19] Williams's conception rather made room for, even if it did not actively emphasize, the deployment of force as well as of economic power, coercion as well as consent, as central means of sustaining class dominance.[20] "Society" or "social process" therefore now amounted for Williams to something much more than a mere renaming of the anthropological concept of "culture" on which he had previously relied.

A still more vital second transition, though never fully formalized, occurred around Williams's complex reformulation of the nature of human self-activity. In *The Long Revolution*, once again, Williams had sought to employ an anthropological concept of culture, encompassing "[t]he art . . . as an activity, with the production, the trading, the politics, the raising of families,"[21] as the constitutive agency of the social process. What happened to this generalizing thrust? By the mid-1970s, in a crucial restatement, much the same range of activity came to be reconceived in terms of "productive forces" and, crucially, of "production"[22] per se:

> The social and political order which maintains a capitalist market, like the social and political struggles which created it, is necessarily a material production. From castles and palaces and churches to prisons and workhouses and schools; from weapons of war to a controlled press: any ruling class, in variable ways though always materially, produces a social and political order. These are never superstructural activities. They are the necessary material production within which an apparently self-subsistent mode of production can alone be carried on.[23]

Williams was striving not so much, as he once had done, to circumvent as now to positively transcend, the historically embedded legacy of "base and superstructure." His unique reintegration of these categories was developed, as Perry Anderson was to comment, "not on the usual grounds that the ideal sphere of the latter was indefensibly reduced to its material supports, but rather because if anything the former was wrongly narrowed and abstracted by the exclusion from it of the forces of cultural production"; thus, "Williams taxed Marxism with too little rather than too much materialism."[24]

It should be stressed that Williams's emerging revision concorded with a tenacious—and, from the perspective of institutionalized socialism, often a heretical—tradition, which sought its inspiration in Hegel and in the young Marx. The latter had written in one place that "the human essence . . . is the ensemble of the social relations";[25] and, in another, that "[r]eligion, family, state, law, morality, science, art, etc., are only *particular* modes of production, and fall under its general law."[26] Thereafter this tenet was approached by Morris in the 1880s and 1890s, and by the philosophers Herbert Marcuse (in 1933)[27] and Georg Lukacs. The latter came to assert that productive activity—labor—had fundamental ontological significance. Productive activity became for him what C. J. Arthur calls the "primary mediation" through which the self-creation of humankind occurs.[28] As Lukacs put it in regard to humankind's evolutionary "leap to labour"—that is, to social being and thus to history—labor acts as the essential condition and agency of the ongoing metabolism between society and nature:

> Through labour, a teleological positing is realized within material being, as the rise of a new objectivity. The first consequence of this is that labour becomes the model for any social practice. . . . [29]

Akin to Marcuse, Lukacs could never quite bring himself to place art, science, and other activities of a purported "higher" and "relatively autonomous" kind unreservedly within the province of labor; labor is given the status of "model" rather than "source" or "agency."[30] Yet, during the 1970s and early 1980s, Williams was ranging toward just this idea: that labor constitutes the comprehensive category of human self-activity, operative at once across the whole range of "intellectual" pursuits—art, law, science, and religion—as well as within more familiar precincts of directly "economic" production.

Williams's incipient attempt to unify "intellectual" and "manual" labor within a single conceptual framework can be detected in several ways. There is, first, his very tentative and limited assimilation of "information," within the context of a brief treatment of contemporary economic trends:

> In a modern capitalist economy, and its characteristic kind of social order, the cultural institutions of press and publishing, cinema, radio, television and the record industry, are no longer, as in earlier market phases, marginal or minor, but, both in themselves and in their frequent interlock or integration with other productive institutions, are parts of the whole social and economic organization at its most general and pervasive.[31]

Such was the sweep of these tendencies that Williams was moved momentarily to contemplate a point of synthesis between "culture" and "information." "Information processes," he wrote, at the very end of *Culture*—assimilating what he found useful in postindustrialism and, perhaps, in the associated radical critique of "information"—"have become a qualitative part of economic organization." Yet at once he also noticed that this meant that "a major part of the whole modern labour process must be defined in terms which are not easily theoretically separable from the traditional 'cultural' activities."[32] "Culture" and "information" thus specified overlapping aspects or segments of a single

historical continuum of practice, and the latter concept—"practice"—
made no concessions to the reification of "intellectual" labor.

In a discussion of "new forms of cultural production," symp-
tomatically, Williams emphasized that with ever-increasing "professional specialization" not only writers, actors, and designers, but also
"cameramen, sound recordists, editors and a whole range of people with
ancillary skills," as well as "electricians, carpenters, [and] logistical
staff," became "indispensable."[33] Williams's revisionary effort around
"production" comported increasingly well, too—unlike Hall's—with research which emphasized the political economy of communication media.[34] Perhaps most crucially, for Williams "work" explicitly began to
verge on being a medium in which signifying and nonsignifying elements together attained, in any discrete case, a specific gravity. To get at
this, he introduced what he called "the metaphor of solution"—a capa-
cious and insightful usage, intended to underline that "manifestly signifying institutions, practices and works" were "deeply present" in other
activities, and vice versa. This formulation, evidently taken over from an
earlier effort to explicate the "structure of feeling," now correspondingly
began to verge on an unprecedented and welcome specificity.

Is it going too far to suggest that Williams's formulation meant that
each social practice within the vast array of human production creates its
own specific suspension of "intellectual" and "manual" elements—
thought and activity combined? The ongoing assimilation of the work of
the Soviet psychologist Lev Vygotsky offers significant support for such a
conception, by attempting to show how, on the level of individual development, language merges repeatedly with and into activity. "Our
analysis accords symbolic activity a specific *organizing* function that
penetrates the process of tool use and produces fundamentally new
forms of behavior," writes Vygotsky.[35] For Vygotsky, the central role in
shaping the child's development is played by a notion of self-activity that
is all but identical to an integral concept of labor. The latter's distinctive
realm is thus properly demarcated by what Vygotsky called the "higher
psychological functions"—verbal thought, intellectual speech, voluntary memory and attention, rational volition—functions whose own
development he associated specifically with the above-mentioned convergence of language and tool (including body) use. In an important
extension, other scholars—working in light of Vygotsky's approach—
have argued that "everyday cognition"[36] pervades activity across the
entire range of the division of labor.

We might also recall here the century-old arguments offered by
Joseph Dietzgen and Baptist Hubert. Thinking, following Dietzgen, is
labor, only because and insofar as it is performed by an embodied sensuous agent; turning to Hubert, no matter how mundane or "unskilled,"
labor—practice, human self-activity, call it what you like—*always* contains its portion of thought. "Intellectual" labor, or what Dietzgen

termed "brainwork," cannot be considered a separate ingredient or thing; rather, following Hubert, it is coextensive with "labor." Significa-tion, on this view, exists not as a separate and autonomous practice, nor even as half of a composite construct which also encompasses activity; it is, rather, again an organic dimension of an ontologically prior category of social labor.[37] Labor, in turn, has been embodied through the course of history in innumerable concrete activities, some of which we are in the significant habit of calling "intellectual" labor.

This book has tried to show that when we confuse this convenience of nomenclature with the activities themselves, we commit ourselves to pursuing a chimera. In contrast, an inclusive, integral concept of "labor" points in a more promising direction. Yet this idea of "labor" as the full range of practice engaged in by a sensuously self-active social subject is not yet simply a plum ripe for picking. Only if a series of additional conceptual dislodgments can be effected, will a long-obstructed road once again be thrown open.

Ensconced notions of "play" and "leisure" comprise one such area of engagement. We have before us a century and more of feminist argu-ment that domestic work should count as "real" labor,[38] to dissuade us from over-hasty dismissal of activity that seems remote or peculiar when placed only in light of dominant—and dominating—categorizations. Some recent works of feminist communication research may be utilized to draw out this point. Feminist scholars have turned to study mass-media audiences to counteract a general and longstanding marginaliza-tion. Women, by virtue of their relative historical absence from such positions, long could not be studied as programmers and network ex-ecutives; but they could be taken seriously as viewers, listeners, and readers.[39] This feminist effort to attend to the audience comes as a wholly welcome initiative; it is about time that this vast domain of social self-activity, ceded for so long solely to market researchers and political pollsters, should be reclaimed for critical inquiry. Placing gender at the center of renewed theorization of the audience is equally necessary, for only by doing so can analysis take up the concrete historical modalities of the social division of labor.

It needs to be underlined, however, that the abiding tendency to reify "intellectual" labor has arisen as well within this context. The feminist turn toward the audience is sometimes founded on an act of abstraction, wherein by something approaching sheer assumption an overarching realm of signification comes to be equated solely with the sphere of consumption—or what Ien Ang goes so far as to distill into a realm of "use value" putatively separated by a rigid barrier from the domain in which "exchange value" predominates. Inquiry then comes to revolve around how and why audience members make meanings as they do,[40] as if this question could be given a valid answer without systematic scrutiny of the role of gender within media production, which of course is replete with its own originating limits and pressures. Indeed, by reproducing the very dichotomy between consumption and production that is itself institutionalized by the culture industry, such research may truncate its own critical potential, and ironically introduce affinities with the very researchers whose manipulative interventions into audience reaction and response helped to resubordinate women in the home after the Second World War. So much has been aptly noted by John Clarke:

> [T]his view of cultural creativity highlights consumption as an active social practice and relegates exchange and commodity relations to the background. What we see is the excess of signs, not the conditions of production, distribution and exchange which make them available. The effect, ironically, is to replicate that view of capitalism which capitalism would most like us to see: the richness of the market-place and the freely choosing consumer. The other side—the structures of production and the inequalities of access to the market-place—are missing, and these absences emphasize the "free-floating" quality of the sign, making it available for any use or meaning that may be attached to it. . . . In a sense, these approaches miss the structured secondariness of consumption.[41]

Yet this imputed "secondariness" in its turn hints at a familiar put-down: capitalism precedes and overrides patriarchy. How might we redirect ourselves away from this approaching cul-de-sac? Only, I think, by moving expressly against the familiar dichotomy between "production" and "consumption," toward the sort of scheme I am proposing. Are we not entitled to insist that, in this context, "production" itself requires not one but two moments: the first centering on the media as sites of institutionalized cultural production, and the second on audience-members as producers who contribute to their own self-understanding?[42] If so, then we must expend significantly greater effort in cultivating the study of audience members not simply as viewers or readers, engaging in repeated acts of spectatorship, but rather as persons whose labors include paying attention to the media.[43] We must ready ourselves to contemplate a more exotic range of activities in this way.

A further revision must also be contemplated. With Williams's vital thesis, that productive activity extends to both base and superstructure, to "intellectual" as well as "manual" practice, an overt apparatus through which to apprehend and analyze "production" becomes indispensable. A vast body of human activity remains informal; but, as anthropologists long have known, this does not mean it is disordered or ad hoc. In order to comprehend the disparate expanse of practice that is society, we will need means with which to describe and classify this interrelated and dynamic complex of historically determinate human activities. "[T]he difficulty is," Williams himself was to note, "that if we . . . describe productive forces as all and any activities in the social process as a whole, we have made a necessary critique but, at least in the first instance, lost edge and specificity. To go beyond this difficulty will be a matter for later argument. . . ."[44] Williams died without having fully and explicitly surmounted this challenge. Yet he did commence on the work of building toward such a theorization; indeed the problem of endowing "production" with a determinate form lay close to the heart of his continuing intellectual endeavor. In *Culture*, once more, we find the provisional results:

> [W]e can distinguish, in the whole range of social practice, different and variable measures of distance between particular practices and the social relations which organize them. . . . Some forms of work, including . . . some forms of cultural work, operate outside the conditions of wage-labour. . . . Thus the hypothesis of degree of distance between the conditions of a practice and the most immediately organized forms of social relations seems to be a useful working procedure in the differential sociology of the range of practices which compose a culture and a society.[45]

"Culture," plainly, needs to be pursued not solely on the plane of intersubjectivity or experience, but also in more specific and determinate terms: "the social relations which organize . . . particular practices."

This nascent formulation harmonizes with a suggestion on offer from kindred revisionist historians: that distinct social relations cohere around discrete labor systems:[46] homework and unfree labor of various kinds, as well as wage-earning; independent commodity production as well as a range of different systems of production for use.[47] It is apparent that, in the context of his own special interest—literary signifying systems—Williams was already reaching to concretize "productive activity" in just such terms. His book *Culture* (1981) relied, albeit "provisionally," on a nomenclature that made room not only for specific "means of production" and for "institutions" such as "patronage," but also for what Williams specified as artisanal, post-artisanal, market professional, and corporate professional systems of labor.[48] As Williams insistently recognized, even today it is patently untrue that capitalism excludes all else but waged labor, that artisanal systems of labor have been dispensed with, and that the commodity form has specifically become all-pervasive within the "cultural" sector.[49] The study of institutionalized communication—that is, of that portion of the division of labor whose work is formally communication—must try, correspondingly, to comprehend the full range of this variety, by working to recognize and explicate all of the labor systems which shape and limit communication processes; that is, by never ceasing to attend to the relations of production that directly "organize" so much—though still by no means all—of our cultural practice. The nature and range of diverse labor systems, and the interlocks and tensions among them, must become subjects of enduring study.

By means of these organizing labor systems, finally, many signifying practices may be situated within a wider field of social relationships. We need to be careful here, because we are verging on the vexed concept of social totality. Yet we cannot afford to abdicate the intellectual responsibility—and humility—that some such generalizing effort permits us to assume. The needs to interrelate and to assign priority to local developments are not lightly forsaken; indeed it is arguable that they cannot ever really be relinquished—they are only more or less explicit or hidden. Recognition of the need to seek out such interrelationships was never far from the center of Williams's continuing inquiry.

Having been burned during the 1960s for not sharply distinguishing the idea of a common culture from the existing complex of capitalist institutions, however, Williams acted to distance his emerging theorization from any prior assumption of an expressive totality. He did so, first, by trying to pluralize what had earlier comprised a unitary conception— so as, for example, to attend to what he now significantly came to call "the complex relation of differentiated structures of feeling to differentiated classes."[50] Thereafter, even this remnant evidently came to be abandoned; in a major work on "Culture" published in 1981, the term "structure of feeling" is never even introduced, despite obvious occasions for doing so.[51] With an eye on the reality of uneven historical development after the early 1970s Williams likewise began to explore the idea of "residual" and "emergent" cultural forms; while through notions of "alternative," "oppositional," and "dominant" cultural forms and practices he sought newly explicit means of demarcating what he had not always been able to emphasize should be seen as sustained, relationally structured differences within social experience. But there are more direct indications of this relinquishment—or was it actually a redefinition?—of social totality. Williams began self-consciously to utilize "[t]he idea of totality . . . [as] a critical weapon '*against* 'the growing dominance of capitalist economic activity and its values over all other forms of human activity."[52] In 1977, for example, he wrote: "[*N*]*o mode of production and therefore no dominant social order and therefore no dominant culture ever in reality includes or exhausts all human practice, human energy, and human intention.'*"[53] Leavis's yearning for a spurious organic community of yesteryear here might be said to have metamorphosized, somehow, into a space in which Williams's own abiding hopes for a common culture managed to subsist. But what principle(s), if not solely those attending the wage relationship, interrelated and systematized "human practice" across this surplus expanse? How might there be introduced ordering principles across "the social formation"? Doubtless "hegemony" functioned as the mainstay of the loose framework which Williams provided for addressing these questions. But his seeming inability to pose the issues directly suggests that we have here arrived at an outermost border of his evolving thought.

Relations of production within and around communication institutions exist only within an environing social field or formation. How is the latter to be apprehended? How, in turn, may we adequately engage the unrelievedly dynamic process that has been "historical capitalism"?[54] To meet the well-taken objection—that "capitalism" in fact coexists with labor systems beyond the wage relation, and on which indeed the latter itself may be partly dependent—plainly we may not assign primacy, as a matter of prior doctrine, to one or another determinate system of labor. Work performed under a wage contract thus can have no ontological preference over, for example, domestic work, peasant production, or slave labor. If we now cease to insist, a priori, on the achieved universality of one particular form of labor—the wage relation—then we really have no choice but to analyze production as it occurs across society's observable span. Only in this way can we give concrete definition—active historical pressures and limits—to Thompson's claim that "the logic of capitalist process has found expression within all the activities of a society, and exerted a determining pressure upon its development and form. . . ."[55] In this context, finally, we may look to "culture"/"information" as the site at which longstanding historical pressures toward the capitalization of production are presently undergoing a decisive expansion.[56] But *that* story must await its own time.

Notes

Preface

1. Robert K. Merton, "On Sociological Theories of the Middle Range," in idem, *Social Theory and Social Structure* (1945; New York, 1968), 39–72.

2. This latter point made by Dallas Smythe, "Communications: Blindspot of Western Marxism," *Canadian Journal of Political and Social Theory* 1 (3) (Fall 1977): 1–27.

3. Peter Golding and Graham Murdock, "Theories of Communication and Theories of Society," *Communication Research* 5 (3) (July 1978): 339–56.

4. Martin Jay, *Marxism and Totality: The Adventures of a Concept from Lukacs to Habermas* (Berkeley, 1984).

5. Raymond Williams, *Keywords: A Vocabulary of Culture and Society*, rev. ed. (New York, 1983), 176–79.

6. Harry Braverman, *Labor and Monopoly Capital: The Degradation of Work in the 20th Century* (New York, 1974), 126.

7. Fredric Jameson, *The Political Unconscious* (Ithaca, 1981), 9.

8. On this point, which receives further attention in the conclusion to this book, Hannah Arendt asserts: "[T]the seemingly blasphemous notion of Marx that labor (and not God) created man or that labor (and not reason) distinguished man from the other animals was only the most radical and consistent formulation of something upon which the whole modern age was agreed." Hannah Arendt, *The Human Condition* (Chicago, 1958), 86.

9. Cf. Braverman, *Labor and Monopoly Capital*, 45–58.

10. Dan Schiller, "Enlightenment, Mass Deception, and Beyond in Communication History," George Gerbner Lecture in Communications, Annenberg School of Communications, University of Pennsylvania, Philadelphia, April 22, 1988.

Chapter One. Communication and Labor

1. John Dewey, *The Public and Its Problems* (1927; rpt., Athens, n.d.), 8.

2. Harry Braverman, *Labor and Monopoly Capital: The Degradation of Work in the 20th Century* (New York, 1974), 13.

3. Edward Bellamy, *Looking Backward 2000-1887* (1888; Cleveland, 1946), 54–55.

4. The standard work is Sean Wilentz, *Chants Democratic: New York City & the Rise of the American Working Class, 1788–1850* (New York, 1984).

5. Dan Schiller, *Objectivity and the News: The Public and the Rise of Commercial Journalism* (Philadelphia, 1981), 32–46. For the exclusionary aspect of artisan republicanism in its bearing on the press, see Alexander Saxton, *The Rise and Fall of the White Republic: Class Politics and Mass Culture in 19th-Century America* (London, 1990), 95–108.

6. Richard Kielbowicz, *News in the Mail* (Westport, 1990).

7. U.S. Congress, Senate, 23d Congress, 2d Session, Senate Document 86: 112, in U.S. Congress, Senate, 48th Congress, 2d Session, Executive Document No. 40, *History of the Railway Mail Service; A Chapter in the History of Postal Affairs in the United States*, 16.

8. David Montgomery, *The Fall of the House of Labor* (New York, 1987), 328; James Gilbert, *Designing the Industrial State: The Intellectual Pursuit of Collectivism in America, 1880–1940* (Chicago, 1972), 7, 26, 61–62.

9. John L. Thomas, *Alternative America: Henry George, Edward Bellamy, Henry Demarest Lloyd and the Adversary Tradition* (Cambridge, 1983).

10. Laurence Gronlund's *The Cooperative Commonwealth* was first published in 1884. A direct influence on, among others, trade union and socialist leaders such as Eugene Debs and Kate Richards O'Hare and on the radical journalist J. A. Wayland, this work also itself gave a specific inflection to diverse existing strands of radical social criticism. See Stow Persons, "Introduction," in Gronlund, *The Cooperative Commonwealth*, ed. Stow Persons (Cambridge, 1965), vii–xxvi; Elliott Shore, *Talkin' Socialism: J. A. Wayland and the Role of the Press in American Radicalism, 1890–1912* (Lawrence, Kansas 1988); Mark Pittenger, *American Socialists and Evolutionary Thought, 1870–1920* (Madison, 1993), 43–63.

11. James R. Green, *Grass-Roots Socialism* (Baton Rouge, 1978); Norman Pollack, *The Just Polity: Populism, Law, and Human Welfare* (Urbana, 1987); Robert C. McMath, Jr., *American Populism: A Social History 1877–1898* (New York, 1993).

12. Leon Fink, *Workingmen's Democracy: The Knights of Labor and American Politics* (Urbana, 1983); Montgomery, *Fall of the House of Labor*. On the "cooperative commonwealth" idea see especially pp. 203, 281–90; Kim Voss, *The Making of American Exceptionalism: The Knights of Labor and Class Formation in the Nineteenth Century* (Ithaca, 1993).

13. Mari Jo Buhle, *Women and American Socialism, 1870–1920* (Urbana, 1983); Ken Fones-Wolf, *Trade Union Gospel: Christianity and Labor in Industrial Philadelphia, 1865–1915* (Philadelphia, 1989); Kathryn Kish Sklar, *Florence Kelley and the Nation's Work: The Rise of Women's Political Culture, 1830–1900* (New Haven, 1995); Arthur Lipow, *Authoritarian Socialism in America: Edward Bellamy & the Nationalist Movement* (Berkeley, 1982); Nell Irvin Painter, *Stand-*

ing at Armageddon: The United States, 1877–1919 (New York, 1987); David Nord, "The Experts versus the Experts: Conflicting Philosophies of Municipal Utility Regulation in the Progressive Era," *Wisconsin Magazine of History* 58 (3) (Spring 1975): 219–36.

14. David Montgomery, *Citizen Worker: The Experience of Workers in the United States with Democracy and the Free Market during the Nineteenth Century* (Cambridge, 1993) is the most recent and synoptic assessment of this tradition, which infused 19th-century U.S. working-class movements for reform.

15. One partial exception to this claim is Linda Lawson, *Truth in Publishing: Federal Regulation of the Press's Business Practices* (Carbondale, 1993), which characterizes reform efforts around the commercial press as falling within a shared "Progressive" impulse. Robert W. McChesney's study of a later phase of the reform effort, centering around radio, must also be noted: *Telecommunications, Mass Media, and Democracy: The Battle for the Control of U.S. Broadcasting, 1928–1935* (New York, 1993). I survey and explicate the popular movement to restructure telecommunications around the turn of the century in Dan Schiller, "'Everybody's Common Means of Communication'?: Rethinking the Public Service History of U.S. Telecommunications, 1894-1919," paper presented to the Annual Meeting of the Organization of American Historians, April 14–17, 1994, Atlanta. A study of struggles around the structure and content of the early film industry is promised from Steven Ross.

16. Lambert A. Wilmer, *Our Press Gang; Or, A Complete Exposition of the Corruptions and Crimes of the American Newspaper* (Philadelphia, 1859), 14.

17. See Lawson, *Truth in Publishing*, 12–44. Though the statistical series are not comparable, they give a general sense of the movement toward corporate control: in 1899, corporations owned 17% of U.S. newspapers and periodicals, but by 1909 corporations controlled over 71% of the newspaper industry's revenues. Alfred M. Lee, *The Daily Newspaper in America: The Evolution of a Social Instrument* (New York, 1937), 197.

18. Thomas Ainge Devyr in U.S. Congress, Senate, 48th Congress, Committee on Education and Labor, *Report of the Committee of the Senate upon the Relations between Labor and Capital, and Testimony Taken by the Committee* (Washington, 1885), II:835.

19. John Jarrett in ibid., I:1165.

20. Edward King in ibid., II:80–81, 82.

21. King, in ibid., II:82.

22. On the emergence of a working-class press in this period, see Jon Bekken, "'No Weapon So Powerful': Working-Class Newspapers in the United States," *Journal of Communication Inquiry* 12 (2) (Summer 1988): 104–19; and idem, "The Working-Class Press at the Turn of the Century," in William S. Solomon and Robert W. McChesney, eds., *Ruthless Criticism: New Perspectives in U.S. Communication History* (Minneapolis, 1993), 151–75; Shore, *Talkin' Socialism*; Green, *Grass-Roots Socialism*, 128–43. On the Populists' use of the newspaper and their critique of the commercial press, see Theodore Mitchell, *Political Education in the Southern Farmers' Alliance 1887–1900* (Madison, 1987), 96–112.

23. King, in *Report on Relations between Labor and Capital*, II: 82–83.

24. See, for example, Henry George in ibid., I: 480–88; Richard Hinton in ibid., II: 412; Daniel H. Craig in ibid., II: 1268–70, 1279. For a cogent analysis of

the common class interest that animated the tie between Western Union and the AP, and the opposition that recognition of this overlap provoked, see James G. Smart, "Information Control, Thought Control: Whitelaw Reid and the Nation's News Services," *Public Historian* 3 (2) (Spring 1981): 23–42. The best-documented study of the 19th-century Associated Press unfortunately removes the news agency too far from its social, as opposed to business, context. Popular criticisms are thus arbitrarily subordinated to the narrower interests of publishers, politicians, and telegraph magnates. Menahem Blondheim, *News over the Wires: The Telegraph and the Flow of Public Information in America, 1844–1897* (Cambridge, 1994).

25. Richard B. Du Boff, "The Telegraph and the Structure of Markets in the United States, 1845–1890," *Research in Economic History*, vol. 8 (Detroit, 1983), 253–77; see also idem, "The Telegraph in Nineteenth-Century America: Technology and Monopoly," *Comparative Studies in Society and History* 26 (4) (Oct. 1984): 571–86.

26. Richard B. Du Boff, "The Rise of Communication Regulation: The Telegraph Industry, 1844–1880," *Journal of Communication* 34 (3) (Summer 1984): 52–66 at 58–59.

27. Lester G. Lindley, *The Constitution Faces Technology: The Relationship of the National Government to the Telegraph 1866–1884* (New York, 1975), 160–62.

28. Ann Moyal, "The History of Telecommunication in Australia: Aspects of the Technological Experience, 1854–1930," in Nathan Reingold and Marc Rothenberg, eds., *Scientific Colonialism: A Cross-Cultural Comparison* (Washington, D.C., 1987), 40.

29. Richard B. Du Boff, "Business Demand and the Development of the Telegraph in the United States, 1844–1860," *Business History Review* 54 (4) (Winter 1980): 467; for European comparisons, Eric Hobsbawm, *The Age of Capital* (New York, 1975), 48–68.

30. Nathaniel P. Hill (Senator), "Postal Telegraph," a report submitted to the U.S. Senate, May 27, 1884, in Hill, *Speeches and Papers on the Silver, Postal Telegraph, and Other Economic Questions* (Colorado Springs, 1890), 189.

31. U.S. Congress, House of Representatives, 51st Cong., 2d Sess., *Report of the Postmaster-General*, Executive Document 1, Part 4 (Washington, 1890), 113.

32. Gene Fowler, *A Solo in Tom-Toms* (New York, 1946), 83; for the contrast between "social" uses of the telegraph in Europe and the United States, see also Charles A. Sumner, *The Postal Telegraph: A Lecture Delivered at Dashaway Hall, San Francisco, Oct. 12, 1875* (San Francisco, 1879), 4.

33. AT&T *Annual Report 1911* (New York, 1912), 37.

34. Hill, "Postal Telegraph," 190.

35. Sumner, *The Postal Telegraph*, 1.

36. William Appleman Williams, *Contours of American History* (Chicago, 1966), 337.

37. Fink, *Workingmen's Democracy*, 31.

38. ". . . I am not afraid," Hinton continued, "of a government that cooperates with the people in an endeavor to correct the evils that may grow up in any community." In *Report of Relations between Labor and Capital*, II: 405–6.

39. William E. Unrau, *Tending the Talking Wire* (Salt Lake City, 1979), 12. In California, Nevada, and Utah, aboriginal groups also had a record of attacking mail coaches and post riders throughout the 1850s; "A Brief History of the Mail

Service, Settlement of the Country, and the Indian Depredations Committed upon the Mail Trains of George Chorpenny on the Several Routes between Salt Lake and California from May 1st, 1850, to July 1860" (n.p., n.d.).

40. James Weinstein, *The Decline of Socialism in America 1912–1925* (New Brunswick, 1984), 139.

41. Blondheim, *News over the Wires*, 71–95.

42. Donald Bruce Jackson, comp. *National Party Platforms*, rev. ed., vol 1: *1840–1956* (Urbana, 1978), 65.

43. Blondheim, *News over the Wires*, 187. The news-telegraph monopoly's scandalous intervention into the watershed election and post-election "compromise of 1876," which announced the final end of Reconstruction, are likewise related in Blondheim, *News over the Wires*, 177–84.

44. The fractious development of news agencies is covered, in great descriptive detail, by Richard A. Schwarzlose, *The Nation's Newsbrokers*, vol. 2: *The Rush to Institution: From 1865 to 1920* (Evanston, 1990), esp. 33–107, 131–212. Also useful are Blondheim, *News over the Wires*, 143–68; and Smart, "Information Control, Thought Control."

45. Richard Hinton in *Report on Relations between Labor and Capital*, II: 430–31. See, at the other end of the period, Amos Pinchot, "The Associated Press," *The Masses* 5 (April 1914): 18–19.

46. U.S. Congress, Senate, 41st Cong., 2d Sess., Mis. Doc. No. 13, 1869–1870, *Resolutions of the National Typographical Union* (Washington, D.C., 1870), 81. Also see *Report of the Proceedings of the 17th Annual Session of the National Typographical Union*, Held in Albany, N.Y., June 7–11, 1869 (Cincinnati, 1869), 35, 51–52. The evidence for narrow forms of collusion between the AP news agency and Western Union appears mixed. On one hand, the close interlock between the two clearly could generate strategic press attacks on government ownership, replete with denunciations of contemporary European experiences, when proponents of nationalization appeared to be gaining ground. Western Union President Orton, for example, requested and received an editorial in the *New York Tribune* that pointed up the ostensible shortcomings of the just-nationalized English postal telegraph, in a successful attempt to defeat nationalization legislation in the 1870 Congress. Writing to Whitelaw Reid, who was second in command at the *Tribune* and a coming power at the AP itself, Orton stated: "let me record my thanks for the prompt and efficient support which the Tribune has given, and please say to Mr. Greeley how grateful I am for the generous response he has always made to every request of mine. . . . I trust you will not be slow to advise me whenever occasion arises for me to render yourself, or the Tribune, a service." Lindley, *Constitution Faces Technology*, 110, 162. On the other hand, Postmaster General Wanamaker in 1890 went out of his way to call attention to the "strong endorsement of the press of the country" for a postal telegraph. Of 289 newspaper articles which had come to his notice, no less than 209, he claimed, "were for postal telegraphy." As we will see, it would be useful to know what proportion of the 289—and, especially, of the 209—held AP franchises. U.S. Congress, House of Representatives, 51st Cong., 2d Sess., *Report of the Postmaster-General*, Executive Document 1, Part 4 (Washington, D.C., 1890), 113. There is no doubt that, in a looser but perhaps more significant sense, the AP and Western Union tie animated and sought to sustain a common class interest. See especially Smart, "Information Control, Thought Control."

47. R. H. Curl, "Government Telegraphs," *Typographical Journal* 2 (10) (Jan. 1, 1891): 2.

48. In *Report on Relations between Labor and Capital*, I: 480–88, 928–29.

49. The continuing political interventions of typographical unions in questions of communication have not been adequately traced. "When congress and the administration reach the conclusion that the time is ripe for taking over the wire service of the country," boasted a committee of union printers in 1918, "the International Typographical Union can justly claim to be the one labor organization that has consistently and persistently advocated this step for the past quarter of a century." Committee on Postal Telegraph and Telephone Service, "Reports of Officers to the 64th Session of the International Typographical Union," Scranton, Pennsylvania, August 12–17, 1918, Supplement to *Typographical Journal* (August 1918): 273. On the other hand, significant differences erupted within the printing trades unions, as in 1912 when Chicago's ITU local affiliate refused to cooperate with a strike against the Hearst papers by more militant pressmen. See Philip Taft, "The Limits of Labor Unity: The Chicago Newspaper Strike of 1912," *Labor History* 19 (1) (Winter 1978): 100–129.

50. Blondheim, *News over the Wires*, 162.

51. Thomas Ainge Devyr in *Report on Relations between Labor and Capital*, II: 839–40.

52. Gronlund, *Cooperative Commonwealth*, 71, 90.

53. Ibid., 202, 90, 163.

54. Ibid., 164.

55. Edward Bellamy, "'Looking Backward' Again," *North American Review* (March 1890), in Thomas, *Alternative America*, 273; Lipow, *Authoritorian Socialism*, 224.

56. Still, Gronlund wrote, it would require at least two further changes "to make it so fully." First, the agency's salary structure would need far-reaching revision: "In the Cooperative Commonwealth, the Postmaster General will not receive $10,000 while letter carriers must be satisfied with $800." Second, appointments to jobs within the Post Office, akin to those throughout society, "will be made from below": "[T]he letter-carriers will elect their immediate superiors; these, we will say, the postmasters and these in turn the Postmaster General." Gronlund, *Cooperative Commonwealth*, 109, 132, 153.

57. Ibid., 111. The same confident pride in postal service remained apparent into the 1910s at least. See U.S. Congress, Senate, 63d Cong., 2d Sess., Senate Document 399, *Government Ownership of Electrical Means of Communication* (Washington, D.C., 1914).

58. Marion Butler in 1898; quoted in Wayne E. Fuller, "The Populists and the Post Office," *Agricultural History* 65 (1) (Winter 1991): 11.

59. One historian subtitles his study of the Post Office "enlarger of the common life"; he also chronicles how, during the period between 1865 and 1890, the Post Office inaugurated free mail delivery in towns of at least 10,000, developed a postal money-order system, and undertook other significant organizational reforms. Wayne E. Fuller, *The American Mail: Enlarger of the Common Life* (Chicago, 1972), 71–76. For a discussion detailing how the new second-class mail privileges inadvertently underwrote the unprecedentedly wide-ranging circulation of Populist publications—periodicals in which, it should be added, the need for a nondiscriminatory and accessible system of intercom-

munication by telegraph was stressed—see Fuller, "Populists and the Post Office," 1–16. One demand for further enlargement of Post Office responsibilities, common in the labor movement at the time, is especially salient: elimination of private banks and their replacement by government-owned postal savings banks. Another endeavor, in which Congressman David Lewis, a key figure in the movement to nationalize the telephone in the 1910s, played a pivotal part, was the successful campaign for a parcel post. Joining metropolitan retailers and Grangers in that cause were the National American Woman's Suffrage Association, the Equal Suffrage Association of the District of Columbia, and the Pennsylvania Federation of Labor. The effort to enlarge the range of beneficiaries of postal services thus again continued into the 1910s. U.S. House of Representatives, 62d Cong., 1st Sess., Parcels Post, *Hearings before Subcommittee No. 4 of the Committee on the Post Office and Post Roads, June 1911* (Washington, D.C., 1911), esp. at 166, 168, and 117.

60. Henry George in *Report on Relations between Labor and Capital*, I: 480–81; Richard T. Ely, *Socialism: An Examination of Its Nature, Its Strength and Its Weakness, with Suggestions for Social Reform* (New York, 1894), 265.

61. Daniel J. Czitrom, *Media and the American Mind* (Chapel Hill, 1982), 25–29. See also Lindley, *Constitution Faces Technology*.

62. *Report on Relations between Labor and Capital*, I:213, 147. During the contemporaneous strike against Western Union, McClelland, a member of the Brotherhood of Telegraphers and Secretary of the Knights of Labor, "deserted his own union near the end . . . and charged that the strike was unwise in its inception." Vidkunn Ulriksson, *The Telegraphers: Their Craft and Their Unions* (Washington, D.C., 1953), 48.

63. Edwin Gabler, *The American Telegrapher: A Social History, 1860–1900* (New Brunswick, 1988), 204–8.

64. H. C. Frantz, "Make the Journal a Weekly–Telegraph Nationalization—Organization," *Typographical Journal* II (19) (May 15, 1891): 2–3.

65. "Government Control of Telegraphs," *Typographical Journal* II (15) (March 16, 1891): 4.

66. U.S. Congress, House of Representatives, 51st Cong., 2d Sess., *Report of the Postmaster-General*, Executive Document 1, Part 4 (Washington, D.C., 1890), 112.

67. Ibid., 113. See also Ulriksson, *Telegraphers*, 56–57; McMath, *American Populism*, 118, 141,167.

68. *Report of the Postmaster-General* (1890), 8.

69. For example, see David A. Wells, *The Relation of the Government to the Telegraph* (New York, 1873); Frank Parsons, *The Telegraph Monopoly* (Philadelphia, 1899); Richard T. Ely, "Why the Government Should Own the Telegraph," *Arena* 15 (Dec. 1895): 49–54.

70. Gideon Tucker, probably a journalist, in 1883 testified eloquently to the changes of heart that were transpiring: "The United States Government should own and work telegraph wires for public use as an adjunct of the postal system. It should own and run interstate transportation systems. I began life as a State-rights Democrat, fearing governmental interference and centralization, and especially the Federal Government. But this is as different a world from that into which I was born as though it were another planet. There is now no way to protect the people from the monopolies of almost demoniac power which they

have created but by and through the action of Government. If you say this is unconstitutional which is demanded by our supreme necessities, the reply is that constitutions can be amended, and that they must be made to conform from time to time to new popular wants." In *Report on Relations between Labor and Capital,* II: 906.

71. P. J. Maguire in ibid., I: 345.

72. Ibid., I:345–46. See also Alfred H. Seymour, a longtime telegraph operator, in ibid., I: 385–86.

73. H. W. Orr, in ibid., I: 178–79.

74. McClelland in ibid., I: 148.

75. Schiller, "'Everybody's Common Means of Communication'?''; Meighan Maguire's ongoing dissertation research into telephone system development in San Francisco should shed additional light on local efforts to place the telephone utility under public service obligations.

76. N. G. Warth to Woodrow Wilson, Oct. 6, 1913, U.S. National Archives and Records Administration RG 60 Box 38, 60-1-0 Section 6.

77. Johnson, *National Party Platforms.*

78. *Report on Relations between Labor and Capital,* II: 194.

79. Ibid., II: 196–97.

80. David F. Noble, *America by Design* (New York, 1977). Also see Paul Israel, *From Machine Shop to Industrial Laboratory: Telegraphy and the Changing Context of American Invention, 1830–1920* (Baltimore, 1992).

81. *Report on Relations between Labor and Capital,* II: 193–94, 196.

82. Gronlund, *Cooperative Commonweath,* 33.

83. *Report on Relations between Labor and Capital,* I: 147.

84. Gronlund, *Cooperative Commonwealth,* 75. For links between technological invention and artisanal labor, see Nicholas K. Bromell, *By the Sweat of the Brow: Literature and Labor in Antebellum America* (Chicago, 1993), 40–58.

85. *Report on Relations between Labor and Capital,* I: 1095.

86. Ibid., II: 188.

87. Ibid., II: 189.

88. Jurgen Kocka, *White Collar Workers in America 1890–1940* (London, 1980), 45–46. An early emphasis on the salience of this trend was given in Richard Hofstadter, *The Age of Reform* (New York, 1955), 148–73.

89. In Bromell, *By the Sweat of the Brow,* 28.

90. Kocka, *White Collar Workers,* 83, 136–37, 147–53.

91. Fink, *Workingmen's Democracy,* 24. Local assemblies of the Knights of Labor accepted as members not only factory workers, but also self-employed businessmen, and farmers, artisans, and middle-men, and unpaid women domestic workers. Kocka, *White Collar Workers,* 55, 299.

92. Gronlund, *Cooperative Commonwealth,* 101, original emphasis.

93. Dr. A. Douai in *Report on Relations between Labor and Capital,* II: 719.

94. Susan Levine, *Labor's True Woman: Carpet Weavers, Industrialization, and Labor Reform in the Gilded Age* (Philadelphia, 1984), 10, 39, 63, 103–4, 106–8, 121, 126–27; Voss, *Making of American Exceptionalism,* 72–89.

95. Kocka, *White Collar Workers,* 66–68, 71–73, 84–85, 97–101, 131–32, 257–58; cf. David M. Gordon, Richard Edwards, and Michael Reich, *Segmented Work, Divided Workers: The Historical Transformation of Labor in the United States* (Cambridge, 1982).

96. Montgomery, *Fall of the House of Labor*; Braverman, *Labor and Monopoly Capital*.

97. I survey political economy's attempts to wrestle with the concept of intellectual labor in a companion work in progress. Dan Schiller, "The Information Commodity from Grub Street to the Information Highway."

98. The history of pervasive social degradation of manual labor is developed by Stuart M. Blumin, *The Emergence of the Middle Class: Social Experience in the American City, 1760–1900* (Cambridge, 1989), esp. 122–23. The commanding work on the distinction between mental and manual labor in antebellum literary discourse is now Bromell, *By the Sweat of the Brow*, esp. 22, 39; the quote is from Jonathan A. Glickstein, *Concepts of Free Labor in Antebellum America* (New Haven, 1991), 7. I owe this latter reference to Michael Bernstein.

99. A different index of this change: "The half-million store clerks and clerical office workers of 1880 had tripled by the end of the century, and by far the greatest numbers of additions were in the lowest-paying jobs that offered the least chance of promotion or salary improvement." Blumin, *Emergence of the Middle Class*, 291. Illuminating studies of different facets of this larger movement include: Braverman, *Labor and Monopoly Capital;* Margery W. Davies, *Women's Place Is at the Typewriter: Office Work and Office Workers, 1870–1920* (Philadelphia, 1982); Cindy Sondik Aron, *Ladies and Gentlemen of the Civil Service: Middle-Class Workers in Victorian America* (New York, 1987); Dale L. Johnson, ed., *Class and Social Development: A New Theory of the Middle Class* (Beverly Hills, 1982); Kocka, *White Collar Workers*.

100. McMath, *American Populism*, 192; Fones-Wolf, *Trade Union Gospel*, 20, 80–82, 102.

101. Quintin Hoare and Geoffrey Nowell Smith, eds. and trans., *Selections from the Prison Notebooks of Antonio Gramsci* (New York, 1971), 8.

102. Baptist Hubert in *Report on Relations between Labor and Capital*, II: 946.

103. Joseph Dietzgen, *The Nature of Human Brain Work: An Introduction to Dialectics*, trans. Ernest Untermann (Vancouver, 1984), 28. Marx called Dietzgen "one of the most gifted workers I know," and wrote that his book was an "independent achievement" which, despite a "certain confusion," "contained much that was excellent, and—as the independent product of a worker—even admirable." Engels concurred that Dietzgen's book testified to "a remarkable instinct to think out so much that is correct on the basis of such inadequate studies." Karl Marx and Frederick Engels, *Collected Works*, vol. 43 (New York, 1988), 149, 154–55, 173, 153.

104. Anson Rabinbach, *The Human Motor: Energy, Fatigue, and the Origins of Modernity* (Berkeley, 1992). The signal exception to this generalization is William Morris. See E. P. Thompson, *William Morris: Romantic to Revolutionary* (New York, 1961), esp. 800. Even Morris, however, found no true path all the way through the question. See William Morris, "Useful Work versus Useless Toil," in Asa Briggs, ed., *William Morris: News from Nowhere and Selected Writings and Designs* (Harmondsworth, 1986), 117–36.

105. Walter L. Adamson, *Marx and the Disillusionment of Marxism* (Berkeley, 1985), esp. 40–105; Rabinbach, *Human Motor;* Marshall S. Shatz, *Jan Waclaw Machajski: A Radical Critic of the Russian Intelligentsia and Socialism* (Pittsburgh, 1989); Stanley Pierson, *Marxist Intellectuals and the Working-Class*

Mentality in Germany, 1887–1912 (Cambridge, 1993); Carl Levy, ed., *Socialism and the Intelligentsia 1880–1914* (New York, 1987).

106. For the institutional context, Laurence Veysey, *The Emergence of the American University* (Chicago, 1965).

107. George E. Mont, "Socialization of Industry—No. 2," *The Citizen* (Los Angeles) 5, no. 364 (21), (Oct. 13, 1912). Harry W. Laidler, the executive director of the League for Industrial Democracy (which John Dewey joined in 1921), made the argument for "a cooperative commonwealth" as late as 1935. Harry W. Laidler, *Socializing Our Democracy: A New Appraisal of Socialism* (New York, 1935), 161.

108. Edward Alsworth Ross, "The Suppression of Important News," *Atlantic Monthly* 105 (March 1910): 303–11.

109. Parsons, *Telegraph Monopoly*; Ely, "Why Government Should Own the Telegraph." Thanks to Michael Bernstein for this point concerning the history of economic thought.

110. Thorstein Veblen, *The Theory of the Leisure Class* (1899; New York, 1926), 40–44, 97. For a new edition of Veblen's classic work, *The Engineers and the Price System*, Daniel Bell noted in an introduction in 1963 that "[t]he distinction between productive and unproductive labor, between industrial and pecuniary employments, runs as a peculiar thread through the writings of . . . [Veblen], and reflects at bottom the hatred—and fear—felt by the artisan mentality toward metropolitan life." Daniel Bell, "Introduction to the Harbinger Edition," in Thorstein Veblen, *The Engineers and the Price System* (New York, 1963), 32.

111. Thorstein Veblen, *Absentee Ownership and Business Enterprise in Recent Times: The Case of America* (New York, 1964), 300, 305.

112. Thorstein Veblen, *The Engineers and the Price System* (New York, 1921), 7–8.

113. Veblen, *Absentee Ownership*, 310; Veblen, *Engineers and the Price System*, 110, 109; Bell, "Introduction," 32.

114. Dorothy Ross, *The Origins of American Social Science* (Cambridge, 1991), 117, 133. Mary Furner, *Advocacy and Objectivity: A Crisis in the Professionalization of American Social Science, 1865–1905* (Lexington, 1975). According to one historian of the contemporary professoriate, "class and ethnic background, as well as professional ideology, training, and function, served to justify high standards of living. The idea of serving truth and community gave those justifications a gloss of anti-materialistic idealism." Frank Stricker, "American Professors in the Progressive Era: Incomes, Aspirations, and Professionalism," *Journal of Interdisciplinary History* 19, no. 2 (1988): 251.

115. Ross, *Origins*, 117–18. Recounting the circumstances of Bemis's dismissal from the University of Chicago in 1895, John Dewey wrote to his wife that he had no doubt that the university's president, William Rainey Harper, was "afraid of hurting the feelings of the capitalists, and sees the external money side of the Univ. and is relatively purblind to the real advances of life." In Robert B. Westbrook, *John Dewey and American Democracy* (Ithaca, 1991), 91.

116. Ross, *Origins*, 101–2.

117. This composite is drawn from Westbrook, *John Dewey*; Andrew Feffer, *The Chicago Pragmatists and American Progressivism* (Ithaca, 1993); Lewis S. Feuer, "John Dewey and the Back to the People Movement in American

Thought," *Journal of the History of Ideas* 20 (4) (Oct.–Dec. 1959): 545–68; George Dykhuizen, "John Dewey and the University of Michigan," *Journal of the History of Ideas* 23 (4) (Oct.–Dec. 1962): 513–44; Neil Coughlan, *Young John Dewey: An Essay in American Intellectual History* (Chicago, 1975), 90–93; C. Wright Mills, *Sociology and Pragmatism: The Higher Learning in America* (New York, 1964), 279–324; and Larry A. Hickman, *John Dewey's Pragmatic Technology* (Bloomington, 1992), 167.

118. Westbrook, *John Dewey*, 315, 454; John Dewey, "A Great American Prophet" (1934), in Dewey, *The Later Works, 1925–1953*, vol. 9: *1933–1934*, eds. Jo Ann Boydston, Anne Sharpe, and Patricia Baysinger (Carbondale, 1986), 102–6.

119. The most useful accounts are Czitrom, *Media;* John Durham Peters, "Satan and Savior: Mass Communication in Progressive Thought," *Critical Studies in Mass Communication* 6 (3) (Sept. 1989): 247–63 at 252–54; Westbrook, *John Dewey*, 51–58; Coughlan, *Young John Dewey*, 93–108; Feffer, *Chicago Pragmatists*, 82–86.

120. David H. Burton, ed., *Progressive Masks: Letters of Oliver Wendell Holmes, Jr., and Franklin Ford* (Newark, 1982), 11–22; 111, 114. It is symptomatic of scholarly neglect of the concurrent popular critique of communication that Ford's ideas are said to have affected Dewey through more of less isolated combinations of Ford's own "dynamic" personality and Dewey's "susceptibility"—what Coughlan calls, somewhat admiringly, his "lifelong weakness for quacks." Coughlan, *Young John Dewey*, 96; Westbrook, *John Dewey*, 52; Fred. H. Matthews, *Quest for an American Sociology: Robert E. Park and the Chicago School* (Montreal, 1977), 22; Czitrom, *Media*, 104, allows that Ford's ideas were a "curious mixture of press reform, syndicalism, and half-baked socialism."

121. Westbrook, *John Dewey*, 52–53.

122. For evidence of Ford's continuing commitment, see the letters collected in Burton, ed., *Progressive Masks*.

123. Franklin Ford, *Draft of Action* (Ann Arbor, July 1, 1892), 58. Even as the nation's leaders contemplated a growing imperial role, Ford's international ambitions were also overt—notwithstanding his "Maine to California" meta- phor. Developments in the United States, thus, would only "prepare the way for the organization of its intelligence and the correlation therewith of the intelligence of the whole world." Ford closed his work with this admonishment: "Great significance is bound up in the fact that it is English-speaking men who are to bring intelligence to a centre and distribute it. In this is finally certified the power resting in the hands of England and the United States jointly. Mr. Gladstone, writing of the English and American peoples, said: 'They with their vast range of inhabited territory, and their unity of tongue, are masters of the world, which will have to do as they do.'" Ibid., 20, 58.

124. Ibid., 28, 29.

125. Dorothy Ross, "Socialism and American Liberalism: Academic Social Thought in the 1880's," in Donald Fleming, ed., *Perspectives in American History*, vol. XI: *1977–1978* (Cambridge, 1978), 31–32, 58–60, 73; Gilbert, *Designing the Industrial State*, 26, 34, 37; Lipow, *Authoritarian Socialism*, 91–92, 161, 185, 196. Franklin Ford's brother, Corydon, went on to edit the Bellamyite journal, *The Coming Nation*. Lipow, ibid., 108.

126. In Winifred Raushenbush, *Robert E. Park: Biography of a Sociologist* (Durham, 1979), 18; see also Hanno Hardt, *Critical Communication Studies: Communication, History and Theory in America* (London, 1992), 42–60.

127. Ibid., 21.

128. Matthews, *Quest for an American Sociology*, 20.

129. A man who specifically sought, in historian Dorothy Ross's description, "to dissolve the bonds of class" in a "particularistic and promiscuous array" of "vocational types," Park, she generalizes, "always tried to justify the capitalist order." Ross, *Origins*, 363, 307, 305.

130. In Coughlan, *Young John Dewey*, 145.

131. Peters, "Satan and Savior," 249–50.

132. John Dewey to William James, June 3, 1891, in Ralph Barton Perry, *The Thought and Character of William James: As Revealed in Unpublished Correspondence and Notes, Together with His Published Writings*, vol. 2: *Philosophy and Psychology* (Boston, 1935), 518, in Raushenbush, *Robert E. Park*, 19.

133. In John Dewey, *The Middle Works, 1899–1924*, vol. 9: *1916, Democracy and Education*, ed. Jo Ann Boydston, intro. Sidney Hook (Carbondale, 1980), xx, xxiii. "A democracy," wrote Dewey, "is more than a form of government; it is primarily a mode of associated living, of conjoint communicated experience. The extension in space of the number of individuals who participate in an interest so that each has to refer his own action to that of others, and to consider the action of others to give point and direction to his own, is equivalent to the breaking down of those barriers of class, race, and national territory which kept men from perceiving the full import of their activity." Ibid., 93.

134. Westbrook, *John Dewey*, 53.

135. Mills, *Sociology and Pragmatism*, 375–76.

136. John Dewey, "The Reflex Arc Concept in Psychology," in idem, *The Early Works, 1882–1898*, vol. 5: *1895–1898, Early Essays* (Carbondale, 1972), 108, 97.

137. Feffer, *Chicago Pragmatists*, 149. See also Westbrook, *John Dewey*, 67–70. Dewey's critique of the reflex arc provided an indispensable foundation for Mead, who spent much of the next three decades, according to Neil Coughlan, learning how to argue "that man is social *before* he is individual, that our awareness of others precedes our awareness of ourselves, and that, indeed, certain aspects of our distinctively human behavior, particularly our consciousness of *meaning*, can be accounted for only if we accept the fact that man is an intrinsically social being." Coughlan, *Young John Dewey*, 149.

138. George Herbert Mead, *On Social Psychology* (Chicago, 1956), 243.

139. I follow Hickman, *John Dewey's Pragmatic Technology*, 166–95, though without Hickman's endorsements of Dewey's solutions.

140. A point made well by James W. Carey, "Commentary: Communications and the Progressives," *Critical Studies in Mass Communication* 6 (3) (Sept. 1989): 276–77.

141. Dewey, *Public and Its Problems*, 146–47, 126.

142. Ford, *Draft of Action*, 16, 6, 8.

143. In Westbrook, *John Dewey*, 54. For comments suggesting that this remained a viable idea for Dewey, see *Public and Its Problems*, 182–83; cf. Dewey, "Intelligence and Power" (1934), in Dewey, *Later Works*, 107–10.

144. In Coughlan, *Young John Dewey*, 125.

145. Feffer, *Chicago Pragmatists*, 180.

146. Dewey, *Democracy and Education*, 210.

147. Ibid., 264, 270.

148. Hickman, *John Dewey's Pragmatic Technology*.

149. Thus "work" might be identified momentarily with inquiry or intelligence, as in the following: "What is work—work not as mere external performance, but as attitude of mind? It signifies that the person is not content longer to accept and to act upon the meanings that things suggest, but demands congruity of meaning with the things themselves." John Dewey, *How We Think* (Buffalo, 1991), 162–63. Or, on the other hand, but equally ephemerally, "art" might be called "a process of production." John Dewey, *Experience and Nature* (New York, 1958), xv.

150. Dewey, *Democracy and Education*, 260.

151. Ibid., 146, 147, 158.

152. In Park's subsequent sociology of news this same proclivity is confirmed and amplified. Retaining Ford's "conviction that communication was the essential cohesive force in modern society, and that by improving the quality of news transmission the quality of the total society could be raised," Park came to deploy "communication" squarely within the tradition of "liberal exceptionalism" that predominated across the contemporary social sciences. Matthews, *Quest for an American Sociology*, 25, 29.

153. Feffer, *Chicago Pragmatists*, 244–45, 247.

154. Dewey, *Democracy and Education*, 7. This passage is frequently quoted as a means of establishing Dewey's early relevance to communication study, as in Czitrom, *Media*, 108.

155. Dewey, *Public and Its Problems*, 152.

156. Cf. Westbrook, *John Dewey*, 81; cf. Dewey, *Public and Its Problems*, 161–62, 169.

157. Feffer, *Chicago Pragmatists*, 117–46. Also see Westbrook, *John Dewey*, 150–94, 401.

158. Dewey, *Public and Its Problems*, 211. For more extensive discussion of the pretense of individuality, in psychology and philosophy, see ibid., 88, 102, 158, 186–91.

159. Coughlan, *Young John Dewey*, 129.

160. Dewey, *Public and Its Problems*, 146.

161. Ibid.

162. In 1909 Mead wrote that "the probable beginning of human communication was in cooperation . . . where conduct differed and yet where the act of the one answered to and called out the act of the other." Thus, as Feffer comments, Mead purported to solve Dewey's earlier difficulties concerning the origins of cooperative intelligence: "Communication (hence humanness) did not begin in prudence or competition, or in imitation, but in constructive cooperation, suggesting that sociability likewise did not emerge as a prudent strategy for individual adaptation but was present with the appearance of language." Feffer, *Chicago Pragmatists*, 239. Also see Coughlan, *Young John Dewey*, 113–33, 149–50.

163. In his *Experience and Nature* (1925), quoted in Czitrom, *Media*, 108. Much has been made of this by James W. Carey, *Communication as Culture* (Boston, 1989), 13ff.

164. Dewey, *Democracy and Education*, 7, 14.

165. Ford, *Draft of Action*, 48.

166. Ibid., 1, 2.   ⁕

167. Dewey, *Public and Its Problems*, 179.

168. Ibid., 169.

169. For the wider usage achieved by this idea, see Gary Cross, *Time and Money: The Making of Consumer Culture* (London, 1993), 52–53.

170. Dewey, *Public and Its Problems*, 169, 114, 123, 139, 126.

171. Feffer, *Chicago Pragmatists*, 233, 252, 223; Lipow, *Authoritarian Socialism*, 196–97, 265.

172. In Coughlan, *Young John Dewey*, 145.

173. Dewey, *Public and Its Problems*, 154–55.

174. Feffer, *Chicago Pragmatists*, 269. See also Dewey, *Public and Its Problems*, 110; Westbrook, *John Dewey*, 205, 309–11, 315–16. On Mead, see, in addition: Andrew Feffer, "Sociability and Social Conflict in George Herbert Mead's Interactionism, 1900–1919," *Journal of the History of Ideas* 51 (2) (April–June 1990): 233–54; Dmitri N. Shalin, "G. H. Mead, Socialism, and the Progressive Agenda," *American Journal of Sociology* 93 (4) (Jan. 1988): 913–51; Gary A. Cook, "The Development of G. H. Mead's Social Psychology," *Transactions of the Charles D. Peirce Society* 8 (3) (Summer 1972): 167–85.

175. Richard Hofstadter, *The Age of Reform* (New York, 1955), 148–63; Patten and George in Gilbert, *Designing the Industrial State*, 45, 81; Clark, Ely, and Bellamy in Pittenger, *American Socialists*, 31, 37, 43, 69; for a more extensive discussion of Bellamy's relationship to the new middle class, see Lipow, *Authoritarian Socialism*, 64, 96–159.

176. Gronlund, *Cooperative Commonwealth*, 237–38; Ford, *Draft of Action*, 52.

177. Gronlund, *Cooperative Commonwealth*, 201–2.

178. Ford, *Draft of Action*, 55.

179. Ross, *Origins*, 237. For a brief discussion of Dewey's views on "social science and social control," see Coughlan, *Young John Dewey*, 157.

180. And this emphasis long remained within reach, as in this 1976 formulation: "Post-industrial society is organized around knowledge, for the purpose of social control and the directing of innovation and change. . . ." Daniel Bell, *The Coming of the Post-Industrial Society* (New York, 1976), 20.

181. Ross, *Origins*, 236, 233, 247–56.

182. Robert H. Wiebe, *The Search for Order, 1877–1920* (New York, 1967), 151; Braverman, *Labor and Monopoly Capital*.

183. Ronald Steel, *Walter Lippmann and the American Century* (New York, 1981).

184. Czitrom, *Media*, 112. Dewey's ultimate judgment concerning the failure of "Thought News"—the first promised offering from Ford's more encompassing intelligence trust—is of interest. It was, simply, that it comprised "an overenthusiastic project which we had not the means nor the time to carry through," and one that was "too advanced for the maturity of those who had the idea in mind." Nearly sixty years had passed, yet Dewey still came no closer than he had in 1890 to confronting the social relations that had concretely obstructed the project's success and, indeed, underlain its conception. Westbrook, *John Dewey*, 57.

185. Laidler, *Socializing Our Democracy*, 270.

186. In Westbrook, *John Dewey*, 401.

Chapter Two. **The Anomaly of Domination**

1. J. Michael Sproule, "Propaganda Studies in American Social Science: The Rise and Fall of the Critical Paradigm," *Quarterly Journal of Speech* 73 (1) (Feb. 1987): 62, 65–66; Philip M. Taylor, "Propaganda in International Politics, 1919–1939," in K. R. M. Short, ed., *Film and Radio Propaganda in World War II* (London, 1983), 17–47. A benchmark study is Harold Lasswell, *Propaganda Technique in the World War* (New York, 1927).

2. Joseph V. Femia, *Gramsci's Political Thought* (Oxford, 1987), 24.

3. Terry Eagleton, *Ideology* (London, 1991), 116.

4. Perry Anderson, "The Antinomies of Antonio Gramsci," *New Left Review* 100 (Nov. 1976–Jan. 1977): 46, 41. A useful overview of the evolution of Anderson's own thinking is Gregory Elliott, "Olympus Mislaid? A profile of Perry Anderson," *Radical Philosophy* 71 (May/June 1995): 5–19.

5. J. Michael Sproule, "Progressive Propaganda Critics and the Magic Bullet Myth," *Critical Studies in Mass Communication* 6 (3) (Sept. 1989): 235–36. Dan Schiller, *Objectivity and the News: The Public and the Rise of Commercial Journalism* (Philadelphia, 1981), 182–89. "Not hyperbolically and contemptuously, but literally and with scientific precision," wrote Upton Sinclair, "we define Journalism in America as the business and practice of presenting the news of the day in the interest of economic privilege." Upton Sinclair, *The Brass Check* (Pasadena, 1919), 222.

6. Edward L. Bernays, *Propaganda* (New York, 1928), 27, 9, 11, 19–20. Already particularly prominent were the intimate connections forged between mass media and promotional and sales campaigns by big corporations. During the Depression of the 1930s, when—as Danielian put it—the primary concern of business shifted toward "political survival," public relations blossomed into a more ubiquitous corporate art. N. B. Danielian, *AT&T: Story of Industrial Conquest* (New York, 1939), 332. Alan Raucher, *Public Relations and Business* (Baltimore, 1968).

7. A point I take from Sproule, "Progressive Propaganda Critics" and "Propaganda Studies." For brief affirmations that this is, indeed, a caricature, see Ellen Wartella and Byron Reeves, "Historical Trends in Research on Children and the Media: 1900–1960," *Journal of Communication* 35 (2) (Spring 1985): 118–33 at 121–22; Todd Gitlin, "Media Sociology: The Dominant Paradigm," *Theory and Society* 6, no. 2 (Sept. 1978): 210.

8. In addition to Sproule references noted in the previous footnote, see Jacqueline Marie Cartier, "Wilbur Schramm and the Beginnings of American Communication Theory: A History of Ideas" (Ph.D. dissertation, University of Iowa, 1988), 22; Lucien W. Pye, ed., *Communications and Political Development* (Princeton, 1963), 13. Jesse G. Delia, "Communication Research: A History," in Charles R. Berger and Steven H. Chaffee, eds., *Handbook of Communication Science* (Newbury Park, 1987), 20–98, esp. 65–66, 22, 24–54; Daniel J. Czitrom, *Media and the American Mind* (Chapel Hill, 1982), 91–146.

9. Wartella and Reeves, "Historical Trends," 122.

10. Sproule, "Progressive Propaganda Critics," 233.

11. Perhaps above all in works by Edward S. Herman and Noam Chomsky, such as their *Manufacturing Consent: The Political Economy of the Mass Media* (New York, 1988).

12. Frederick E. Lumley, *The Propaganda Menace* (New York, 1933).

13. O. W. Riegel, *Mobilizing for Chaos: The Story of the New Propaganda* (New Haven, 1937), 211.

14. Sproule, "Propaganda Studies," 74. Cf. Steven H. Chaffee and John L. Hochheimer, "The Beginnings of Political Communication Research in the United States: Origins of the 'Limited Effects' Model," in Michael Gurevitch and Mark R. Levy, eds., *Mass Communication Review Yearbook Volume 5* (Beverly Hills, 1985), 75–104 at 97, 95.

15. Sproule, "Propaganda Studies," 66.

16. A journalistic exposure of the unprecedented growth and invasiveness of corporate public relations, published in 1938, asserted that, in response to the widespread loss of confidence in American business generated by the Depression, business had found in public relations "a new social force" aimed specifically at restoring the faded legitimacy of the market system. "This campaign is distinguished from innumerable previous compaigns by one fact: it is not designed to gain a competitive advantage or to favor the interests of one man, firm, or industry independently of the rest of business; this campaign, and the basic movement of which it is the expression, are designed to establish business as a whole securely in what business men believe to be its rightful place in the national polity." In "selling" the public on this "general philosophy"—"sufficiently extensive to guide our every public action, social, political, and economic"—U.S. business insisted "that business management cannot be supposed to have interests differing basically from labor's, the consumer's, or the general public's; which, in turn, implies that the principles which guide the present management of business cannot be overturned, replaced, or materially altered (except, in special cases, by management itself) without causing the country to cease to function as a going concern." S. H. Walker and Paul Sklar, "Business Finds Its Voice," *Harpers* 176, (Jan. 1938): 113–23 at 113; idem, Part II: "Motion Pictures and Combined Efforts," *Harpers* 176 (Feb. 1938): 317–29 at 317; Part III: *Harpers* 176 (March 1938): 428–40. A full-scale study of the rise of public relations—a sorely neglected component of U.S. communication history—is promised from Stuart Ewen.

17. Malcolm M. Willey and Stuart A. Rice, "The Agencies of Communication," in Report of the President's Research Committee on Recent Social Trends, *Recent Social Trends in the United States* (New York, 1933), 216–17.

18. Harold D. Lasswell, "The Propagandist Bids for Power," *American Scholar* 8 (July 1939): 357.

19. Harold D. Lasswell, "The Study and Practice of Propaganda," in Lasswell, Ralph D. Casey, and Bruce Lannes Smith, *Propaganda and Promotional Activities: An Annotated Bibilography*, prepared under the direction of the Advisory Committee on Pressure Groups and Propaganda, the Social Science Research Council (1935; Chicago, 1969), 27.

20. Robert K. Merton, Marjorie Fiske, and Alberta Curtis, *Mass Persuasion: The Social Psychology of a War Bond Drive* (New York, 1946), 1, 185, 188.

21. Propaganda analysis indeed may be seen, therefore, as Carey and Sproule have separately argued, as a home-grown version of ideology critique—

a carryover into the 1930s of Progressive-era beliefs—but it was not free of the accent of class, which these writers suggest was only imported with alien ideologies. Carey, "Communications and the Progressives," 278–79; Sproule, "Progressive Propaganda Critics," 228.

22. Michael E. Brown, Randy Martin, Frank Rosengarten, and George Snedeker, eds., *New Studies in the Politics and Culture of U.S. Communism* (New York, 1993).

23. Carlos Blanco Aguinaga, "On Modernism, from the Periphery," unpub. ms., 1994, 16. A vivid memoir of the League of American Writers during the late 1930s is Franklin Folsom, *Days of Anger, Days of Hope* (Niwot, Colo., 1994).

24. Paul Buhle, *Marxism in the United States* (London, 1987), 179. These concurrent shifts in cultural theory and practice are insightfully scrutinized in Rita Barnard, *The Great Depression and the Culture of Abundance: Kenneth Fearing, Nathaniel West, and Mass Culture in the 1930s* (Cambridge, 1995). *Partisan Review*, oriented toward Trotsky and highly critical of the Soviet Union and the U.S. Communist Party, published articles on media and propaganda in Germany and the Soviet Union. Ignazio Silone, "The School for Dictators," *Partisan Review* 6 (1) (Fall 1938): 20–41; and Dwight Macdonald, "Soviet Society and Its Cinema," *Partisan Review* 6 (2) (Winter 1939): 80–95. It also published an influential early article on mass culture and a historical assessment by Rorty of the decline of "muckrake" journalism. See Clement Greenberg, "Avant-Garde and Kitsch," *Partisan Review* 6 (5) (Fall 1939): 34–49; and James Rorty, "The Socialization of Muckraking," *Partisan Review* 6 (5) (Fall 1939): 90–101. In addition to film reviews, *New Masses*, aligned with the Communist Party, devoted significant space both to criticism of mainstream commercial journalism and to telecommunications. For the former, see the series of articles by Robert Terrall on the newspaper press: "Mrs. Ogden Reid's Paper," *New Masses* 31 (5) (April 25, 1939): 13–15; "Don't Mention Scripps to Howard," *New Masses* 31 (7) (May 9, 1939): 7–9; "Nobody Appreciates Mr. Stern," *New Masses* 31 (9) (May 23, 1939): 8–10; "Hearst Is Still Alive," *New Masses* 31 (12) (June 13, 1939): 3–7; "Who Reads Hearst?," *New Masses* 31 (13) (June 20, 1939): 9–12. For the latter, Douglas Ward, "Our Telegraph Monopoly," *New Masses* 32 (2) (July 4, 1939): 15–16.

25. I know of no works of scholarship which attempt systematically to explore this crucial set of developments across the communication industry. One of the most important features of this unionization drive was to challenge the established division of labor; ongoing doctoral research by Dennis Mazzocco will help us to understand better the contemporary efforts made to organize radio's technical workers into CIO-affiliated industrial unions.

26. See, for example, "Radio Cleans House," *New Republic* 99, no. 12 (July 1939); Jerome H. Spingarn, "These Public-Opinion Polls," *Harpers* 178 (Dec. 1938): 92–104; Dickson Skinner, "Music Goes into Mass Production," *Harpers* 178 (April 1939): 484–90; Walker and Sklar, "Business Finds Its Voice," 113; idem, "Motion Pictures and Combined Efforts," 317. *PM* devoted regular sections to "movies," "the press," and "radio," which made room for both program criticism and labor news. One should also mention here the attempt to create a left-liberal magazine for the mass market—called *Ken—the Insider's World*—whose projected press department, overseen by George Seldes, was to comprise around a third of the magazine, and to feature monthly investigations, whose

emphasis "was always to be on suppressed news." "When *Ken* announced a left-of-center policy," wrotes Seldes in his exposure of how the journal had nonetheless succumbed to pressures from advertisers and big business, "250,000 advance buyers appeared." Seldes himself went on to publish and edit *In fact*, a newsletter that attained a peak circulation of 176,000 in 1947. Randolph T. Holhut, ed., *The George Seldes Reader* (New York, 1994), 337–44.

27. Relying on the unprecedented documentation produced by a full-blown FCC investigation, N. B. Danielian proffered a gracefully grim economic history of the U.S. telephone industry, emphasizing AT&T's instinct to predation. In a reprise of Ernest Gruening's study of propaganda by the electrical utility industry, itself beholden to the findings of the Federal Trade Commission, Danielian detailed the telephone giant's unremitting effort to "mold the public mind." Danielian, *AT&T;* Ernest Gruening, *The Public Pays: A Study of Power Propaganda* (New York, 1931). By connecting propaganda to class interest, even researchers who explicitly eschewed "any ethical evaluation of labor or employer propaganda" undoubtedly contributed to problematizing its place within public discourse. Selden C. Menefee, "Propaganda and Symbol Manipulation," in George W. Hartmann and Theodore Newcomb, eds., *Industrial Conflict: A Psychological Interpretation* (New York, 1939), 456–96.

28. U.S. Congress, Senate, 76th Cong., 3d Sess., Temporary National Economic Committee, Investigation of Concentration of Economic Power, Monograph No. 21, *Competition and Monopoly in American Industry* (Washington, D.C., 1940); and ibid., Hearings Pursuant to Public Resolution No. 113, Part 30, *Technology and Concentration of Economic Power* (Washington, D.C., 1940).

29. U.S. Congress, Senate, 76th Cong., 1st Sess., Committee on Education and Labor, *Report of the Committee on Education and Labor*, No. 6, Part 6, pursuant to Special Resolution 266 (Washington, D.C., 1939), as cited in Alex Carey, "Reshaping the Truth: Pragmatists and Propagandists in America, "*Liberation* (July/Aug. 1977): 12–17.

30. Over 1200 of the nation's 1950 dailies in 1936 supported the Republican presidential candidate, A. M. Landon, according to Lee, *Daily Newspaper in America*, 182. On newspaper publishers' antagonism to Roosevelt, see Betty Winfield, *Roosevelt and the News Media* (Urbana, 1990), 127–54. For the larger subject of capital's hostility to the New Deal, see Kim McQuaid, *Big Business and Presidential Power from FDR to Reagan* (New York, 1982), 18–61.

31. George Michael, *Handout* (New York, 1935), 3, 15. See also Winfield, *FDR and the News Media*, 91–92; and Robert S. Mann, "Capital Corps No Propaganda Victim, Writers Tell Journalism Teachers," *Editor & Publisher* 69 (1) (Jan. 4, 1936): 1, 2, 12.

32. Scott Donaldson, *Archibald MacLeish: An American Life* (Boston, 1992), 356–57.

33. Walker and Sklar, "Business Finds Its Voice," Part III, 434.

34. "Special Train Correspondents See Roosevelt 1936 'Landslide,'" *Editor & Publisher* 69 (44) (Oct. 31, 1936): 4; and "Round the Next Corner," ibid., 28.

35. The only accurate predictor of Roosevelt's 46 state "avalanche," according to *Editor & Publisher*, was Democratic Campaign Manager James Farley. Bice Clemow, "Roosevelt's 46-State Sweep a Surprise Even to Nation's Blase Press," *Editor & Publisher* 69 (45) (Nov. 7, 1936): 4.

36. "Publishers Comment on Election," *Editor & Publisher* 69 (45) (Nov. 7, 1936): 7.

37. Walker and Sklar, "Business Finds its Voice," Part III, 434.

38. Mike Davis, *Prisoners of the American Dream* (London, 1986), 5, 52–73.

39. "The Press and the People—A Survey," *Fortune* 20 (2) (Aug. 1939): 64.

40. In Lee, *Daily Newspaper in America*, 182.

41. In Winfield, *FDR and the News Media*, 132.

42. C. Wright Mills, "Mass Media and Public Opinion," in Irving Louis Horowitz, ed., *Power Politics and People: The Collected Essays of C. Wright Mills* (New York, 1963), 577.

43. Ibid.

44. Ibid., 593–94.

45. James L. Baughman, *Henry R. Luce and the Rise of the American News Media* (Boston, 1987), 117, 107, 111. By 1937, Luce himself had grown strongly hostile to Roosevelt's program and rhetoric. Winfield, *FDR and the News Media*, 114.

46. Edward L. Bernays, "Views on Postwar Responsibility of the American Press," *Journalism Quarterly* 22 (3) (Sept. 1945): 255–62 at 256.

47. "The Press and the People," 65, 70, 72.

48. Statistics on radio receivers in Christopher H. Sterling and Timothy R. Haight, *The Mass Media: Aspen Institute Guide to Communication Industry Trends* (New York, 1978), 367, Table 670-A. Between 1934 and 1935 some leading consumer products companies markedly increased their broadcast advertising budgets—from $969,236 to $2,104,697 for Procter & Gamble; from $1,450,575 to $1,948,509 for General Foods; and from $1,191,577 to $1,928,860 for Ford Motor Company. "Gravure Linage and Colored Comic Space Both Up Nearly 20%," *Editor & Publisher* 69 (3) (Jan. 18, 1936): 6.

"Turn Yo' Radio On" by Leadbelly (Huddie Ledbetter) in *Gwine Dig a Hole to Put the Devil In*, Library of Congress Recordings, vol. 2 (Rounder 1045), recorded by Alan Lomax © 1991.

49. By 1940 more than 30% of broadcast stations were owned by newspapers. Christopher H. Sterling and John M. Kittross, *Stay Tuned: A Concise History of American Broadcasting*, 2d ed. (Belmont, 1990), 191. Quote taken from John Tebbel and Sarah Miles Watts, *The Press and the Presidency* (New York, 1985), 435, 446–47.

50. Winfield, *FDR and the News Media*, 109–10.

51. This accessibility went far beyond Roosevelt's thirty-one-odd "Fireside Chats." The extent of radio's orientation to the New Deal is a prime subject for additional study. In 1936, the chairman of the Republican National Committee sent an open letter to NBC and CBS in which he "castigated" the radio networks "for refusing to sell time for presentation of political skits" produced, in this election year, by the Republicans themselves. The Republicans turned instead to WGN, a station owned by the arch-reactionary Chicago *Tribune*, which they paid to dramatize a program entitled "Liberty at the Crossroads," which dealt chiefly with the public debt and "the agricultural problem." James L. Butler, "Chain Stations Rebuff Republicans on Demands for Air Time," *Editor & Publisher* 69 (3) (Jan. 18, 1936): 20. Through ventures such as the Columbia Workshop, on the other hand—CBS's experimental division—more than a few

of those who later might be labeled "premature anti-fascists" found means of reaching significant audiences. One leading historian asserts that radio commentators were "especially interventionist." Baughman, *Henry R. Luce*, 120. One immediate reason for this accessibility was doubtless that the radio networks went through the Depression carrying a significant proportion of unsponsored airtime. James L. Baughman, *The Republic of Mass Culture* (Baltimore, 1992), 19.

52. Leila A. Sussmann, "Labor in the Radio News: An Analysis of Content," *Journalism Quarterly* 22 (3) (Sept. 1945): 207–14.

53. Robert W. McChesney, "Press-Radio Relations and the Emergence of Network, Commercial Broadcasting in the United States, 1930–1935," *Historical Journal of Film, Radio and Television* 11 (1) (1991): 41–57; Gwenyth Jackaway, "America's Press-Radio War of the 1930s: A Case Study in Battles between Old and New Media," *Historical Journal of Film, Radio and Television* 14 (3) (1994): 299–314.

54. Lee, *Daily Newspaper in America*, 195.

55. Winfield, *FDR and the News Media*, 146.

56. Harold L. Ickes, *America's House of Lords: An Inquiry into the Freedom of the Press* (New York, 1939), x; George Seldes, *Lords of the Press* (New York, 1938).

57. Donaldson, *Archibald MacLeish*, 356.

58. William J. Buxton, "The Political Economy of Communications Research," in Robert E. Babe, ed., *Information and Communication in Economics* (Boston, 1994), 147–75 at 168. This role, it has been argued, had been broadly characteristic of foundations before the interventionist New Deal. Barry D. Karl and Stanley N. Katz, "The American Private Philanthropic Foundation and the Public Sphere 1890–1930," *Minerva* 19 (1981): 236–70.

59. Paul F. Lazarsfeld, *Radio and the Printed Page: An Introduction to the Study of Radio and Its Role in the Communication of Ideas* (New York, 1940), xii.

60. Walker and Sklar, "Business Finds Its Voice," Part III, 434, 430.

61. Lasswell, "Study and Practice of Propaganda," 10; E. L. Bernays, "Molding Public Opinion," *Annals* (1935): 84, both in Brett Joseph Gary, "American Liberalism and the Problem of Propaganda: Scholars, Lawyers, and the War on Words, 1919–1945" (Ph.D. dissertation, University of Pennsylvania, 1992), 85, 88.

62. Jean M. Converse, *Survey Research in the United States: Roots & Emergence 1890–1960* (Berkeley, 1987).

63. Paul F. Lazarsfeld, Bernard Berelson, and Hazel Gaudet, *The People's Choice: How the Voter Makes Up His Mind in a Presidential Campaign* (New York, 1944), xxix.

64. Ibid., 158.

65. Ibid., 50.

66. Walker and Paul Sklar, "Business Finds Its Voice," Part III, 427; and Part II, 120.

67. Gary, "American Liberalism," 182.

68. In ibid., 187.

69. Harold D. Lasswell, "The Structure and Function of Communication in Society," reprinted in Wilbur Schramm and Donald F. Roberts, *The Process and Effects of Mass Communication*, rev. ed. (Urbana, 1971), 84.

70. Gary, "American Liberalism," 183.

71. Ibid., 221–32. For MacLeish's background and wartime role see Donaldson, *Archibald MacLeish*, 262–365.

72. Gary, "American Liberalism," 230–31.

73. Cf. Sproule, "Propaganda Studies," 72. Lazarsfeld, *Radio and the Printed Page*, xvii.

74. In Gary, "American Liberalism," 276.

75. Ibid., 261, 270.

76. U.S. Federal Communications Commission, *Public Service Responsibility of Broadcast Licensees* (Washington, D.C., 1946); Commission on Freedom of the Press, *Report* (Chicago, 1946). On the FCC, see Richard J. Meyer, "Reaction to the 'Blue Book,'" in Lawrence W. Lichty and Malachi C. Topping, *American Broadcasting: A Source Book on the History of Radio and Television* (New York, 1975), 589–602; on Hutchins, Jerilyn S. McIntyre, "Repositioning a Landmark: The Hutchins Commission and Freedom of the Press," *Critical Studies in Mass Communication* 4 (2) (June 1987): 136–60.

77. Actively complicit in this later reversal, significantly, were the dominant media themselves, whose changing stance thereby nominally recapitulated, even as it substantively undercut, efforts during the 1940s to transmute the tenor of the press so as to emphasize its "social responsibility." For a specific demonstration of this flip-flop in the dominant media's stance, see Richard B. McKenzie, *Times Change: The Minimum Wage and the* New York Times (San Francisco, 1994). Arguing from within the terms of the right-wing critique, the economist McKenzie shows that the *Times* editorially opposed minimum wage legislation all the way through the New Deal, turning to embrace it only in 1950; in a second about-face, the paper rejected as outmoded the theory that lay behind the minimum wage, beginning in 1977.

78. "In my credo with reference to our newspapers," wrote Ickes, "is embedded the sincere belief that if editorial direction were left to the editors and reporters there would be little occasion for criticism." Ickes, *America's House of Lords*, vii–viii.

79. Herbert I. Schiller, *Communication and Cultural Domination* (White Plains, 1976), 24-45.

80. Dallas Smythe, *Counterclockwise: Perspectives on Communication*, edited by Thomas Guback (Boulder, 1994), 34.

81. Blanche Wiesen Cook, *The Declassified Eisenhower* (New York, 1980).

82. Paul Baran and Paul Sweezy, *Monopoly Capital* (New York, 1966).

83. Elaine Tyler May, *Homeward Bound* (New York, 1986); George Lipsitz, *"A Rainbow at Midnight": Class and Culture in Cold War America* (New York, 1982); Ellen Schrecker, *No Ivory Tower* (New York, 1986); Joel Kovel, *Red Hunting in the Promised Land* (New York, 1994).

84. It may be noted that one of the founding figures in the establishment of academic communication study devoted a book-length study to the impact of Cold War mobilization on academic social scientists. See Paul F. Lazarsfeld and Wagner Thielens, Jr., *The Academic Mind: Social Scientists in a Time of Crisis* (Glencoe, 1958).

85. Looking back during a later interview, the Yale-based author of the most influential social psychological text on propaganda in the 1930s, Leonard Doob, reported that by 1960 "he would not have dreamed of using propaganda as a significant theoretical term." It was, Doob declared, too crude; by which he

meant it had been rendered insufficiently scientific. Sproule, "Propaganda Studies," 78 n. 54; Delia, "Communication Research," 59.

86. Christopher Simpson, *Science of Coercion: Communication Research and Psychological Warfare, 1945–1960* (New York, 1994), 23.

87. Willard D. Rowland, Jr., *The Politics of TV Violence Research: Policy Uses of Communication Research* (Beverly Hills, 1983); Converse, *Survey Research;* Delia, "Communication Research," 58–59.

88. It should be noted, however, that, at the same time, within the classified deliberations of the U.S. international propaganda apparatus there was apparently little difficulty in conceding that "propaganda" was the appropriate designation. See, for example, Leo Bogart, *Premises for Propaganda* (New York, 1976)—a study originally commissioned by the U.S. Information Agency in 1953 "to help plan its own program of research," whose purpose was "to identify and articulate the 'operating assumptions,' explicit and implicit, that guided or underlay the daily work decisions of the Agency's propaganda personnel. . . ." Wilbur Schramm, Paul Lazarsfeld, and Joseph T. Klapper and other principal figures in the concurrent transition from "mass persuasion" to"communication research" were all connected directly as consultants and researchers with U.S. propaganda agencies, as detailed by Simpson, *Science of Coercion.* see also Bogart, *Premises*, vii, xx, 1.

89. This transition did not lack for some prior guidance. Sproule has shown how, for example, overzealous propaganda analysts began to find themselves isolated, in a harbinger of the coming postwar "emergency." Hadley Cantril, a founder of "empirical" communication study, began backpedaling from his association (as a board member) with Alfred M. Lee's Institute for Propaganda Analysis after he became concerned that this affililation might somehow discredit him in the eyes of the Rockefeller Foundation—of whose largesse his own Princeton Radio Project was a beneficiary. And when, still before U.S. entry into World War II, Lee's institute was singled out for attack by the Dies committee in Congress as a supposed Communist-front group, Cantril altogether severed his ties with it. Sproule, "Propaganda Studies," 70, 72. But sensations of anti-fascist unity during wartime momentarily suppressed such portents. Jowett's recent research into the origins of the Payne Fund Studies of movies supports the idea that this research constituted an early attempt to shift discussion of film as a social force into a more academic social scientific register. Jowett, "Social Science as a Weapon," 1992.

90. Dorothy Ross, *The Origins of American Social Science* (Cambridge, 1991).

91. See, for example, Arthur W. Kornhauser, "Analysis of 'Class' Structure of Contemporary American Society—Psychological Bases of Class Divisions," in George W. Hartmann and Theodore Newcomb, *Industrial Conflict: A Psychological Interpretation* (New York, 1939), 199–264, which employed a typology of classes drawn from the Soviet leader and theoretician Nicholai Bukharin.

92. C. Wright Mills, *The Sociological Imagination* (New York, 1959). Although, significantly, some mainstream studies of the 1950s continued to employ this language.

93. Cartier, "Wilbur Schramm," 160.

94. Mills, "Mass Media and Public Opinion," 577; Lazarsfeld, Berelson, and Gaudet, *People's Choice*, 5.

95. Elihi Katz and Paul F. Lazarsfeld, *Personal Influence* (1955; New York, 1964), 15–30.

96. Paul F. Lazarsfeld and Robert K. Merton, "Mass Communication, Popular Taste and Organized Social Action," in Lyman Bryson, ed., *The Communication of Ideas* (New York, 1948), 95–118, at 96 and 97.

97. Lazarsfeld's close affiliations, through the 1930s, with the left-wing Institute for Social Research, largely vitiates efforts to absolutize the familiar dichotomy between "administrative" and "critical" research—a dichotomy Lazarsfeld himself introduced, mainly as an attempt to exhibit solidarity in the popular-front atmosphere of the wartime emergency. For a compelling treatment of this important intellectual relationship, see Rolf Wiggershaus, *The Frankfurt School: Its History, Theories, and Political Significance* (Cambridge, 1994), 236–46.

98. Lazarsfeld and Merton, "Mass Communication, Popular Taste," 101–5.

99. Ibid., 107.

100. Ibid., 111.

101. Ibid., 113.

102. Ibid., 115–16.

103. Ibid., 117.

104. Ibid., 117–18.

105. Joseph T. Klapper, *The Effects of Mass Communication* (Glencoe, 1960). Also see Rowland, *Politics of TV Violence*, 72: and Gitlin, "Media Sociology."

106. Joseph T. Klapper, "Mass Media and the Engineering of Consent," *American Scholar* 17 (4) (Autumn 1948): 419–29 at 419–20.

107. Klapper, "Mass Media," 422.

108. Ibid.; Klapper, *Effects of Mass Communication*, x, 13.

109. Klapper, *Effects of Mass Communication*, 252.

110. David C. McClelland, *The Achieving Society* (New York, 1961), 50.

111. Katz and Lazarsfeld, *Personal Influence*. For an exception that proves the rule, see John W. Riley, Jr., and Matilda White Riley, "Mass Communication and the Social System," in Robert K. Merton, Leonard Broom, and Leonard S. Cottrell, Jr., eds., *Sociology Today: Problems and Prospects* (New York, 1959), 537–78. Riley and Riley argued that individual communicators and the recipients of their messages had been located primarily only in relation to "diverse primary groups." However, a "less developed" but no less crucial line of research, they asserted, would have to begin from the fact that, "just as the audience is not composed of discrete individuals, neither is it composed of discrete primary groups. These smaller, solidary groupings must also be viewed in their interdependence with one another and as belonging to some still more inclusive system. . . . the relevant theory also invokes wider structures and longer-term changes which include and also transcend the individual or the primary group as such." Ibid., 554. Klapper termed the highly schematic model provided by Riley and Riley for situating mass communication "within a social system" "particularly provocative." Klapper, *Effects of Mass Communication*, 296 n. 3.

112. Katz and Lazarsfeld, *Personal Influence*, 16.

113. It is perhaps worth recalling that Cooley, who himself also had been quick to dismiss the relevance of social class to the American context, boasted in 1898 in the privacy of his journal, at the advent of the Spanish-Cuban-American War, that the conflict "makes me proud of the race and the American stock." His

adumbration of "the primary group" aimed to provide nothing less than the concept of human nature needed "for a new liberal society." Ross, *Origins*, 242, 245, 244.

114. Katz and Lazarsfeld, *Personal Influence*, 63.

115. Klapper, *Effects of Mass Communication*, 3.

116. Katz and Lazarsfeld, *Personal Influence*, 114–15, 140–45, 245, 258, 276–79.

117. Ibid., 225, 224. The gendered categories and conceptions of this era of research have not received the scrutiny they merit. For another instance, see McClelland, *Achieving Society*, where a so-called "need for achievement," in turn associated with economic growth, is identified and universalized from a sample including only boys.

118. On Lynd's explicit decision to study Muncie, owing to its small proportion of African Americans, immigrants, Catholics, and Jews, see Richard Wightman Fox, "Epitaph for Middletown: Robert S. Lynd and the Analysis of Consumer Culture," in Fox and T. J. Jackson Lears, eds., *The Culture of Consumption* (New York, 1983), 111. The People's Choice study selected Erie County, Ohio, for study in part because "it was relatively free from sectional peculiarities," which seems to have meant—the authors later state—that its population was "almost all native-born white." Lazarsfeld, Berelson, and Gaudet, *People's Choice*, 3, 10. For "sectional peculiarities," Katz and Lazarsfeld, *Personal Influence*, 335.

119. Not especially surprisingly, "status" turned out to play the "least important" role of three different indicators in predicting opinion leadership. Katz and Lazarsfeld, *Personal Influence*, 220–22, 225–26, 322–24.

120. Robert K. Merton, "Patterns of Influence: Local and Cosmopolitan Influentials," in idem, *Social Theory and Social Structure* (New York, 1968), 466, 469, 472.

121. The subtitle of Katz and Lazarsfeld, *Personal Influence*. It should be noted, however, that the field's continuing major concern for content analysis comprised an important, unbroken continuity with the war period and even earlier.

122. See Gitlin, "Media Sociology," 237–39, who argues that Mills had "not yet grasped," as he would a decade later (in *The Power Elite*), "the emergence of a high-consumption society," and Irving Louis Horowitz, *C. Wright Mills: An American Utopian* (New York, 1983), 77–81.

123. Gitlin, "Media Sociology"; Mills, *Power Elite*, 316.

124. Abbe Mowshowitz, *On the Market Value of Information Commodities I: The Nature of Information and Information Commodities*, Management Report Series No. 90 (Rotterdam, 1991), 6.

125. Klaus Krippendorff, "Paradox and Information," in Brenda Dervin and Melvin J. Voigt, eds., *Progress in Communication Sciences*, vol. 5 (Norwood, N.J., 1984), 50.

126. For a spectacular example, purporting to present an integrated analysis of the roles of information, matter, and energy, in "systems" ranging from cell to society, see James G. Miller, *Living Systems* (New York, 1978). Also moving far too effortlessly across these levels is James Beniger, *The Control Revolution* (Cambridge, 1986).

127. Wilbur Schramm, "Information Theory and Mass Communication," *Journalism Quarterly* 32 (Spring 1955): 135.

128. Steve J. Heims, *The Cybernetics Group* (Cambridge, 1991), 183. 187, 192–93.

129. Heims, *Cybernetics Group;* L. David Ritchie, *Information* (Newbury Park, 1991). "It is generally agreed," Abbe Mowshowitz asserts, "that Shannon's measure . . . is limited in its applicability." Mowshowitz, *On the Market Value of Information Commodities*, 1.

130. Wilbur Schramm, "The Nature of Communication between Humans," in Schramm and Donald F. Roberts, eds., *The Process and Effects of Mass Communication*, rev. ed. (Urbana, 1971), 7, 5.

131. Katz and Lazarsfeld, *Personal Influence*, 16.

132. Robert B. Shoemaker, "The London 'Mob' in the Early Eighteenth Century," *Journal of British Studies* 26 (3) (July 1987): 273–304. See also Asa Briggs, "The Language of 'Mass' and 'Masses' in 19th-Century England," in *The Collected Essays of Asa Briggs*, vol. 1: *Words, Numbers, Places, People* (Urbana, 1985), 34–54. For a kaleidoscopic account, which unfortunately chooses not to distinguish radical from conservative modalities of the class-based concern over mass culture, see John Carey, *The Intellectuals and the Masses* (New York, 1992). Also see Raymond Williams, *Culture and Society, 1780–1950* (New York, 1966), 297; Patrick Brantlinger, *Bread and Circuses: Theories of Mass Culture as Social Decay* (Ithaca, 1983); William Kornhauser, *The Politics of Mass Society* (New York, 1959), 21–38; Delia, "Communication Research," 66.

133. Notably through Robert E. Park, whose dissertation (1904), "The Crowd and the Public," "analyzed and accepted the nature and social setting of the crowd, as defined by LeBon, Sighele, and other conservative European social theorists." Czitrom, *Media*, 114. A useful study, which I learned of too late to incorporate fully into the present text, is Paul R. Gorman, "The Development of an American Mass Culture Critique" (Ph.D. dissertation, University of California, Berkeley, 1990).

134. Joan Shelley Rubin, *The Making of Middlebrow Culture* (Chapel Hill, 1992), 1–33; Steven J. Ross, "Struggles for the Screen: Workers, Radicals, and the Political Uses of Silent Film," *American Historical Review* 96 (2) (April 1991): 333–67; Roy Rosenzweig, *Eight Hours for What We Will* (Cambridge, 1983), 191–221; Garth S. Jowett, "Social Science as a Weapon: The Origins of the Payne Fund Studies, 1926–1929," *Communication* 13 (1992): 211–25; Herbert Blumer, "Moulding of Mass Behavior through the Motion Picture," in James F. Short, Jr., *The Social Fabric of the Metropolis* (1935; Chicago, 1971), 131–37.

135. Robert E. Park et al., *An Outline of the Principles of Sociology* (New York, 1939), 242.

136. Louis Wirth, "Consensus and Mass Communication," *American Sociological Review* 13 (1) (Feb. 1948): 1–15.

137. Daniel Bell, *The End of Ideology* (Glencoe, 1960), 21. Andrew Ross quite rightly qualifies this depiction to take proper note of the renewed affirmation of pluralism through which Cold War liberals sought to distance 1950s America from any hint of "totalitarianism." Andrew Ross, *No Respect: Intellectuals and Popular Culture* (New York, 1989), 55.

138. The extraordinary success achieved by Packard's book is usefully ex-

plored in a recent biography: Daniel Horowitz, *Vance Packard and American Social Criticism* (Chapel Hill, 1994).

139. Roald Dahl, *Charlie and the Chocolate Factory* (1964; New York, 1988), 145.

140. Dwight Macdonald, "A Theory of 'Popular Culture,'" *Politics* 1, no. 1 (1944): 22.

141. Dwight Macdonald, "A Theory of Mass Culture" (1953), in Bernard Rosenberg and David Manning White, eds., *Mass Culture: The Popular Arts in America* (Glencoe, 1957), 62; James Gilbert, *A Cycle of Outrage: American Reaction to the Juvenile Delinquent in the 1950s* (New York, 1986).

142. Cited in Ross, *No Respect*, 105. Lazarsfeld and Merton disparaged the view expressed, they said, at a symposium in the late 1940s "that 'the power of radio can be compared only with the power of the atomic bomb.'" Paul F. Lazarsfeld and Robert K. Merton, "Mass Communication, Popular Taste, and Organized Social Action," in Lyman Bryson, ed., *The Communication of Ideas* (1948; New York, 1964), 95.

143. The social sources of these anxieties will repay further investigation; but any inventory must emphasize both the spectacular postwar rise of mass consumerism on the suburbanized family unit, and the uneasily coupled secular migration of married women into the paid labor force. The fact that increasing numbers of married women were taking paid work, however, seems not to have been connected with the concerns about media representations—above all, television violence—that began to erupt at this time. Lynn Spigel, *Making Room for TV* (Chicago, 1992); Gilbert, *Cycle of Outrage*; Ross, *No Respect*, 42–64. That some leading researchers—Lazarsfeld and Merton among them—were turning away from the study of mass media during the 1950s was undoubtedly also a factor.

144. Paul F. Lazarsfeld, "Mass Culture Today," in Norman Jacobs, ed., *Culture for the Millions* (Princeton, 1959), xii. Lazarsfeld's position was consonant with the perspective he offered with Merton in 1948: "there can be no doubt that the women who are daily entranced for three or four hours by some twelve consecutive 'soap operas,' all cut to the same dismal pattern, exhibit an appalling lack of esthetic judgment. Nor is this impression altered by the contents of pulp and slick magazines, or by the depressing abundance of formula motion pictures replete with hero, heroine and villain moving through a contrived atmosphere of sex, sin and success." Lazarsfeld and Merton, "Mass Communication, Popular Taste, and Organized Social Action," 108–9.

145. Robert and Helen Lynd, *Middletown: A Study in Modern American Culture* (New York, 1929).

146. As argued by Fox, "Epitaph for Middletown," 101–41.

147. Francis Mulhern, *The "Moment" of Scrutiny* (London, 1981).

148. Michael Wreszen, *A Rebel in Defense of Tradition* (New York, 1994), 37, 42–43, 348.

149. James Rorty, *Our Master's Voice: Advertising* (New York, 1934), x, 373–85 passim.

150. There is no question that, as one often-perceptive account has it, "attacks on mass culture permeate[d] the Left throughout the 1960s and 1970s." Gary Cross, *Time and Money: The Making of Consumer Culture* (London,

1993), 189. I would argue that most of the key elements in the critique of mass culture remain publicly prevalent down to the present day.

151. See Carey, *Intellectuals and the Masses;* Macdonald, "A Theory of 'Popular Culture,'" 20–23; Macdonald, "A Theory of Mass Culture," 59–73. Valuable here are Brantlinger, *Bread & Circuses:* 200–203; and Donald Lazere, ed., *American Media and Mass Culture: Left Perspectives* (Berkeley, 1987), 7–8. F. R. Leavis had identified "standardization" and "levelling-down" as inexorable features of British decline in 1929. Mulhern, *The "Moment" of Scrutiny,* 49. Rorty declared that the advertiser-supported press, functioning as an effective agent of "cultural stultification" on behalf of business, also acted to "level all cultural values to the common denominator of emulative acquisition and social snobbism." Rorty, *Our Master's Voice,* 31.

152. Macdonald, "A Theory of Mass Culture," 61–62.

153. Macdonald, "A Theory of 'Popular Culture,'" 20, 21.

154. Also worth noting here was the growing convergence in U.S. public thought between fascism and Communism. See Les K. Adler and Thomas G. Paterson, "Red Fascism: The Merger of Nazi Germany and Soviet Russia in the American Image of Totalitarianism," *American Historical Review* 75 (4) (April 1970): 1046–64.

155. "The Russian masses like the Hollywood type of film," wrote Macdonald: "A film studio can be a dream factory, whether it is on the shores of the Black Sea or of the Pacific." Dwight Macdonald, "Soviet Society and Its Cinema," *Partisan Review* 6 (2) (Winter 1939): 86, 85. Macdonald's discussion of popular culture as indoctrination appears in his "A Theory of 'Popular Culture.'" "If kitsch is the official tendency of culture in Germany, Italy and Russia, it is not because their respective governments are controlled by philistines, but because kitsch is the culture of the masses in these countries, as it is everywhere else. The encouragement of kitsch is merely another of the inexpensive ways in which totalitarian regimes seek to ingratiate themselves with their subjects. Since these regimes cannot raise the cultural level of the masses—even if they wanted to—by anything short of a surrender to international socialism, they will flatter the masses by bringing all culture down to their level. . . . Kitsch keeps a dictator in closer contact with the 'soul' of the people. Should the official culture be one superior to the general mass-level, there would be a danger of isolation." Clement Greenberg, "Avant-Garde and Kitsch," *Partisan Review* 6 (5) (Fall 1939): 46–47. It was "non-communist leftists," according to one recent historian, who most avidly supported enlarging the social base for paternalistic but noncommercial leisure practices—embracing churches, concerts, museums, libraries, and adult education—hoping by this means "not only to broaden their political base beyond the narrow social world of labour through the appeal of enhanced recreational and cultural programmes, but to wage a cultural battle with 'totalitarians.'" Cross, *Time and Money,* 100, 105–14.

156. Horkheimer and Adorno's crucial essay was not translated into English until 1972, but some earlier work in a similar vein was accessible, for instance, T. W. Adorno, "Television and the Patterns of Mass Culture," in Bernard Rosenberg and David Manning White, eds., *Mass Culture: The Popular Arts in America* (Glencoe, 1957). The products of U.S. mass culture, in the form of Hollywood films, were abundantly available in interwar Europe and, not least,

in Berlin and Vienna. For an argument that Adorno's concept of culture industry was unrelated to any particular aversion to popular culture, see Peter Uwe Hohendahl, "The Frozen Imagination: Adorno's Theory of Mass Culture Revisited," *Thesis Eleven* 34 (1993): 17–41.

157. Max Horkheimer and Theodor W. Adorno, *Dialectic of Enlightenment* (New York, 1972), 122.

158. Theodor W. Adorno, "Culture Industry Reconsidered," *New German Critique* no. 6 (Fall 1975): 12, 18.

159. Leo Lowenthal, *An Unmastered Past* (Berkeley, 1987), 186; Adorno, "Culture Industry Reconsidered," 12; Horkheimer and Adorno, *Dialectic of Enlightenment*, 120–67.

160. Macdonald, "A Theory of Mass Culture."

161. Barnard, *The Great Depression and the Culture of Abundance*, 132, 186, 211; Cf. Alan M. Wald, *Writing from the Left: New Essays on Radical Culture and Politics* (London, 1994), 120.

162. Rorty, *Our Master's Voice*, 279–80.

163. Ibid., 30, 18, 73, 33.

164. Ibid., 291.

165. Ibid., 75, 104–6

166. Ibid., 133.

167. Ibid., 394.

168. For a critical discussion of this, a dominant strand in explanations of European fascism, see Val Burris, "The Discovery of the New Middle Classes," in Arthur J. Vidich, ed., *The New Middle Classes* (New York, 1995), 16, 24–46. For an extensive and insightful study of the comparative historical proclivity, among U.S. white-collar strata, to accept authoritiarian rule, see Jurgen Kocka, *White Collar Workers in America 1890–1940: A Social-Political History in International Perspective* (London, 1980). Kocka emphasizes that white-collar identity became a problem in U.S. public discussion in the 1930s, decades later than it did in Germany. Ibid., 200–206.

169. Wilhelm Reich, *The Mass Psychology of Fascism* (New York, 1970), 10–19; Wiggershaus, *Frankfurt School*, 173; Hans Speier, *German White-Collar Workers and the Rise of Hitler* (New Haven, 1986), 9.

170. Lewis Corey, *The Crisis of the Middle Class* (1935; New York, 1992), 286. On Corey, see Paul M. Buhle, *A Dreamer's Paradise Lost* (Atlantic Highlands, N.J., 1995). In Sinclair Lewis's novel, *It Can't Happen Here* (New York, 1935), fascism can be seen as a struggle for the soul of the middle class: the anti-fascist protagonist is an aging, small-town New England newspaper editor, while his spineless, deal-making son—in marked contrast to his willful and principled daughter—becomes a collaborator.

171. Harold D. Lasswell, "The Psychology of Hitlerism," *Political Quarterly* 4 (1933): 374, 375, 383, 384, 377.

172. Corey, *Crisis of the Middle Class*, 261, 280, 272.

173. Robert A. Brady, *The Spirit and Structure of German Fascism* (1937; New York, 1969), 23. "[P]ractically all the 'white collar' salaried and professional classes," wrote Brady, were to be found within "the great mass of the middle-class." The latter, lacking "any forces, organization, or principles to unite it, made up of the hesitant, the confused, and the compromising elements of society," comprised the decisive social force in the run-up to fascism: "The real

significance of the Nazi Party lay in the fact that it had a certain following amongst the amorphous and hesitant central mass, and that it reflected in its confused platform the very state of mind in which the bulk of the citizens found themselves. Ideal for the purposes to which it was to be put, there was a plank in the Nazi platform to meet the prejudices of nearly every group to be appealed to, and it conducted its campaigns so as to combine a proper degree of idea-dulling fanaticism with further confusion of the issues." Ibid., 18, 20. Herbert I. Schiller suggested that I should emphasize the significance of this now unfortunately obscure work. Brady, it also should be noted, was an important and direct influence on a pioneering figure in radical communication study, Dallas Smythe.

174. Erich Fromm, *Escape from Freedom* (1941; New York, 1969); Bruno Bettelheim, "Individual and Mass Behavior in Extreme Situations," *Journal of Abnormal and Social Psychology* 38 (4) (Oct. 1943): 451–52, original emphasis.

175. Wiggershaus, *Frankfurt School*, 378–80.

176. Mills, "Mass Media and Public Opinion," 584.

177. Ibid., 582–83.

178. It is worth emphasizing that, taking account of slight differences in chronology and of divergent starting points, both Macdonald and Horkheimer and Adorno likewise subsequently blunted—and in the latter case perhaps even censored—their pointed wartime criticisms of capitalist cultural production as serving the purpose of class domination. For the former, see Lazere, *American Media and Mass Culture*, 7–8; for the latter, Wiggershaus, *Frankfurt School*, 401.

179. There were as well, predictably, significant intellectual disagreements on the character of the culture industry between the members and hangers-on of the Frankfurt School—a point recently emphasized, by Martin Jay, "Mass Culture and Aesthetic Redemption: The Debate between Max Horkheimer and Siegfried Kracauer," in Seyla Benhabib, Wolfgang Bonss, and John McCole, eds., *On Max Horkheimer* (Cambridge, 1993), 365–86.

180. Siegfried Kracauer, *From Caligari to Hitler: A Psychological History of the German Film* (Princeton, 1947), v.

181. Institute of Social Research, "Research Project on Anti-Semitism," *Studies in Philosophy and Social Science* 9, no. 1 (1941): 125. Franz Neumann, *Behemoth: The Structure and Practice of National Socialism* (New York, 1942), 436–37. See also: Martin Jay, "The Jews and the Frankfurt School: Critical Theory's Analysis of Anti-Semitism," in Anson Rabinbach and Jack Zipes, eds., *Germans and Jews since the Holocaust* (New York, 1986), 287–301; and John B. Thompson, *Ideology and Modern Culture* (Stanford, 1990), 101–101, for a more general treatment of this point.

182. Herbert Marcuse, *One-Dimensional Man* (Boston, 1964), 8.

183. The sources of this preconditioning were, it is true, left vague in the varied formulations of Frankfurt School writers.

184. Bell, *End of Ideology*, 27–28.

185. C. Wright Mills, *The New Men of Power: America's Labor Leaders* (1948; New York, 1971), 3, 15, 30.

186. Mills, *Power Elite*, 309–10. My treatment of Mills is generally indebted to Horowitz, *C. Wright Mills*. Mills's approach to the power elite was anticipated in his first major study, in his comments on the views of "the independent left"—with whom his own affinities lay: "They see coming a great coalition of business, labor, and government; they see bureaucracy everywhere and they are

afraid. To them unions seem one more bureaucratic net ensnaring the people, part of the whole alien and undemocratic apparatus of control. All the bureaucratic elite, in labor as in business and government, are against the rank and file; they are trying to manage it, and it is immoral that man should be the object of management and manipulation. He is the root, and he is being choked." Mills, *New Men of Power*, 18.

187. Horowitz, *C. Wright Mills*, 257.

188. Arthur J. Vidich, "Foreword," in Speier, *German White-Collar Workers*, xv.

189. C. Wright Mills, *White Collar* (New York, 1951), 65, 72, 71.

190. Horowitz, *C. Wright Mills*, 231.

191. Fritz Machlup, *The Production and Distribution of Knowledge in the United States* (Princeton, 1962), 381, 382.

192. Mills, *White Collar*, dust jacket.

193. Ibid., 110. It bears mention that this same linkage emerged in the semiotic discussion of "myth" propounded in France by the critic Roland Barthes at the same time: "The political alliance of the bourgeoisie and the petite-bourgeoisie has for more than a century determined the history of France; it has rarely been broken, and each time only temporarily (1848, 1871, 1936). This alliance got closer as time passed, it gradually became a symbiosis; transient awakenings might happen, but the common ideology was never questioned again. . . . By spreading its representations over a whole catalogue of collective images for petit-bourgeois use, the bourgeoisie countenances the illusory lack of differentiation of the social classes: it is as from the moment when a typist earning twenty pounds a month *recognizes herself* in the big wedding of the bourgeoisie that bourgeois ex-nomination achieves its full effect." Roland Barthes, *Mythologies* (1957; New York, 1975), 141. See also Louis-Jean Calvet, *Roland Barthes: A Biography* (Bloomington, 1995), 123, 143.

194. This critical assessment was fully in keeping with Mills's overall intellectual propensity: "Always and everywhere," writes his leading biographer, "Mills's pragmatism overwhelmed his Marxism." Horowitz, *C. Wright Mills*, 216.

195. David Caute, *The Great Fear: The Anti-Communist Purge under Truman and Eisenhower* (New York, 1979).

196. Brady, *Spirit and Structure*, 22, original emphasis. Horkheimer in David Held, *Introduction to Critical Theory: Horkheimer to Habermas* (Berkeley, 1980), 52. Held himself quotes from Max Horkheimer, "Die Juden und Europa," *Zeitschrift fur Sozialforschjung* 8, nos. 1–2 (1939): 115. Thanks to Lora Taub for recalling this reference.

197. Rosenberg and White, *Mass Culture*.

198. "The masses are exploited culturally as well as economically. . . . The deadening and warping effect of long exposure to movies, pulp magazines and radio can hardly be overestimated. . . . this culture-pattern stamped deep into the modern personality, much deeper than conscious political ideas, is a factor always to be reckoned with." Macdonald, "A Theory of 'Popular Culture,'" 22.

199. George Gerbner, "Violence in Television Drama: Trends and Symbolic Functions," in George A. Comstock and Eli A. Rubinstein, eds., *Television and Social Behavior: Reports and Papers, vol. 1: Media Content and Control*, a Techni-

cal Report to the Surgeon General's Scientific Advisory Committee on Television and Social Behavior (Rockville, Md., 1972), 30.

200. George Gerbner, "The Social Role of the Confession Magazine," *Social Problems* 6 (Summer 1958): 31, 40; see also idem, "The Social Anatomy of the Romance-Confession Cover Girl," *Journalism Quarterly* 35 (Summer 1958): 299–306; idem, "Content Analysis and Critical Research in Mass Communication," *AV Communication Review* no. 6 (Spring 1958): 85–108.

201. George Gerbner, "The Structure and Process of Television Program Content Regulation," in Comstock and Rubinstein, eds., *Television and Social Behavior*, 386, 412.

202. C. Wright Mills, "The Cultural Apparatus" (1959) in Mills, *Power, Politics & People*, ed. Irving Louis Horowitz (New York, 1967), 413.

203. Bell, *End of Ideology*, 38, 25.

204. Mills, *Power Elite*, 315.

205. Ibid., 3. In an earlier formulation, Mills had written: "The people, even as they act, are more like spectators than actors." Mills, "Mass Media and Public Opinion," 583.

206. Mills, *Power Elite*, 324, 315.

207. Macdonald, "A Theory of Mass Culture," 71.

208. Mills, *White Collar*, 148.

209. Marcuse, *One-Dimensional Man*, xv, xiii, 18. Marcuse's views were echoed by Stanley Aronowitz, who wrote that "the pervasive character of capitalist commodity relations and of the technological rationality upon which they are based tends to reduce social relations and social consciousness to a single dimension: their instrumental value in terms of maintaining the structure of social domination." Aronowitz, *False Promises* (New York, 1973), 9. Marcuse subsequently developed the theme that domination might be offset in a hypostasized "aesthetic dimension"—immanent in which he identified a transcendant utopian impulse. Herbert Marcuse, *The Aesthetic Dimension* (Boston, 1974).

210. Herbert I. Schiller, *Mass Communications and American Empire* (New York, 1969), 147–64, esp. 158.

211. Raymond Williams, *The Country and the City* (New York, 1973), 117.

212. The distinction among "categorical," "relational," and "formational" notions of class, originating in the work of Ralph Miliband, is brought home for communication study in Vincent Mosco, *The Political Economy of Communication: Rethinking and Renewal*, forthcoming.

213. Stuart Hall, "The Rediscovery of 'Ideology': Return of the Repressed in Media Studies," in Michael Gurevitch, Tony Bennett, James Curran, and Janet Woollacott, eds., *Culture, Society and the Media* (London, 1982), 59, 61.

214. Ibid., 61. Connecting with this view was the widely heralded notion that the U.S. was becoming "a middle-class society," the majority of whose citizens were blessed with unprecedented income and abundant leisure time. Leo Bogart, *The Age of Television* (New York, 1956), 2–5. Bogart (viii) wrote that television "has not, however, transformed the values which Americans hold dear. It has taken the features already most expressive of our culture and has heightened and intensified their impact upon the daily life of the average person. There is nothing in the content of television programming which is not already vividly apparent in the motion pictures, radio, magazines or the press; TV is saying the same things, but in a much louder and more insistent voice."

215. Gitlin, "Media Sociology," 207.

216. The concept of mass society still today supplies a largely hidden lodestone of poststructuralist argument—for example, in the claim that "the depth and importance of communications media is evident when it is realized that contemporary mass society in its present form is inconceivable without the printing press." Mark Poster, *The Mode of Information: Poststructuralism and Social Context* (Chicago, 1990), 8.

217. Mills, *Power Elite*, 324.

218. Aronowitz, *False Promises*, 95, 102.

219. Julianne Burton and Jean Franco, "Culture and Imperialism," *Latin American Perspectives Issue* 16, no. 5 (1) (Winter 1978): 3.

220. Williams, *Culture and Society*, 328.

221. Jonathan M. Wiener, "Radical Historians and the Crisis in American History, 1959–1980," *Journal of American History* 76, no. 2 (Sept. 1989): 409.

222. Paul Baran and Paul Sweezy, *Monopoly Capital* (New York, 1966). It was only in 1973, on the other hand, that Victor Perlo's *The Unstable Economy* (New York) appeared and revisited the issue of structural instability.

223. It is illuminating to compare this passage as well with remarks made by Lazarsfeld and Merton in their classic 1948 article: "Economic power seems to have reduced direct exploitation and turned to a subtler type of psychological exploitation, achieved largely by disseminating propaganda through the mass media of communication. This change in the structure of social control merits thorough examination. . . . The manifest concern over the functions of the mass media is in part based upon the valid observation that these media have taken on the job of rendering mass publics conformative to the social and economic status quo." Lazarsfeld and Merton, "Mass Communication, Popular Taste and Organized Social Action," 109.

224. Herbert Marcuse, "The Question of Revolution," *New Left Review* 45, (Sept.–Oct. 1967): 6.

225. Theodor W. Adorno, *Prisms* (1967; Cambridge, 1992), 26.

226. Jay, *Marxism and Totality*, 212, 270–71.

227. Reich, *Mass Psychology*, 3–33.

228. Bell, *End of Ideology*, 38.

229. Fredric Jameson, "Reification and Utopia in Mass Culture," *Social Text* 1 (1) (1979): 132; Michael Denning, "The End of Mass Culture," *International Labor and Working Class History* 37 (Spring 1990): 9.

230. Dallas Smythe, *The Structure and Policy of Electronic Communications* (Urbana, 1957), set the pattern. Some of Smythe's other work has been collected in a volume edited by Thomas Guback, *Counterclockwise: Perspectives on Communication* (Boulder, 1994). For two later works of political economy see Thomas Guback, *The U.S. International Film Industry* (Indianapolis, 1969); and Schiller, *Mass Communications and American Empire*.

231. Dallas W. Smythe, "Some Observations on Communications Theory" (1954), reprinted in Denis McQuail, ed., *Sociology of Mass Communications* (Harmondsworth, 1972), 25.

Chapter Three. **The Opening Toward Culture**

1. Eric R. Wolf, "American Anthropologists and American Society," in Dell Hymes, ed., *Reinventing Anthropology* (New York, 1974), 251–63; Robin

Blackburn, ed., *Ideology in Social Science* (New York, 1973); Jesse Lemisch, *On Active Duty in War and Peace* (n.p., n.d.).

2. Tamar Liebes and Elihu Katz, *The Export of Meaning: Cross-Cultural Readings of* Dallas (New York, 1990), v. 4.

3. Liebes and Katz actually concede much of this point themselves, but in a tacit form. They propose three reasons for the "worldwide success of American television." The first is the supposed "universality, or primordiality, of some of its themes and formulae"; second is "the polyvalent or open potential of many of the stories." The third contributing factor is presented as though it were just one more dimension of their own theory, rather than an essential plank in the approach they seek to discredit: "the sheer availability of American programs in a marketplace where national producers—however zealous—cannot fill more than a fraction of the hours they feel they must provide." Liebes and Katz, *Export of Meaning*, 5.

4. Ien Ang, *Watching* Dallas: *Soap Opera and the Melodramatic Imagination* (London, 1985).

5. James Rorty, *Our Master's Voice: Advertising* (New York, 1934), 288.

6. Clement Greenberg, "Avant-Garde and Kitsch," *Partisan Review* 6 (5) (Fall 1939): 41. Herbert I. Schiller has observed that Lerner, Schramm, and other U.S. international communication scholars of the 1950s and 1960s "had no doubt that the modern media and the new information technologies were means of great potential influence." Herbert I. Schiller, *Culture, Inc.: The Corporate Takeover of Public Expression* (New York, 1989), 141.

7. Daniel Lerner, *The Passing of Traditional Society* (Glencoe, 1958), 52, 56.

8. Ibid., 52, 54. Wilbur Schramm was even blunter: "No one who has seen modern communication brought to traditional villages will ever doubt its potency." Schramm even worried about the ethical issues of using mass media to encourage "productive" attitudes among the peoples of poor countries: "Are we advocating that mass communication should be used in the developing countries to manipulate people?" His answer—really only a rationalization—was that "change is inevitable." Wilbur Schramm, *Mass Media and National Development* (Stanford, 1965), 20,35.

9. Lucien W. Pye, ed., *Communications in Political Development* (Princeton, 1963), 15, 19.

10. In Schramm, *Mass Media*, 51.

11. Pye, *Communications in Political Development*, 10, see also 25–27. See also Christopher Simpson, *Science of Coercion* (New York, 1994), 90–92.

12. This formulation is a composite based on W. W. Rostow, *The Stages of Economic Growth* (Cambridge, 1960); Lerner, *Passing of Traditional Society;* Schramm, *Mass Media;* Robert C. Hornik, *Development Communication* (New York, 1988), 15; Alex Inkeles and David H. Smith, *Becoming Modern: Individual Change in Six Developing Countries* (Cambridge, 1974); and David C. McClelland, *The Achieving Society* (New York, 1961).

13. Herbert I. Schiller, *Mass Communications and American Empire* (New York, 1969), 13–16. At the dawn of the postwar era, David Sarnoff, chairman of RCA's board, claimed: "When television has fulfilled its destiny, man's sense of physical limitation will be swept away, and his boundaries of sight and hearing will be the limits of the earth itself. With this may come a new horizon, a new philosophy, a new sense of freedom and greatest of all, perhaps, a finer and

broader understanding between all the peoples of the world." Cited in Lynn Spigel, *Making Room for TV* (Chicago, 1992), 214 n. 46. Parallel conditions were apparent in the domestic scene. In the United States itself, wrote Schiller, the "cultural process" had emerged as society's "deepest concern"; the intractable difficulty was once again that marketplace domination "largely removed [it] from general consideration and public decision-making." Schiller, *Mass Communications*, 151.

14. Harry Magdoff, "Colonialism (c. 1450–c. 1970), Part II: European Expansion since 1763," *The New Encyclopaedia Britannica*, 15th ed., Macropaedia, vol. 4 (Chicago, 1974), 904–5.

15. John Tomlinson, *Cultural Imperialism* (Baltimore, 1991), 34.

16. Schiller, *Mass Communications*, 16.

17. One eminent analyst thus wrote casually of "countries where people work harder and therefore reach a higher level of economic development." McClelland, *Achieving Society*, 52. Wilbur Schramm, incorporating Daniel Lerner's defining work, wrote: "This is the dynamic of social development as Lerner sees it: a nucleus of mobile, change-accepting personalities; then a growing mass media system to speed the ideas and attitudes of social mobility and change; then the interaction of urbanization, literacy, industrialization, and media participation to bring modern society into being." Schramm, *Mass Media*, 47.

18. A fact celebrated without reflection in the mass market press of the U.S.—still the epicenter and self-interested supplier of transnational culture—on a regular basis. See Rone Tempest, "American TV—We Are the World," *TV Guide* 41 (27) (July 3, 1993): 8–14.

19. Mitchell Stephens, "Pop Goes the World," *Los Angeles Times Magazine*, Jan. 17, 1993, pp. 26, 24, 34. The deliberate suppression of native languages other than English has of course been a regular feature of policy *within* the United States, most recently, for example, in Alaska, where just two of the twenty languages that once flourished are considered viable candidates for survival. Lee Dye, "Alaskans Speak Out to Save Dying Languages," *Los Angeles Times*, July 7, 1994, p. A7.

20. Herbert I. Schiller, *Communication and Cultural Domination* (White Plains, 1976), 17.

21. Anthony Brewer, *Marxist Theories of Imperialism: A Critical Survey*, 2nd ed. (London, 1990), 109–99, quotes at 130, 281. For a useful explication of the emergence and metamorphosis of dependency theory, first articulated in the mid- to late 1960s by Latin American economists, see Magnus Blomstrom and Bjorn Hettne, *Development Theory in Transition* (London, 1984).

22. Ernesto Laclau, *Politics and Ideology in Marxist Theory* (1971; London, 1977), 15–50; Brewer, *Marxist Theories*, 179–82, 225–84; Aidan Foster-Carter, "The Modes of Production Controversy," *New Left Review* 107 (Jan.–Feb. 1978): 47–77.

23. Tomlinson, *Cultural Imperialism*, 2; cf. Frederick Buell, *National Culture and the New Global System* (Baltimore, 1994), 7–8.

24. Aijaz Ahmad, *In Theory: Classes, Nations, Literatures* (London, 1992). The entire intellectual register was different: "We know," wrote Sartre about the Third World in a famous preface, "that it is not a homogeneous world; we know too that enslaved peoples are still to be found there, together with some who have achieved a simulacrum of phony independence, others who are still fight-

ing to attain sovereignty and others again who have obtained complete freedom but who live under the constant menace of imperialist aggression. . . ." Jean-Paul Sartre, "Preface" to Frantz Fanon, *The Wretched of the Earth* (New York, 1968), 10.

25. Fred Fejes, "Media Imperialism: An Assessment," *Media, Culture & Society* (3) (1981): 284–85.

26. Raquel Salinas and Leena Paldan, "Culture in the Process of Dependent Development: Theoretical Perspectives," in Kaarle Nordenstreng and Herbert I. Schiller, eds., *National Sovereignty and International Communication* (Norwood, 1979), 84.

27. "One avenue of research that shows hope of progress particularly to communication researchers," he continued, "is the work by literary scholars and some communication researchers which attempts to explicate the symbolic universe that is contained in the content of the mass media in dependent societies and relate this to the overall system of dependency. . . . Such works are useful to communication researchers in that they establish a baseline for the content of the media which enables researchers to say something about the products of the transnational media in dependent societies. The next step—going from a discussion of the content of the popular media to a study of its actual impact on the lives and human relationships of Third World populations—is, of course, an extremely difficult step. . . ." Fejes, "Media Imperialism," 286, 287. I remember conversations during 1978–79 in which Peter Golding, then of the Centre for Mass Communication Research at the University of Leicester, chafed at the difficulty of finding funds to underwrite such a study—which, he believed, would be of inestimable value—in an African national context.

28. Schiller, *Communication and Cultural Domination*, 85 (original emphasis). For a massive compendium of the same era, in which the links between "communication and class struggle" were explicit and sustained, see Armand Mattelart and Seth Siegelaub, *Communication and Class Struggle*, 2 vols. (New York, 1979, 1983).

29. Tomlinson, *Cultural Imperialism*, 70–75.

30. Schiller, *Communication and Cultural Domination*, 16–17, quoting Evelina Dagnino, "Cultural and Ideological Dependence: Building a Theoretical Framework," in F. Bonilla and Robert Girling, eds., *Struggles of Dependency* (Stanford, 1973). The projected social transformation of Chile, a state which, like most other South American nations, had achieved formal political independence during the 19th century, rested not on an armed movement for national liberation but on the electoral victory of Salvador Allende, within a continuing context of parliamentary democracy. This context offered many important lessons for radical analysts of communication and cultural production. The Chilean counterrevolution succeeded with strong support from the CIA and other state agencies, and from the American corporate community, most especially including the then communications conglomerate ITT; however, the relentless attack on the Allende Popular Unity government by the domestic media, and the domestic social classes for which they spoke, could not be, and were not, overlooked. Schiller, *Communication and Cultural Domination*; Armand Mattelart and Michelle Mattelart, *Rethinking Media Theory* (Minneapolis, 1992), 180–82.

31. Herbert I. Schiller, "Computer Systems: Power for Whom and for What?," *Journal of Communication* 28 (4) (1978): 192.

32. Schiller, *Communication and Cultural Domination*, 9, original emphasis.

33. Amilcar Cabral, "National Liberation and Culture," the Eduardo Mondlane Memorial Lecture, delivered at Syracuse University, New York, Feb. 20, 1970, in idem, *Unity and Struggle* (New York, 1979), 144.

34. Ibid., 143.

35. Ibid., 149; and Patrick Chabal, *Amilcar Cabral: Revolutionary Leadership and People's War* (Cambridge, 1983), 185.

36. Chabal, *Amilcar Cabral*, 185–86. Throughout the earlier period of colonial rule, as metropolitan radical analysts became aware, first and foremost through the work of Frantz Fanon, imperialism already had interrupted and reshaped aspects of the "traditional" cultures of the new nations. The colonial era's substantial forms of cultural domination—racializing forms were by far the most well-observed—were, however, limited. Most African and Asian indigenous peoples, for example, continued to speak in their own tongues, and to be ignorant of the languages used by colonialists. The practices of colonial cultural domination, no matter how pernicious, existed within a relatively well-defined and restricted sphere. Frantz Fanon, *Black Skin, White Masks* (1952; New York, 1967).

37. Cabral, "National Liberation," 152.

38. Frantz Fanon, *The Wretched of the Earth* (1961; New York, 1968), 315, 209, 233.

39. Ibid., 245–46.

40. Schiller, *Mass Communications*, 110.

41. Raymond Williams, *Culture and Society, 1780–1950* (1958; New York, 1966), 312.

42. Mattelart and Mattelart, *Rethinking Media Theory*, 175–76.

43. Fanon, *Wretched of the Earth*, 222–23.

44. Schiller, *Communication and Cultural Domination*, 86.

45. The Cuban movie *Lucia* tried to insist on just this point: that it was only after the revolution that continuing conflicts over gender inequality could hope to find a supportive context for transcendence.

46. Edward W. Said, *Culture and Imperialism* (New York, 1993), 268.

47. Fanon, *Wretched of the Earth*, 166, 175, 152–53, 200.

48. Ngugi wa Thiong'o, *Barrel of a Pen: Resistance to Repression in Neo-Colonial Kenya* (Trenton, 1983), 80.

49. Ibid.

50. Ibid., 80–85.

51. Once more, however, the beginnings of significant recognition lay, already, within the critique of cultural imperialism. See Mattelart and Siegelaub, *Communication and Class Struggle*, vol. 2: *Liberation, Socialism* (New York, 1983).

52. Robert Kavanagh, *Theatre and Cultural Struggle in South Africa* (London, 1985); Eugene Van Erven, *The Playful Revolution: Theatre and Liberation in Asia* (Bloomington, 1992).

53. Frantz Fanon, *Studies in a Dying Colonialism* (New York, 1967), 83, quoted in Schiller, *Mass Communications*, 66.

54. These points emerge in desultory fashion from different sources. They are not to be taken as coterminous with the critique of cultural imperialism, but as exemplary of it. See, in particular, Schiller, *Mass Communications*; idem, *Com-*

munication and Cultural Domination; Many Voices, One World (MacBride Report) (London, 1980); Armand Mattelart, *Multinational Corporations and the Control of Culture* (Sussex, 1979); Alan Wells, *Picture-Tube Imperialism?* (Maryknoll, N.Y., 1972); Jeremy Tunstall, *The Media Are American* (Beverly Hills, 1977); Thomas H. Guback and Tapio Varis, *Transnational Communication and Cultural Industries* (Paris, 1982).

55. Fanon, *Wretched of the Earth*, 203, quoted in Schiller, *Mass Communications*, 162.

56. Everett M. Rogers, "Communication and Development: The Passing of the Dominant Paradigm," *Communication Research* 3, no. 2 (April 1976): 213–40.

57. Schiller, *Mass Communications*, 121–22.

58. Kaarle Nordenstreng, *The Mass Media Declaration of UNESCO* (Norwood, 1984).

59. Schiller, *Communication and Cultural Domination*, 84–89, makes explicit mention of such issues.

60. Ahmad, *In Theory*, 40. This theme has been a regular preoccupation of leading contemporary novelists. In anglophone and francophone African contexts, see Ngugi Wa Thiong'o, *Devil on the Cross* (London, 1982); and Sembene Ousmane, *The Last of the Empire* (London, 1983); Chinua Achebe, *Anthills of the Savannah* (New York, 1988).

61. Nordenstreng, *Mass Media Declaration of UNESCO*. This of course is not to imply that critical research in international communications has not continued, but only to say that its ability to energize and influence the larger field has been attenuated. For a recent example of continuing radical revisionism in this subfield, see Gerald Sussman and John Lent, *Transnational Communications* (Newbury Park, 1991).

62. Williams, *Culture and Society*, 312.

63. Stuart Hall, "The Emergence of Cultural Studies and the Crisis of the Humanities," *October* 53 (Summer 1990): 11–23 at 12; Patrick Brantlinger, *Crusoe's Footprints: Cultural Studies in Britain and America* (New York, 1990); Michael Denning, "The Academic Left and the Emergence of Cultural Studies," *Radical History Review* 54 (Fall 1992): 21–47; John Clarke, *New Times and Old Enemies* (London, 1991), 1–19, esp. 10–11; Richard Hoggart, *The Uses of Literacy* (1957; New York, 1970); Williams, *Culture and Society*; Raymond Williams, *The Long Revolution* 2nd ed. (Harmondsworth, 1965); E. P. Thompson, *William Morris Romantic to Revolutionary* (1955; New York, 1961); E. P. Thompson, *The Making of the English Working Class* 2nd ed. (Harmondsworth, 1968); E. P. Thompson, "The Long Revolution," *New Left Review* 9 (May–June 1961): 24–33; and 10 (July–Aug. 1961): 34–39. Indispensable complements to Hall's essay in *October*, cited in this footnote, are Raymond Williams's discussions in "The Future of Cultural Studies," which was produced from a transcript of a lecture, and "The Uses of Cultural Theory," both in Williams, *The Politics of Modernism* (London, 1989).

64. "Indeed, it can hardly be stressed too strongly that Cultural Studies, in the sense we now understand it, for all its debts to its Cambridge predecessors, occurred in adult education: in the WEA, in the extramural Extension classes. . . . as a matter of fact, already in the late forties, and with notable precedents in army education during the war . . . Cultural Studies was extremely active in

adult education." Williams, *Politics of Modernism*, 154. See also Hall, "Emergence of Cultural Studies," 12.

65. E. P. Thompson, *The Poverty of Theory* (London, 1978), 199.

66. Richard Hoggart and Raymond Williams, "Working Class Attitudes," *New Left Review* 1 (Jan.–Feb. 1960): 26.

67. Raymond Williams, "Working Class Culture," *Universities and Left Review* 1 (2) (Summer 1957): 30.

68. Stuart Hall, "The 'First' New Left: Life and Times," in Robin Archer et al., eds., *Out of Apathy* (London, 1989), 26, 27.

69. In ibid., 37.

70. "This category of culturalism is constructed from some sloppy and impressionistic history. . . . In the mid-1950s Richard Hoggart's attitude to Marxism was one of explicit hostility, Raymond Williams's was one of active critique, Stuart Hall's (I would surmise) was one of sceptical ambivalence, whereas, from 1956 onwards, the Reasoner group, with which was associated, closely or loosely, a number of Marxist historians . . . was attempting to defend, re-examine and extend the Marxist tradition at a time of political and theoretical disaster." E. P. Thompson, "The Politics of Theory," in R. Samuel, ed., *People's History and Socialist Theory* (London, 1981), 397. See also Hall, "The 'First' New Left," 21–23.

71. Hoggart, *Uses of Literacy*, 280, 23–24.

72. Hall, "Emergence of Cultural Studies," 12. Compare Stuart Hall, "A Sense of Classlessness," *Universities and Left Review* 1 (5) (Autumn 1958): 27–32.

73. For a thoroughgoing treatment, see Francis Mulhern, *The Moment of Scrutiny* (London, 1979).

74. Raymond Williams, "Fiction and the Writing Public," *Essays in Criticism* 7 (4) (Oct. 1957): 422–23, 425.

75. Raymond Williams, "Class and Voting in Britain," *Monthly Review* 11 (9) (Jan. 1960): 327.

76. Williams, *Culture and Society*, 283.

77. Thompson, *William Morris*.

78. Thompson, "The Long Revolution."

79. Thompson, *Making of the English Working Class*, 9–10, 11.

80. Thompson, "Peculiarities of the English," in idem, *Poverty of Theory*, 85, original emphasis.

81. For an extended and provocative treatment of Thompson's thinking, see Perry Anderson, *Arguments within English Marxism* (London, 1980).

82. Editorial, *Universities and Left Review* 1 (1) (Spring 1957): i.

83. Raymond Williams, "The British Elections," *The Nation* 199 (8) (Sept. 28, 1964): 155.

84. Editorial, *Universities and Left Review* 1 (1) (Spring 1957): i.

85. Stuart Hall, "The Supply of Demand," in E. P. Thompson, Kenneth Alexander, Stuart Hall, Alasdair MacIntyre, Ralph Samuel, and Peter Worsley, *Out of Apathy* (London, 1960), 70. Thanks to Michael Meranze for making available this text.

86. Hall, "Emergence of Cultural Studies," 12.

87. Williams, "British Elections," 156.

88. Raymond Williams, "Notes on Marxism in Britain since 1945," *New Left Review* 100 (Nov. 1976–Jan. 1977): 87.

89. Williams, "Class and Voting in Britain," 327.

90. Ibid.

91. Williams, *Culture and Society*, 324, 323.

92. Williams, "British Elections," 154; Raymond Williams, *Politics and Letters* (London, 1981), 414.

93. Williams, *Politics and Letters*, 14–15.

94. Raphael Samuel, "Born-Again Socialism," in Archer et al., eds., *Out of Apathy*, 57.

95. Williams, *Politics and Letters*, 107, 115, 364.

96. V. G. Kiernan, "Culture and Society," *The New Reasoner* 3 (Summer 1959): 82, 83. The quote about "masses" comes from Williams, *Culture and Society*, 300.

97. Williams, *Long Revolution*, 329.

98. Ibid., 201.

99. The notion of reformism is clarified as "the belief in the possibility of attaining socialism by gradual and peaceful reforms within the framework of a neutral parliamentary State." Anderson, *Arguments*, 176–77.

100. Williams, "Working Class Culture," 31–32.

101. Williams, *Culture and Society*, 325.

102. Williams, "Working Class Culture," 31–32.

103. Williams, "British Elections," 156.

104. As is movingly evident in the final essays in Williams, *Politics of Modernism*.

105. Williams, *Politics and Letters*, 362.

106. Williams, "Class and Voting in Britain," 333.

107. Which in turn, he dispiritedly conceded in the wake of a third straight Labour defeat in 1959, "was just too difficult." Williams, "Class and Voting in Britain," 330.

108. Raymond Williams, "Working Class Culture," *Universities and Left Review* 1 (2) (Summer 1957): 29.

109. Williams, *Culture and Society*, 295.

110. Thompson, "The Long Revolution," 25–26.

111. Williams, *Long Revolution*, 54.

112. Ibid., 11.

113. Williams returned to this central conviction over and over again. His book *Modern Tragedy*, to take one example, announced that his discussion of this subject would begin "with the modern experiences that most of us call tragic, and . . . try to relate these to tragic literature and theory. . . ." Raymond Williams, *Modern Tragedy* (Stanford, 1966), 14.

114. Thompson, "The Long Revolution," 27, 28. Thompson's language recalls Williams's own earlier discussion: "The next step in thinking . . . must be in a different direction, for Eliot has closed almost all the existing roads." Williams, *Culture and Society*, 243.

115. Williams, *Long Revolution*, 63.

116. As Stuart Hall later put this, Williams's approach "rescued culture from its residual status as the mere expression of other forces: but at the expense of a radical relativism, skirting the problem of determination." Hall, "Cultural

Studies and the Centre: Some Problematics and Problems," in Centre for Contemporary Cultural Studies, *Culture, Media, Language* (London, 1980), 28.

117. Williams, *Long Revolution*, 63, 62.

118. Williams, *Culture and Society*, 320. "A man cannot be interpreted in terms of some original sin of class; he is where he is, and with the feelings he has; his life has to be lived with his own experience, not with someone else's." Ibid., 292. And, in 1961: "Comparative studies of different societies have added to our historical evidence to show how various are the learned systems of behaviour and attitudes which groups of human beings adopt. Each of these systems, while it lasts, is the form of a society, a pattern of culture to which most of its individual members are successfully trained." Williams, *Long Revolution*, 98.

119. Williams, *Long Revolution*, 54, 56.

120. Ibid., 61.

121. "Any theoretical account of the analysis of culture," wrote Williams, "must submit to be tested in the course of actual analysis." *Long Revolution*, 70. Williams thereby established a crucial point of common ground with Thompson.

122. Ibid., 55.

123. Ibid., 11–12.

124. Ibid., 139.

125. Raymond Williams, *Drama from Ibsen to Brecht* (London, 1968), 17–18.

126. Martin Jay, *Marxism and Totality: The Adventures of a Concept from Lukacs to Habermas* (Berkeley, 1984), 14. Jay notes that "[a]side from several suggestive references to culture as a 'whole way of life' in the early work of Williams, totality did not really enter the English debate until the Althusserian wave of the 1970s." Jay, *Marxism and Totality*: 4 n. 7. Cf. Stuart Hall, "Culture, the Media and the 'Ideological Effect,'" in James Curran, Michael Gurevitch, and Janet Woollacott, *Mass Communication and Society* (London, 1977), 319–20.

127. Raymond Williams, "Literature and Sociology: In Memory of Lucien Goldman," *New Left Review* 67 (May-June 1971): 10.

128. Georg Lukacs, *History and Class Consciousness* (Cambridge, 1971), 27. For discussion of Lukacs's concept of the totality in this work, see Jay, *Marxism and Totality*, 102–27.

129. Ibid., 109.

130. Lukacs, *History and Class Consciousness*, 92. Lukacs himself wrote that "[t]he journalist's 'lack of convictions,' the prostitution of his experiences and beliefs is comprehensible only as the apogee of capitalist reification." Ibid., 100. Yet those inclined to Althusser's structural Marxism (of which more in the next chapter) sometimes faulted Lukacs for neglecting "the whole institutional superstructure of bourgeois class power: parties, reformist trade unions, newspapers, schools, churches, families. . . ." For Lukacs, in this account, "the bourgeoisie maintains its ideological rule, not through the corporeal communication of its political organizations, voluntary associations, press or educational systems but solely through the ghostly discourse of commodities." Gareth Stedman Jones, "The Marxism of the Early Georg Lukacs," in New Left Review, *Western Marxism: A Critical Reader* (London, 1978), 40. For a useful account of Lukacs's life, see Arpad Kadarkay, *Georg Lukacs: Life, Thought, and Politics* (Cambridge, 1991).

131. Williams, "Literature and Sociology," 11.

132. Mark Poster, *Existential Marxism in Postwar France from Sartre to Althusser* (Princeton, 1975), 270–76.

133. Karl Marx, *Preface to a Contribution to the Critique of Political Economy* (New York, 1970), 21.

134. Lukacs, *History and Class Consciousness*, 262, original emphasis. For an unsympathetic but still useful discussion of this claim, see Jones, "Marxism of the Early Georg Lukacs," 44–45.

135. Williams, *Culture and Society*, 325.

136. Thompson, "The Long Revolution," 31. With all due respect to the concern for lived experience—which was, Thompson agreed, also an "interesting" and "refreshing" aspect of *The Uses of Literacy*—Williams, like Hoggart, appeared to be trying to substitute a flair for literary-sociological criticism as a surrogate for substantive social history. Thompson, "The Long Revolution," 32. Thompson's criticisms resurrected those leveled at Raymond Williams by Victor Kiernan in his review of *Culture and Society* for *The New Reasoner*—a journal Thompson coedited. V. G. Kiernan, "Culture and Society," *The New Reasoner* (Summer 1959): 74–83.

137. Thompson, "The Long Revolution," 34.

138. Raymond Williams, *Culture* (Glasgow, 1981), 85.

139. Williams, *Culture and Society*, 320.

140. Williams, *Long Revolution*, 314–15.

141. Louis Althusser, *For Marx* (1969; London, 1990), 203; Louis Althusser and Etienne Balibar, *Reading Capital* (London, 1970), 186–87.

142. Willaims, *Long Revolution*, 64.

143. Williams, "British Elections," 154; Williams, *Long Revolution*, 84–85; Williams, *Modern Tragedy*, 17. For a variation of this attempt to privilege art within the context of the structure of feeling, see Williams, "Literature and Sociology," 14.

144. Williams, "Working Class Culture," 32.

145. Williams, *Communications*, 3d ed. (Harmondsworth, 1976), 182.

146. Perry Anderson, *English Questions* (London, 1992), 176.

147. Williams, *Politics and Letters*, 373, 375, 376–77.

148. Thompson, *Making of the English Working Class*, 13.

149. Fanon, *Wretched of the Earth*, 314.

150. Williams, *Long Revolution*, 10.

151. Williams, *Modern Tragedy*, 80.

152. Stuart Hall, "The New Revolutionaries," in T. Eagleton and B. Wicker, eds., *From Culture to Revolution* (London, 1968), 208, 219.

153. Raymond Williams, ed., *May Day Manifesto 1968* (Harmondsworth, 1968), 57, 43, 70, 66.

154. Williams, *Communications*, 182, 183.

155. See, for example, Schiller, *Communication and Cultural Domination*, 50–51, 106; Raymond Williams, *Marxism and Literature* (New York, 1977), 136.

156. Williams, *May Day Manifesto*, 9, 15–16.

157. Williams concluded presciently in early 1965 that a "critical period" had commenced the previous October, "with Labour's narrow victory": "An extraordinary instability of politics, reflecting the deep and postponed tensions of the society itself, seems now ahead of us. In this situation, the development of

the British Left is again open and active." Raymond Williams, "The British Left,"
New Left Review 30 (March–April 1965): 26.

158. Williams, *Communications*, 181. Already in 1966 he had hinted at
an even stronger position, writing of Britain as "a society powered by great
economic inequality and by organised manipulation." Williams, *Modern
Tragedy*, 79.

159. Hall, "New Revolutionaries," 182, 207, 217.

160. Williams, "Culture and Revolution: A Response," in Eagleton and
Wicker, eds., *From Culture to Revolution*, 297.

161. Williams, "Culture and Revolution: A Comment," in ibid., 31, 30.

162. Williams, "Culture and Revolution: A Response," 297.

163. Williams, "Culture and Revolution: A Comment," 29.

164. Williams, "Culture and Revolution: A Response," 297–98.

165. Ibid., 298–99.

166. Ibid., 308.

167. Stuart Hall, Chas Critcher, Tony Jefferson, John Clarke, and Brian
Roberts, *Policing the Crisis: Mugging, the State, and Law and Order* (London,
1978), 318.

168. Williams, "Notes on Marxism," 87.

169. Stuart Hall, "Gramsci and Us," *Marxism Today* 31 (6) (June 1987): 21.

170. Alexander Cockburn, "Introduction," in Alexander Cockburn and
Robin Blackburn, eds., *Student Power/Problems, Diagnosis, Action* (Baltimore,
1969), 16.

171. Juliet Mitchell, "Women: The Longest Revolution," *New Left Review*
40 (Nov.–Dec. 1966): 11–37.

172. Hall, "Gramsci and Us," 20.

173. Hall, "Cultural Studies and the Centre," 38. According to Grossberg,
the denizens of Hall's Centre for Contemporary Cultural Studies were, as early as
1968, "exploring issues of the gendered relations of power, without assuming
that these were merely epiphenomenal expressions of deeper, more real,
bottom-line economic or class relations." Lawrence Grossberg, "Cultural
Studies vs. Political Economy: Is Anyone Else Bored with This Debate?," *Critical
Studies in Mass Communication* 12 (1) (March 1995): 77. Thanks to Lora Taub for
this timely reference.

174. Stuart Hall, "Cold Comfort Farm," in idem, *The Hard Road to Renewal*
(London, 1988).

Chapter Four. The Contraction of Theory

1. Anson Rabinbach, *The Human Motor* (Berkeley, 1992), 72–83.

2. Maurice Cornforth, in E. P. Thompson, "Caudwell," in Ralph Miliband
and John Saville, eds., *The Socialist Register 1977* (New York, 1977), 240.

3. By purporting to take "the same givens" as classical Marxism, according to an authoritative study, Sartre's existentialist Marxism was enabled "to
avoid a rigorous analysis of Marx's concept of the means of production." Mark
Poster, *Existential Marxism in Postwar France from Sartre to Althusser* (Princeton,
1975), 270. Western Marxism, wrote one of its own maverick representatives,
displayed "an almost exclusive preoccupation with superstructural questions,
and conspicuous lack of concern for the material and economic base. . . ."

Alfred Sohn-Rethell, *Intellectual and Manual Labour* (London, 1978), xii. That there existed a "sociological deficit" in Critical Theory—lately underlined by Axel Honneth and other writers—may be inferred from the following earlier admission that ". . . if the work of Adorno nowhere yields that bald statement about the administered world which would seem to be its presupposition, if he nowhere takes the trouble to express in outright sociological terms that theory of the structure of the 'institutionalized society' which serves as a hidden explanation and essential cross-reference for all the phenomena under analysis, this is to be explained not only by the fact that such material belongs to a study of the infrastructure rather than of ideological materials, and that it is already implicit in classical Marxist economics, but above all by the feeling that such outright statements, such outright presentations of sheer *content*, are stylistically wrong. . . ." Fredric Jameson, *Marxism and Form* (Princeton, 1971), 54; Axel Honneth, "Max Horkheimer and the Sociological Deficit of Critical Theory," in Seyla Benhabib, Wolfgang Bonss, and John McCole, eds., *On Max Horkheimer* (Cambridge, 1993), 187–214; and Moishe Postone and Barbara Brick, "Critical Theory and Political Economy," in ibid., 215–56. Following Perry Anderson, it is reasonable to see this "deficit" as a concomitant feature of Western Marxism's general divorce from political practice. But why this divorce occurred initially requires further explanation. Perry Anderson, *Considerations on Western Marxism* (London, 1979), 42–48 at 44.

4. See also Perry Anderson, "The Antinomies of Antonio Gramsci," *New Left Review* 100 (Nov. 1976–Jan. 1977): 41–46.

5. Fredric Jameson, *Postmodernism; Or, The Cultural Logic of Late Capitalism* (Durham, 1990), xviii.

6. Martin Jay, *Marxism and Totality: The Adventures of a Concept from Lukacs to Habermas* (Berkeley, 1984), 109.

7. Jay, *Marxism and Totality*, 212, 270–71.

8. Sohn-Rethell, *Intellectual and Manual Labour*, 34.

9. See, for example, in addition to later references, James O'Connor, "Productive and Unproductive Labor," *Politics and Society* 5 (3) (1975): 297–336; Erik Olin Wright, *Class, Crisis and the State* (London, 1978), 30–61; Ian Gough, "Marx's Theory of Productive and Unproductive Labour," *New Left Review* 76 (Nov.–Dec. 1972): 47–72. Ernest Mandel gives strong hints of an emphasis on the existence of the wage relation as the key arbiter of labor's productive status, but even here there are qualifications. Mandel, *Marxist Economic Theory* (New York, 1968), I: 191–92, 206.

10. Nicos Poulantzas, *Classes in Contemporary Capitalism* (London, 1975), 211, 213, 214, 222.

11. Harry Braverman, *Labor and Monopoly Capital: The Degradation of Work in the 20th Century* (New York, 1974), 410–23.

12. Paul A. Baran and Paul M. Sweezy, *Monopoly Capital* (New York, 1966), 130–31, 141.

13. Ali Rattansi, *Marx and the Division of Labour* (London, 1982), 139.

14. Braverman, *Labor and Monopoly Capital*, 13.

15. Stuart Hall, "A Sense of Classlessness," *Universities and Left Review* 1 (5) (Autumn 1958): 27, 32. Around the same time, Williams cited Marx's distinction between base and superstructure to make the point "that changes in the

latter are necessarily subject to a different and less precise mode of investigation." Williams, *Culture and Society*, 266.

16. Stuart M. Hall, "The New Conservatism and the Old," *Universities and Left Review* 1 (1) (Spring 1957): 22, 21.

17. Hall, "A Sense of Classlessness," 26.

18. George Orwell, *The Lion and the Unicorn* (London, 1941), 112, 54. Cf. Cross, *Time and Money*, 74. Hall, as we shall see, later took up Orwell's implied suggestion, in an in-depth study of *Picture Post*.

19. Hall, "A Sense of Classlessness," 31 (order of quotations altered). The previous year Hoggart had concluded about "an emerging classlessness" that "in at least one sense we are indeed becoming classless—that is the great majority of us are being merged into one class. We are becoming culturally classless." Hoggart, *Uses of Literacy*, 279.

20. Hall, "The Supply of Demand," 81, 83.

21. Stuart Hall, "The New Revolutionaries," in T. Eagleton and B. Wicker, eds., *From Culture to Revolution* (London, 1968), 182–222.

22. Williams, *Culture and Society*, 298.

23. Raymond Williams, "Notes on Marxism in Britain since 1945," *New Left Review* 100 (Nov. 1976–Jan. 1977): 87.

24. During Hall's stint as editor of *New Left Review*, in 1960–61, Williams defended his policy of according emphasis on "new cultural styles . . . in a language that differed from the typical left magazine" against pressures emanating from editorial board members, notably including Thompson, who thought that the journal should take up a more traditional political role in the movement. Willaims, *Politics and Letters*, 365.

25. Hall, "The Supply of Demand," 86. 96, 93, 95–96.

26. Stuart Hall and Paddy Whannel, *The Popular Arts* (New York, 1965), 15, original emphases. The connection of this work to the National Union of Teachers is appropriately emphasized by John Storey, *An Introductory Guide to Cultural Theory and Popular Culture* (Athens, 1993), 60.

27. Hall and Whannel, *Popular Arts*, 67.

28. Ibid., 45.

29. Ibid., 363.

30. Ibid., 384.

31. Ibid., 380, 382. In this work, the debt to Leavis, as much as to Williams, is unmistakable, a point aptly emphasized by Storey, *Guide to Cultural Theory*, 44.

32. Stuart Hall, "The Social Eye of Picture Post," *Working Papers in Cultural Studies* no. 2 (1971/72): 89, 87, 103.

33. Hall, "The Social Eye," 100–101, original emphasis.

34. Stuart Hall, Chas Critcher, Tony Jefferson, John Clarke, and Brian Roberts, *Policing the Crisis: Mugging, the State, and Law and Order* (London, 1978).

35. Stuart Hall, "Signification, Representation, Ideology: Althusser and the Post-Structuralist Debates," *Critical Studies in Mass Communication* 2 (2) (June 1985): 97.

36. Hall, "Williams Interviews," 313–14, original emphasis. Hall's attempt to work through the theoretical issues surrounding the idea of a complex totality is best expressed in Stuart Hall, "Marx's Notes on Method: A 'Reading' of the '1857 Introduction,'" *Working Papers in Cultural Studies* 6 (1974): 132–70, and

Stuart Hall, "The 'Political' and the 'Economic' in Marx's Theory of Classes," in Alan Hunt, ed., *Class and Class Structure* (London, 1977), 15–60.

37. Alex Callinicos, *Marxism and Philosophy* (Oxford, 1983), 95, as quoted in Gregory Elliott, "Introduction" to Louis Althusser, *Philosophy and the Spontaneous Philosophy of the Scientists* (1965; London, 1990), xii.

38. Hall, "The Rediscovery of 'Ideology,'" 83. In the pages of the theoretical journal of the British Communist Party, Hall later repeated this assertion: "[D]o not fall into the trap of the old mechanical economism and believe that, if you can only get hold of the economy, you can move the rest of life. The nature of power in the modern world is that it is *also* constructed in relation to political, moral, intellectual, cultural, ideological, sexual questions." Stuart Hall, "Gramsci and Us," *Marxism Today* 31 (6) (June 1987): 20–21, original emphasis.

39. These are reviewed in Peter Golding and Graham Murdock, "Ideology and the Mass Media: The Question of Determination," in Michele Barrett, Philip Corrigan, Annette Kuhn, and Janet Wolff, *Ideology and Cultural Production* (London, 1979), 198–224.

40. Stuart Hall, "Introduction to Media Studies at the Centre," in Center for Contemporary Cultural Studies, *Culture, Media, Language* (London, 1980), 118.

41. Louis Althusser and Etienne Balibar, *Reading Capital* (London, 1970), 13.

42. Louis Althusser, *For Marx* (London, 1990), 113. For Hall's appreciative comment, see Stuart Hall, "Rethinking the 'Base-and-Superstructure' Metaphor," in Jon Bloomfield, ed., *Papers on Class, Hegemony and Party* (London, 1977), 68.

43. Louis Althusser, "Contradiction and Overdetermination," *New Left Review* 41 (Jan.–Feb. 1967): 31, 32, original emphasis.

44. Louis Althusser, "Theory, Theoretical Practice and Theoretical Formation: Ideology and Ideological Struggle," in Althusser, *Philosophy and the Spontaneous Philosophy*, 6. See also Althusser and Balibar, *Reading Capital*, 58.

45. Althusser, "Theory, Theoretical Practice," 23.

46. Ibid., 24.

47. Althusser, *For Marx*, 233, original emphasis.

48. Althusser, "Theory, Theoretical Practice," 25. "What does it mean, then, to say that ideologies are basically *unconscious?*" asks Althusser's onetime collaborator, Etienne Balibar, in a recent essay: "Not that they would *lack* consciousness: rather, they produce forms of consciousness for individuals and groups, that is, modes of representation, modes of 'being in the world' and subjective identities, always already knit together with *non-representative* elements (such as hopes, fears, beliefs, moral or immoral values, moves toward liberation or domination—possibly both). In doing so they must depend on conditions that no 'subject' can ever master or create himself: material constraints from the division of labor, the forms of property, etc., and the no less material constraints of language, desire, sexuality, etc. Ideologies are the various *historical* forms in which unconscious conditions can be elaborated to allow individuals and groups to imagine their own practices." Etienne Balibar, "The Non-Contemporaneity of Althusser," in E. Ann Kaplan and Michael Sprinker, *The Althusserian Legacy* (London, 1993), 10. This entire collection contains much useful material.

49. Terry Eagleton, *Ideology* (London, 1991), 148.

50. "If in its totality ideology expresses a representation of the real destined to sanction a regime of class exploitation and domination," wrote Althusser in 1965, "it can also give rise, in certain circumstances, to the expression of the *protest of the exploited classes* against their own exploitation." Althusser, "Theory, Theoretical Practice," 30. Also see Althusser, "Ideology and Ideological State Apparatuses," an essay published in Britain in 1971, and available in Louis Althusser, *Lenin and Philosophy* (New York, n.d.), 127–86.

51. Hall, "Marx's Notes on Method," 147. This formulation, it is worth emphasizing, allowed Hall to return, through a side door, to a space he could cohabit with Williams, even as the battles over "empiricism" were being waged: "concrete relations and conjunctions." For Althusser's use of this same passage in Marx, see Althusser, *For Marx*, 206. n. 45.

52. Ignorant of a more knowledgable historical assessment, I would offer as an early evidence of this idea's utilization by British radicals an essay by the socialist-feminist Juliet Mitchell, which appeared in *New Left Review* as early as 1966. What, asked Mitchell, was the solution to the impasse in socialist thinking regarding women? "It must lie in differentiating woman's condition, much more radically than in the past, into its separate structures, which together form a complex—not a simple—unity. This will mean rejecting the idea that woman's condition can be deduced derivatively from the economy or equated symbolically with the society. Rather, it must be seen as a *specific* structure, which is a unity of different elements" wrote Mitchell, making direct citation to Althusser's work. Juliet Mitchell, "Women: The Longest Revolution," *New Left Review* 40 (Nov.–Dec. 1966): 16.

53. Stuart Hall, "Culture, the Media and the 'Ideological Effect,'" in James Curran, Michael Gurevitch, and Janet Woollacott, eds., *Mass Communication and Society* (London, 1977), 315, 316.

54. Hall, "Culture, the Media and the 'Ideological Effect,'" 319, original emphasis.

55. That this was a collective effort stands out with particular clarity when we recall the little-known work, written by one of Hall's associates at the Centre for Contemporary Cultural Studies, Charles Woolfson, *The Labour Theory of Culture* (London, 1982).

56. Hall, "Culture, the Media and the 'Ideological Effect,'" 318, original emphasis.

57. David Montgomery, *Workers' Control in America* (Cambridge, 1979).

58. Vincent Mosco and Andrew Herman, "Radical Social Theory and the Communications Revolution," in Emil G. McAnany, ed., *Communications and Social Structure: Critical Studies in Mass Media Research* (New York, 1981), 58–84; see also Vincent Mosco, *Pushbutton Fantasies* (Norwood, 1982), 119–38.

59. James D. Halloran, Philip Elliott, and Graham Murdock, *Demonstrations and Communication: A Case Study* (Harmondsworth, 1970); Philip Elliott, *The Making of a Television Series: A Case Study in the Sociology of Culture* (London, 1972); Jeremy Tunstall, *Journalists at Work: Specialist Correspondents, Their News Organisations, News Sources, and Competitor-Colleagues* (London, 1971); Peter Golding and Philip Elliott, *Making the News* (London, 1979); Philip Schlesinger, *Putting "Reality" Together* (London, 1978). A rare (U.S.) effort to apply the same techniques of analysis to non-news production is Michael Intintoli,

Taking Soaps Seriously (New York, 1987). This research converged with a series of related U.S. studies, influenced by phenomenological and organizational sociology. See Gaye Tuchman, "Objectivity as a Strategic Ritual: An Examination of Newsmen's Notions of Objectivity," *American Journal of Sociology* 77 (1971–72): 660–79; Harvey Molotch and Marilyn Lester, "News as Purposive Behavior," *American Sociological Review* 39 (1974): 101–12; idem, "Accidental News," *American Journal of Sociology* 81 (2) (1975): 235–60.

60. Dallas W. Smythe, "Communications: Blindspot of Western Marxism," *Canadian Journal of Political and Social Theory* 1 (3) (Fall 1977): 1–27. Smythe was far from alone in his effort to treat consumption as labor; for another significant attempt along these lines see James O'Connor, "Productive and Unproductive Labor," *Politics and Society* 5 (3) (1975): 297–336, esp. 314–15.

61. *Jean Baudrillard: Selected Writings,* ed. Mark Poster (Stanford, 1988), 21. One authority writes that, for Baudrillard, "the imperatives of an entire system of needs and objects require a vast labor to learn about the products, to master their use and to earn the money and leisure to purchase and use them. Consumption is thus productive activity" and even "a kind of labor." Douglas Kellner, *Jean Baudrillard: From Marxism to Postmodernism and Beyond* (Stanford, 1989), 13, 19.

62. Althusser, "Theory, Theoretical Practice," 16.

63. Althusser, *Philosophy and the Spontaneous Philosophy,* 82.

64. Althusser, "Theory, Theoretical Practice," 30–31, original emphasis. However, Althusser also added, "the Party refuses to reserve the knowledge of theory as a monopoly for some specialists, leaders and intellectuals. . . ." Ibid., 41. The link between intellectuals, as the supposed bearers of correct theory, and the working class, as the purported bearer of practice, as I have already asserted, has been of long and deeply problematic standing within Marxism.

65. Althusser, "Theory, Theoretical Practice," 37–38, original emphasis.

66. Cf. ibid., 16.

67. Althusser, "On Theoretical Work: Difficulties and Resources" (orig. 1967), in Althusser, *Philosophy and the Spontaneous Philosophy,* 51, 45.

68. Althusser, "Theory, Theoretical Practice," 26.

69. Althusser and Balibar, *Reading Capital.* For "anthropological ideology of labour," 172.

70. Ibid., 59.

71. Jay, *Marxism and Totality,* 394, 399–401.

72. See Gregory Elliott, "Althusser's Solitude," in E. Ann Kaplan and Michael Sprinker, eds., *The Althusserian Legacy* (London, 1993), 26; and Ted Benton, *The Rise and Fall of Structural Marxism: Althusser and His Influence* (London, 1984), 36.

73. In Elliott, "Althusser's Solitude," 31. See also Sebastiano Timpanaro, *On Materialism* (London, 1980), 170, 176.

74. Frederick J. Newmayer, *The Politics of Linguistics* (Chicago, 1986), 6, 28.

75. Fredric Jameson, *The Prison-House of Language* (Princeton, 1973), 106.

76. "For there is not one side of theory, a pure intellectual vision without body or materiality—and another of completely material practice which 'gets its hands dirty,'" writes Althusser in regard to the concept of practice. Althusser and Balibar, *Reading Capital,* 58.

77. Thompson, *Poverty of Theory*.

78. Williams, "Notes on British Marxism," 90. Later, Williams would use even tougher language. See Williams, *Politics of Modernism*, 170–71.

79. Williams, "Notes," 87–88. Williams's target was of course not simply Althusser but, closer to home, the current of literary and cultural theory then represented by Terry Eagleton, *Criticism and Ideology* (London, 1978).

80. Williams, *Culture*, 28, 29.

81. Althusser, *For Marx*, 166; quoted in Hall, "Rediscovery of 'Ideology,'" 77. Hall characteristically justified the new approach by arguing that "the media have penetrated right into the heart of the modern productive and labour process itself." Hall, "Culture, the Media and the 'Ideological Effect,'" 340.

82. Hall, "Signification, Representation, Ideology," 98.

83. Though, Hall conceded without any further specification, "[c]ertain insights were indeed to be gained from that approach." Hall, "Rediscovery of 'Ideology,'" 68. For a less extreme version of this position, which nonetheless emphasizes that "[t]he institution-societal relations of production must pass under the discursive rules of language for its product to be 'realized,'" thereby initiating a moment "in which the formal rules of discourse and language are in dominance," Stuart Hall, "Encoding/Decoding," in Center for Contemporary Cultural Studies, *Culture, Media, Language* (London, 1980), 130.

84. Hall, "Encoding/Decoding," 128.

85. Hall, "Rediscovery of 'Ideology,'" 68.

86. Ibid. For Althusser's formulations, *For Marx*, 166–67, 173, 182–83.

87. Stuart Hall, *The Hard Road to Renewal* (London, 1988), 9.

88. Benton, *Rise and Fall of Structural Marxism*, 42.

89. Hall, "Signification, Representation, Ideology," 103–4, original emphasis.

90. Ibid., 103. In 1980, Hall noted of Foucault's concept of discourse that, despite its attractive features, it remained "highly ambiguous," because it "blurs the key issue—if all 'practices' are mediated by language, what aspect of a practice is not language?—and favours a slide between these different meanings without confronting them. . . ." Hall, "Cultural Studies and the Centre," 286 n. 97. Hall nonetheless soon began to incorporate Foucault's concept, even as he sought to pull back toward what remained, for him, happier ground: "Discourse is about the production of knowledge through language. But it is itself produced by a practice: 'discursive practice'—the practice of producing meaning. Since all social practices entail meaning, all practices have a discursive aspect. So discourse enters into and influences all social practices." But how, then—given that, as Hall properly concedes, the chief advantage of "discourse" is that it works against ensconced dualisms "between thought and action, language and practice"—do practices "enter into and influence" discourse itself? In Hall's portrayal of 1985, the emphasis still runs all the other way. As "discursive practice" becomes the heir of "signifying practice," The latter's new Foucauldian raiment acts, characteristically, mainly to protect against the thought of truly mutual constitution. Signification instead is restored as an implicitly separate dimension. Stuart Hall, "The West and the Rest: Discourse and Power," in Stuart Hall and Bram Gieben, eds., *Formations of Modernity* (Cambridge, 1992), 291. This volume preserves the tension that is characteristic of Hall's endeavor, in that

it situates discourse within the field of "four major social processes . . . : the political, the economic, the social and the cultural." Ibid., 1.

91. In his previous spirited defense of a social totality comprised of distinct but "differentiated" instances. Hall, "Marx's Method," 147–51.

92. Hall, "Signification, Representation, Ideology," 100.

93. Jay, *Marxism and Totality*, 412.

94. Antonio Gramsci, *Selections from the Prison Notebooks* (New York, 1971), 8.

95. Hall, "Cultural Studies and the Centre: Some Problematics and Problems," 30.

96. E. P. Thompson, "Caudwell," in Miliband and Saville, eds., *Socialist Register 1977*, 242.

97. Larry Grossberg, *We Gotta Get Out of This Place* (New York, 1992), 43, 47. Hall's later criticism of the engagement with structuralism never concedes this point: [T]he impact of structuralism, one must repeat, does not consist of positions unqualifiedly subscribed to. We must acknowledge a major theoretical intervention. . . . It obliged us really to rethink the 'cultural' as a set of practices: to think of the material conditions of signification and its necessary determinateness." Hall, "Cultural Studies and the Centre: Some Problematics and Problems," 31.

98. "What is the nature of this ideology which can inscribe such a vast range of different positions and interests in it, and which seems to represent a little bit of everybody. . . . What Thatcherism, as an ideology, does, is to address the fears, the anxieties, the lost identities, of a people." Hall, "Gramsci and Us," 19.

99. E. Veron, quoted in Hall, "Rediscovery of 'Ideology,'" 71, 70. This tendency to exaggerate ideology's domain in turn was attacked, without confronting the need to place "the specificity of the cultural" on a distinctly different basis, in Nicholas Abercrombie, Stephen Hill, and Bryan S. Turner, *The Dominant Ideology Thesis* (London, 1980). Cf. Eagleton, *Ideology*, 149.

100. John Fiske, "Television: Polysemy and Popularity," *Critical Studies in Mass Communication* 3 (4) (Dec. 1986): 405, 392.

101. Cf. Jay, *Marxism and Totality*, 390.

102. Stuart Hall, "Recent Developments in Theories of Language and Ideology: A Critical Note," in Centre for Contemporary Cultural Studies, *Culture, Media, Language*, 157–62; and Chris Weedon, Andrew Tolson, and Frank Mort, "Introduction to Language Studies at the Centre," in ibid., 177–85. The reformulation toward "semiology and the theory of the subject" was exemplified by Rosalind Coward and John Ellis, *Language and Materialism* (London, 1977).

103. "[T]hough ideology and language were intimately linked, they could not be one and the same thing." Hall, "Rediscovery of 'Ideology,'" 80.

104. Hall, "Cultural Studies and the Centre," 283 n. 58.

105. Hall, "Rediscovery of 'Ideology,'" 65.

106. Stuart Hall, "The 'Political' and the 'Economic' In Marx's Theory of Classes," in Alan Hunt, ed., *Class and Class Structure* (London, 1977), 23.

107. Hall, "Marx's Notes," 151. On the other side of the historical divide announced by Prime Minister Thatcher's unrelenting counterattack on the British working class, furthermore, Hall's socialism generated unease about the

more glaring forms of idealism which were now running rampant through academe. He wished to be "dissociated," Hall now declared, from "the discourse theoretical approach to the analysis of whole social formations, or . . . the idea that the production of new subjectivities provides, in itself, an adequate theory of ideology (as opposed to a critical aspect of its functioning)." Stuart Hall, "Authoritarian Populism: A Reply to Jessop et al.," *New Left Review* 151 (May–June 1985): 121. See also Hall, *The Hard Road to Renewal*, 10. Around this same time Hall also characterized cultural studies as having made a "headlong rush into structuralism and theoreticism." "Stuart Hall: Discussion," in Cary Nelson and Lawrence Grossberg, eds., *Marxism and the Interpretation of Culture* (Urbana, 1988), 69. With the disclaimer that he had never assumed "economic questions to be residual or unimportant," and the ability to point to real although limited evidence, certainly throughout the 1970s, that the synthetic study favored by Williams retained legitimacy in the Centre's work, Hall now offered this rather sympathetic self-justification: "I work on the political/ideological dimension (a) because I happen to have some competence in that area, and (b) because it is often either neglected or reductively treated by the left. . . ." Hall, "Authoritarian Populism," 121. The closest Hall would come to an integrative synthesis was to unite "culture," now inflected toward "ideology," with the state; a displacement of the economic which drew criticism by the end of the 1970s from Peter Golding and Graham Murdock: "Stuart Hall, like Williams, maintains that questions of economic determination are central to a Marxist sociology of culture. However, unlike Williams they make no significant appearance in his substantive analysis of the contemporary mass media. They are announced and placed in a theoretical bracket." Golding and Murdock, "Ideology and the Mass Media," 204.

108. David Morley, *Television, Audiences and Cultural Studies* (New York, 1992); Hall et al., *Policing the Crisis*.

109. Paul Willis, *Learning to Labor* (1977; New York, 1981), 192.

110. Carey, *Communication as Culture*, 51.

111. James W. Carey, "Communications and Economics," in Robert E. Babe, ed., *Information and Communication in Economics* (Boston, 1994), 325, 329.

112. Wilbur Schramm and Donald F. Roberts, *The Process and Effects of Mass Communication*, 3d ed. (Urbana, 1971), 5. Murdock and Golding took issue with this approach in their 1978 article, "Theories of Communication and Theories of Society."

113. Stuart Hall, "Negotiating Caribbean Identities," *New Left Review* 209 (Jan./Feb. 1995): 12–13.

114. Hall et al., *Policing the Crisis*, 55. John Fiske's conception of language filters Hall through Foucault and Bakhtin: "Language is a crucial site of struggle, for of all our circulation systems it is the one with the widest terrain of operation. It works extensively across the globe and across the nation to spread its own preferred ways of thinking, and intensively to carry the same cultural work into the innermost areas of consciousness. A language is a historical product and has inscribed within it the knowledges that serve the interests of the social formations who have dominated that history. Though it is a resource available to all members of a society, it is neither neutral, nor equally available." John Fiske, *Power Plays, Power Works* (London, 1993), 31.

115. Hall, "The Structured Communication of Events," 4–5. This insight became the core of the work on audiences of David Morley, now collected in Morley, *Television, Audiences and Cultural Studies.*

116. Carey, "Communications and Economics" makes countervailing power the centerpiece of his effort. It is worth underscoring again that the concepts of language adopted by cultural studies may themselves be viewed as comprising a dynamic selective tradition, perhaps most notably in that they almost uniformly insist on structural approaches, above all, that of de Saussure and his descendants. British cultural studies tolerated quite different conceptions of language through the 1970s, after which, characteristically, its option became more fixed. For a recent statement by Carey of his general position, see James W. Carey, "Abolishing the Old Spirit World," *Critical Studies in Mass Communication* 12 (1) (March 1995): 82–89. Other more recent attempts have also been made to boot up such formalistic concepts of shared experience. Take, for example, the highly visible research on "media events." In these so-called "high holidays of mass communication"—the Olympics, the funeral of John F. Kennedy—dramatizations of a putative "sacred center" are said to rehearse "consensual values" and to "integrate" and "reconcile" society. Daniel Dayan and Elihu Katz, *Media Events: The Live Broadcasting of History* (Cambridge, 1992), 1–12. I owe this point to Susan G. Davis, "Media Events," *Library Quarterly* 60 (1) (Jan. 1993): 129–31.

117. E. P. Thompson, *Customs in Common* (London, 1991), 6. Thompson's insistence that there is, indeed, a "whole" merits underlining.

118. Hall discusses his relationship with Williams in Hall, "Williams Interviews"; also see Hall, "Signification, Representation, Ideology," and Stuart Hall, "Culture, Community, Nation," *Cultural Studies* 7 (3) (Oct. 1993): 349–63.

119. Raymond Williams, "Developments in the Sociology of Culture," *Sociology* 10 (3) (Sept. 1976): 505.

120. Williams, *Culture*, 14.

121. Althusser, "Contradiction and Overdetermination," 33.

122. Williams, "Developments in the Sociology of Culture," 505.

123. In further testimony to the fluidity of the moment that produced this intellectual separatism, it bears mention that Ernesto Laclau—one of its leading proponents—was also a leading early adherent of a return within Marxism to the relations of production, and away from the very widely accepted "circulationist" positions of, for example, Immanuel Wallerstein and Andre Gundar Frank. Ernesto Laclau, *Politics and Ideology in Marxist Theory* (London, 1977), 15–50.

124. Adrian Mellor, "Discipline and Punish? Cultural Studies at the Crossroads," *Media Culture and Society* 14 (4) (Oct. 1992): 663–70 at 664, 665. Evidence that "less abrasive" variants are in the wings comes, among other works, via Fred Inglis, *Cultural Studies* (Oxford, 1993).

125. Jane M. Gaines, *Contested Culture* (Chapel Hill, 1991), 243.

126. One significant source of institutional support in the United States was to be the Rockefeller Foundation. During the 1930s and early 1940s, recall, Rockefeller largesse proved crucial to what soon developed into the dominant research orientation in communications—through Hadley Cantril, Paul F. Lazarsfeld, and others. Now the Rockefeller Foundation also chose to become a significant player in another emergent field. It funded a variety of interdisciplinary centers, principally (though not only) at elite research institutions; and not,

significantly, at the community colleges and comprehensive four-year institutions where most working-class and minority students were enrolled. See "Fellowships," *Chronicle of Higher Education* (Oct. 14, 1992): A15.

127. Hall, "Cultural Studies and the Centre: Some Problematics and Problems," 26.

128. Hall continues that this was simply "politics by other means," but the use of "retreat" remains pivotal. Stuart Hall, "The Emergence of Cultural Studies and the Crisis of the Humanities," *October* 53 (Summer 1990): 12.

129. Hall, "Emergence of Cultural Studies," 12.

130. Perry Anderson, *English Questions* (London, 1992), 238. See also Perry Anderson, "Components of the National Culture," in Alexander Cockburn and Robin Blackburn, eds., *Student Power/Problems, Diagnosis, Action* (Baltimore, 1969), 268–76.

131. Perry Anderson, *In the Tracks of Historical Materialism* (London, 1983), 33, 68, 74.

132. Ahmad, *In Theory*, 192.

133. Graham Murdock, "Across the Great Divide: Cultural Analysis and the Condition of Democracy," *Critical Studies in Mass Communication* 12 (1) (March 1995): 91.

134. For some indications, see Ellen Meiksins Wood, *The Retreat from Class* (London, 1986).

135. Hall, "Gramsci and Us," 16.

136. Stuart Hall, "Notes on Deconstructing 'The Popular,'" in Raphael Samuel, ed., *People's History and Socialist Theory* (London, 1981), 238.

137. John Fiske, in "Popular Cultures: Summary Perspectives," *civitas: Cultural Studies at MIT*, 2, no. 3 (Spring 1993): 12.

138. George Lipsitz, *A Life in the Struggle* (Philadelphia, 1988).

139. Fredric Jameson, "Reification and Utopia in Mass Culture," *Social Text* 1 (1) (1979): 139.

140. John Fiske, "Television: Polysemy and Popularity," 392. One often might have difficulty distinguishing why one "struggle" should be seen as better than the next. The effect of even a well-intentioned stress on resistance, as Richard Butsch observes, is therefore often to "erase questions of domination . . . from the agenda." Richard Butsch, "Introduction: Leisure and Hegemony," in idem, ed., *For Fun and Profit* (Philadelphia, 1990), 5. See Mike Budd, Robert M. Entman, and Clay Steinman, "The Affirmative Character of U.S. Cultural Studies," *Critical Studies in Mass Communication* 7, no. 2 (June 1990): 169–84.

141. Fiske, *Power Plays*.

142. Edward Said, *Culture and Imperialism* (New York, 1992), retreats from this earlier position. Bill Ashcroft, Gareth Griffiths, and Helen Tiffin, *The Empire Writes Back: Theory and Practice in Post-Colonial Literatures* (London, 1989). See Ahmad, *In Theory*.

143. Paul Gilroy, *The Black Atlantic* (Cambridge, 1993), 31, 32.

144. The best work on this general subject is Oscar H. Gandy, Jr., *The Panoptic Sort: A Political Economy of Personal Information* (Boulder, 1993). A congenial counterpart is Stuart Ewen, *All Consuming Images* (New York, 1988).

145. For journalistic accounts of media articulation toward gays, minorities, and women, respectively, see Andrew Jacobs, "Mainstream Advertisers

Dare Speak Their Names in Formerly Taboo Media," *San Diego Union-Tribune,* May 22, 1994, p. I 1; Bruce Horovitz, "Major Sponsors Warming Up to the Gay Games," *Los Angeles Times,* June 7, 1994, p. D1; Bruce Horovitz, "More Advertisers Are Tailoring TV Spots to Ethnicity of Viewers," *Los Angeles Times,* May 3, 1994, p. D1; Catherine Jordan, "Go Ahead, Make Her Day," *Los Angeles Times,* April 26, 1994, p. D1. As I write, even as affirmative action is under siege, "ethnic marketing" appears to be still gaining ground. Leah Rickard and Jeanne Whalen, "Retail Trails Ethnic Changes," *Advertising Age,* May 1, 1995, p. 1, 41.

146. A reliance that Hall condemned for always threatening to slide back into "a complex class reductionism." Hall, "Cultural Studies and the Centre," 38. See also Joan Scott, *Gender and the Politics of History* (New York, 1988). For some pointed dissents to the "cultural racism" that underlay some left positions, see Paul Gilroy, *There Ain't No Black in the Union Jack* (Chicago, 1987), 49–50; Hall, "Culture, Community, Nation," 357–61; for a further extension see Gauri Viswanathan, "Raymond Williams and British Colonialism: The Limits of Metropolitan Cultural Theory," in Dennis L. Dworkin and Leslie G. Roman, *Views Beyond the Border Country: Raymond Williams and Cultural Politics* (New York, 1993), 217–30.

147. Hall, "Culture, Community, Nation," 361.

148. Fiske, *Power Plays,* 43.

149. Krishan Kumar, *Prophecy and Progress: The Sociology of Industrial and Post-Industrial Society* (Harmondsworth, 1978), 235.

150. Marshall S. Shatz, *Jan Waclaw Machajski: A Radical Critic of the Russian Intelligentsia and Socialism* (Pittsburgh, 1989); for Bell's allusion to this tradition, Daniel Bell, *The End of Ideology* 2nd ed. (Cambridge, 1988), 355–57. For a useful bibliographic assessment, see Alvin W. Gouldner, *The Future of the Intellectuals and the Rise of the New Class* (London, 1979), 94–101.

151. Bell not only had spent years covering "labor" for Luce's *Fortune* magazine, but also had grown unusually familiar, both through study and via personal association (among others, with Lewis Corey and Max Nomad), with the enigmas introduced specifically into Marxism by the need to grapple with "intellectual" work.

152. The latter accorded special emphasis to the "distinctive language behavior," or "culture of discourse," and to the similarly anomalous "human capital," said to be embodied in the new class. Gouldner, *Future of Intellectuals,* 7, 5, 21–27.

153. Daniel Bell, "Introduction to the Harbinger Edition," in Thorstein Veblen, *The Engineers and the Price System* (New York, 1963), 34–35.

154. Thorstein Veblen, *The Engineers and the Price System* (New York, 1921), 28.

155. Ibid., 132, 133, 55; Bell, "Introduction," 28.

156. Lewis Corey, *The Crisis of the New Middle Class* (New York, 1992), 323, 194; cf. 349.

157. Harold D. Lasswell, "The Psychology of Hitlerism," *Political Quarterly* 4 (1933): 376–77.

158. Michael Rogers Rubin and Mary Taylor Huber, *The Knowledge Industry in the United States, 1960–1980* (Princeton, 1986), 194–95.

159. "The proliferation of new jobs in the mass-culture industries and in the growing college and university system had helped the intellectuals to become

absorbed into the permanent war economy" was the way in which Hofstadter, a historian, characterized the leading criticism of these developments. Richard Hofstadter, *Anti-Intellectualism in American Life* (New York, 1963), 394, 396.

160. Ibid., 6.

161. Ibid., 21.

162. Bell, "Introduction," 29, 34, 35.

163. Daniel Bell, "The Third Technological Revolution," *Dissent* 36 (2) (1989): 169.

164. Bell, *End of Ideology*, 44, 45.

165. Daniel Bell, *The Coming of Post-Industrial Society* (New York, 1976), 112, 109.

166. Robert W. Lucky, *Silicon Dreams* (New York, 1989), 5.

167. Harlan Cleveland, *The Knowledge Executive* (New York, 1985), 33, 25, 34, 29.

168. Frank Webster and Kevin Robins, *Information Technology: A Luddite Analysis* (Norwood, 1986), 33. Jameson, too, points out aptly that theories of postindustrial society "have the obvious ideological mission of demonstrating, to their own relief, that the new social formation in question no longer obeys the laws of classical capitalism, namely, the primacy of industrial production and the omnipresence of class struggle." Fredric Jameson, *Postmodernism; or, The Cultural Logic of Late Captialism* (Durham, 1991), 3.

169. Bell, *Coming of Postindustrial Society*, 107, 108.

170. Daniel Bell, "The Social Framework of the Information Society," in Michael L. Dertouzos and Joel Moses, eds., *The Computer Age: A Twenty-Year View* (Cambridge, 1979), 178; cf. Webster and Robins, *Information Technology*, 32–48.

171. Bell, "Social Framework," 168.

172. Cf. Burton W. Adkinson, *Two Centuries of Federal Information* (Stroudsburg, Pa., 1978), 29–78.

173. An African American packinghouse worker and trade unionist interviewed at his home in Chicago in the mid-1960s (Studs Terkel, *Division Street America* (1967; New York, 1993), (134–135)) "walks over to the piano, removes the plastic cover, and noodles some roughhewn blues chords as he talks.

" 'I call this culture. That's my best definition of culture. When people are oppressed, sometimes they have to have some way . . . Mahalia [Jackson] is a typical example of what I'm trying to say. Like when my mother died, her music made me cry, but it gave me hope.' "

174. John P. Sears, "With Nixon: 'Politics Is Great—Except for People,' " *Los Angeles Times*, April 24, 1994, p. M6.

175. Daniel Bell, "The Eclipse of Distance," *Encounter* 20 (5) (May 1963): 54; idem, *The Cultural Contradictions of Capitalism* (New York, 1976), xi, 12.

176. Bell, *Cultural Contradictions*, xii, xv, 10–15; cf. Fred Block, *Postindustrial Possibilities: A Critique of Economic Discourse* (Berkeley, 1990), 7.

177. Eileen Marie Mahoney, "Negotiating New Information Technology and National Development: The Role of the Intergovernmental Bureau for Informatics" (Ph.D dissertation, Temple University, 1986).

178. See Gingrich's "Forward" to Alvin and Heidi Toffler, *Creating a New Civilization* (Atlanta, 1995), 13–18; and Richard J. Herrnstein and Charles Murray, *The Bell Curve: Intelligence and Class Structure in American Life* (New York,

1994). The intellectual context for the latter work is comprehensively established in Russell Jacoby and Naomi Glauberman, eds., *The Bell Curve Debate: History, Documents, Opinions* (New York, 1995). A shorter but equally pungent critical reception is accorded in Steven Fraser, ed., *The Bell Curve Wars: Race, Intelligence, and the Future of America* (New York, 1995).

179. Herbert I. Schiller, *Mass Communications and American Empire* (New York, 1969), 33.

180. John Fekete, "McLuhanacy: Counterrevolution in Cultural Theory," *Telos* no. 15 (Spring 1973): 77. It is worth noting that such linkages were growing rather widespread. An often-cited radical media manifesto of the period opened with these words: "With the development of the electronic media, the industry that shapes consciousness has become the pacemaker for the social and economic development of societies in the late industrial age. It infiltrates into all other sectors of production. . . ." Hans Magnus Enzensberger, "Constituents of a Theory of the Media," *New Left Review* 64 (Nov.–Dec. 1970): 13.

181. Herbert I Schiller, *Who Knows: Information in the Age of the Fortune 500* (Norwood, 1981); idem, *Information and the Crisis Economy* (New York, 1988); idem, *Culture, Inc.* (New York, 1989). Hamid Mowlana, George Gerbner, and Herbert I. Schiller, eds., *Triumph of the Image* (Boulder, 1992); Webster and Robins, *Information Technology*; Mosco, *Pushbutton Fantasies*; idem, *The Pay-per Society* (Norwood, 1990); Dan Schiller, *Telematics and Government* (Norwood, 1982).

182. See, for example, J. Davis and M. Stack, "Knowledge in Production," *Race & Class* 34 (3) (Jan.–March 1993): 1–14; Tessa Morris-Suzuki, "Capitalism in the Computer Age," *New Left Review* 160 (Nov.–Dec. 1986): 81–91; and Nicholas Garnham, *Capitalism and Communication* (London, 1990), 38–40.

183. Mark Poster, *Foucault, Marxism and History: Mode of Production versus Mode of Information* (Oxford, 1984).

184. Mark Poster, *Existential Marxism in Postwar France from Sartre to Althusser* (Princeton, 1975), esp. 52–75.

185. Althusser, "On Theoretical Work," 62, see also 45–46; and cf. Althusser and Balibar, *Reading Capital*, 171–72.

186. Michel Foucault, *Remarks on Marx: Conversations with Duccio Trombadori* (New York, 1991), 98.

187. Foucault, *Remarks on Marx*, 101–2.

188. Ibid., 101.

189. "[W]hat was lacking here," he said in this later account, "was this problem of the 'discursive regime,' of the effects of power peculiar to the play of statements. I confused this too much with systematicity, theoretical form, or something like a paradigm." Michel Foucault, "Truth and Power," in Paul Rabinow, ed., *The Foucault Reader* (New York, 1984), 55.

190. Foucault, *Remarks on Marx*, 85–86. A useful examination of this encounter may be found in Poster, *Existential Marxism*.

191. Rabinow, *Foucault Reader*, 59.

192. Michel Foucault, *The Order of Things* (New York, 1973), 168, 217.

193. Michel Foucault, *The Use of Pleasure* (New York, 1990), 7.

194. Foucault, *Order of Things*, 252, 257.

195. Ibid., 261. For the CP's continuing reliance on "the formula of increasing pauperization," see Poster, *Existential Marxism*, 362.

196. Foucault, *Order of Things*, 261.

197. E. P. Thompson, "An Open Letter to Leszek Kolakowski," idem, *Poverty of Theory*, 159.

198. This characterization is a composite, based on Karl Marx, *Economic and Philosophic Manuscripts*, in Loyd D. Easton and Kurt H. Guddat, eds., *Writings of the Young Marx on Philosophy and Society* (Garden City, 1967), 332, quoted in Poster, *Existential Marxism*, 67; and from ibid., 66; Adamson, *Marx and the Disillusion of Marxism*. For the dissenters, see Thompson, "Caudwell," 228–76; and Williams, *Marxism and Literature*.

199. Jean Hyppolite, *Studies on Marx and Hegel* (New York, 1969), 138. Hyppolite's discussion of the process of immiseration occurs on 79–80, and is also discussed by Poster, *Existential Marxism*, 30–31.

200. Hyppolite, *Studies*, 80.

201. Ibid., 87.

202. Foucault, *Order of Things*, 341.

203. Michel Foucault, "L'Intellectuel sert à rassembler les idées," *Liberation*, May 26, 1973, quoted in Didier Eribon, *Michel Foucault* (Cambridge, 1991), 253.

204. See Poster, *Existential Marxism*, for Lefebvre, 238–60, esp. 241, 246; for Sartre, 72–105, 161–205, 282; for Hyppolite, 18–32, and also Hyppolite, *Studies*, 87.

205. Jurgen Habermas, *Communication and the Evolution of Society* (Boston, 1979), 135, 138. One trenchant critic writes that, for Habermas, "the Marxian concept of social labor is reduced to 'instrumental action' and, ultimately, to the productive forces, and the Marxian categories of relations of production and superstructure are reduced to the developmental domain of symbolic interaction. This latter move leads Habermas to ignore everything but the communicative aspects of relations of production, or else to reconceive their other aspects in communicative terms (capitalistic property relations and other structures of domination, for example, as 'distortions' of communication). Even more important, Habermas is forced to ignore both the normative and symbolic aspects of productive force development and the purposive-rational aspects of the development of systems of communicative action." Adamson, *Marx and the Disillusion of Marxism*, 141. See also Anthony Giddens, "Labour and Interaction," in John B. Thompson and David Held, eds., *Habermas: Critical Debates* (Cambridge, 1982), 149–61.

206. Jay, *Marxism and Totality*, 512–14.

207. Foucault's work made sustained opportunistic reference to the totality of "bourgeois society." In presenting Foucault's attack on totality as mainly a methodological injunction I follow Gary Gutting, "Michel Foucault: A User's Manual," in Gary Gutting, ed., *The Cambridge Companion to Foucault* (Cambridge, 1994), 1–27, esp. 21. On similar grounds, criticism of Foucault by Hall in 1980 held that the former's "agnosticism about the connections between discursive formations remains troublesome and ambiguous." Hall, "Cultural Studies and the Centre," 286 n. 98.

208. Michel Foucault, "Politics and Ethics: An Interview," in Rabinow, *Foucault Reader*, 375–76, original emphases.

209. Michel Foucault, "Polemics, Politics, and Problemizations," in ibid., 385, 386.

210. Foucault was to suggest that the intellectual moment of French structuralism had centered on the question of ". . . to what extent is it possible to conduct a theoretical, rational, scientific program of research that can surpass the laws and dogmatism of dialectical materialism?" Foucault, *Remarks on Marx*, 95.

211. Michel Foucault, *The Archaelogy of Knowledge* (New York, 1972), 125, 29.

212. Foucault, for example, later criticized semiology's approach to the conflictful event, for which war was the prototype, as "a way of avoiding its violent, bloody, and lethal character by reducing it to the calm Platonic form of language and dialogue." Foucault, "Truth and Power," 57.

213. Foucault, *Archaelogy of Knowledge*, 229.

214. Mark Poster, "Foucault's True Discourses," *Humanities in Society* 2 (2), 1979, 157.

215. Poster, "Foucault's True Discourses," 156; and idem, *Foucault, Marxism and History*.

216. Hall found, as we saw, that he needed to identify means of distinguishing his preferred variant of cultural studies from those of rivals who, ironically, had only transmuted his own longstanding affinities into ironclad assumptions. For a strong sense of Hall's awareness of this tension, see Stuart Hall, "Re-Thinking the 'Base-and-Superstructure' Metaphor," in Jon Bloomfield, ed., *Papers on Class, Hegemony and Party* (London, 1977), 43–72.

217. Fiske, *Power Plays*, 14–15.

218. Hall, "Signification, Representation, Ideology," 106.

219. Fiske, *Power Plays*, 48.

220. Jameson, *Prison-House of Language*, 194.

221. Baudrillard's propensity for "setting up a straw-man Marx" with regard to human needs and in other respects is documented well by Douglas Kellner, *Jean Baudrillard: From Marxism to Postmodernism and Beyond* (Stanford, 1989), 35, 36, 41.

222. Jean Baudrillard, *The Mirror of Production* (St. Louis, 1975), 123.

223. Ibid., 17, 19, 20.

224. Ibid., 33, 31, original emphasis.

225. Ibid., 118–19, 42–43, 58, 109.

226. Kellner, *Baudrillard*, 52.

227. Baudrillard, *Mirror*, 51.

228. Ibid., 107, 99, 108.

229. Ibid., 130.

230. Kellner, *Baudrillard*, 1–32, is helpful in explicating this feature of Baudrillard's early writing.

231. Baudrillard, *Mirror*, 121, 120, 144, 122. Baudrillard's extensive debt to Lefebvre is apparent here, as the latter emphasized that, out ot the twin crises of depression and fascism, advertising and propaganda emerged to effect a "gigantic *substitution*": "For work and for the worker as subject (individual and collective) the consumer has been substituted." In Poster, *Existential Marxism*, 253.

232. See, for example, Mark Poster, *The Mode of Information: Poststructuralism and Social Context* (Chicago, 1990). Moving toward Poster's version of the same convergence was the sociologist Fred Block's depiction of "the choice of the label *postmodern* or *postindustrial* to describe the intellectual project of con-

structing" a theory capable of making sense of "people's experience" today. Block, *Postindustrial Possibilities*, 4.

233. Joan Shelley Rubin, *The Making of Middlebrow Culture* (Chapel Hill, 1992), 7.

234. Clifford Geertz, "The Impact of the Concept of Culture on the Concept of Man" (orig. 1966), in idem, *The Interpretation of Cultures* (New York, 1973), 49. The incongruent relation posited by Geertz and Bell between the two adjoining concepts, "culture" and "information," was likewise preserved, without explication, in radical thought, when Herbert I. Schiller wrote, "The nucleus of culture in a highly industrialized society . . . [is] information itself. . . ." Herbert I. Schiller, *Information and the Crisis Economy* (Norwood, 1984), 77.

235. Herein are combined several vital strands, including an emphasis on experience, characteristically sundered entirely from social class, and associated most strongly with technology. "I call this new world of information, communications, and entertainment machines an information culture. I use the term 'information culture' because these machines, and the social structures that they are part of, have come to define our culture, at least as much as ethnicity, race, or geography. How we feel about the world around us, about one another, even about ourselves has been changed by these machines and the way we've chosen to use them." Steven Lubar, *InfoCulture* (Boston, 1993), 4.

236. How times change! In an earlier discussion of France's May–June days of 1968, Poster had looked to "the proletarianization of the old middle class, the technicians, and the white-collar workers in service industries [to] prepare these groups to be able to identify their own situations with those of students and blue-collar workers." Poster, *Existential Marxism*, 396.

237. Poster, *Mode of Information*, 29, 30.

238. Ibid., 33.

Chapter Five. Toward a Unified Conceptual Framework

1. "Among School Children," in Richard J. Finneran, ed., *The Collected Poems of W. B. Yeats* (New York, 1989), 217; cited in E. P. Thompson, *William Morris: Romantic to Revolutionary* (New York, 1961), 801–2.

2. Raymond Williams, "Problems of Materialism," *New Left Review* 109 (May–June 1978): 17.

3. As anticipated by a participant in the Birmingham debates during the 1970s. Charles Woolfson, *The Labour Theory of Culture* (London, 1981).

4. Raymond Williams, "Notes on Marxism in Britain since 1945," *New Left Review* 100 (Nov. 1976–Jan. 1977): 88.

5. Ibid., 88–89.

6. Stuart Hall, "The Williams Interviews," in Manuel Alvarado, Edward Buscombe, and Richard Collins, eds., *The Screen Education Reader* (New York, 1993), 317.

7. Means of communication, for example, Williams argued, should be approached as actively developing means of production—but they were not to be construed as the only means of production. Raymond Williams, "Means of Communication as Means of Production," in idem, *Problems of Materialism and Culture* (London, 1982), 50–63.

8. Raymond Williams, *Politics and Letters* (London, 1981), 364.

9. Ibid., 364.

10. Ibid., 362.

11. Raymond Williams, *Marxism and Literature* (New York, 1977), 87–88.

12. Raymond Williams, "Marxism, Structuralism and Literary Analysis," *New Left Review* 129 (Sept.–Oct. 1981): 64–65.

13. Raymond Williams, *Culture* (n.p., 1981), 207–10, original emphasis.

14. Ibid., 145, original emphasis.

15. Hall, "Williams Interviews," 313.

16. Williams, *Marxism and Literature*, 94.

17. Hall, "Williams Interviews."

18. "Williams has submitted some of his own culturalist positions to a self-critique far more thoroughgoing than any that I offered in 1961," observed Thompson in 1981: "today I am very close indeed to Raymond Williams on critical points of theory." E. P. Thompson, "The Politics of Theory," in R. Samuel, ed., *People's History and Socialist Theory* (London, 1981), 399. On culture as "a way of struggle," see Thompson, "The Long Revolution," 33. Thompson gave tacit hints that he had moved toward Williams's position in an essay from the mid-1970s: "For value will be found, most often, in particular historical contexts, and in particular men and women's struggle with, or adjustment to, or love for, other particular women and men." Thompson, "Caudwell," in Ralph Miliband and John Saville, eds., *The Socialist Register 1977* (New York, 1977), 256.

19. "Gramsci always insisted that hegemony is *not* exclusively an ideological phenomenon. There can be no hegemony without 'the decisive nucleus of the economic.'" Stuart Hall, "Gramsci and Us," *Marxism Today* 31 (6) (June 1987): 20. For Gramsci, wrote Hall as early as 1980, "'[h]egemony' retains its base in the way the productive life of societies is organized." Hall claimed that the use of the concept by the Centre for Contemporary Cultural Studies could be distinguished from that of Williams (supposedly in *Marxism and Literature*), who tried to "restrict it to questions of 'cultural power' and ideology." Stuart Hall, "Cultural Studies and the Centre: Some Problematics and Problems," in Centre for Contemporary Cultural Studies, *Culture, Media, Language* (London, 1980), 36 and 286 n. 94.

20. "[T]he empirically unsustainable emphasis on the *state* ideological apparatus can be replaced by the more plausible proposition of control of the ideological apparatus by a dominant *class*, working in general institutional and market terms as well as (or rather than) directly through state organizations." Williams, *Culture*, 222. The importance of the balance between coercion and consent is emphasized by Perry Anderson, "The Antinomies of Antonio Gramsci," *New Left Review* 100 (Nov. 1976–Jan. 1977): 5–78, esp. 44–49.

21. Williams, *Long Revolution*, 63.

22. Williams, *Marxism and Literature*, 90–94.

23. Ibid., 93. Williams had similarly written that "labor," through the early modern period, had in its most general usage meant "all productive work." Only as capitalism developed did it acquire the specialized meaning of work for wages. Raymond Williams, *Keywords* (New York, 1983), 177.

24. Perry Anderson, *English Questions* (London, 1992), 239. Cf. Williams, *Marxism and Literature*, 92–94.

25. Karl Marx, "Theses on Feurbach," in Karl Marx and Frederick Engels, *Selected Works* (New York, 1980), 29.

26. Karl Marx, "Economic and Philosophic Manuscripts of 1844," in Karl Marx and Frederick Engels, *Collected Works 3, Marx and Engels: 1843–44* (Moscow, 1975), 297. For commentary on the young Marx's concept of labor, see Douglas Kellner, *Jean Baudrillard* (Stanford, 1989), 41, 53; Rabinbach, *Human Motor*, 72–83; Adamson, *Marx and the Disillusion of Marxism*, 81–82.

27. Herbert Marcuse, "On the Philosophical Foundation of the Concept of Labor in Economics," *Telos* no. 16 (Summer 1973): 9–37.

28. C. J. Arthur, *Dialectics of Labour: Marx in His Relation to Hegel* (Oxford, 1986), 5.

29. Georg Lukacs, *The Ontology of Social Being: Labour* (London, 1980), 39, iv, 3.

30. See, for example, ibid., 57, 118.

31. Williams, *Culture*, 54.

32. Ibid., 231, 232.

33. Ibid., 114–15.

34. Concerning his projected sociology of culture, Williams wrote in 1981, "there is also direct overlap with economic analysis, and this is becoming especially important in work on modern capitalist cultural organizations and especially the 'media.' The recent development of a 'political economy of culture' (see Schiller (1969), Murdock and Golding (1974), Garnham (1977)) is especially necessary and welcome, and should be seen as not only distinct from, but complementary to, a cultural sociology." Ibid., 31–32. Reference was to Herbert I. Schiller, *Mass Communications and American Empire* (New York, 1969); Peter Golding and Graham Murdock, "For a Political Economy of Mass Communication," in Ralph Miliband and John Saville, eds., *Socialist Register 1973* (London, 1974), 205–34; and Nicholas Garnham, "Towards a Political Economy of Culture," *New Universities Quarterly* (Summer 1977), extended and developed in idem, "Contribution to a Political Economy of Mass Communication," *Media Culture & Society* 1 (2) (1979).

35. L. S. Vygotsky, "Tool and Symbol in Child Development," in his *Mind in Society: The Development of Higher Psychological Processes*, ed. Michael Cole, Vera John-Steiner, Sylvia Scribner, and Ellen Souberman (Cambridge, 1978), 24. For useful secondary works, see: David J. Bakhurst, "Social Memory in Soviet Thought," in David Middleton and Derek Edwards, eds., *Collective Remembering* (London, 1990), 203–26; James V. Wertsch, *Vygotsky and the Social Formation of Mind* (Cambridge, 1985); and Rene Van Der Veer and Jaan Valsiner, *Understanding Vygotsky: A Quest for Synthesis* (Oxford, 1991).

36. Sylvia Scribner, "Studying Working Intelligence," in Barbara Rogoff and Jean Lave, eds., *Everyday Cognition: Its Development in Social Context* (Cambridge, 1984), 9–40. Thanks to Michael Cole for this suggestion.

37. Cf. Len Doyal and Roger Harris, "The Practical Foundations of Human Understanding," *New Left Review* 139 (May–June 1983): 59–78.

38. An important historical study of the origins of this development in the U.S. context is Jeanne Boydston, *Home & Work: Housework, Wages, and the Ideology of Labor in the Early Republic* (New York, 1990).

39. Lynn Spigel, *Make Room for TV: Television and the Family Ideal in Postwar America* (Chicago, 1992), 5. Ien Ang, *Watching* Dallas: *Soap Opera and the*

Melodramatic Imagination (London, 1985): esp. 17–20; Janice A. Radway, *Reading the Romance: Women, Patriarchy, and Popular Literature* (Chapel Hill, 1991). Radway's romance readers, deeply committed to the ethic of bourgeois achievement and self-striving, attempted regularly to distinguish their own efforts at education and self-instruction from the supposedly inferior and unrewarding activity of soap opera viewing. The two genres thus would appear to manifest significant interconnections in social class terms. A rare effort to connect gender with class in the context of media audiences is Andrea L. Press, *Women Watching Television: Gender, Class, and Generation in the American Television Experience* (Philadelphia, 1991).

40. Both Ang and Spigel evince a strong tendency to substitute texts as supposed surrogates for the experience of audience members—which in turn acts as a substitute for the more encompassing theorizations at which each of the two writers hints. Ang's reliance on personal letters in which her correspondents express, in lesser or greater detail, their feelings about *Dallas,* moreover, suffers from the same subjectivism that is evinced by the absence, in Spigel, of any discussion of the institutional placement and biases of the women's magazines that comprise a mainstay of her evidence. This latter point stands out with particular clarity as a result of a recent useful study of such magazines. Ellen McCracken, *Decoding Women's Magazines: From* Mademoiselle *to* Ms. (New York, 1993).

41. John Clarke, *New Times and Old Enemies* (London, 1991), 85, 102.

42. Cf. Dallas Smythe, "Communications: Blindspot of Western Marxism," *Canadian Journal of Political and Social Theory* 1 (3) (Fall 1977): 1–27; and idem, "Rejoinder to Graham Murdock," *Canadian Journal of Political and Social Theory* 2 (2) (Spring–Summer 1978): 120–27, both collected in Dallas Smythe, *Counterclockwise: Perspectives on Communication,* ed. Thomas Guback (Boulder, 1994).

43. Where women have worked in great numbers and in obvious ways as producers of a communications commodity—as telephone operators, for example—feminist scholars have been free to effectuate salutary and significant junctures of just this kind. Michele Martin, *"Hello, Central?": Gender, Technology, and Culture in the Formation of Telephone Systems* (Montreal, 1991); Stephen Norwood, *Labor's Flaming Youth: Telephone Operators and Worker Militancy, 1878–1923* (Urbana, 1990). Such connections have also been forged by studies of working-class women's film-going around the First World War, which situate the intersections between gender inequality and domination in a context of generational, ethnic, and social class conflicts. Elizabeth Ewen, "City Lights: Immigrant Women and the Rise of the Movies," *Signs: Journal of Women in Culture and Society* 5 (3) (Supplement, 1980): S45–65; Kathy Peiss, *Cheap Amusements* (Philadelphia, 1986), 139–62; Roy Rosenzweig, *Eight Hours for What We Will* (Cambridge, 1983), 191–221.

44. Williams, *Marxism and Literature,* 93.

45. Williams, *Culture,* 189–91.

46. I am relying here, among other things, on continuing research by Marcus B. Rediker and Peter Linebaugh. I think it might be shown that Edward Thompson was thinking along similar lines during the later 1970s. At the University of California, San Diego, Lora E. Taub's doctoral dissertation utilizes the idea of labor systems to analyze the first capitalist culture industry—that which developed through Elizabethan theatre—and there will be more on labor sys-

tems in my own work-in-progress, "The Information Commodity from Grub Street to the Information Highway."

47. As I write, Lawrence Grossberg (drawing on the thinking of John Clarke) likewise observes that "[p]roduction cannot simply be the capitalized manufacture of cultural commodities." Lawrence Grossberg, "Cultural Studies vs. Political Economy: Is Anybody Else Bored with this Debate?," *Critical Studies in Mass Communication* 12 (1) (March 1995): 74. Thanks to Lora Taub for this reference.

48. On the issue of "means of production," Williams only continued to retain *May Day Manifesto*'s concern for communication technologies as forces of production, which he had thereafter gone so far as to claim might enable transnational corporate capital at points "to affect, to alter, and in some cases control our whole social process." Raymond Williams, *Television: Technology and Cultural Form* (London, 1974), 151.

49. As, notwithstanding, proponents of the Frankfurt School continue to proclaim. Stanley Aronowitz claimed that "[t]he appropriation of all culture in the service of commodity production is the distinguishing feature of late capitalism." Stanley Aronowitz, *False Promises* (New York, 1973), 15; as we found in an earlier chapter, the critic Fredric Jameson concurred; Jameson, "Reification and Utopia in Mass Culture," *Social Text* 1 (1) (1979): 131, 134. For Williams, *Culture*, 46, 50.

50. Williams, *Marxism and Literature*, 128, 134.

51. For example, Williams, *Culture*, 76.

52. Williams, "Literature and Sociology," 11.

53. Williams, *Marxism and Literature*, 125, original emphasis.

54. Immanuel Wallerstein, *Historical Capitalism* (London, 1983).

55. E. P. Thompson, *The Poverty of Theory* (London, 1978), 254.

56. Bernard Miege, *The Capitalization of Cultural Production* (New York, 1989).

Index

Academia: and academic freedom, 23–24; cultural studies in, 157–60; institutionalization of communication as scholarly discipline in, 55–64; limitations in nineteenth-century thinking of, 4; and post-industrial theory, 166; and pretensions to privileged knowledge, 36; in Progressive Era, 24–38; and propaganda studies, 42, 43, 51, 52–53, 54–64; and teachers as intermediaries, 106; and telegraph controversy, 14. *See also specific person or institution*

Academic freedom, 23–24
Adams, Henry Carter, 24, 29
Adamson, Walter, 20
Addams, Jane, 24
Adorno, Theodor, 67–68, 72–73, 84–85, 134
Advertising: and cultural imperialism, 125; and cultural studies, 115; and culture industry, 65, 69; as news, 6–7; as parasitism, 70; and productivity, 23; and propaganda, 43, 50, 57, 58, 59, 84; radio versus newspaper, 48; and "salesmanship," 23; and structural Marxism, 161

African Americans, 4, 81, 83
Ahmad, Aijaz, 105, 158
Althusser, Louis. *See* Structural Marxism
America's House of Lords (Ickes), 49
Anderson, Perry, 40, 123, 133–34, 158, 190
Ang, Ien, 193
Anti-Monopoly Party, 10
Anti-Semitism, 71, 72, 73
Apprenticeship system, 19
Aronowitz, Stanley, 83
Arthur, C. J., 191
Associated press, 7, 8, 10–11
AT&T: antitrust case against, 54
Audience ratings, 50, 51
Authoritarianism, 40, 129, 130

Bakunin, Mikhail, 162
Barnard, Rita, 68
Barthes, Roland, 149, 151

163, 164, 165–66, 167, 168–70, 171, 172, 184; and post-structuralism, 182–83, 184; and structural Marxism, 150, 184; and unified conceptual framework, 187, 191–92, 197
Intellectual labor: and anti-intellectualism, 164–65; and cultural imperialism, 100, 102, 104, 105; and cultural studies, 107, 108, 110, 117, 131, 184, 192, 194; and Deweyan instrumentalism, 30–31; limitations in nineteenth-century thinking about, 4; and Marxism/socialism, 132, 133, 135, 136; and mass culture, 40–41, 69, 71, 75–77, 81, 84; and organized intelligence, 77; ownership of, 15–17; and patent system, 15–17; and post-industrial theory, 137, 161, 162, 163, 164–65, 170, 184, 187; and post-structuralism, 172, 173, 174, 176–77, 181, 184, 187; and propaganda, 84–85; and structural Marxism, 145, 146–47, 151, 152, 153, 160, 184, 187; and unified conceptual framework, 185, 186, 187, 192–94; white-collar workers as, 41; in World War II, 40–41. *See also* Labor
"Intelligence trust," 25–27, 35–36
Interpersonal communication. *See* Personal influence
Inventors, 15–17
Isolationism, 45, 54

Jakobsen, R. O., 152
James, William, 27
Jameson, Fredric, 86, 148, 180
Jarrett, John, 6
Jay, Martin, 85, 119, 120, 148, 151
Joseph, Keith, 130
Justice Department, U.S., 45, 53, 54

Katz, Elihu, 42, 58, 60–61, 62, 64, 82–83, 90
Kazan, Elia, 65
Kelley, Florence, 24

Kellner, Douglas, 182
King, Edward, 6–7
Klapper, Joseph, 58–60
Knights of Labor, 13, 18, 19, 20
Kocka, Jurgen, 19
Kracauer, Siegfried, 73
Krauss, Michael, 94
Krippendorff, Klaus, 63

Labor: and cultural imperialism, 100, 102, 104, 105; and cultural studies, 107, 108, 110, 117–18, 122, 131, 155, 182, 191–92, 194, 195–96; definition of, 17–22; and Deweyan instrumentalism, 4, 24, 25, 28–35, 37–38; diversity of, 195–96; in early nineteenth century, 4–5; and ethnicity, 19; and feminism, 193–94; and French social thought, 173; limitations in nineteenth-century thinking about, 4; and Marxism/socialism, 19, 21–22, 85, 132–37, 173, 183, 187; and mass culture, 74–77, 81–82, 84–85, 134; and opinion leaders, 62; and post-industrial theory, 132, 137, 163, 166–68, 170, 171, 184, 187; and post-structuralism, 132, 172, 173–74, 175–78, 179, 180–81, 182, 183–84, 187; and producer republicanism, 4–5, 17, 19–20, 22–23, 25, 30, 32, 38, 186; productive and unproductive, 17–19, 22–23, 135–36; and structural Marxism, 132, 138, 145–46, 149, 150, 151–52, 153, 155, 158, 174, 184, 187; and unified conceptual framework, 182, 186, 187, 191–94, 195–96, 197; universality of one form of, 197. *See also* Intellectual labor; Manual labor; Organized labor
Labor and Monopoly Capital (Braverman), 146
Labour Movement. *See* Organized labor
Labour Party (Britain), 110–11, 112–13, 114, 115, 122, 123, 124, 128, 130, 137